THE RUINS OF THE NEW ARGENTINA

MARK A. HEALEY

THE RUINS OF THE NEW ARGENTINA

Peronism and the Remaking of San Juan after the 1944 Earthquake

Duke University Press

Durham and London   2011

© 2011 Duke University Press

All rights reserved

Designed by Heather Hensley

Typeset in Adobe Garamond Premier Pro by
Keystone Typesetting, Inc.

Library of Congress Cataloging-in-Publication Data
appear on the last printed page of this book.

PER MAGDALENA. T'ESTIMO TANT.

CONTENTS

ILLUSTRATIONS

Maps

ACKNOWLEDGMENTS

The first words of this book were written in Barcelona, followed by a torrent of other words, typed out on eight computers in a dozen homes in as many years, in Spain, Argentina, and the United States. My friends know that along the way I have become a connoisseur of the acknowledgments in books, looking for the most gracious and artful way to render tribute to the host of witnesses, colleagues, allies, and supporters who were so essential to a project that is formally attributed only to me. But on this point I must admit a small defeat: clever formulas have failed me, and so I can only turn to the familiar list, the small written attempt to honor a greater debt.

The institutions are a good place to start. This project has been generously funded by fellowships from Duke University, the Fulbright Commission, the Social Science Research Council (with the American Council of Learned Societies), the Woodrow Wilson International Center for Scholars, the United States Department of Education, the Conference of Latin American Historians, and the Woodrow Wilson National Foundation. I have also received ample support as a postdoctoral scholar and faculty member from New York University, the University of Mississippi, and the University of California, Berkeley. In particular, of course, I am grateful to Valerie Millholland and Miriam Angress at Duke University Press for believing in this book and guiding it into its final form.

In research on Argentina, and on Latin America in general, the very availability of sources is never a given, and thus I owe a great deal to the librarians and archivists who made this work possible at all. All of the institutions they capably run are named in the bibliography.

In Buenos Aires, I owe a deep debt to Graciela Milani, for offering shelter, guidance, and sustenance, and also to Facundo, Juan Manuel, and Oscar Rodríguez Pérsico for their company over the years. Jorge and Virginia Lanza took me in as their own; I am grateful for wine, conversation, and the joyous use and abuse of Allen wrenches, not to mention the genio and enthusiasms of Federico, Jerónimo, and Valentina.

From our first meeting, Anahí Ballent has selflessly shared her superb insights and exhaustive research on architecture and Peronism. Her openness and camaraderie, along with that of Adrián Gorelik and Graciela Silvestri, have been an invaluable help and encouragement. Jorge Liernur and Juan Molina y Vedia kindly allowed me access to private papers they held. Lila Caimari and Mirta Lobato have been gracious mentors. Lucas Rubinich and the *banda del CECyP*, Alex Laje, Fernanda Velázquez, María Baliero, Eduardo Jakubowicz, Laura Radetich, *Comandante* Fernando García, and Moira Mackinnon were excellent compañeros along the way.

In Mendoza, Susana Ramella de Jefferies opened her home and her father's papers to me, and I greatly enjoyed our debates on religion, Peronism, and the historian's craft. I also benefited from discussions with Enrique Zuleta Alvarez, Florencia Ferreira de Cassone, Marcela Aranda, Esteban Fernández, Margarita Gascón, and particularly Diego Escolar, a wonderful friend and wise critic.

In San Juan, I would like to thank Carlos and Rubi Díaz, the late José and Felipe Santamaría, the late Dora Roitman de Schabelman, and the Allub family–Sarui, Ximena, and the late Leopoldo–for their hospitality and kindness. Luis Garcés and Nelly de León were invaluable guides into local politics, architecture, and cuisine, as well as models of scholarship and political engagement. Graciela Gómez and Hugo Basualdo shared their own research and later invited me to teach an oral history course to an inspiring cohort of students. I am particularly grateful to everyone who agreed to be interviewed on their experiences of Peronism and rebuilding.

Along the way, I was blessed with the friendship and example of other scholars of Argentina, especially Adriana Brodsky, Alistair Hattingh, James Cane-Carrasco, Javier Auyero, Steve Levitsky, and Oscar Chamosa. Nancy Westrate blazed a trail. Oscar Bragos retrieved obscure documents. From Brazil, Cathy Karr-Colque, Bebel Delgado, and Bryan McCann sent moral support and motivational music. From Chile, Jody Pavilack offered wise advice. From France, Rob Maxwell dispatched mysterious requests and wonderful wine.

I am grateful to junior colleagues who assisted with research: Aldo Gaete, Fabiana González, Laura Zambrini, Katharine French-Fuller, and the amazingly resourceful Adrianna Catena. Leopoldo Mazuelos Corts and Juan Carlos Bataller kindly provided permissions and copies for key images. Debra Wong and Bill Nelson produced a series of splendid maps.

Friends and colleagues at our various stops across the United States have kept me grounded and sane: I deeply appreciate the compañerismo of María Teresa and Mike Palmer, Chris and Sandy Franks, Kelly Lyn Logue, Will Jones, Margie Brache, Adriana Johnson, Jody Pavilack, Kecia and Mohamed Ali, Ivonne Wallace-Fuentes, Tom Rogers, Jefferson Cowie, Scott Littlehale, Ernesto Semán, Claudio Benzecry, Amy and Mathew Randall, Doug Sullivan-González, and all of the Wednesday bar night gang—Ann Claycombe, Jake Selwood, Wayne Lee, Rhonda Mawhood, Philippe Rosenberg, and Jennifer Terni.

Everything I know about Peronism I learned through the teaching and example of Daniel James. He has shaped the questions and approach of this work in fundamental ways and proven an excellent guide all through the long march. Above all, he kept me from the natural path of trying to reproduce his work, pushing me instead to pursue something further afield and remaining patient as I defined and refined that something.

John French was equally important in my intellectual formation. His hands-on style was an excellent complement to Danny's more philosophical approach; his intense dedication to students, and sense of responsibility for us, has been a blessing and an example. For years, John has been a tireless fount of enthusiasm and support—if sometimes offered rather early in the morning—as well as a rigorous and always constructive critic. It was only because John and Danny placed their confidence in me that I came to deserve it.

This book has benefited from thoughtful readings by Daniel James, John French, Tulio Halperín, Oscar Chamosa, Bryan McCann, Ernesto Semán, Diego Escolar, James Cane-Carrasco, Will Jones, Javier Auyero, Daniel Levinson-Wilk, and Claudio Benzecry. It has also been enriched by specific suggestions from Alberto Moreiras, Gabriela Nouzeilles, Thomas Bender, Sukhdev Sandhu, William Marotti, Danna Kostroun, Mark Sheftall, and Greg Grandin. Two anonymous readers for Duke University Press offered useful thoughts. I appreciate the insights from each of the scholarly venues where I have presented this work: at the Universidad de Buenos Aires, the Universidad de San Andrés, the Universidad Nacional de San Juan, the International Center for Advanced Studies at New York University, the Latin American Labor History Conference at Duke University, and meetings of the American Historical Association, American Society for Environmental History, and Latin American Studies Association. At Berkeley, I am especially grateful for comments from William Taylor, David Henkin, Mark Brilliant, John Connelly, Maureen Miller, Rebecca McClennan, Kerwin Klein, Mark Peterson, and Peter Zinoman. Mark Brilliant deserves particular recognition for offering not only astute observations but steady comradeship in many early morning runs. My graduate students have been a great encouragement. Above all, I owe a special debt to Margaret Chowning, for her repeated, rigorous, and at times heroic readings and critiques.

My family has been amazingly supportive of my work over the years, even through unexpected turns, and especially in the crucial final stretch. Many observations were first aired in conversations with my cousin Pam, brother Brian, and sister Janice over the years, and their encouragement has been a great resource. My parents, Alan and Sharon, have been kind throughout, whether in discussing the larger ideas at play, carefully proofreading the text, or spiriting away Mateu and Julia for a "mystery trip" so I could write. The hospitality of our Catalan family—especially Enriqueta Parera, Pilar Giribets, and Pilar Parera i Giribets—has also been a wonderful help, especially at the very beginning and end.

Our children, Mateu and Julia, have grown up in the shadow of this book, and though they hardly realize it, their joy and chaotic energy have been essential to bringing this to a worthy close. I greatly look forward to future frolics with them, now that it is done.

Finally, and most importantly, Magdalena Parera i Giribets has been an anchor and a beacon through these years, encouraging, cajoling, enticing me as I took the work in new directions and finally brought it back to safe harbor. I simply could not have done it without her patience, presence, and love—and this is the debt I most look forward to repaying.

ACRONYMS

AAD: Agrupación de Arquitectos Democráticos (Group of Democratic Architects)

AGN: Archivo General de la Nación

AHASJ: Archivo Histórico Administrativo de San Juan

BHN: Banco Hipotecario Nacional (National Mortgage Bank)

CAI: Centro Argentino de Ingenieros (Center of Argentine Engineers)

CINVA: Centro Interamericano de Vivienda y Planeamiento (Inter-American Center for Housing and Planning)

CNV: Comisión Nacional de Vivienda (National Housing Commission)

DDF: Departamento de Documentos Fotográficos

GOU: Grupo de Oficiales Unidos (Group of Officers United)

INPRES: Instituto Nacional de Prevención Sísmica (National Seismic Prevention Institute)

IPV: Instituto Provincial de Vivienda (Provincial Housing Authority)

MOP: Ministerio de Obras Públicas (Ministry of Public Works)

PDN: Partido Demócrata Nacional (Conservatives)

PRO: Public Records Office

SCA: Sociedad Central de Arquitectos (Central Society of Architects)

STP: Secretaría de Trabajo y Previsión (Secretariat of Labor and Social Welfare)

UBA: Universidad de Buenos Aires (University of Buenos Aires)

UCR: Unión Cívica Radical (Radical Civic Union)

UCRB: Unión Cívica Radical Bloquista (Bloquistas, Cantonistas)

UCRI: Unión Cívica Radical Intransigente (led by Frondizi, anti-Liberating Revolution)

UCRP: Unión Cívica Radical del Pueblo (led by Balbín, pro-Liberating Revolution)

USNA: United States National Archives

INTRODUCTION

"One's first impression is of grapes everywhere," a visitor to the Argentine wine belt reported in 1942, "numerous *bodegas* (wineries) . . . and everything—houses, fences, stores, factories, even the provincial capitol—built of adobe brick."[1] Timeless as this landscape might have seemed, it was a recent creation. The Spanish had planted vines when they arrived in the neighboring provinces of San Juan and Mendoza, but wine had become the engine of the local economy only in the last sixty years, after the completion of the railroad from Buenos Aires, over a thousand kilometers to the east.[2]

The rise of the wine industry was swift and impressive, but also unbalanced, and brutal. It was the product of politics as much as ecology, the regional variant of the national liberal project first articulated by the great San Juan intellectual Domingo Sarmiento in the 1840s. Sarmiento had argued in *Facundo*, a foundational text for liberals across Latin America, that the isolation and "barbarism" of the Argentine interior could only be redeemed through "civilization" by force. He advocated decisive action to subdue the "barbarous" masses and introduce the commerce, agriculture, railways, immigrants, and schools that might eventually make them into a worthwhile citizenry. In 1852, Sarmiento's allies overthrew Juan Manuel de Rosas, a strongman who had dominated national politics for a generation. Sarmiento went on to serve as a general, governor, minister, ambassador, and finally president, as his political generation enacted much of the liberal program, turning the country from a backwater into an economic powerhouse.[3]

As Sarmiento had imagined, the greatest benefits of the liberal project accrued to Buenos Aires and its surrounding plains, the Pampas, which became the heartland of export agriculture. The cities and countryside of this

Argentina, 1944

core region came to hold two-thirds of the national population. But the interior was remade as well. By the late nineteenth century, a new San Juan elite of immigrant entrepreneurs and old notables imported vines, workers, and know-how from Europe to sow a dense cluster of vineyards on this sparsely occupied terrain. The provincial government auctioned off land and dug irrigation canals, private and public capital built railroads, and the national government erected protective tariffs. The wine industry became the mainstay of San Juan's economy, and vineyards expanded to cover half the cultivated land, a twelve-fold increase over six decades. As Mendoza grew even more, Argentina soon had the fifth-largest wine industry in the world, producing largely for the domestic market.[4]

Sarmiento had hoped that wine would be San Juan's "salvation," and it certainly did transform the province, though hardly into the stable, educated,

1 Vineyard, San Juan province, 1930s. CREDIT AGN.

and prosperous place he had envisioned.[5] Instead, liberalism had yielded a landscape of flourishing vineyards and ramshackle dwellings. For all the prosperity the wine boom brought the elite, it left most of the province landless, impoverished, and only intermittently employed. This was a social order of "rooted vines and uprooted men," in a dissident's succinct formula.[6] While these failings were especially evident in San Juan, they were present across the nation. The liberal project had begun with the remaking of the interior. As this book will show, the Peronist overthrow of that project would begin here as well.

The rule of the winery elite had certainly faced challenges. After the passage of universal male suffrage in 1912, a local populist movement led by two brothers, Aldo and Federico Cantoni, three times had won the governorship and launched progressive reforms—only to be overthrown by the winery elite and their national allies. By the early 1940s, after a decade of soaring unemployment and bitter struggles, the winery elite was holding on through violence and fraud. For all the changes in the countryside, the provincial capital of San Juan retained a decidedly traditional air, with narrow streets and colonial churches. But this was a precarious stability, and as the visitor in 1942 had noted, even the palaces were built of clay.

In less than a minute on the evening of 15 January 1944, an earthquake reduced this adobe city to rubble, leaving perhaps ten thousand dead and half the province homeless. The city had dozens of engineers, a handful of architects, and no building code: nearly all those adobe structures collapsed into dust. As the disaster made clear, the prosperity of the province had been built on recklessness as well as injustice.

This was an indictment of the old political order, and a spur for the new order to come. Only six months before, a military coup had ended thirteen years of repressive and fraudulent—though nominally democratic—governments and proclaimed a new future of order, virtue, and "social justice." Now the military regime had a chance to make good on those promises. The day after the earthquake, the recently installed secretary of labor went on national radio to announce a relief collection for victims. The collection mobilized tens of thousands and proved a signal success, launching the public career of the secretary, Colonel Juan Domingo Perón.

Building on the relief collection, Perón would assemble a broad movement that would win him the presidency in democratic elections two years later, and go on to dramatically remake the country's political institutions and social structure, leaving Argentina with the strongest welfare state in Latin America and one of the most powerful labor movements in the world—but also a deeply divided and unstable political system. In power or in exile, Perón would remain the dominant figure on the national stage until his death in 1974, and the resilient and contradictory movement he founded is the central presence in Argentine politics to this day. Understanding Peronism, in turn, has been a major task of Argentine history and social science.

The San Juan earthquake provides an evocative opening to the best scholarly biography of Perón, by the historian Joseph Page—indeed, it often earns prominent mention in accounts of Peronism.[7] The earthquake marked the beginning of a crucial partnership: at a benefit concert one week later, Perón met Eva Duarte, the future Evita Perón. The relief collection was the first step in forging Perón's enduring alliance with the poor, the earliest sign that, as the popular slogan later put it, "Perón delivers." As he argued, "On a social plane, most Argentines are comparable to the homeless of San Juan," and the social agenda launched there would soon expand to all Argentines.[8] Moreover, the mass mobilization of Peronism would lead opponents and supporters alike to describe the movement as a kind of political earthquake, an "uprising of the subsoil of the fatherland" that overturned what "until then had seemed unshakeable."[9]

Yet the recognition of the earthquake's importance has been as shallow as it is widespread.[10] After using San Juan as his opening stage set, Page drops the province entirely from his book—and this is not an isolated oversight. In the vast literature on Peronism, the worst disaster in national history has been reduced to an anecdote. It is as if the mere announcement of relief were enough to rebuild an entire province.

Four Moments of the Ruins

This book examines the shattering and galvanizing experience of the earthquake: the world it exposed, the transformations it inspired, and the legacies it left. This is a study of how one city and province were unmade and remade by disaster and rebuilding. Casting a seemingly familiar political landscape in a new light, I explore the territorial strategies of an expanding state and foreground the importance of apparently peripheral locales. But this is far more than a local study. What I uncover is a central event, not only in provincial history but in national history as well. I expose not only a great social trauma but also a political cause, and a massive rebuilding effort, the landmark project for a generation of architects, engineers, and planners. The destroyed province, I argue, was a crucial site in forging and testing—and ultimately limiting—the Peronist project for transforming the nation.

In various ways, this book ultimately underscores the primacy of politics in the history of Argentina in these years. But I also offer an expanded understanding of politics, reaching geographic areas and social sectors, from architects and engineers to provincial journalists and elites, little addressed by scholars until now. And this expanded understanding of politics is built on a new emphasis on its underpinnings in urban and especially environmental history.

For all the studies of Peronism, there has been virtually no examination of how it remade local structures of power—or how localities shaped or constrained the national movement. While many scholars have seen Peronism as a key moment in the formation of the Argentine state, few have examined that state in action, as I do here. Similarly, the handful of excellent works on Argentine modernist architecture and planning have focused entirely on Buenos Aires, but I argue that what is distinctive about this moment is the national vocation of modernism, the degree to which architectural ambitions extended across national territory, as exemplified in the rebuilding of San Juan. And just as I look at the state in action, so I study architects and engineers in action, tracing the contours of everyday practice, political alliance, and social commitment. As I establish here for the first time, modernism and architecture were key to Peronism as a national project. Understanding the transformation of San Juan, as place and as idea, during this period gives us insight into both the promise and limits of Peronism that previous scholars have missed, because they were centered on Buenos Aires, focused on labor, and often more attentive to what Peronism became than the contingent process through which it emerged.

In this book, I analyze four moments in the interplay between the history of San Juan after the earthquake and the broader history of Argentina under Perón. Each moment can be expressed as a play on the title, *The Ruins of the New Argentina*. First, the ruins were an invitation to transformation, to building a new Argentina, more just, inclusive, and resilient. Second, they became a laboratory for forging that transformative project, and also for revealing its limits. Third, as rebuilding faltered, eighteen months after the quake, the ruins would become instead a measure of the failure of transformation, an indictment of Perón. But fourth, with Perón's electoral victory in 1946, rebuilding would finally, if slowly, get underway, along far less ambitious lines than at first, more accommodating than undermining local elites. And this is the final meaning of the phrase: the rebuilt city as the ruins of the promise of a New Argentina.

The arc of this argument provides the organizing structure for the book. In part 1, "Revelations among the Ruins," I show how the ruins of San Juan inspired the rise of Perón and his visions for a New Argentina. In chapter 1, I examine the durable inequality and political fragility that the wine boom had brought the province. In chapter 2, I turn to the disaster itself, arguing that it sharpened local divisions even as remedying its effects became a unifying national cause. I show how the earthquake's devastation discredited local elites, revealed the extent of national poverty, and inspired calls for transformation. Chapter 3 offers the first scholarly account of how the relief campaign launched Perón's political career. While other regime leaders spoke of submission and sacrifice, attempting to paper over conflicts by asserting their authority, Perón produced a new kind of authority by building a broad campaign to aid earthquake victims. This was where Perón became Perón, I argue, introducing himself, his labor bureaucracy, and his broader social agenda to the public, even as he maneuvered and consolidated power within the state.

In part 2, "The Cornerstone of the New Argentina," I argue that San Juan became a laboratory for building a different nation. In chapter 4, I examine what led the state to consider a radical rebuilding of the city and region, why architects were particularly drawn to this project, and what they proposed. Crucially, this was not only a matter of building new kinds of homes but also of creating a new social geography—a more diversified economy, a less concentrated population, a more egalitarian social order and, most controversially, a new location. Yet even in ruins, San Juan was far from a blank slate, as designers and state authorities soon discovered. In chapter 5, I turn to the reaction of fractious local elites who were unified for the first time by the threat of radical reform and the possible return of the provincial populist movement. In order to blunt the threat, they attempted to co-opt military authorities, making common cause with national objectives but arguing for a much narrower version of local rebuilding. Instead of reimagining the city, they claimed, the military need only build sturdy homes out of concrete. In chapter 6, I show how emergency housing in San Juan was the first step in the Peronist project to make housing a right. But I also show how emergency housing allowed the local elite to secure its position. Even as architects and reformist military officials pushed for radical rebuilding, local elites recruited engineers and less ambitious military figures as allies. A military confident of its power proved reluctant to mobilize broad support, and at the very moment provincial elites seemed defeated, they managed to battle radical rebuilding to a draw. This first half of the book thus presents San Juan as the place where Perón's ambitious vision for transformation emerged, and also where it began to falter.

In part 3, "From Leading Case to Exemplary Failure," I show how and why the project for a new San Juan stalled just as labor reforms and mass mobilization began to produce a New Argentina. Chapter 7 begins with the most radical proposal for rebuilding yet, a high point of Argentine modernism and an attempt to reconfigure social power and the spatial structure of the province. But riven by design disputes and political rivalries, progressively detached from the national ambitions of Perón, the schemes for transformation ultimately broke apart. In chapter 8, I show how the ruins of San Juan became a potent symbol, particularly for the opposition to the military government Perón led. This is also the moment at which architects found that their vision for the future was losing its purchase with state officials and the local public. In chapter 9, I argue that just as the ruins of San Juan became a central symbol in national political debate, the substantive dispute over how to transform the province was sidelined. When Perón finally did mobilize popular support in San Juan, it was too late for that support to connect up with a rebuilding project.

Part 4, "Rubble or No Rubble, We Want Perón," traces the national triumph of Perón's project, but the failure of an expansive vision of rebuilding for San Juan. In chapter 10, I show how the elected Peronist government that took office in 1946 based its authority on renouncing radical rebuilding and embracing Conservative elites. In chapter 11, I explore how Peronism finally built a coherent political project in San Juan, enlisting modernist architects to produce a vastly less ambitious but finally enduring vision for rebuilding the province. In chapter 12, I show how after Perón's overthrow, a Conservative engineer nicknamed "the Bulldozer Kid" rebuilt San Juan along more modest lines, as a shadow of what it might have been. In this sense, the rebuilt San Juan represents the ruins of the promise of a New Argentina. Yet this failure was also productive. The rebuilt city was a far more egalitarian, stable, and peaceful place than before the earthquake, one of the few examples worldwide of an "anti-seismic" city. San Juan was ultimately rebuilt, and transformed, though hardly in the ambitious way architects, state officials, and local activists had first imagined.

Before turning to the conceptual innovations of this work, one more comment about its structure. The first half of this book reveals for the first time the intimate links between the project for a new city and the project for a New Argentina, telling a story of perhaps unexpected convergence. The second half of this book, however, is a tale of divergence, as the model for the New Argentina turns into an afterthought. Ultimately, then, this book is as much about divergence as convergence. I show how the periphery shaped the national movement, decentering our accounts of Peronism. But I also follow how the national movement reshaped the periphery, especially after the initial bond between local and national transformation had frayed and broken, and rebuilding had taken a less ambitious—but still consequential—course. This is not only a story of how Peronism was born from the rubble; it is also a story of how Peronism was lived amid the enduring rubble, and despite it.

This book innovates across four conceptual domains: region and nation; disasters and rebuilding; architecture, housing, and planning; and Peronism and political culture. In each area, particularly disaster and architecture, it pushes the existing literature in new and unexplored directions. But one of its chief innovations is simply bringing—and holding—these domains of scholarship together. Until now, each has been pursued in isolation: sketches of individual disasters, monographic studies of particular architects, capsule provincial histories, and a self-contained literature on Peronism. But this isolation is a scholarly convention which impedes our understanding of the historical process itself.

Ultimately, this is an account of how a range of political actors—sometimes allied, sometimes opposed—grappled with the fundamental challenge of raising up a destroyed city and province. This rebuilding is an analytic problem in itself, worthy of interpretive weight, and not simply a subsidiary matter. Continuing to pursue individual strands of scholarship in isolation is a flawed approach, as is assuming, for instance, that the dominant approaches that do explain much about Peronism explain everything worth knowing. It means not only missing the point of this complex experience but also reproducing the narrowness of thought and inflexibility of approach which ultimately hampered rebuilding, as we will see. In short, there are larger lessons here in how to think about disasters and planning, and not simply in how to interpret the provincial and technical dimensions of Argentine politics. This is not about four separate parallel stories. Each of these processes is tightly linked to the emergence of a new national structure of power and expertise. We can look for Peronism not only in the movement itself but also in the broader imprint it left on Argentine society and landscape.

Region and Nation

Argentina in 1944 consisted of fourteen provinces with just over fourteen million people. This population was not evenly distributed across national territory. Roughly speaking, one could divide the population into three: one third lived in the city of Buenos Aires and its suburbs; another third lived elsewhere in the four Pampas provinces; and the last third were scattered across the ten provinces of the interior (and, in much smaller numbers, the nine federal territories). By virtually any measure of wealth or social development, from average income to literacy rates to infant mortality, the city of Buenos Aires and the core areas of the Pampas far outpaced the interior. Any indicator of economic power would underscore the massively dominant position of Buenos Aires—number of factories, size of banks, availability of electrical power—and it was, after all, the center of national politics as well.[11]

Yet there was a paradox here, as the interior could sometimes compensate for its economic weakness with political power. Argentina had one of the most concentrated patterns of settlement and development in the Americas, but it also had by far the most federalist constitutional design. For example, the ten interior provinces, with just under a third of the population, controlled three-quarters of the senate. This disproportion had been a deliberate act by the framers of the 1853 constitution, giving greater power to less favored areas in order to check the voracious ambitions of Buenos Aires and to promote a more balanced pattern of national development. It had produced stability, but hardly more even growth. Instead, this mechanism had given national backing to provincial elites. This pattern was evident from early on, but particularly marked in the two decades after 1880 when provincial elites took over the national state. The clearest example was the combination of tariff barriers, infrastructure investments, and official credit that enabled the rise of the sugar industry in Tucumán (and later Salta and Jujuy) and the wine industry in Mendoza and San Juan.[12]

The continual lament at the neglect of the interior was a legitimate complaint, because basic improvements and public investments, like sewers and schools, were indeed lacking. But it was also a (perhaps cynical) strategy for power, as provincial elites consistently used this rhetoric to strengthen their position, often at the expense of the remainder of their provinces.

The national state was more directly present in the provinces through the practice of intervention. After the upheaval of the independence era, the (revised) 1853 constitution had established that if "the republican form of government" was under threat in a province from subversion, corruption, or misbehavior, the national authorities could "intervene" in the province, remove its authorities, and appoint new ones. In theory, this was a temporary device for protecting established authorities. But in practice it became a common mechanism for putting friendly administrations in power. An essential coercive tool in the liberal state-building project, intervention became even more useful to the democratically elected Radical party after 1916, as they tried to overcome Conservative persistence and their own divisions in the provinces, and it was endlessly employed by the Conservative governments after 1930.

Given this larger picture, it is striking how the provinces vanish from studies of national history around 1880, just when their elites begin to colonize the national state. While historians often agree with Sarmiento that the interior holds the key to understanding much of the political and social dynamics of the nation in the nineteenth century, they rarely have assigned much importance to provincial dynamics in the twentieth. At most, they have examined how national processes played out in provincial settings. But with a few valuable exceptions, the interior remains "largely unexplored territory for historians of twentieth-century Argentina."[13]

This oversight is particularly notable for Peronism. Despite the importance of the interior to its project and electoral base, for many years Peronism was studied from the center. The few studies of Peronism in the interior characterized it as either a small-scale replica of the national movement or as a local front for conservative infiltration; only as this book neared completion has careful empirical work begun to appear.[14]

The general neglect of the interior has two ironic components in San Juan. First, while national histories take little account of San Juan, the national state has not displayed a similar indifference. "No province has suffered more . . . from federal interventions in its political life," one local historian claimed, and the record is indeed striking. From the first elections with universal male suffrage in 1916 to the fall of the last military government in 1983, San Juan was ruled by nineteen governors elected by the people—and thirty-eight interventors appointed by the national government.[15] Not one elected governor finished his term.[16] But while this might initially seem like evidence of the wanton abuse of national power, as the local historian suggested, those interventions were more often invited by local actors than arbitrarily imposed by the national state. They were a way for local elites to achieve by force what they could not win by ballot.

Second, while local politics have dropped out of national histories, they have produced a rich provincial historiography, largely focused on the populist political movement founded in the 1920s by Federico and Aldo Cantoni.[17] But while Cantonismo was born from opposition to a nationally imposed governor, endured near-constant conflict with national administrations, and is often described as a forerunner of national politics—as a "regional harbinger of Perón"—it has remained a folkloric episode within a national narrative still centered on Buenos Aires.[18] This tendency has been reinforced by the narrow scope of studies of Cantonismo, which have concentrated on its early years and provincial setting, rather than exploring its broader parallels, national alliances, or larger legacies. The repeated analogies to Peronism are emblematic. Scholars have made sweeping comparisons of the structural features and ideological programs of Cantonismo in the 1920s and Peronism in the 1940s. But they have not examined how the two interacted, for instance by considering how the earlier experience of Cantonismo shaped the later experience of Peronism in San Juan. As a result, they reinforce the notion that Cantonismo is a movement with exclusively local effects, and that Peronism is a movement with exclusively national causes.

Instead, I argue that the provinces are important spaces for producing the political. The earthquake itself is a powerful example of a provincial event shaping national trajectories. The earlier experience of Cantonismo was not only a precedent for Peronism but also a constraint on it. After enduring Cantonismo, and failing to overcome it, local Conservatives were eager to ally with Peronism—in order to check Cantoni. The overall impact of these dynamics on rebuilding suggests the value of examining such provincial spaces. By taking these areas seriously, moreover, we can develop a more comprehensive understanding not only of Peronism but of the nation as a whole.

Disaster and Rebuilding

"Earthquakes are not disasters in themselves," the Mexican seismologist Cinna Lomnitz reminds us, "structures make them so."[19] Lomnitz is literally speaking of physical structures, such as buildings, and these will indeed be at the center of this book. He is arguing against the common view which, in describing an event as a natural disaster, attributes its cause exclusively to the workings of the nonhuman world. It is only human presence, and the failure of human constructions, that make seismic events into natural disasters. Beyond the physical structures, as Lomnitz emphasizes, part of the responsibility can also be found in social structures, the relations of power that place certain groups in harm's way. If these social structures are often invisible or taken for granted, a major disaster can bring them into view—and open them to challenge. Disasters can be revelations, for those who experience them and for those who examine them later.

In scholarship, and in the popular imagination, disasters lead a double life. On the one hand, disasters are commonly assumed to produce swift and comprehensive transformations, which is why unexpected political or social changes are so often described metaphorically as "earthquakes." But the question of what changes earthquakes actually bring is left unexamined.

At the same time, disasters are also invoked as an example of trivial and routine change, epiphenomena of little interest and no consequence. When English newspaper editors were asked to name the least important headline ever, the winner was "Small Earthquake in Chile: Not Many Killed."[20] In this sense, disasters are often naturalized, rendered invisible, as their effects are ruled either unimportant or simply inevitable.

Thus disasters lead this unexamined double life, serving as metaphors both for dramatic change and for unremarkable stasis, with only sporadic attention paid to their actual dynamics and effects. In the case of San Juan, which after all does border Chile, we can see how this double analytic life has worked: a widespread acknowledgment of the disaster's importance, coupled with complete incuriosity about its effects. In fairness, perhaps this incuriosity is not so surprising. "Major seismic events are almost universally associated in the short term with perceptions of whole-scale and rapid change," John Dickie notes, but in the long term "the failure of those expectations to bear fruit in the aftermath of real quakes is almost equally widespread."[21]

This makes San Juan a particularly rich subject for study. For here we have a direct connection between the expectations for renewal in the aftermath and an enduring national movement, and also a clear, if paradoxical, relationship between that movement and the eventual (and partial) renewal of the stricken province. In short, San Juan is an excellent site for a comprehensive study of disaster and rebuilding, an approach that does not take a snapshot view but pursues a dynamic examination of historical process.

This book thus goes beyond the lively recent work by historians on disasters, in Latin America and elsewhere, which are mostly case studies using particular disasters as windows into society.[22] These works have critiqued the idea of a "natural disaster," emphasizing the social, political, and even cultural processes that put certain populations at risk from geological or climatic events. But they isolate disasters in two key ways. First, they tend to focus on the disaster as a singular, discrete event, rather than examining the disaster and recovery together, as an ongoing process and a contested field of action. Second, these studies take disasters as illustrations but not initiators of larger trends. In short, they view disasters as windows rather than crucibles. It is certainly true that many disasters do have only isolated impact and are primarily of interest as illustrations of already-known social or political processes. But others, like San Juan, have played a large role in remaking politics and places. For as the geographer Alejandro Rofman noted twenty years ago, nearly every attempt at comprehensive state planning in Latin America began as a response to natural disaster. Across the region, Rofman pointed out, the interventionist state emerged under the sign of catastrophe.[23]

One way of thinking about disaster and rebuilding is through the trope of a locality under assault by rapid change—first from the destruction, then from the reconstruction. Such a vision of tradition besieged by modernity runs through the handful of local accounts from San Juan.[24] This approach obviously echoes not only parochial rhetoric but also major traditions in social scientific thought. Many sociological works on disasters, for example, examine how unified communities respond to the impact of disruptive outside forces.[25] A more sophisticated version of this opposition underlies James Scott's influential account of how state designs for modernity have systematically disregarded local knowledge and experience.[26] And there will be much here that could suggest such a reading, in the brutal experience of disaster, the prolonged disruptions of the aftermath, the prideful schemes of designers, or the forceful actions of distant state authorities.

But the primary thrust of this book is different. Nothing about the local was so isolated or bounded as this image would suggest. On the contrary, vineyards dominated the landscape and winemakers dominated the polity due to national arrangements, from the construction of railroads and establishment of tariffs to the brutal suppression of reformist groups. Local knowledge was of how to build in adobe, a technique that resulted in thousands of deaths. Framing the issue as tradition versus modernity fails to understand that local tradition was itself a modern product, and a particularly flawed one at that. Framing the issue as the local versus the national accepts the terms local elites have preferred, because it obscures the key question of local power. It also silences those who embraced national projects for eminently local reasons. In the aftermath of devastation, with the perfidy of local elites exposed, those reasons could be quite compelling.

In this book, I argue for the importance of San Juan not as a window but as a crucible: this disaster drove the emergence of a major political movement, the reconfiguration of regional power, and the reshaping of the technical field, as well as the material remaking of the city.[27] I thus examine precisely the interaction between the local and national, as political authorities, technical experts, and local activists confronted the material challenges of rebuilding. In short, this book looks closely but critically at the promise of modernization offered by architects and state officials, keeping a focus throughout on how that promise resonated, or failed to resonate, and how local power relations were implicated in it. I take the power of these visions of national transformation seriously, which means taking architecture and engineering seriously.

Architecture, Housing, and Planning

Structures are obviously central to both disasters and rebuilding, as Lomnitz reminds us, particularly the physical buildings that are the most obvious evidence of collapse or recovery. But as the fall of the adobe structures underscores, the question of how to build again did not have an easy or obvious answer. While the destruction of the city served as a political indictment, the restoration of the city was not solely a political challenge but a technical and material one as well. For these reasons, architecture and engineering were implicated in rebuilding from the beginning.

But there were also larger political and institutional reasons for architects and engineers to join this debate. For both professions, especially for architecture, the earthquake came at a moment of change, when professional practice was turning from the design of isolated monumental buildings toward the provision of social housing and the planning of whole urban environments. This was a transnational shift in architecture, broadly associated with modernism, which played out with particular intensity in Argentina. Here a small profession previously centered on the city of Buenos Aires, led by exiles and immigrants and driven by aesthetic ideas associated with Europe, was giving way to a growing field led by the native-born, receptive to nationalist projects, and increasingly concerned with building and planning for the interior. For engineers, a similar shift had taken place a decade earlier—but led to quite different political commitments in debates over rebuilding. In both cases, San Juan was a decisive test for their visions of how to build not only stronger houses but a stronger nation, now that the nineteenth-century liberal project was apparently exhausted.

The architects (and to a lesser extent engineers) involved in planning San Juan were a broad sample of the strongest voices in the largest professional community in the Western Hemisphere, outside of the United States. This is thus a decisive chapter in the history of the profession, as well as in the history of the technical capacity of the Argentine state—and the relationship between the two.

Understanding the competing visions for the future city requires taking design seriously, first of all, but also looking closely at the ways design is entangled with and deployed by the state. This requires moving beyond both the idealist approach common to architectural and planning history, which overlooks how politics and institutions condition design, and the reductionist approach frequent in cultural and political history, which reduces form to a reflection of politics. On the contrary, it is precisely because form is not directly reducible to politics that the relationship is so complex. The political use of architecture involves the selection, encouragement, and deployment of certain design elements (but not others), rather than the simple derivation of formal practices from social or political ones. The architectural use of politics, in turn, has to do with harnessing the powers of the state to advance particular design solutions.

This book builds on rich recent work on architecture in Argentina, particularly by Anahí Ballent.[28] Focused on the Peronist era, she shows how the professional concerns of designers and the social concerns of the state converged on three key areas—architecture, housing, and the city. This period of alliance and intricate struggles, Ballent demonstrates, structured both the later political course of architecture as a practice and the material policies of the state, even as both architects and Peronists subsequently attempted to tell their own histories in terms of autonomous actions and solutions. Limiting her study to Buenos Aires, Ballent explores the complexities of the relationship at the center of national power, but she does not touch on the largest architectural project and professional dispute during the decade—the reconstruction of San Juan.

Peronism

Scholars have studied Peronism for sixty years, but in many ways the field remains remarkably open, as major issues have not yet received scholarly attention.[29] The initial terms of the debate were set by essayists and, above all, sociologists, the first scholars to produce detailed studies.[30] Marked by an assumption that Peronism was a pathological outcome, these studies focused on the structural analysis of class dynamics. Over time, they took greater account of political and historical contingency, but they never lost a focus on labor, with an emphasis on structural factors, and a conceptual concern with origins, devoting far more attention to Perón's early career than to the period after 1946 when the movement consolidated power.

Until recently, the historian Mariano Plotkin observed, much of the literature offered a "monolithic image" that Perón "controlled every aspect of Argentine life," with "no evidence of tension within the regime."[31] Any newspaper from the time would have dispelled this image: for all the attempts at control, even the official press offered daily evidence of cross-cutting conflicts not easily reduced to polarized oppositions between the regime and its critics. Yet scholars largely ignored this rich material. Instead, scholarly energy focused far more on explaining Peronism in theory, premised on stylized understandings of its social base and political project, than on examining Peronism in practice—a choice which, as Mariano Plotkin noted, reflected "the endurance of the vision of Peronism as a kind of pathology."[32] Only in the last two decades have historians taken the lead in this debate, subjecting those stylized understandings to empirical critique.

From the sixties on, the richest strand in the literature focused on labor. This was because unions had become decisive political actors with Perón, and because the pioneering sociologist Gino Germani had defined the political allegiances of labor as the central question requiring explanation. Germani explained workers' support of Perón in terms of backwardness and irrationality; others later argued more convincingly for workers' economic self-interest.[33] The work of Daniel James was particularly innovative, showing the inner workings of unions to be far more dynamic, contested, and contingent than previous accounts had allowed. He underscored the grassroots mobilization of a movement long portrayed as dominated from above, while showing how that rank-and-file initiative could be channeled into demobilizing projects. Perhaps most importantly, James sketched out a more nuanced social history of Peronism that was attentive to symbolic action and cultural imaginaries.[34]

The past two decades have seen many case studies. Perhaps the most important examined Peronism and the Catholic Church, showing how Catholic activism expanded dramatically after 1930, exercised decisive influence over Peronism, and ended up in opposition.[35] Others have reexamined earlier commonplaces, like the propaganda apparatus, cultural strategies, and education policy of the regime.[36] This has given way to imaginative work on the press, popular music, and mass culture.[37] There have also been the first examinations of the functioning of political parties during these years, exploring the contested emergence of Peronism and, more recently, the opposition.[38] Topical studies have begun to explore state policies in more detail, especially on economic, health, and social matters.[39] Most important for our purposes here, of course, are the works on architecture and housing.

These works have restored Peronism to the larger sweep of Argentine history, as a particularly intense, traumatic, and productive moment within a longer trajectory. They have underscored continuities, especially with the fraudulent governments of the preceding years, while clarifying the points of rupture and departure. Many Peronist tools for state action and political mobilization were forged under the previous order. The crucial change was not in the tools themselves but in how and where they were deployed.

But in all these case studies, we have begun to lose sight of Peronism as a totality, of how each piece relates to others. The work on the Church, for example, does a splendid job of tracing how an elitist attack on liberalism became plebian and radical through its embrace of social justice, and ultimately connected up with the labor movement. But labor and the Church remain autonomous entities, studied by different scholars, with the relationship between them largely unspecified. To understand this complex ensemble, scholars have effectively learned to hold constant all but one or two variables for the purposes of their study, producing results that are illuminating but limited.

For all the recent output, there remain major lacunae in our understanding of the most important political movement in twentieth-century Argentina. First, our comprehension of the state is still fragmentary and often abstract, based more on deploying normative categories, examining rhetorical strategies, and invoking the life histories of a few key actors than on examining how policies were made and enacted on the ground. Recent works have clarified how the state expanded up to 1946 but only begun to follow these processes through the elected Peronist administration. By examining the unmaking and remaking of San Juan over the course of two decades, this book offers a comprehensive and integrated account of state policy, however fragmented, incomplete, and contradictory that state policy was.

Second, rebuilding the city required actors at the time to make political connections between matters normally viewed separately, connecting projects, organizing interests, and blocking opposing alliances. This book will take up this theme for the largest design project and central professional dispute of the decade, the reconstruction of San Juan.

Third, our understanding of the political dynamics of the period is still biased toward the center, and toward Perón himself. This may be justifiable, but it presumes what it needs to demonstrate, the primacy of the center as the political motor for change. Rather than taking Peronism as a monolith, we need to understand how the movement came together, building on which forces, and in what contexts. Though this book will not offer a comprehensive analysis of the rise and fall of Perón—many aspects of Peronism are not examined here, from gender to economic policy, and other well-understood aspects are passed over lightly, such as labor politics, military policy, or Church-state relations—it offers a path back to totality by focusing on the making of Peronism in and through one place.

As we will see, there are many familiar actors in sanjuanino Peronism: organized workers, reformist military officers, opportunistic politicians, and Catholic activists. There are also some who are far less familiar, such as modernist architects and conservative landowners. San Juan is certainly not representative of the country as a whole, but it offers a singularly revealing vantage point on the Peronist state, as no other province felt the force of federal power or the push and pull of Perón's promises of change quite so intensely. By narrowing in on one province, and particularly on one city, we can examine Peronism as a project on an intimate scale that also resonated nationally. Furthermore, because the disaster cast the totality of the city itself into question, leading many to rethink each of its components and how they related to each other, this is a particularly rich site to examine the textures of local political and social life under Peronism, its promise, contradictions, and limits.

Sources and Structure

Before turning to the work itself, a brief comment on its sources and overall shape is in order. It is based on three years of field research, conducted in a score of libraries and archives in Argentina (in San Juan, Mendoza, and Buenos Aires), Chile, England, and the United States. Because this is fundamentally a political story, the key sources here would be, in a perfect world, the archives of the powerful and expanding national state. But in Argentina, these are largely unavailable to scholars. The Archivo General de la Nación (AGN) has only one collection on the Perón years, built around public letters responding to Perón's radio request in 1951 for projects to include in his Second Five-Year Plan. Considering that this single broadcast message generated several hundred boxes of archival material, one can only imagine the rich sources buried or lost inside the working archives of government ministries or the Archivo Intermedio, the storage facility for the AGN. Indeed, when a small piece of the

Archivo Intermedio was opened to scholars as I was finishing the book, I found a dozen highly useful Interior Ministry documents—surviving fragments of a missing series of weekly reports submitted over decades. As things stand, though, scholars have minimal access to the internal workings of national agencies: meeting minutes, internal memos, and policy debates have vanished or remain hidden. Even the scraps found by others can later disappear: for eight years I tried to chase down a diplomatic file an earlier scholar had cited on Church-state conflicts after the earthquake, and despite the assistance of a top ministry aide, I failed.[40] These archival gaps undoubtedly produce gaps in interpretation, mysteries that can be resolved indirectly if at all.

Secretive as it kept its inner workings, though, the Argentine national state loudly proclaimed its policies and achievements—above all during Peronist rule. Such printed speeches, press releases, pamphlets, reports, official journals, and technical bulletins have been singularly valuable, although it is worth underscoring that, as there is no central repository for such items, my collection was gathered patiently over years from many locations. Beyond official self-promotion, the sharp politicization of the period resulted in intense debates about government actions—at the time, after Perón was overthrown, and after that overthrow turned disastrously sour—which ultimately brought a significant number of internal government documents into the public record. Finally, and fortunately for this study, provincial states are far less secretive, making the provincial archive invaluable, despite somewhat haphazard organization, as suggested by its long-standing (but now rectified) division into two categories, Miscellaneous 1 and Miscellaneous 2.

Equally important were the technical publications of architects, engineers, and builders. In addition, I have made extensive use of the private papers of four architects—Fermín H. Bereterbide, Ernesto Vautier, Jorge Ferrari Hardoy, and José M. F. Pastor—and two leading politicians—Senator Pablo Ramella and Deputy Ramón Tejada. While only the Ferrari Hardoy and Ramella papers are organized, all offered valuable clues to the inner logic of disputes and negotiations within the technical and political fields, provided sketches and preliminary versions of drawings published elsewhere, and contained internal government documents otherwise unavailable.

Along with examining these private papers I conducted oral history interviews. While often extraordinarily rich sources in their own right, in this book I employ them more to flesh out the larger stories of disaster, architecture, and politics rather than to explore in depth the complex terrain of subjectivity and memory.

Finally, in many ways the backbone of the study is the popular press. This work is based on a comprehensive reading of all the newspapers with regular correspondents in San Juan for the six years bracketing the earthquake and key moments thereafter. This includes two national papers of record, the regional paper in Mendoza, and the four main local papers. Beyond this, I examined a wide range of bulletins, broadsheets, and magazines, including the official publications of Communists, Socialists, and the archdiocese of Buenos Aires. Drawing on this diverse range of sources, I return to a hidden corner of an extensively studied period in Argentine history, to show the complexity and vitality of the struggle to rebuild a city and remake a nation in the wake of tragedy.

This book is a narrative, and that merits a few words of closing explanation. It is divided into four parts, and each of those is divided into three chapters. Each of the parts begins with a preface that surveys the argument so far and outlines its direction in the coming chapters. Some of the chapters are relatively self-contained, tracing the arc of an argument from beginning to end, while others find their larger meaning, and the full weight of their argument, only in the context of the book as a whole. Rather than trying to separate out the strands of my argument thematically—first a chapter on buildings, then a chapter on the elite, then a chapter on popular politics—I have tied them together in chronological sequence.

This is partly a question of style, but it is also a matter of methodology. I have chosen a narrative approach to capture an important aspect of the experience. As I have argued, disasters scramble the ways that fields of knowledge and historical actors relate to each other. Thus to cleanly separate the social from the technical, to isolate the project to build a labor movement from the debates over how to build stronger houses, is to miss precisely what was at stake in this historical moment.

PART 1

REVELATIONS AMONG THE RUINS, EARLY 1944

Out across the city of San Juan, late on the summer evening of 15 January 1944, the sociable hour had arrived: there was a wedding at the Concepción parish, early shows at the cinemas, families out for a stroll, and modest folk drinking and playing cards in the bars. In the downtown cafes, one topic dominated all conversation: the latest shift in provincial political power. For the eleventh time in ten years, a new man was taking the reins of provincial government, and no one knew quite what to expect.

Six months before, on 4 June 1943, the military had overthrown a corrupt Conservative regime. But for all the promises of dramatic change and calls to unity, regime leaders were divided in their ambitions, and especially in their opinions on the Second World War. While a smaller group largely favored the Allies and saw themselves as caretakers, charged with cleaning up a corrupt political system and returning power to civilians, a rival group strongly defended neutrality, saw themselves as revolutionaries, and aspired to more far-reaching changes. The smaller group included a few Army generals and nearly all the officers in the Navy; the larger group was led by a core of mid-rank Army officers who had formed a secret military lodge, the Group of Officers United (GOU). The hard-liners in the GOU played a minor role in the coup but a major role in barracks struggles and cabinet crises afterward. By the end of 1943, this group, joined by civilian nationalists, Catholic integralists, and a few fascists, had finally prevailed. On New Year's Eve, the government had dissolved all political parties, implemented censorship of the press, and established mandatory religious education. These three actions were body blows against central institutions of liberal Argentina—political parties, newspapers, and public schools—and pointed toward a very different future, authoritarian, illiberal, and Catholic.[1]

David Uriburu, the new interventor in San Juan, was in keeping with this harsh new tone: he was a pro-Axis nationalist lawyer, a former officer in the political police, and the nephew of General José Uriburu, the leader of the 1930 coup which had overthrown the last legitimately elected government. He was certainly a change from the previous interventor, a clean-government naval officer who had chosen, surprisingly, to draw his cabinet from the local leadership of a national antifascist organization. In his first speech, Uriburu declared liberalism bankrupt. "The dispossessed classes already know that liberal institutions were the instrument of financial powers in their work of oppression and injustice," he claimed. "Now we bring the Glad Tidings" of a government that rejects liberalism to embrace what is "morally and materially right and just." He declared that "we bring disappointment to those . . . waiting in the shadows, hoping our action will serve their interests," insisting to an audience composed largely of politicians that "politicians of all parties should fulfill their sacrificial duty by leaving public life and returning to the private sphere many should never have left." The military regime, Uriburu announced, has brought to an end "the chances of political parties, of factions, of miniscule interests."[2]

Locals were accustomed to playing along with the political enthusiasms of new interventors, and the winemaker establishment had grown skillful at turning such enthusiasms to their own ends. Proclamations of rupture from above were generally followed by practices of accommodation from below. Uriburu surely recognized this—perhaps that was why he signaled the break so stridently. His proclamations were backed by military force and a broader project. For those in the cafes, fearful of losing their position or eager to gain a new one, deeper changes seemed to be coming. Since the state was by far the province's largest employer, these changes would affect many beyond the chattering classes downtown. And while Uriburu's rhetoric was tailored primarily to wealthy and elitist nationalists like himself, it clearly did resonate with a broader disenchantment with the political and social order.

This world was about to be overturned by a far more powerful force than politics. In the long and tumultuous aftermath, San Juan would be transformed more deeply than Uriburu and his allies had dreamed. This change would emerge from within the military government but take a rather different course than Uriburu had imagined, more controversial, and also far more consequential.

This opening section explores the world about to be destroyed, the experience of destruction, and its immediate local and national aftermath. Chapter 1 examines San Juan through the lens of the wine boom, starting out in the countryside and then moving into the city that controlled it. The focus here is on the boom's enduring strength and polarizing impact, in geographic, social, and ultimately political terms. Chapter 2 turns to the experience of destruction, showing how the earthquake undermined the authority of the local state and widened divides within the community, even as it narrowed some others. Chapter 3 then broadens the focus to the national scene, showing how Perón turned this unanticipated opportunity to his own ends, channeling popular enthusiasm for change into a distinctive military project for transformation. In this way, the ruins of San Juan became an invitation to transform the nation. This began in the world created by the wine boom.

CHAPTER 1

"ROOTED VINES AND UPROOTED MEN"

THE WORLD WINE MADE

San Juan is an arid and sparsely inhabited terrain of mountains and deserts. Less than 1 percent of its surface area is cultivated land. The flats are the driest region in Argentina, receiving less than ten centimeters of annual rainfall. Two river systems cut across this stark landscape, bringing water down from the high Andes, and since before the Spanish conquest, settlement has concentrated in five oases along their course: Valle Fértil in the east, Jáchal in the north, Rodeo in the northwest, Calingasta in the west, and San Juan in the south. Nestled in the gaps between mountain and desert, these oases contain a rich array of microclimates—nearly a quarter of all the distinct ecological zones in the entire country.[1] From these oases, hunting, ranching, and trading circuits crossed the seemingly forbidding mountains and deserts.

The provincial capital stood in the middle of the largest oasis, a broad valley filled with the alluvial soil the river had dragged down from the mountains over centuries. Since its founding in 1562, the city of San Juan had been the formal center of power in the region, but its control over the territory was often nominal at best, particularly in the decades after independence.

The rise of wine in the central valley changed this balance of power. The main oasis filled up with vineyards, and the others faded into irrelevance. The capital city became the center of the winery complex and the main railroad stop, greatly increasing its economic and political power by integrating into national markets. By contrast, the other oases grew weaker and more isolated, failing to forge robust connections to the provincial capital, much less to national markets. The railroad arrived in the capital in 1885, but took another half-century to reach Jáchal—and never made it to Rodeo, Calingasta, or Valle

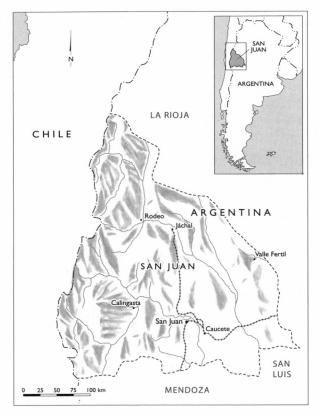

Province of San Juan

Fértil at all. There were not even permanent roads to these other oases until the 1920s.

All these outlying communities were integrated into national markets, but on deeply unequal terms. The once-lively cattle trade with Chile from Calingasta, Rodeo, and Jáchal dwindled in the face of rising tariffs, greater political obstacles, and a shrinking pool of buyers. The grain mills of Jáchal faded away, unable to compete with the much larger Buenos Aires enterprises, which enjoyed easy access to capital and cheap Pampas wheat. The mines scattered across the mountains hobbled along without reliable power, investment, or transportation, producing little beyond sustenance for nearby towns. The mines inspired utopian rhetoric, to be sure, but few sustained attempts at development, even though San Juan had sizable known deposits—for example, of marble, mica, copper, iron, wolfram, and gold—and the one mining school in the republic, founded in the capital by liberal governor Domingo Sarmiento.[2]

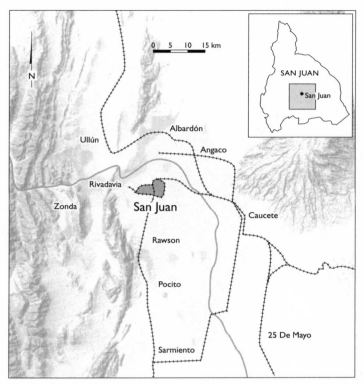

Central valley of San Juan Province

In practice, staking the province's future on grape monoculture meant leaving behind everything outside the central valley. Migrants made their way to the one dynamic pole, and by 1944, 90 percent of the province lived in the central valley, in the shadow of the vines.[3]

The Central Valley

This landscape was ruled by the wineries, and above all by the twenty largest firms. Only these twenty, the *bodegas exportadoras*, shipped wine out of the province under their own label. Located primarily along the rail lines that circled the capital, they accounted for three-quarters of the industry's production and an even larger share of its profits. The largest wineries, like that of Bartolomé del Bono, were integrated complexes employing hundreds of workers and producing millions of liters of wine annually. Towering over the fields, these structures were the physical expression of the social power wielded by their owners, the bodegueros (winemakers), the cluster of families which had come to dominate local economics and politics.[4]

2 Del Bono winery, San Juan province, ca. 1940. CREDIT AGN.

Beyond the bodegas exportadoras, there were about three hundred smaller wineries. These operations generally employed a handful of workers, produced a few thousand liters annually, and sold their output either to the exportadoras or to wholesalers in Buenos Aires or Rosario. Smaller bodegas were more geographically dispersed than their larger rivals, spread out across the central valley, with fewer than half around the capital.[5] More vulnerable to market fluctuations than the large producers, the small bodegas often shut down in bad years, leaving about two hundred and fifty in operation during any given harvest. Still, running a winery was a profitable business, and many small-time bodegueros were among the wealthiest people in the province.

Surrounding the wineries were the vineyards themselves, a dense patchwork across the valley floor. In this model of mass production of wine, most grapes were grown by independent viñateros (growers), not the wineries themselves. Vineyards did not vary in plantings: they all grew the same varietals, with little concern for quality. But they did vary in size: there were about two hundred large, a thousand medium, and four thousand small vineyards.[6] The largest covered almost 40 percent of the acreage, the middle ones another 40 percent, and the smallest—more than two-thirds of all properties—just over 20 percent.[7]

The largest viñateros employed sharecroppers and hired hands, but most relied on family labor, hiring solely for the harvest. Whatever their size, viñateros faced a common structural bind: they lacked storage capacity and thus were forced to sell their entire crop to wineries at every harvest. Every year, wineries bought most of the grapes they processed—usually about four-fifths—from independent growers.[8] Because of their size, bodegas exportadoras accounted for most of these purchases, although nearly all wineries bought some grapes. With five thousand growers effectively selling to a handful of wineries, power rested with the bodegas exportadoras, who were decisive in setting prices. The persistent tendency toward overproduction of grapes only strengthened their position. At the end of the harvest, each viñatero needed to sell his entire production or let it spoil—a powerful incentive to lower prices in falling markets. In good years, viñateros could earn better returns than most other agricultural producers in the country, but in bad years, wineries could easily force them to swallow losses. The viñateros kept at the game in the hopes of striking it rich in a bonanza year, and they cushioned themselves from losses by squeezing what they could from sharecroppers and agricultural workers. Needless to say, these arrangements only increased the power of the bodegueros.[9]

Grapes were not the only crop grown in San Juan: interspersed with the vineyards were orchards of plums and peaches, fields of tomatoes and onions, and even the occasional stand of the once-dominant wheat and alfalfa. Closer in to the capital, truck farms grew vegetables for the local market. There were also a few clusters of specialized production outside the central valley, such as apples and onions in Calingasta. But these operations were small-scale and distinctly secondary to the grape. Tellingly, grape production was fully industrialized, but the province did not have a single plant to process other fruits or vegetables.[10]

Overall, grape monoculture brought fabulous new fortunes to the largest winemakers and a shallower prosperity to a broad range of middling groups in the industry itself (small bodegueros and viñateros), the larger world of commerce (bankers, professionals, merchants, clerks, and skilled tradesmen), and local government (teachers and provincial employees). The winery elite was overwhelmingly urban and counted in its ranks many immigrants, most of the older patrician families, and more than a few of their once-poor cousins.

Yet the major trend of these decades was towards increased inequality. At the onset of the boom, rural property ownership had been more evenly distributed in San Juan than anywhere else in the country, but since then the absolute number of landowners had declined, even as the population had tripled. The average size of holdings remained small, because vineyards were used so intensively, but they were held by fewer people. Where once 30 percent of the economically active population had owned land, now only 8 percent did.[11]

During the grape boom, many smallholders lost their land, while gauchos and farmhands were driven from relatively settled and permanent positions into migrant and seasonal work. By the 1940s, harvest workers employed for two months a year constituted three-quarters of the agricultural workforce. Powerful structures of domination and a weakly diversified economy had created a floating population of unskilled labor, employed primarily in the countryside but increasingly living on the impoverished outskirts of the capital.[12]

The brutal inequality of this social order was evident in the low wages and harsh lives of the majority. All available sources—official documents, press reports, and popular memories—attest to widespread misery, especially during the wine industry's cyclical crises of overproduction, most recently in the 1930s, when San Juan and Mendoza had the highest unemployment in the nation. There are no reliable surveys of wealth and income, but public health statistics are telling. The province had one of the country's highest concentrations of doctors, but its second-worst infant mortality rate.[13] Nearly three-quarters of those called up for the draft were rejected as physically unfit— almost three times the national rate.[14] Life expectancy here was half that for Buenos Aires, one prominent doctor calculated, and had actually declined during the wine boom. Disease mortality rates for San Juan were comparable to those of Buenos Aires seventy years earlier. "The extraordinary industrial development that has marvelously transformed every other value," the doctor observed, "has proven incapable until now of doing anything for the value of our human lives."[15] Indeed, it had actively devalued them. For the doctor, whose father and grandfather had been leading bodegueros and governors, this was a bitter conclusion to reach. But it aptly captured the dynamism and brutality of this social order, particularly in the provincial capital, which had always been the fortress of the prosperous and was increasingly becoming the refuge of the impoverished as well.

The City of Statues

Entering the city from the valley, the landscape changed from green to gray. One left the vineyards behind, passed through ramshackle suburbs, and crossed a threshold of poplars to enter a world of high walls, narrow streets, and few trees. This was "a city of dried mud," as one local described it: "dull, faded, and ochre." For two urbanists hired in 1942 to draft a master plan, it was a "stubbornly dry" city lacking public space and civic grandeur, "spiritually and physically degraded" by heat and grit.[16]

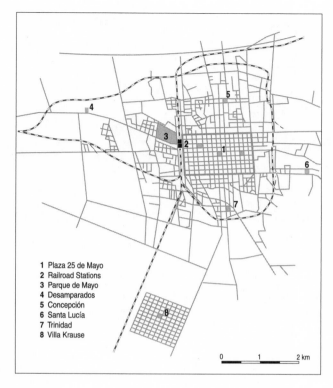

1 Plaza 25 de Mayo
2 Railroad Stations
3 Parque de Mayo
4 Desamparados
5 Concepción
6 Santa Lucía
7 Trinidad
8 Villa Krause

0   1   2 km

City of San Juan,
1942

Locals and outsiders alike portrayed San Juan as a kind of open-air museum of national history, suffused with "that somber and melancholy feeling" of being "a little lost in time." It was the third-oldest city in the country, with a skyline punctuated by twenty-one churches. Its streets were laid out on the traditional Spanish colonial model, a checkerboard grid nine blocks by thirteen blocks, and still lined by adobe houses, as all the streets of the republic once were. At the center of the grid was a plaza and along its outside edges were the four avenues that had long marked the limit of civilized society. The sculptures of liberal heroes in the downtown plazas were only a generation old, but many observers already found them ancient, marking San Juan as a "city of statues" haunted by a musty "sense of the fatherland."[17]

Yet this nostalgic air was the product of recent decisions. Fifty years before, on 27 October 1894, a powerful earthquake had struck the city. The quake killed only twenty people but caused extensive damage, even to the recently built seat of government. The governor appointed a commission of geologists to study rebuilding. He clearly had the precedent of neighboring Mendoza in mind: after that city was devastated by an earthquake in 1861, it was rebuilt on

3 Downtown San Juan, late 1930s. Photo from northwest, facing southeast. Plaza 25 de Mayo in upper right corner. Note patios inside houses, irregular street fronts, narrow streets. CREDIT *REVISTA CUYO*.

a new site, two kilometers to the west, and in dramatically different form, with wide streets lined by trees and canals. The 1894 quake left San Juan "a constant danger, an open grave," with nearly every building damaged and many collapsed, observed the geologist Leopoldo Gómez de Terán, the director of the mining school. The commission he led produced a geological survey and an ambitious proposal to rebuild the city "on a new basis," with wide streets, better construction, and a new site—on higher and firmer ground to the west. A second commission concurred, arguing that "leaving things as they were . . . is almost criminal" and rebuilding on a new site would be less expensive. Endorsed by the governor, the proposal required legislative approval and national funding. This early in the wine boom, San Juan was still a small city, lacking expensive infrastructure such as paving, sewers, or electricity.[18]

But all the geologists did not agree, and one prominent professor from Córdoba argued that moving the city was pointless, since the entire province had seismic activity. Instead of a new site, he endorsed new building techniques: better materials, stronger joints, and a ban on the tall façades that had collapsed into the streets.[19] In light of this counterproposal, local political rivalries, and a lack of national support, the legislature voted down the governor's ambitious idea—and went on to reject laws to widen the streets or require improved construction methods.[20]

"Never was there a more opportune time to move the city," Gómez de Terán's assistant observed fifty years later. Instead, the city was rebuilt on the same layout using the same techniques.[21] In the following decades, the city became much larger and denser, doubling in area and increasing tenfold in population. In the center, larger properties were divided up, internal patios built over, and irrigation canals closed off. Workshops replaced gardens in the middle of many blocks. Many property owners benefited from the growth, as two-thirds of the population were renters.[22]

With the rise of the wineries and the influx from the countryside, the city spread out beyond the four avenues, absorbing garden plots, small vineyards, and the neighboring towns of Concepción to the north, Santa Lucía to the east, Trinidad to the south, and Desamparados to the west. By 1944, the capital and suburbs held nearly one hundred thousand people, just under half the provincial population. This was the most pronounced case of urban primacy in the republic: the capital was twenty times larger than the second city.[23]

Outside the four avenues, the city looked quite different. This new urban landscape was dominated by the railroad and the scores of wineries alongside it. These tracks, the backbone of industrial San Juan, encircled the city just past the four avenues, tying its economy together while splitting its neighborhoods apart. Out here, the rough uniformity of downtown houses gave way to a haphazard accretion of shacks and bodegas, and the strict geometry of the central streets fractured into an irregular array of pathways, alleys, and the occasional avenue. There were pockets of wealth, especially in Desamparados to the west, which had clusters of fashionable chalets and a few country mansions enveloped by the expanding city. There were also older and denser sections, like Concepción to the north, which seemed like tattered variations on the city center. But most of the suburbs were poor, filled with the dried mud shelters that the impoverished majority called home. One measure of the social distance from center to periphery is average life span: the province calculated it at thirty-eight years inside the four avenues and seventeen in the suburbs just outside.[24] When they looked closely at such areas, even Conservatives were forced to admit that "popular housing in San Juan, in the immense majority of cases, is incompatible with elemental conditions of human dignity and health."[25]

Almost every building in the province, from the Cathedral down to the most modest home, was made from dried mud and straw—but they were not all built the same way. Larger and more symbolically important structures were built from adobe bricks, as were most urban dwellings. Over the course of the wine boom, elaborate façades executed in masonry replaced many of the austere whitewashed street fronts of the past. But these innovations were limited to the façade—one nationalist architect later derided the style as "Louis XIV in front, the gaucho Juan Moreira out back"—and represented precisely the building technique the geologists had wanted to ban.[26] The houses behind were still laid out in traditional fashion, with a high wall along the street followed by a series of rooms and patios stretching back to an interior garden. Their basic structure was also the same: massive load-bearing walls composed of solid blocks of sun-dried adobe joined together by mud mortar and covered with an outer layer of lime plaster. The thick walls and the heavy roofs perched atop them enabled little heat or cold to pass through, a crucial virtue in this desert climate, keeping houses cool in the day and warm at night. While there were more or less refined versions of this construction, all partook of the cultural value placed on solidity, as massive structures rooted in the earth that sheltered a private world of shadowy rooms and intimate patios against an often harsh and threatening outside.

By contrast, out in the countryside, or on the city's poorer fringes, most homes were built of quincha, an indigenous technique refined during Spanish colonial rule. The weight of a quincha building was carried by a light frame of logs or trunks; instead of solid adobe brick, the walls were a web of twigs woven together and smeared with a mixture of mud, straw and animal excrement. The roof was made in a similar way. Rather than presenting a massive wall to the outside world, quincha offered a thin and fragile screen, often rough, irregular, and apparently unsanitary. Because it was light, quincha was held to offer little shelter, and since it was inexpensive, it was often portrayed as a sign of primitiveness and penury. For decades, local elites had drawn a strong contrast between the solid and the frail, the finished and the rough, the cultured and the barbaric, making a rancho of quincha into the very image of rural backwardness—and moral degradation. Replacing such homes with something more solid and sanitary was the individual aim of many striving workers and the long-standing rhetorical goal of reform-minded elites.

Even if nearly all of San Juan was built from dirt, quincha was regarded as especially improper. Critiques of quincha were unconcerned with structural design; they drew on science only to portray quincha (with some basis) as a breeding ground for disease. Yet fierce denunciations yielded little in specific initiatives in housing or public health. Rather than spurring efforts at reform, this discourse primarily served to draw a sharp line between city and country, between the civilized and proper downtown and the grimy and barbarous outskirts.

Just as local urban culture prized traditional construction, it valued traditional locations. The city was lacking in public amenities, and had only one small park, located just outside the four avenues, with a pond, a copse of trees, equestrian statues, and the provincial stadium. There were other spaces for sociability, from the six smaller plazas—two inside the four avenues, and one in each of the four surrounding towns—to the sports clubs outside the center, the bars and cheap pensions across from the railroad station, or the clutter of shops and stalls around the municipal market. But for many sanjuaninos, especially the wealthy, there was only one proper place to gather.

The heart of the city remained the Plaza 25 de Mayo. It was not the precise spot where the Spaniards had planted their banner in 1562—that was twenty-five blocks north, in what was now the flood-prone suburb of Concepción—but it was the starting point for everything in provincial life. This was the local seat of authority, a space framed by the columns of official buildings, sheltered by a canopy of trees, and always surrounded by a file of parked cars.

Two statues of local heroes anchored the square: the patriotic cleric Fray Justo Santa María de Oro and the anticlerical intellectual Domingo Faustino Sarmiento, arguably the most influential liberal thinker in nineteenth-century Latin America. As one of the signatories of the Argentine declaration of independence and a firm advocate of republican government, Fray Justo placed the Church at the heart of national history. Sarmiento, for his part, was first a relative and protégé of the Oro family, then a writer, politician, and president. Here he was cast as a man of ideas. Unlike the other statesmen in plazas across the city, who stood proudly or sat tall in the saddle, Sarmiento was portrayed humbly, seated in a chair, with two small children at his side to recall his establishment of free and secular public education across the nation. Much of the outward-looking liberal project he advocated had triumphed, from immigrants and exports to railroads and schools. The statue seemed to confirm the wisdom of his ideas.

Wine had brought prosperity but not stability. The statue of Sarmiento was still marked by bullets from the overthrow of Cantoni ten years before. Politics in San Juan remained a blood sport, and however placid and traditional the plaza seemed, it was also the site of threats, gunfights, and assassinations. This was where winery rule had been consolidated—and where it had been most fiercely contested.

The secular and spiritual powers faced each other across the square: along

4 Plaza 25 de Mayo, north side, late 1930s. Building with columns is Club Social. CREDIT AGN.

the east side stood the provincial government, the legislature, and the courts, and along the west side, the Cathedral, the seminary, and the archbishop's palace. Every major civic institution was on the plaza or nearby, including the iconic buildings of the two social clubs, seven of the eight banks, and the main library. Here were all five cinemas, dozens of shops, and the professional, business, and political organizations that bound the elite together, such as Catholic Action, the Medical Association, the Rotary Club, and the Chamber of Commerce.

Nearly all the elite did business and resided downtown: thirteen of the fifteen leaders of the provincial coup against Cantoni in 1934, for example, lived inside the four avenues, on the west side of the city, and within a few blocks of the plaza.[27] This elite comprised bodegueros, viñateros, and liberal professionals. These categories overlapped to a significant degree, both because the leading winemaking (and to a lesser extent grape-growing) families made sure their children became professionals and because the surest way for a professional to confirm his respectability was by purchasing a vineyard. For their part, liberal professionals, with or without a traditional background, were also increasingly important in politics. They numbered about five hundred in all, including one hundred and twenty in law, one hundred and sixty in medicine, fifty in construction, and two hundred in agro-industry. While doctors and lawyers were the largest group, engineers and enologists were becoming increasingly important, as they could earn their degrees at the only

5 Del Bono family, ca. 1940. Bartolomé del Bono in back row. COURTESY FUNDACIÓN BATALLER.

institutions of higher education in the province, the mining and enology schools recently incorporated into the University of Cuyo.[28]

Traditional families remained powerful in the legal professions, the press, and cultural institutions. As elsewhere in the interior, these families carefully (and often imaginatively) traced lineages back to original Spanish settlers, endlessly retelling the roles of prominent ancestors in the founding of the nation, men with surnames like Oro, Sarmiento, del Carril, Videla, and Godoy. For all these past glories, however, traditional families were gradually losing control overall.

Relatively few immigrants had reached San Juan, but they had become central to the elite. At the high point in 1914, first-generation immigrants were only 14 percent of the local population—compared to 32 percent of Mendoza and 49 percent of the city of Buenos Aires.[29] Still, sizable contingents of Spaniards, Italians, Germans, Syrio-Lebanese, and Jews had established a foothold at the outset of the wine boom and later gained prominence in every local profession except law—and especially in winemaking itself. By 1944, fifteen of the twenty largest wineries were owned by the children of immigrants (and foreign capital owned two more).[30] Perhaps more remarkably, children of immigrants controlled the most powerful political forces in the province—Juan Maurín and Santiago Graffigna led the Conservatives, and Federico and Aldo Cantoni the Bloquistas.

Winemakers and professionals usually ran their businesses from the con-

6 Del Bono Building,
San Juan, late 1930s.
CREDIT AGN.

verted front rooms of traditional houses, spaces marked by a kind of shabby
gentility. But there were a handful of striking buildings. The most imposing
was the sleek Art Deco edifice across from the Cathedral. Modern in style and
occupants, the Del Bono Building was one of the city's few reinforced concrete buildings, along with the Ford dealership and the archbishop's palace.
Owned by Bartolomé del Bono, the son of Italian immigrants who was the
province's wealthiest man and second-largest winemaker, it housed several
leading institutions: the winemakers' association, the engineering association,
the Italian consulate, the finest men's clothing store, and many professional
offices. The basement held the broadcasting studios of the more potent of the
two local radio stations.

What tied the plaza together as a social space were the cafes, the centerpiece
of the local civic imaginary and "operational headquarters" of provincial politics.[31] Here the powerful met to hatch schemes and debate the events of the
day, and middling sorts came to drink and gossip and watch. Cafe chatter was
a motor of civic life, what one observer called "a kind of living spoken journal-

7 Plaza 25 de Mayo, late 1930s. From left: Cine Cervantes, Casa España, Archbishop's Palace, Cathedral, Del Bono Building. CREDIT AGN.

ism" intimately linked to the formal written kind.[32] Moreover, every Sunday, the main plaza was still the site of the *retreta*, when unmarried local young men and women circled the plaza in opposite directions, flirting and joking while the municipal band played. Every town in the province had its own retreta, but only this one merited detailed commentary in the next day's society columns.

San Juan had a lively and often fierce press which sold few papers but wielded great influence.[33] Unlike many larger cities, where the commercial press had broken free of direct political ties, here newspapers remained openly partisan institutions. Thus the broad contours of the political landscape were clearly reflected in the institutions of the press.

The clerical wing of the Conservative Party was dominated by the largest bodegueros, intimately tied to Catholic Action and led by engineer Santiago Graffigna. All the top leaders were closely related: Graffigna ran the third-largest winery; his uncle Bartolomé del Bono ran the second-largest, and his brother-in-law Francisco Bustelo ran the fifteenth-largest. Graffigna's brother Alberto was the director of their paper, *Tribuna*, the official Conservative Party organ, and another brother-in-law had been director of the Graffigna football club and mayor until the 1943 coup.

The rival "liberal" group was led by Juan Maurín, whose immigrant father had been a pioneering bodeguero, founder of the Club Social, and governor. Maurín was one of the province's largest landowners, with extensive vineyards in Caucete. His group drew support from a broad range of smaller viñateros and bodegueros, as well a few of the largest. They were liberal in their ideological references, reflexively siding with the Allies, sometimes allying with the secular-minded Socialists and Radicals, and defending their positions by invoking Sarmiento rather than Catholic social doctrine. Indeed, Maurín's wife was a direct descendent of the liberal hero, and his father-in-law had written the "Hymn to Sarmiento" schoolchildren across the nation sang daily. They had a daily named *La Acción*, founded in 1937 by the Zunino family, who were bankers, merchants, and owners of a hardware store a block away from the Del Bono Building.

There were other papers, from a dwindling traditionalist daily to the broadsheets sporadically issued by Catholics, Socialists, and the Chamber of Commerce. But beyond the two Conservative dailies, only one other publication mattered. This was the one newspaper not located on the plaza, the lightning rod of local politics: *La Reforma*, the evening daily of the Cantonis.

An Unruly Reform

The dissident center of power in the province was ten blocks off the plaza, along one of the four avenues that marked the old city limits. That was where the main building in the Cantoni compound stood, with the brothers' medical practice upstairs, the *La Reforma* newsroom downstairs, and the printing press behind. Their mother's home was next door and a gate in the back led to Federico Cantoni's house on the other side of the block. There was another medical office across town, where Elio lived, but all the things that held together their political project were right here in disorderly proximity, along with reminders of the violence it had provoked—bullet holes in the walls, weapons in the closets, a bombed-out printing press in the back, and secret escape tunnels leading to the convent next door.[34]

From their first appearance on the provincial stage, the Cantonis had been bold and committed reformers. Their father was an Italian geologist who taught at the mining school, and all three brothers graduated from the medical school of the University of Buenos Aires. Each challenged the prevailing ethos, but in distinctive ways. The quiet Elio ran the practice and stayed on the political margins. The cerebral Aldo was the ideologue: he started out as a member of the Socialist Party, helped to found the breakaway International Socialist (later Communist) Party, and then returned to his home province to write speeches and craft a political program. But Federico was the orator and visionary, a disheveled man possessed of boundless confidence, powerful charisma, and a bone-crushing handshake.[35]

8 Federico Cantoni
(center), ca. 1925.
CREDIT AGN.

Their birth and training would have easily won them a position within the local elite, but they chose instead to attack it from outside. Rather than building their medical practice among the prominent, for instance, they won a reputation by attending to the poor, often free of charge. While their rivals condemned the poor and their homes as hopelessly degraded, the Cantonis made improving the lives and residences of the poor their cause. Just as important as the fact that they cared for the poor was the way they did it. In contrast with the distant and authoritarian manner of most doctors at the time, who regarded their poorer patients as marginally capable of managing their own lives, the Cantonis cultivated an intimate and egalitarian style. Published accounts and popular anecdotes contrasted the reticence of regular doctors to even enter the homes of the poor with the eagerness with which the Cantonis rushed in, hearing complaints, offering advice, sharing a meal, and leaving gifts. Whatever the accuracy of these individual stories, the strength of the Cantonis' appeal was indicated by the documented presence of photo-

9 Cantoni brothers: from left, Aldo, Federico, Ursulina Boot (their mother), and Elio, ca. 1930. CREDIT AGN.

graphs of the brothers, and especially Federico, in humble dwellings across the province.[36]

As early as 1919, Federico Cantoni took up the cause of the poor majority, declaring that "the hour has come for the class of top hats and polished shoes to disappear from government, making way for the sweaty and smelly masses in *alpargatas*."[37] Turning markers of elite disdain—like the *alpargata*, the cheap shoe of the poor—into symbols of pride, the Cantonis brought the popular sectors to the center of local politics. With their charismatic flair and bold initiatives, the Cantonis stood in stark contrast to their elitist, staid, and divided opponents from the Conservative, Radical, or Socialist parties. Committed to expanding the rights of the many against the power of the few, they attacked the power of the bodegueros across the board, winning every legitimate election for two decades. Challenging both the social and spatial concentration of power, they won the support of nearly everyone outside the central valley and a solid majority within it. Only the capital city government itself resisted their advance, and once the property qualifications for municipal elections were removed, even this Conservative bastion fell. This was a modernization that came from the periphery.

Cantonista success was a result of policy as well as personality. The brothers were advocates of radical reform, admirers of Sarmiento and Stalin, as

Federico told a Chilean reporter in 1945.[38] Social rights were at the heart of their program: they established a minimum wage, the eight-hour day, legal recognition for unions, old-age pensions, and disability insurance; they greatly expanded and improved education and medical care; they granted women the vote for the first time, and enshrined all these rights in a progressive new constitution in 1927. On many issues, labor rights and female suffrage in particular, Cantonismo was a national pioneer, indeed the most radical government in the country at the time. Moreover, these laws were effectively, if sometimes unevenly, enforced, due to popular mobilization and Cantonista willingness to use brute force when necessary.

Carrying out these reforms had required forging a more powerful state, which meant a break with local tradition. While the winemaker elite in neighboring Mendoza had built a state with broad authority to tax and regulate, their counterparts in San Juan had remained more divided and less ambitious. Mendoza had far outpaced San Juan in building public infrastructure like canals and schools. Thus when the Cantonis' populist allies, the Lencinas, came to power in Mendoza, they were able to simply redirect the spending of an already powerful state. This option was not open to the Cantonis.

Instead, Cantonismo created a modern state virtually ex nihilo, massively increasing taxation and spending. Taxes on grapes and property were particularly important. By their second administration, the Cantonis had quintupled the provincial budget (see appendix).[39] Along with expanding social rights, they had launched an ambitious program of public works designed to strengthen the state, unify the province, and diversify its economy. The major aim was promoting alternatives to grape monoculture. The Cantoni administrations built the first permanent roads to the outlying corners of the province—Calingasta, Jáchal, and Valle Fértil. In many places, they built the first schools and medical posts as well. They promoted several industrial enterprises with state support, from a marble quarry to an ill-starred attempt at sugar beet cultivation, as well as smaller-scale agricultural experiments with a broad variety of crops and animals. In this spirit, they carried out several colonization projects with the dual aim of providing dignified homes for workers and distributing the population more evenly across the province. Some of this was self-interested, of course, enabling the Cantonis to build a patronage network of contractors and functionaries, reward the faithful with state housing, and even personally benefit from the new roads (Aldo bought land in Calingasta and Federico near Jáchal). But ultimately, this patronage only strengthened support for projects that benefited the province as a whole.[40]

Important as these projects on the periphery were, particularly because they marked the state's first effective presence there, the Cantonis also undertook major public works to democratize power within the grape zone. The Cantonis expanded the main hospital, constructed new schools, and created a new infrastructure of leisure spaces, from a concrete stadium in the capital to the first provincial park, ten kilometers away. Most dramatically, the Cantonis built a cooperative state winery, the largest edifice in the province, in order to break bodeguero power by providing grape growers with storage, stable prices, and a buyer of last resort. Such efforts made clear how expanding state authority had coincided with expanding citizenship rights, giving Cantonismo the opportunity to genuinely respond to popular demands while also building an impressive patronage machine.

The Cantoni years were marked by cycles of intense partisan conflict and social struggle. Political instability was nothing new to San Juan, a fractious and insubordinate land where, since 1820, seven governors had been assassinated while in office. But after the Cantonis, local politics became far more participatory and consequential. Rhetorically fierce struggles between small political cliques gave way to ideologically defined contests between larger political organizations. Cantonismo built the first political machine in the San Juan, extending down to "sergeants" and "corporals" on each block, and quickly became the only party with mass support—in 1926, for example, Aldo Cantoni won 74 percent of the vote. This success forced rivals to build their own networks and, equally importantly, to find national allies to compensate for local weakness. As a result, despite all its reforms, Cantonismo failed to overcome the local tradition of bitter partisan conflict—and ultimately only deepened and strengthened it.

The Cantonis' political ferocity and intense localism made the opposition search for outside allies far easier. Despite their rhetorical defense of equal citizenship, the Cantonis governed with little regard for the niceties of the law or the civil liberties of their opponents. The original sin of the movement was a political murder: after narrowly avoiding death at police hands in 1921, Federico Cantoni orchestrated the assassination of the man responsible, Governor Amable Jones, and although arrested and charged, he successfully mounted his first gubernatorial campaign from his jail cell. This violence was not obscured by Cantonistas. The masthead of *La Reforma* read: "Oderint Dum Metuant," or "Let Them Hate, So Long as They Fear." The Cantonis made popular resentment into a strategy of rule, and while their reforms won them some surprising allies—notably the local bishop, Orizali, normally no friend to outspoken atheists—they generally governed by threat

10 Conservative leaders of coup against Cantoni, February 1934. Note future senator Santiago Graffigna (tall figure, fourth from left), future vice-governor Oscar Correa Arce (fifth from left), and future governor Juan Maurín (last on right). CREDIT AGN.

and intimidation more than by negotiation or debate. Whatever the progressive pedigree of their policies, their style of rule was portrayed by local opponents and national observers as familiar thuggery poorly disguised by Latin aphorisms, a straightforward regression to the barbaric past. Nearly every other political party regarded the Cantonis as demagogues and brutes, heirs of Rosas, "a godless and lawless montonera" in the words of one Conservative deputy.[41] The dominant wing of the national Radical Party never forgave Cantoni for killing their local champion, Governor Jones, or stealing their electoral base. The national judiciary proved consistently hostile, repeatedly striking down labor and social reforms as unconstitutional. However strong its popular support, Cantonismo had a weak hold on institutional power and was only able to survive through a series of cynical and fragile national alliances of convenience.[42]

From the standpoint of the provincial elite, Cantonismo overturned all that was right, bringing insolence to workers, wealth to the undeserving, and punitive taxes to the virtuous. Divided amongst themselves, unable to win at the ballot box, and reluctant to adapt to the new context of mass politics, the provincial elite fell back on familiar strategies. First came the assassination attempts—eventually six or more against Aldo or Federico—and then the persistent and ultimately successful attempts to lobby the national authorities to intervene in the province.[43]

None of the three Cantoni administrations (1923–25, 1926–28, 1932–34) finished its term; all three were removed by the national authorities. The brothers held office for only six years. After each overthrow, the new authorities attempted to roll back the changes by purging the public administration and harassing and arresting party activists. The repression grew more intense over time: the first intervention was relatively moderate and brief, the second pursued an extensive campaign of fraud, beatings, and assassination that greatly discredited the Radical Party then holding national office, and the third began with an insurrection that left thirty-one dead yet still failed to finish off Cantoni.

Fragile Restoration

The provincial coup that overthrew Federico Cantoni in February 1934 brought together the entire opposition, from Conservatives to Radicals to Socialists, under the banner of "God, Fatherland, Home."[44] Impressed by this remarkable show of unity, and oddly persuaded that Cantonismo would disappear once it was ejected from office, some elites hoped to forge a broad-based project for conservative modernization. The starting point was the reversal of the recent social transformation: labor laws became a dead letter, as wages dropped and brutal working conditions returned. For long afterward, the late 1930s would be remembered as a time of particularly intense penury.

Beyond cutting wages, however, elites failed to agree on the outlines—or even the necessity—of a modernizing project and soon reverted to familiar habits of plunder and factionalism. Within months of winning staged elections, the liberal wing of Conservatives, led by Juan Maurín, had outmaneuvered their rivals to seize the state for themselves. Before long, frustrated at the persistence of popular Cantonismo, these self-styled champions of order launched a brutal campaign of repression—including two bombings of *La Reforma*, another attempted assassination of Federico Cantoni, trumped-up criminal investigations, and beatings and murders in the countryside—that soon devolved into broader violence against any and all political opponents.

Lacking a persuasive countervision, unable to agree even on how to rewrite the constitution passed under Cantoni, Conservatives settled for enfeebling and defrauding the provincial state. Some Cantonista reforms were dismantled: the sugar beet refinery was leveled, its state-of-the-art machinery sold for scrap. Others were retained but turned to perverse ends, as teaching positions in schools became the centerpiece of Conservative patronage, the state-owned

winery a device for increasingly elaborate swindles, and the labor department a tool for harassing rivals, since nearly all employers now violated labor law. Instead of the Cantonista policy of requiring each doctor to provide some free medical care, the Conservatives built a centralized public assistance program that guaranteed income for their medical allies. Rather than repealing the female vote, they formed "women's civic clubs" to exclude female Bloquistas, falsify voter registrations, and steal elections.

The most symptomatic reversal was in the wine industry. The collapse of consumption after 1929 had brought on the industry's worst cyclical crisis yet. Cantoni had forcefully intervened to prop up the price of grapes, obliging private wineries to buy from viñateros at a set price and, via the state winery, storing away excess production for future sale. These policies protected growers at the expense of large wineries, and the Conservatives naturally scrapped them. Instead, the national state established a powerful new agency, the Junta Nacional de Vino, staffed it with bodeguero allies, and attacked the problem of persistent overproduction by tearing up thousands of hectares of vines and pouring away millions of liters of wine. Prices recovered, and thanks to their control of the agency, the largest bodegueros were able to reap the benefits without undergoing the indignity of actually having their own grapes and wine discarded. This brutal restructuring strongly benefited the powerful at the expense of everyone else.

Conservative fiscal policies were equally revealing, and equally dependent on national largesse. In 1934, the national government centralized taxation: by opting into the new system, provinces gave up much of their ability to levy their own taxes but received in return a generous portion of the taxes collected by the national government. San Juan was the last province to give up control. Cantoni had naturally refused, but Conservatives signed on eagerly, ensuring there could never be another provincial wine tax and taking advantage of the favorable terms offered by the national government, which assumed much of the provincial debt and set a formula for redistributing tax revenues that gave poorer provinces far more money than they contributed.[45]

With guaranteed resources from Buenos Aires, the governing elites could keep the patronage machine going even without local revenues—and so they quickly stopped collecting taxes. By the late 1930s, the provincial state was bringing in a third of what it was owed—and because rates and assessments had been slashed, it was owed far less than before. The shortfall grew dramatically as the provincial authorities stopped pursuing legal action against evaders.[46]

Outside aid could shore up the power of Conservatives, but not their legitimacy. Like the national regime they depended upon, they muddled through with fraud and intermittent brutality, unwilling to observe the rules of liberal democracy but unable to advance a coherent alternative. Their rule was harsh but fragile. In the decade between the overthrow of Cantoni and the earthquake, San Juan saw eleven administrations come and go—including nine federal interventions.

A Failed Counter-Reform

The only sustained attempt to escape from this legitimacy crisis came from the Catholic Conservatives. It is worth noting that the emphasis on Church social doctrine in the 1930s was new, tied to the broader national process of Catholic renewal. But if elsewhere Catholic Action found its strongest recruits among the middle class, in San Juan it had great success among the bodeguero elite and their client network of professionals and state employees. Consider, for example, the distinguished surnames of the cast of the Catholic Action Christmas pageant, which featured no less than six Graffigna children as well as the offspring of judges, merchants, and bodegueros.[47] These Catholic activists, in turn, would play an important role in formulating a political counter-reform.[48]

Shortly after Cantoni was overthrown, Horacio Videla, a young Catholic lawyer from a traditional family, argued that Conservatives should view Cantonismo as an admonition. It had revealed the weakness and rot of liberalism, which Videla viewed as a "sickening façade" of legality erected "to perpetuate a state of affairs which is unjust and cannot continue." Conservatives needed to present their own reform, Videla insisted, for "we cannot oppose a wave of change that, in defending the disinherited, will finally be the salvation of our bankrupt civilization."[49] While the impulse for reform soon foundered, and Videla and his allies fell back to defending established privilege, they continued to regard the liberal order as a "sickening façade." For Videla's friend Pablo Ramella, a lawyer and Catholic activist, "singing odes to democracy and the sovereign will of the people while carrying out electoral fraud is more pernicious and more irritating than carrying out a coup d'etat and suppressing all political guarantees." Fearful of the return of Cantoni, repulsed by the "moral ambiguity" of liberalism, and increasingly uneasy at the social misery of the province, the Catholic activists pushed for a strong state to forcefully impose social justice and restore proper social hierarchy, in keeping with corporatist principles. "If the avarice of those with wealth or the inertia of those with nothing but their labor are not moved by this call to raise up the province, then the State, a coercive force by its nature," should assume the task. Ramella insisted: "the State is either something that acts . . . or it is nothing."[50]

The city was an important component of their reform. In a lecture in 1935, Ramella had observed with some bitterness that "there must have been a time when the people of San Juan had the will to found their city—the dense and more or less uniform construction proves it—but those who came along later lacked the vision to see that a city that does not renew itself dies." Insisting that a city "must be refounded every day," he had urged his audience to fashion their run-down surroundings into something worthy of their imagination.[51]

Despite the disarray, the decade of Conservative rule had brought major changes to the city. Beyond propping up the provincial administration, the national government also funded long-awaited infrastructure projects. Every street inside the four avenues was paved, the city water system was extended to reach 80 percent of homes, and the first sewer pipes were laid—although only 3 percent of homes were connected before the earthquake. The jewel in the crown was the new city hall, designed by a local architect to echo its counterpart in Buenos Aires, down to the iconic clock tower. All these projects were funded from the national purse but employed primarily local firms, providing tangible benefits for the city while strengthening Conservative patronage powers.[52]

Building on this, the clerical Conservatives made refashioning the city central to their reform. Finally taking power in 1942—with Horacio Videla as vice governor and ideologue—they proposed to industrialize the province, modernize the city, and even build government housing for workers. They also promised to improve, and Catholicize, the educational system. This paternalist version of "social justice" aimed to protect the provincial poor and uproot Cantonista support, thereby reaffirming elite authority in a more "Christian" social order.

However fierce, these calls to virtue were hardly credible. Catholic Conservatives won office using the full toolbox of fraud, including forged electoral rolls, stolen ballot boxes, widespread intimidation, and a few strategic killings. Their leaders were the largest bodegueros, such as Cantoni's archrival Santiago Graffigna, who promoted as private citizens the social ills they denounced as political leaders. In terms of policy, they were more orderly and coherent than the Maurín Conservatives before them but were just as rapacious in their actions.[53] Graffigna, for example, mounted a decade-long legal campaign for a refund of all the wine taxes paid under Cantoni—about forty million pesos' worth, or four times the province's annual budget—even though paying would bankrupt the government to benefit a handful of bodegueros, especially the clerical Conservative leaders themselves.[54] Once in power, their primary concerns revolved around building a patronage machine. Their housing projects were directed at public employees; their education policy aimed to purge the schools of liberal teachers in favor of Catholics and Conservatives. Their proposed urban reforms, like the infrastructure improvements, were concentrated where Conservative support was the strongest, and had little impact on the areas where the city was growing the most, much less on the countryside or outlying small towns.

Two prestigious urbanists, Benito Carrasco and Ángel Guido, were hired to draw up a master plan for San Juan. They proposed a battery of measures to transform the drab city, including parks, a ring highway, and a new civic center, with wide streets and imposing government buildings. Although they saw local housing as generally poor in quality, they had no concerns about adobe, which they regarded as well adapted to the local climate, and their proposed building code only emphasized the importance of making the city look properly traditional, by requiring white walls and red tile roofs for all new construction. "As for the seismic problem," they concluded it was not "technically crucial for San Juan at this time, when anti-seismic construction techniques have achieved a level that guards against major dangers."[55]

Because the master plan could only be fully implemented with sizable expropriations and spending, it met with skepticism from the remainder of the elite, who were reluctant to cede any power over their property. Trimmed down to the civic center and two housing projects, the master plan was legally adopted but not actually implemented—only the housing got underway—before the June 1943 coup removed the Conservatives from power.

This, then, was the city of San Juan on 15 January 1944. In its uneven prosperity and unacknowledged fragility, it was emblematic of much of the country at the time. Whatever its dusty elegance and undeniable modernity, this was a place split by social conflict, built from dried mud, and set on unsteady ground.

CHAPTER 2   IN A BROKEN PLACE

At eleven minutes to nine on 15 January 1944, a local engineer was walking out on the edge of town when the earth suddenly thrust up under him in a long rolling wave, followed by an abrupt sideways jolt that nearly knocked him down. An earthquake that measured 7.4 on the Richter scale had begun. There was a loud crack, and then a roar: the sky filled with dust, and the Andes slipped from view.[1] "It was just an instant, nothing more," a visitor from Mendoza later told a reporter. "There was no warning, no gradual build-up," the visitor continued, "just a great wave, as if something deep down had broken loose. I managed to step out onto the patio, and it was over. But San Juan was in ruins. Suddenly I felt a great anguish inside. I was alone, with a terrifying loneliness. I don't know where I found the strength to tear apart the pieces of the wall, but I felt this mad drive to come back to life, to not stay there, trapped . . . I made it out onto the street, but it was not the street I had known."[2]

Luis Romero was a builder from Buenos Aires who had been surveying local construction. With his task complete, he was relaxing with friends toward the back of a downtown cafe, a few steps from the outside patio. As the band started in on the first tango, the ground started to move, and they scrambled out onto the patio, barely escaping the falling building, and then smashed their way through the remnants of the wall with a metal bar to reach the street. Stepping over rubble and downed electrical lines, Romero and his friends made it to the plaza and turned back to see the cafe go up in an "immense pyre" of flames. From where Romero stood, "the block the café was on, and the next, and the next, and every block as far as we could see was nothing but ruins."[3]

11 City center, 16 January 1944. CREDIT AGN.

Only chance separated the living from the dead. Narratives of survivors return again and again to the narrow escape, to roofs that fell moments later. Two men were playing chess; one was buried, the other unharmed. A man pushed his girlfriend away from a collapsing wall: she woke up in a hotel two days later, he was killed. Another man had been about to take his wife and four children for a walk, but there was a fight, and he left alone. When he made his way back, his house was ruined and his family buried beneath.[4] At one family-run hotel, the owner and staff were manning the front desk, while guests gathered inside for cocktails. When the hotel collapsed, the guests were trapped and the staff found themselves on the sidewalk.[5]

One woman was with her mother when the quake began: "she took me by the hand, neither of us said a word, and we ran across the patio." Then the walls gave way, and everything went dark. Her mother had vanished, and so she set to tearing apart the rubble: "I lost my fingernails, and I found a body, which was hers." With a few slaps she managed to awaken her mother, and then the two of them picked their way out to the street, through the sewing workshop in the front of the building. All seventeen workers there had perished.[6]

More than two hundred were killed at the wedding in the Concepción parish church: the roof smothered those inside, and the walls those outside. Only a few survived: stragglers at the edge of the crowd and a handful in the base of the bell tower spared by the vagaries of the falling structure.[7]

The grimy municipal market, Cantoni's last redoubt, also fell in the quake. "Those luckless souls were surely downing a glass of wine" when their world

12 Interior of Concepción parish church, 16 January 1944. CREDIT AGN.

came apart, the son of a faithful Cantonista later imagined, "telling of distant victories, present miseries, unpredictable lives, and a longing to find comfort in some obscure corner of the provincial budget."[8]

Thousands died indoors or were caught outside by a collapsing façade. Many more were alive but trapped. Fallen wires were everywhere, small fires were breaking out, and on the east side, a ruptured water tank had flooded block after block.

The earthquake left the streets nearly impassable but set survivors in motion—to search for loved ones, to rescue others, or simply to find open space. A telephone operator left the central switch to make sure his wife and baby daughter were safe. He only had to walk a few blocks, but along the way he heard constant moans and "counted at least thirty cadavers." He was more stunned than afraid, he later recalled: "What had happened had not sunk in— there had been no time for it to sink in."[9]

A priest worked his way across the devastation, worrying about his elderly father. Yet "the son in him was held up by the priest in him," as he ministered to the wounded and dying, taking hours to advance a few blocks. Finally, he reached his father, bruised but alive. He pulled a mattress from the wreckage, placed his father on it, and pressed on.[10]

An eighteen-year-old had been dressing for a wedding reception when the quake came. He ran down the hall to rescue his father, dug his brother out of the rubble, then helped pull a neighbor from under a wall. But even so, he "saw at least fifteen people die."[11] A seven-year-old girl accompanied her parents in search of her grandmother, but "of twenty neighbors, fifteen were on the ground dead," she recalled, and the survivors were out on the street "weeping, screaming, desperate, and full of anguish, not knowing if this was the end of the world."[12]

By half past nine, forty minutes after the quake, the city was in complete darkness. There was no moon and no power. With movement difficult and lines of communication down, each block was on its own. The disaster had destroyed the city's infrastructure and overwhelmed its government. The surviving police and firemen did what they could, but there was little coordination or command. For most of the night, the government's effective reach extended about a block past the main plaza.[13]

This central civic space soon filled up with people looking for help, for the missing, or for anywhere free of falling buildings. A Dominican friar patiently made the rounds, ignoring his own head wound to offer consolation and administer last rites. Every few meters there was another body, surrounded by relatives or friends. A doctor appeared early on, and then a handful of medical students. They improvised a surgery on the park benches and set to work under the headlight beams of nearby cars. They broke into a pharmacy for medicine and alcohol, with official approval, and a clothing store for fabric. A half-dozen women spent the night ripping the latest fashions into bandages. In the city's six other plazas, the story was much the same: a scattered presence of doctors, priests, and officials amid a wounded and terrified crowd.[14]

Around ten, contact with the outside world was restored when a contingent from the provincial regiment reached the main plaza. After recruiting civilian volunteers, the soldiers began a more systematic search for those still buried. Soon after, two telephone switch operators finally managed to get through to Mendoza, and a caravan of aid was on its way.[15]

The San Roque hospital had collapsed, and the larger Rawson hospital was heavily damaged. The doctors, nurses, and nuns set up triage and surgery on the sidewalk outside the Rawson. Several local surgeons made it there and remained for days, most notably Federico Cantoni.[16] Operating by the light of kerosene lamps with whatever instruments they could recover, they worked all night, leaving a pile of amputated limbs as a morbid testament to their efficiency.[17] With nearly one thousand people in the small area cleared of rubble, there was hardly room to stand.[18]

At the provincial prison just west of the city, the walls came down, killing seven guards and wounding ten more. With half the guards out of action, the warden went off for police reinforcement, but only found two men. In his absence, the guards had used up their ammunition firing into the air: there was no power, there was no light, and no one knew how many prisoners were injured. Calling the prisoners together, the warden released them to find their families, if they promised to return. Of the nearly four hundred prisoners, all but six—two dead, three seriously wounded, and one to care for them—disappeared into the night. Later, when the warden tried to head into town, he accidentally drove into a ditch, but a group of prisoners pulled his car out, cheering. All but twenty-five prisoners would later return on their own.[19]

Nearby, a young girl was chopping tomatoes and onions for a salad when the quake came. Her mother scooped her and her brother up and they ran out into the woods. Hiding in the trees, they heard the screams and gunfire from the provincial prison. As darkness fell, the gunfire ended, but the voices did not go silent, and they seemed to be drawing near. Waiting for her father to return from downtown, the girl and her family spent the night outdoors, as terrified of escaped prisoners as of the earth's rumbling.[20]

All night the earth shook and the sky threatened rain. Nearly everyone spent the night outdoors, shivering and terrified. Every two hours another aftershock sent survivors scrambling for nonexistent cover.[21] At the industrialist Bartolomé del Bono's mansion, nearly sixty survivors gathered around a bonfire "because the flame, the light, gave strength."[22]

Many sought solace in their faith. In Desamparados, the parish priest was surprised by the arrival of six men, released prisoners, who had come to help. Heading repeatedly back into the ruined church, they rescued statues, images, and candles from the creaking mass of broken beams and walls.[23] Downtown, in a corner of the main plaza, more than fifty women prayed the Rosary together. As a young Dominican monk, Gonzalo Costa had served as the model for the plaza's statue of the patriotic cleric.[24] Now the convent prior, Costa was tireless that night, his white cassock a sign of hope for many. He "gave absolutions of every kind . . . inside houses, in the middle of shapeless piles—absolution to everyone who walked by, terrified, and asked me for it." In the plaza of Santa Lucía, the parish priest led the crowd in praying the Rosary, took confession, and comforted those "convinced with every tremor that the Day of Judgment had come."[25] Not all could provide such comfort. One survivor saw a priest drop to his knees in front of the destroyed Cathedral and cry out "God, what have we done to deserve this?"[26]

At first light, the clouds finally broke, and a light drizzle covered the city. The builder Romero and his companions slowly made their way across town, passing by the ruins of their hotels. "On every street corner during the long walk," Romero saw wounded bodies on the ground and relatives keeping watch over their dead "with small oil lamps and prayers that took on a strange and moving solemnity out in the open air."[27]

By now, the relief effort had begun. With the arrival of aid, the screams and weeping gave way to "absolute silence," as hardly anyone spoke aloud.[28] Some interpreted this quiet as a sign of peaceful resignation.[29] Others saw "no pain, only shock" on the faces of survivors, who "watch[ed] help arrive without enthusiasm, almost with indifference."[30]

Aftermath

Retelling the experience later, survivors offered accounts that were strikingly similar in detail and pattern. These commonalities point to the collective character of the trauma they experienced. In destroying the physical city, the disaster tore apart a symbolic order as well. Each individual story of meaningless deaths also pointed to the destruction of the collective meanings of local life. In returning to the moment of terror and escape, again and again, these stories were pointing to something larger. They were not only narrating the individual trajectories survivors followed out of houses, churches, and cafes. They were also narrating the collective experience of being wrenched from a world that was known and left out in the open, exposed.[31]

"You cannot take a step without coming across a corpse or a wounded body," the provincial secretary of public works declared on 16 January.[32] The thousands of lives lost were the central trauma of the earthquake, but there were other losses as well. Along with loved ones, survivors had lost the social networks and symbolic frameworks that had given their lives meaning. For many, the loss of a home meant the loss of a sense of who they were. The destruction of place only compounded the destruction of so many lives.[33]

Every institution of authority was shattered: the new city hall, courts, legislature, police station, banks, newspaper offices, and twenty of the city's twenty-one churches.[34] Inside the four avenues only a handful of structures stood intact, nearly all of them of reinforced concrete: the Del Bono building, the Ford dealership, a cinema, a hardware store, a few residences, and a new chapel at the Don Bosco School, the one surviving ecclesiastical structure. All

13 Inside the four avenues, 16 January 1944. CREDIT AGN.

around them was the "terrible uniformity of every block, of every street, completely covered with ruins." The city consisted of orphaned walls, vanished buildings, and heaps of rubble. There were only four blocks inside the four avenues where most buildings remained standing.[35] Three days later, the police chief reported that "all construction is practically destroyed and uninhabitable."[36]

Out past the four avenues, the earthquake left a broken landscape of crumbled adobe and tilting electricity poles. Several poorer suburbs, especially Concepción, were even worse off than downtown. Along the railroad tracks, the massive hulks of the bodegas were still upright but with cracked walls, collapsed roofs, and smashed casks and winepresses. Outside the city, across the central valley, the vines were untouched, but much else was in ruins. Towns like Albardón to the north and Caucete to the east, places nestled in the richest bottomlands of the river valley, suffered heavy damage. A government survey later tabulated 92 million pesos in building damages.[37] Of the fifteen thousand homes across the alluvial plain, a local newspaper asked two months later, "How many are still intact? Completely intact, not even one."[38]

The ruins were an indictment of the previous order. "There can be no doubt that the absence of foresight has been the root cause of the destruction of San Juan," a geologist stated flatly.[39] Poor construction with no controls had guaranteed that buildings would collapse. "The authorities were utterly

14 Outside the four avenues, 16 January 1944. CREDIT AGN.

unconcerned with this problem," Judge Pablo Ramella wrote, "and the consequences of this lack of planning and willful negligence is apparent to all."[40] Standing in front of the ruins of the three-year-old city hall, one local observed that many local "buildings should more precisely be called . . . papered-over graves."[41]

The earthquake demonstrated the weakness of institutions along with buildings. The interventor and his aides did not know the city or what to do; police and firemen were dead, missing, or overwhelmed; the political chieftains who had dominated local life were nowhere to be found. Even the local garrison was stranded in the mountains on maneuvers and most could not return for days. This across-the-board failure would later draw intense criticism.

In the short term, the void was filled largely by soldiers and doctors from elsewhere. Troops from neighboring provinces were in the city by sunrise. In the early morning, the regional military commander, Colonel José Humberto Sosa Molina, arrived from Mendoza and placed the province under martial law, pushing aside Interventor Uriburu. By the time the interior minister reached the city in late afternoon, soldiers were patrolling, clearing roads, and digging out victims, and the relief effort was taking shape.

The first teams of doctors had arrived from Mendoza before dawn.[42] During the day, trains brought more medical personnel, led by the national director of public health. Taking over the national high school, one of the few large buildings still standing, they cleared the rubble, filled the classrooms with stretchers, and began an enormous triage operation. The work would ulti-

15 Searching for bodies, January 1944. CREDIT AGN.

mately involve three hundred doctors, one hundred medical students, and three hundred nurses—personnel from across the nation and from neighboring countries.[43] From the improvised facilities in San Juan, they dispatched the more serious cases to Mendoza, where a national hospital nearing completion was fully outfitted in a single day and inaugurated by victims of the earthquake.

The largest medical relief effort in national history, the operation continued for weeks with hundreds of commandeered trucks, dedicated trains, and military cargo aircraft from Argentina and neighboring Chile. It yielded impressive successes, as nearly all the two thousand wounded sent to Mendoza recovered, but also brought further sacrifices. On 20 January, one of the dozens of Chilean relief flights crashed, killing all aboard. In ceremonies in Buenos Aires, Mendoza, and Santiago, these doctors, nurses, mechanics, and pilots were honored as heroes of an inspiring collective effort.[44]

In addition to healing the wounded, the director of public health was concerned about containing infection from what had become a vast open-air grave. Shortly after arriving, he decided to vaccinate the living for typhus and cremate the dead. Given the province's high normal mortality rates, particularly from typhus, this concern was understandable. At first, recovered bodies were publicly displayed for relatives to identify. But as continuing rain and the edginess of military authorities made this more difficult, a new procedure was adopted. Soldiers took the bodies they removed from the wreckage, and even seized the bodies from "anyone they found holding a wake," taking them all to the mass grave.[45] There, soldiers gathered the bodies in piles, doused them with kerosene, and set them aflame.[46]

"Funeral pyres watched by silent, blank-eyed crowds smoke night and day," a North American journalist reported. He claimed to smell burnt flesh while waiting for a train out of town. According to a Chilean reporter, incineration without a coffin was the rule. Few provisions were made for identifying or tracking the victims.[47]

All that many survivors could do was attempt to save their dead. Some tried to make their dead respectable: they went to funeral parlors, "broke in, got a coffin, stuck the corpse in it, took it to the cemetery," marked the site, and left, hoping to evade official attention.[48] One family had lost a son in the quake. They found a coffin and took him to the cemetery, but when the soldiers "saw he wasn't in proper condition to be buried in the niche, they took him away and threw him in the common grave." Already crushed by the loss of her son, the mother never recovered from the loss of his body and died within a year.[49] Others tried to hide the bodies of loved ones. A leading Cantonista spirited away his late mother in the back of a truck; the former Conservative vice governor Horacio Videla snuck his mother's body out to his farm, where he built a mausoleum that held her for ten years, until a proper burial could be arranged.[50]

While everyone recognized the threat of infection, the way bodies were taken powerfully shaped later narratives of the tragedy. "They burned them almost alive," one survivor recalled, describing limbs still moving in piles of burning corpses, and even one body that seemed to be struggling to stand up and break free.[51]

The exact number of victims is impossible to determine. Many had been cremated or buried, one official wrote a month later, "but for the law, those people are not deceased, even though we never hear anything from them, because there is no legal proof of their death."[52] The only legal instrument available was a proceeding initiated by a spouse three years after a disappearance. This was beyond the patience and means of most, and in any case required a surviving spouse. For the many couples whose partnership was not recognized by the law—a third of all births were out of wedlock—it was simply out of the question. Three months after the earthquake, the director of the Civil Registry noted with alarm that "the number of deceased recorded in our books is insignificant."[53]

There would be no comprehensive attempt to determine who had died.[54]

The most authoritative estimate came from the major paper in Mendoza, which published the longest lists of the missing. Drawing on the limited government reports, information from relatives, and local reporting, two weeks after the quake the paper estimated the death toll at 5,000; over the coming months, most reckonings would rise, to settle on the enduring number of 10,000 dead.[55] Official statistics are no help: remarkably, published public health reports record only 3,288 deaths in the province for all of 1944, and a mere 333 for January, figures for an average summer month. No official count was ever made of the single deadliest day in the Argentine twentieth century.[56]

This silence reflected state incapacity more than political intent. This was less a matter of failing to recognize pain than of being unable to name and master it. Significantly, this was not only a failure of the national and provincial state; there would also be a strong local reluctance to name the dead. For half a century, the only memorial to the victims would be a single urn in which the Dominican prior Gonzalo Costa collected whatever ashes he recovered from the common grave.[57]

Trainloads of aid began arriving the day after, but this was not enough. There was no safe water, no reliable electrical power, precious little shelter, and not enough food. Even after confiscating the supplies in local stores, the military authorities could hardly provide everything needed for the nearly hundred thousand homeless. Three days after the earthquake, a North American journalist found the plaza still crowded with bodies, as relief workers with "eyes dust-rimmed, cheeks hollow, parched lips tightly clenched, try to sort out the still critical cases and send them to Mendoza, to Buenos Aires, or to anywhere away from here." He reported their proposed program of action: "evacuate the city, then dynamite what remains. It's impossible to build here again."[58]

Fearful of unrest and disease, the government ordered evacuation that same day, 18 January. This seemed like the final blow. "The overwhelming impression is that San Juan cannot be rebuilt," one reporter wrote in the only article published in Argentina for years to openly question official promises of reconstruction. Many of the wealthy had already left town, headed to other cities or to estates in the largely untouched countryside. What was coming now, the reporter noted, was "the voluntary or forced exodus of fifty thousand souls, most of them with no resources of any kind, as this is a poor city. This will put Argentine generosity to the test."[59]

San Juan seemed to be done for. Free railroad passage was offered to anyone wishing to leave. Rumors of official plans to abandon—or bomb—the city

16 Three women leaving San Juan, January 1944. CREDIT AGN.

spread rapidly.[60] Local branches of businesses with headquarters elsewhere started to dig out and ship back whatever they could recover, ready to give up on the place. "A wave of terror" was sweeping the city, and the authorities could not hold it back.

Thousands gathered at the station, waiting for the twenty-car trains leaving five times daily.[61] Many others took to the road heading south. This refugee city stretched all the way to Mendoza, in the words of one witness, "an endless and ever-increasing procession of carriages of every size and kind bearing families and furniture and objects, from pots to beds to parrots."[62]

This chaotic withdrawal split families and communities apart. Many were forced to leave most possessions behind, taking only what they could carry. For many survivors, swift removal only compounded the violence of losing their loved ones, their home, and their place in the world. A complete list of refugees was never compiled, so no one knew where many survivors had gone. More than a thousand children orphaned by the disaster were dispatched to institutions elsewhere—along with hundreds who had been separated from their parents but not orphaned. Many more children were simply lost. A reporter in Mendoza came across three children who had survived: one could remember nothing but the street number of his former house, a second thought his father was still at work and did not realize he was in another city, and a third could only say his name and met the reporter's gaze with eyes filled with "a river of silence."[63]

17 San Juan orphans in Buenos Aires, January 1944. CREDIT AGN.

Within a few days, tens of thousands would be shipped out by rail.[64] Mendoza alone received eighteen thousand refugees, so taxing local resources that after five days the provincial authorities closed the border.[65] Officials back in San Juan agreed the evacuation had gone far enough, and brought it to an end.

Nearly every disaster produces moments of striking solidarity, a unity forged from joint suffering and work. On the night of the quake there were many acts of local heroism and kindness; in the grim days afterward there was the massive relief effort by national troops and outside doctors.[66]

"There were no neighbors, or acquaintances," one survivor recalled. "We were all like brothers."[67] Amid tottering walls and shifting rubble, many risked their lives to save others—particularly the volunteers, and later soldiers, who rescued many strangers. A few dug themselves out—after twenty hours, a stringer for the United Press extricated himself from beneath a wall—but most were pulled out by others.[68] Dozens of stories tell of those who faithfully tried to save their own: dogs that pulled their masters from the rubble, children who stood watch over the spot where their parents were buried.[69] A man everyone took to be mad set to excavating his buried girlfriend. Driving relentlessly through three meters of rubble, he pulled her out and married her on the spot, with the surrounding crowd as witnesses.[70]

But the experience of disaster can as easily destroy community as renew it. The tragedy created opportunities for abandonment as well as solidarity.

18 Evacuation by train, January 1944. CREDIT AGN.

There were disappearances of another kind in the aftermath: people reported dead who went on to new lives elsewhere, caskets left with the authorities that contained only stones.[71] One volunteer recalled how he and a neighbor found a parched and stunned survivor on the street, gave him water, nursed him back to life, and helped him dig his way back into his ruined house. But when they reached the bedroom of his home, the man swept past the corpses of his family, grabbed his savings from the mattress, clambered out of the building, and ran off.[72]

The day after the quake, Félix Ríos headed downtown, ran into a squad of soldiers, and was drafted to join their rescue team. When they found survivors, they rushed them to the doctors they could find, but as Ríos remembered, "the problem was that virtually all the doctors in San Juan had split for Buenos Aires, as if they had nothing to do here." Three days after the quake, when there was no hope of finding survivors, Ríos saw a foot under the rubble, grabbed it, and felt it move. After digging for an hour, he reached a young woman, who fainted when he pulled her out. The daughter of a landowner from a neighboring province, she had been visiting relatives, but they left her for dead and split for Buenos Aires. Ríos took her to one of the few doctors who had stayed, Federico Cantoni.[73]

As the gratitude of the moment faded, the disaster revealed and deepened social fissures within San Juan. At this defining moment of solidarity, many local notables had simply vanished. There were other stories like the one offered by Ríos, tales of a ruling class so callous, so "miserable" in character, that they abandoned their people and even their own children.[74] Local government officials were ineffective or nowhere to be seen. The intervenor was present but unable to coordinate much; the head of the provincial water department, the largest employer in San Juan, left his post and took his family to Buenos Aires.[75] While some doctors and clerics were prominent in relief work, much of the local elite had either departed or turned to strenuously defending their own interests. The absences and the narcissism were widely and bitterly noted.

Praise for doctors like Cantoni or priests like Gonzalo Costa was tempered by condemnations of others, beginning with the highest local authority of the Church, Archbishop Audino Rodríguez y Olmos. Vacationing five hundred kilometers away in Córdoba when the quake happened, the archbishop did not return to San Juan for a week. He claimed he only learned of the disaster the day after it occurred and was delayed by rain and the refusal of military authorities to allow anyone into the province. When he finally did arrive, he said that his first act was to order his servants to give the money and food in his palace to the needy, "even if it brought him to the level of his subjects, who had nothing."[76]

But his absence was too striking, and his defense unconvincing. He faced the reproof of many locals, the resistance of some priests, and even an unprecedented attempt by the military government to place him under house arrest for negligence. No punishment was finally imposed, but his authority was radically eroded. Even a priest ordained by the archbishop later said, "Why argue? San Juan never forgave him that."[77]

Stories of fleeing doctors, indifferent oligarchs, and absent priests spread quickly. These stories soon prompted establishment papers and clerical publications to offer countervailing accounts of heroic priests and doctors "leaping over piled-up ruins, covered in dust, paying no attention to their garb, overcoming a thousand obstacles."[78] Whatever the truth of these individual accounts, however, the establishment counteroffensive largely failed, because what was at stake was not physical presence but moral leadership. For many, the tragedy only completed the discrediting of local elites and reinforced the claim to authority of those few, men like the Cantonis, who had proven worthy of trust.

CHAPTER 3 "THE MEASURE OF OUR NATIONAL SOLIDARITY"

THE AID CAMPAIGN AND THE RISE OF PERÓN

"All domestic events have paled into insignificance in the face of the terrible San Juan disaster," a British diplomat began his monthly report for January 1944. Yet this recognition had little effect on his analysis: the disaster merited only two sentences, followed by the meat of the report, three detailed pages on local opinions about the Second World War.[1] This diplomatic report was emblematic of how later scholars would treat the earthquake. Like the diplomat, they would acknowledge its impact, only to reduce it to a passing incident in a drama shaped by prior political conflicts—above all by the war. In short, they have recognized the disaster only to dismiss it.

Yet this was a searing experience for the province, and a galvanizing moment for the nation. As I will show, it was also key space for forging the emerging project of Perón. Many saw the earthquake as a radical judgment against an unjust social order. "Bad faith has been made evident," as one architect put it.[2] It also underscored the dominant theme of cultural critique over the previous decade. With Buenos Aires and the Pampas dominating the nation's political economy and cultural imaginary, much of the rest of the country often felt like unknown territory, even to those who lived there. For a decade, essayists from across the political spectrum had portrayed the legitimacy crisis of the political order as a reflection of the deeper identity crisis of a rootless nation of immigrants. In varied ways, these thinkers had called for a break with the transplanted European culture and port mentality of Buenos Aires and a coming to terms with "deep Argentina." But the abstract calls for attending to the soil did not produce any concrete attention to the constant tremors and occasional quakes—such as in 1929 in Mendoza and 1941 in San

Juan—along the Andes. In a sense, the earthquake now represented a particularly brutal return of the repressed, and a chance to recenter the national imaginary.[3]

When news reached them, Secretary of Labor Perón and Vice President Farrell were at a boxing match. They immediately sensed the political urgency and potential of the moment. The military had come to power decrying the corruption and inhumanity of the previous liberal order. In his few public speeches so far, Perón had railed against the previous governments' indifference to popular needs. Speaking over national radio on New Year's Eve, Perón declared that soon "the memory of abandonment, of injustice, of inadequate pay, and of the impossibility of supporting a family with dignity will seem absurd and distant." On becoming secretary of labor and social welfare, he declared that "We are going to pay off our great debt to the suffering and virtuous masses . . . the era of Argentine social policy has begun, and the era of instability and disorder will be left behind forever."[4] Now he had a chance to make good on his promise, far sooner than expected. Faced with bitter evidence of the cost of indifference, the military could now prove its capability and advance its authoritarian project for "social justice." From his strategic position, Perón acted quickly, dispatching the first trains of doctors from Buenos Aires ten hours after the quake.[5]

President Ramírez was at home when he heard the news. Upstaged by his subordinates in public displays of concern, Ramírez decided to declare a day of national mourning—but did not issue the decree until the following afternoon. Faced with the prospect of uneven enforcement, the government then reversed gears and set the mourning to coincide with a presidential visit to San Juan on 17 January.[6] As the rushed-then-delayed decree suggests, regime leaders had a clear sense of the political opportunity, but not of what practical steps to take. There was no government agency charged with emergency response, and no plans or recent precedents. The authorities only knew to assert control, provide relief, and ensure they received the credit. Thus official press releases highlighted the first relief train from Buenos Aires, even though it left the station long after the locally organized relief caravan from Mendoza had reached San Juan.

Purified by Suffering: Official Responses to the Tragedy

Three symbolically powerful acts by national authorities set the tone for national response: the aid collection for victims launched on 16 January, the presidential visit to the devastated city on 17 January, and the many masses for the dead, especially the national one in Buenos Aires on 25 January. Together, the three acts of political theater were the high points of an intense media campaign that filled the papers and airwaves with calls to solidarity and sacrifice.

Behind the rhetoric of unity, of course, each act expressed and advanced rival interests within the regime. "High officials are vying with one another to show their zeal and efficiency in emergency," the U.S. ambassador told Washington, and would use "this publicity to the utmost to divert public opinion from other foreign and domestic issues."[7] The aid campaign was launched first, the day after the quake, and quickly elevated Perón from a second-tier official into a major public figure. His rivals took note and quite deliberately tried to reassert the importance of the highest military and clerical authorities through the other two acts, the presidential visit and the national mass.[8]

Suffused with stern talk of repentance and sacrifice, the speeches at the visit and mass expressed confidence that a purified Catholic nation would emerge from the ruins. The time had come, President Ramírez declared in San Juan, to repudiate liberalism and hew to the deeper values of nationalism, to look inward and recognize "the blame we bear . . . for the evils we must banish forever."[9]

This line of interpretation came across clearly in a national radio address on 24 January by Ramírez's speechwriter, Leopoldo Lugones Junior.[10] On the eve of the Buenos Aires mass for earthquake victims, Lugones recounted the presidential visit as an exemplary narrative of nationalist awakening, drawing heavily on tropes developed by his father. The elder Lugones was the national bard, a poet who began as a Socialist but ended up a nationalist, insistently calling for the military to overthrow the liberal order, producing many proposals when they did seize power in 1930, but finally despairing at the restoration of a corrupt elite.[11] The younger Lugones was also prominent in the short-lived dictatorship after the 1930 coup, not as a poet or advisor but as the head of the Buenos Aires political police, rounding up thousands of activists and dissidents.[12] When the military returned to center stage in 1943, he saw a second opportunity for authoritarian change from above: his proposal for a new secret police was rejected, but he won the ear of the president and saw promise in the earthquake.[13] The earthquake offered an opportunity to advance his austere and authoritarian vision, and, by chance, a key ally was already in place, as Interventor David Uriburu was his former deputy in the political police.[14]

"The first reports about the earthquake in San Juan had just been confirmed," Lugones Jr. began his radio address, when the president issued his first "energetic and prudent" orders. Glossing over the fact that other officials responded first, and the day and a half between the earthquake and the president's departure, Lugones stressed the swiftness of official action. "At no time did the population lack medicine, food, or adequate assistance," he claimed, because efficient soldiers had replaced "politicians accustomed to trafficking in everything, even death."[15]

Insisting that Argentines needed to look inward, Lugones recounted the visit as a voyage of nationalist self-discovery. But he was still thinking in terms of Buenos Aires; his account lingered over the Pampas' "waves of golden wheat . . . herds of gentle cattle . . . and flocks of submissive sheep" and then dispatched the devastated province with a single terse sentence. There, Lugones reported, "from the dust emerged a mass of humans, earthy and tired," to line the path walked by President Ramírez. They did not speak, or act. They simply endured, and waited. In this primal scene of political author- ity, the Argentine people were the stage set, almost part of the soil, and the only actors were efficient, devout, and self-sacrificing soldiers. Lugones's ac- count mentioned only one individual: a stoic local draftee who remained on duty despite losing his entire family.[16]

For Lugones, the defining moment of the visit came during the mass: the officiating priest gave the word, and the president went down on his knees, followed by "a sea of low and humble heads all across the plaza." The spiritual meaning was clear: "Contrite and with heads bowed, those who in a slip of faith had forgotten God in more fortunate days now returned to Him on this horrid date." The political meaning was even clearer. Destruction and repen- tance produced a moment of spiritual unity that reaffirmed the authority of the military ruler.[17]

During his visit, Ramírez spoke to the entire nation by radio, interrupting the religious music of the official day of mourning. The soldier in Ramírez held that true unity was forged on the battlefield. But now he claimed that, if it produced repentance, this tragedy too might bring unity. At the very least, he thought, it had proven that "living in peace" had "not reduced the manly temple of our race." He thus asserted that "we must accept this test that the Almighty sends us as punishment for past errors," and so warned, renounce liberalism and return to the Catholic path.[18]

In the coming weeks, Church and government leaders presented those killed in the earthquake as a sacrificial offering for the sins of liberal Argentina. "The people of San Juan expiated their own vices and those of the entire country," according to Interventor David Uriburu.[19] The province had been "purified by pain," the archbishop declared in a pastoral letter.[20] Recalling a lay leader's prophecy in 1938 that within five years a "communist revolution like

19 Government officials in San Juan, January 1944. Front row, from left, after onlooker: Interior Minister Perlinger; President Ramírez; Finance Minister Ameghino (in suit); Interventor Sosa Molina; Public Works Minister Pistarini. CREDIT AGN.

in Spain" would leave Buenos Aires in flames and all but two churches in ruins, an editorial in the main Catholic newspaper argued that because "San Juan has borne on its shoulders the burdens of an expiatory victim . . . God in his sublime indulgence has pardoned the country."[21]

The next moment in this processional of cross and sword was the mass for earthquake victims in Buenos Aires, a week after the presidential visit and a day after Lugones's radio broadcast.[22] As before, the ceremony filled the air-waves: stations could either broadcast it or go off the air for its duration. Far more than a traditional political ritual in the Cathedral, this was the country's largest open-air mass in a decade, as the Plaza del Congreso, the embodiment of liberal Argentina, "was transformed into the Great Basilica of the Father-land." At the end of the mass, every church bell in the city rang out; the clerical paper exulted that God "has returned to our Argentina her most precious greatness: her Catholic soul."[23]

Officiated by the vicar general of the Army, the ceremony justified and glorified this redemption at military hands. Looking out over the plaza, the vicar general proclaimed: "Here stands the entire Republic: civilian and mili-tary authorities, the Argentine Church with her pastor, the senate of the clergy and the people, all joined by one feeling of faith, pain, and healthy patriotism." His list made an unmistakable point: the only civilian authorities present were those appointed by the military government. Those who had formerly met in the closed national legislature behind him were neither present nor missed. By calling those in the plaza the "senate of the clergy and the people," he suggested no other senate was necessary, now that the proper authorities were in charge.[24] "Argentina has found herself again in the solidarity of pain," he asserted. The vicar general chose less aggressive imagery than the president, but he too saw the earthquake as an exemplary punishment. He imagined the Argentine people kneeling "in every temple in the Republic," pounding their chests "in contrition for past errors," and "lifting their hearts in anguished prayer." After this rededication, "the Fatherland, rising from the ruins" would be "redeemed of its weaknesses."[25]

Yet this redemption by a strong government would not prove as easy as clerical and military leaders thought, nor was the political unity as solid as they claimed. Ultimately, the powerful transformation set in motion with the earthquake would produce an outcome quite different from their nationalist ideals.

If Ramírez had been attentive, he might already have seen the signs back in San Juan. While the presence of the Papal Nuncio, leading the mass, underscored the depth of clerical support, the absence of the local archbishop suggested some difficulties to come. There were more mundane signs: Ramírez closed his speech from San Juan with a minute of silence. But instead of confirming the unity of the nation, this silence highlighted division and fear, as a rumbling aftershock led the crowd to scatter while "only the President and his escort stood still."[26] Lugones suggested this proved the virtue of Ramírez, as "not even imminent danger detains just causes."[27] Yet the incident allows another reading. After Ramírez had called the people to steadfastness and stoicism, his listeners divided and dispersed. After speaking in favor of national unity, Ramírez was left alone.

Coming Together: Perón and the Relief Collection

On the day after the quake, Perón went on national radio to launch a government-led relief drive. He declared the effort "the measure of our national solidarity," inviting every Argentine "to come together to provide all the relief necessary and to proceed with the immediate rebuilding of San Juan."[28] Until this point, Perón had been a background figure in the regime. These broadcasts were the first time many Argentines heard his voice—the beginning, a journalist later tartly observed, of "a decade-long monologue."[29]

Perón offered a vision of hope, in contrast to the stern words of Ramírez and other officials. All stressed the central role of the state, extolled the virtues of the military, and invoked Catholic metaphors of suffering and redemption. But Perón also saw popular involvement as pivotal to any project for transformation. Rather than urging the people to repent and submit, Perón called them to mobilize to remake the country. The architect of this transformation would be Perón himself, and the state agency he now headed, the Secretariat of Labor and Welfare (Secretaría de Trabajo y Previsión, or STP).

Pushing aside charity organizations and decreeing other collections illegal, Perón channeled all aid through the STP. He assigned supervision of the collection to a team of Army officers. All were drawn from the secret military lodge he had cofounded, the GOU, which had played a minor role in the 1943 coup but a major role in barracks struggles afterward, eventually taking over the military government.[30] Entrusting the collection to military officers rather than society ladies was a sharp break with liberal traditions, but the press did not criticize it. This reflects the power of censorship, to be sure, but also the disrepute of the previous order and the hope Perón's actions awakened across the political spectrum. When the collection was launched, a British diplomat noted support for Perón even among pro-Allied businessmen, one of whom had recently been conspiring against the government but now declared that if Perón ran for president in a democratic contest, he would "do everything he could to secure Perón's election." The diplomat added, "The prospect of civilian politicians staging a 'come-back' daily grows more remote."[31]

The relief collection was the public launch of the Secretariat of Labor and Welfare. Less than three months earlier, Perón had taken over the obscure agency, given it greater institutional power, and begun to make it the government's main vehicle for social policy, absorbing a wide range of disparate initiatives into an ambitious bureaucracy.[32] The relief collection was a massive scaling-up of earlier efforts, and the first major campaign for an agency that would soon pioneer many new forms of state action and transform labor relations across the republic. The secretariat plastered its name on every box of aid and every train car headed to San Juan, dispatching over five hundred tons of donations.[33] It provided food every day for forty-five thousand survivors in San Juan—and as many as fifteen thousand refugees elsewhere.[34] Here was the first proof of the later slogan: "Perón delivers."

Perón's speeches give one indication of the importance of the collection to his rising public profile. In the collection of speeches he published a year later, or his later complete works, the sequence is clear: both begin with a handful of addresses at the end of 1943, announcing the new direction for the STP, continue with the national speeches about relief for San Juan in early 1944, and then skip to his address to unions on May Day 1944. After that, the floodgates open, with a flurry of talks to workers, often many per week and sometimes several on the same day. But in the crucial and tumultuous first five months of 1944, as labor leaders kept a wary distance from Perón, his main vehicle for reaching a larger public and for demonstrating the importance and capacity of the STP was the relief collection.[35]

Perón recruited teams of radio and movie stars to walk the most elegant streets in Buenos Aires to collect donations and later joined the teams himself. His willingness to harness the dynamic but disreputable mass media to the military project already made some nervous.[36] But it quickly bore fruit. One week after the tragedy, Perón returned to the stadium where he had first learned of the tragedy to direct a gala benefit concert. That night, he was introduced to Eva Duarte, a radio soap opera actress with a sizable role in his political future.

Official reports on the collection stressed the depth of solidarity, the breadth of participation, and the coordinating role of the national state. "Inspired by the action of the Secretariat of Labor and Welfare," a government publication intoned, "all segments of society—workers, employees, businessmen, industrialists—all united by an identical feeling of solidarity, without distinctions of class or credo, by spontaneous decision, came to offer money or goods to ease the misfortune of their brothers of San Juan."[37] Perón began at the top, canvassing the powerful for donations at a meeting on 17 January with over six hundred business, media, sports, and labor leaders.

But his clear aim was breadth of participation. Posters went up across the country, commemorative stamps were issued, and the lottery, the horse track, and the cinemas all set aside a day of their proceeds for relief. All manner of groups from civil society outdid each other to gather contributions, with charity football games, fashion shows, painting exhibitions, opera extravaganzas, movie premieres, ballet performances, footraces, and plays. The papers were filled with pictures of lines of citizens waiting to contribute, and long lists of those who already had. These daily contribution lists included the obvious institutions of the establishment—banks, newspapers, and manufacturing interests—but also a broad sample of vibrant civil society, from the Boy Scouts and the Association of Jewish Actors of Argentina to Mendoza prison inmates and the Argentine Theosophical Society. There were also generous contributions from abroad, from Chilean naval officers, Brazilian football players, and North American residents of Chile.[38]

"The poor have not been absent," Perón stressed from the beginning, "even those who have nothing offer to march to San Juan to clear the rubble."[39]

Stories of their gifts dominated the press: an injured man gave his crutches, a woman donated her silver rosary, and a seventy-three-year-old shoe shiner outside the War Ministry offered twenty pesos, his entire earnings for the week.[40] The members of many unions donated a day or more of their wages.[41] Many communities gave together, like the working-class neighborhood in Buenos Aires that donated fifteen truckloads of goods.[42]

Even as it produced solidarity, though, the collection also sharpened social oppositions. For the national union confederation, the generosity of workers contrasted with the apparent stinginess of the Buenos Aires elite—a single inheritance settled in April was worth half as much as the entire collection, union leaders pointedly noted—"revealing the deep and humane feelings of the people and the indifference of the moneyed interests."[43]

The campaign intensified as the poverty of the province became more evident. A few days after describing San Juan as "booming," one national paper observed that most survivors were "without resources of any kind, as this is a poor city."[44] Coming off the trains were "people of all social conditions, but especially the humble," another paper wrote, and this "spectacle of weariness, resignation, and desperation" on the front page of every newspaper in Argentina was a "reproduction of refugee scenes from the European war," and a sharp rebuke to optimistic myths of national integration.[45] Standing in a crowd of evacuees, one prominent San Juan reporter wrote in his journal: "People are wandering around, disoriented, like dogs without an owner. These people belong entirely to the humble classes. Is there no one in this city but the humble?"[46]

This poverty had roots far deeper than the immediate tragedy. In laying bare the social structure of one province, the earthquake also drove home the extent of impoverishment across the entire country. Thus the aid for the poor of San Juan was the first step toward aid for the poor of the nation. As Perón noted, it was a call "to work for all the disinherited of Argentina because, on the social plane, the majority of Argentines could be compared to the homeless of the mountain city."[47]

Perón personally met the first train of evacuees to reach Buenos Aires. While other officials talked sternly of sacrifice and endurance, he came with a playful smile, circling the train to take requests and shake hands through the windows. Photographs from that day provide some of the earliest visual records of the intimate rapport he was building with the popular classes. Evacuation meant a brutal uprooting, but these first arrivals had government help to find food, work, and shelter.[48]

Perón was at the center of the relief effort, directing the media campaign

20 Perón meeting train from San Juan in Buenos Aires, January 1944. CREDIT AGN.

and coordinating civil society even as he remained second-in-command at the War Ministry. When he declared the collection "the measure of our national solidarity," he meant it quite literally: a stylized thermometer to track contributions went up next to the Obelisco, at the symbolic center of Buenos Aires. In its first week, the campaign collected twenty-eight million pesos in cash and goods.[49] A strong wind blew down the thermometer, but the collection continued for three months, amassing forty-two million pesos in cash and thirty million pesos in donated goods. Perón called for "popular supervision" of the delivery of aid, but there were few complaints at the time.[50] This collection was such a success, such a stable referent for an unstable government, that when it came to an end, the government launched another, to benefit the poor provinces bordering San Juan. "Having had his hands in other people's pockets once," a British diplomat sneered, "Colonel Perón was getting a taste for it."[51]

The collection "served to demonstrate that Argentine brotherhood is not mere words, but something people feel in the depths of their souls," Judge Pablo Ramella wrote from San Juan.[52] Even the opposition, two years later, described the campaign as forging a "feeling of indestructible national unity," comparing it to the constitutional convention a century before.[53] Later on, opponents would claim that "the people acted out of solidarity for San Juan, not for Colonel Perón," but in 1944, that distinction was not so clear.[54]

Perón directed the relief effort, but he did not travel to San Juan. Rivalries likely kept him out of the presidential entourage, and he may have been reluctant to step away from the seat of power at a turbulent time. His delay in visiting the city surprised officials there but it hardly affected his growing popularity.[55] Moreover, as we will see, Perón astutely employed the support and opportunities gained with the collection to win control of the national state.

The Fall of Ramírez and the Rise of Perón

Since the beginning of the war, the Argentine government had declared itself neutral and worked hard to remain so. The United States wanted Argentina to join the Allies and tended to attribute Argentine neutrality to pro-Axis sentiment among the political leadership. Indeed, military and civilian nationalists often did have Axis sympathies, or at the very least, saw neutrality as a crucial matter of national sovereignty against the imperial control of the Allies, and especially Great Britain. Yet the conflict was not simply between supporters of the Allies and the Axis, as the British themselves saw little point in bringing Argentina into the war and much benefit in keeping neutral beef reaching English ports. In any case, the difficulty of maintaining neutrality against diplomatic pressure and popular sympathy for the Allies had led the Conservative civilian government to declare a state of siege in 1941 that remained in force until 1945.[56]

The complex disagreements about neutrality helped produce the 1943 coup. Two opposing groups had joined together to take power, pro-Allied generals who were unhappy with neutrality and nationalist colonels and majors who feared the next government might end it. The struggle between them continued until the pro-Allied group was outmaneuvered and sacked in October 1943.[57]

Official policy then took a sharp nationalist turn, prompting the United States to push for Argentina's diplomatic isolation. The now-dominant nationalist group, in turn, hatched a plan to purchase weapons from Germany. None of the top officials involved seems to have given much thought to how likely Germany was to actually provide weapons in late 1943, with the Allies advancing in Russia and Italy, or how those weapons might cross the Atlantic. In any case, the scheme's go-between was captured by British intelligence shortly after leaving Buenos Aires, and the British waited until the appropriate moment to press their advantage.[58]

On 15 January, hours before the earthquake, the British ambassador confronted President Ramírez with proof that German agents had violated Argentine neutrality to sell weapons.[59] The British gave Ramírez time to prepare for the break with Germany, perhaps by obtaining his own "confessions." As Ramírez had personally sponsored the violation of neutrality in question, they were offering him a rhetorical lifeline. If he failed to act, they vowed to make the information public, with potentially devastating results. The round-up of German agents began the morning that Ramírez set off for San Juan. The "discovery" of German espionage had undoubtedly delayed his trip—and made it imperative for him to prove his nationalist credentials and turn the disaster to his political advantage. The official response to the earthquake did fortify the regime, but the benefits did not accrue to Ramírez.[60]

As soon became clear, Ramírez had underestimated Perón's strength, both in San Juan and within the national government. The earthquake had struck an area Perón knew well, and relief efforts were led by military officers close to him.[61] In the years before the 1943 coup, Perón had served in several mountain infantry posts, first in Mendoza and later at a supervisory office in Buenos Aires. He was familiar with the local political world. More importantly, his strongest group of supporters had come from the military units there, including his immediate superior, General Edelmiro Farrell, the minister of war, who had personally established the mountain infantry twenty years earlier, and his closest collaborator, Lt. Colonel Domingo Mercante, who had served with Perón at the supervisory office. Perón also benefited from alliances reaffirmed during his year as a military attaché in fascist Italy, particularly with three fellow Axis sympathizers who had joined him there in May 1940—Colonel José Humberto Sosa Molina, General Juan Pistarini, and Colonel Valentín Campero.[62]

The morning after the earthquake, San Juan was placed under martial law; Colonel Sosa Molina, the regional commander, took over from Interventor Uriburu, the ally of Lugones and Ramírez. When martial law was lifted two weeks later, Sosa Molina became interventor, and Uriburu was transferred elsewhere. Meanwhile, Pistarini, the minister of public works, gained authority over evacuating, cleaning up, and rebuilding the city and named Campero as his point man in this effort. By early February, then, Perón's allies from Rome held the three most important posts in the province.

As his grip on San Juan slipped, Ramírez lost control of the national government as well. Having received the British ultimatum just prior to the earthquake, Ramírez delayed his response until after the mass for the earthquake victims. Left with few options, he expressed "shock," severed diplomatic relations with Germany, and closed several pro-Axis and nationalist newspapers.[63] For many junior officers who had come to see neutrality as key to

21 Perón assumes vice-presidency, July 1944. From left, Vice President Perón, Interior Minister Tessaire, Agriculture Minister Mason and wife, Public Works Minister Pistarini and wife. CREDIT AGN.

national sovereignty, this was a betrayal of nationalist ideals and a craven concession to the Allies.

Perón had clearly hoped to ride the San Juan campaign to eventual power, but now he saw a more immediate path forward. A rumor was spread, likely by Perón himself, that Ramírez was about to call up the reserves and actually declare war on the Axis. Discontent was intense among the nationalist and isolationist majority of junior officers, and the GOU, the secret military lodge that had boasted of its unity, was split by factions and formally dissolved.[64] The San Juan campaign provided cover for Perón to mobilize his loyalists against Ramírez by sending them around the country to collect donations— and organize the conspiracy. When the test of strength came, on 24 February, Ramírez's first act was to take the collection away from Perón, but then he overplayed his hand, and ended up resigning at gunpoint.

The new president was General Edelmiro Farrell, Perón's ally and superior, whom Perón soon replaced as war minister, a powerful post in the military regime.[65] Before doing so, Perón dispatched a close ally on a six-day mission to ensure the loyalty of every garrison across the country. Only one garrison was so trustworthy that no visit was required: San Juan.[66]

The response to the San Juan tragedy highlighted the differences in political approach between Ramírez and Perón and enabled the latter to prevail. During the weeks afterward, Ramírez offered authoritarian calls for repentance. His brief visit to San Juan was marked by formality and distance; his advisors evoked a stern commander presiding over "a sea of low and humble heads." By contrast, Perón moved toward the people, stepping out into the streets to personally collect for victims and greet refugees. Rather than emphasizing the obedience of the "humble" to solemn authority, Perón stressed their independence and initiative, offering exemplary stories of popular aid for their countrymen. Ramírez went to San Juan, but understood little of what he saw. Perón stayed in Buenos Aires, but clearly grasped what was at stake in the interior.

It was at this moment that Perón first demonstrated the combination of strategic thinking, conspiratorial skill, and popular appeal that would eventually carry him to the presidency. Over the coming years, Perón would lead a broad and complex movement that would profoundly remake the nation. Clerical and military elements would play crucial roles in this movement, to be sure, but it would be a diverse and shifting coalition that also included strong labor unions, renegade technical elites, and mobilized popular sectors. Brought together by Perón's leadership, this coalition would prove surprisingly powerful for all its internal contradictions.

The earthquake was a crucial moment in Perón's trajectory, even if his later success would overshadow and reshape the drama of the aftermath. Years later, few would recall the symbolically charged masses offered for those killed in the quake. But all remembered the popular musical show given to benefit the survivors, and the woman Perón met there, Eva Duarte, the future Evita.

PART 2

THE CORNERSTONE OF THE NEW ARGENTINA, EARLY 1944

"Nothing was left but "scorched earth," President Ramírez reported when he returned from San Juan on 20 January. The previous social order had proven rootless and deadly. Now the military regime would found a new order, starting with this city whose people the president had found "united, completely united, without political divisions, with their caudillos forgotten and their faith placed in God, the Fatherland and the national government." The extent of the destruction, the illegitimacy of local elites, and the possibilities for dramatic success led him to make rebuilding a national concern. Whatever the cost—"three, four or five hundred million pesos"—he vowed to rebuild the city following "modern urbanism" and taking "all known anti-seismic precautions." The new San Juan would be an earthquake-proof "garden city" with wide streets and housing for all.[1]

Such expansive promises came easily to leaders who aspired to remake the polity, but they were backed by little sense of what rebuilding would actually entail. Regime leaders knew action was necessary but had only a vague idea of what action to take. A newspaper headline captured the moment well: "Reconstruction Will Begin Very Soon; It Is Still Not Known Whether the City Will Be Rebuilt in Same Site."[2]

To act, the state needed experts—architects, planners, and engineers—to explain the disaster, provide a vision for the future, and chart a course forward. The experts saw an opportunity to reshape an entire city, and perhaps to accomplish far more. Starting the day after, many leading architects wrote the highest state official they knew to offer their services.

22 Perón, Pistarini, and other officials, 1944. Labor Secretary Perón in center; Public Works Minister Pistarini on right. CREDIT AGN.

Two architectural teams were recruited through different channels. First, the provincial minister of public works brought three young modernists to San Juan, where they would spend two months quietly exploring emergency solutions and alternative futures. Second, and more importantly, Perón assembled a team of prestigious urbanists in Buenos Aires. The STP had annexed housing to its portfolio six weeks before and already had a demonstration project underway—so Perón turned to the project head, Carlos Muzio, who enlisted his colleague Fermín Bereterbide.

Six days after the disaster, this second team produced a daring proposal for a completely new city, which they presented to Perón and then to the president. Impressed, President Ramírez endorsed the proposal but reassigned the team to work under General Juan Pistarini, the new national minister of public works.

"By presenting a de facto situation that demands immediate solution," Bereterbide and Muzio declared, "the San Juan earthquake—like the bombings in Europe—makes the work of urbanism easier." Modern planners had long denounced cities like San Juan for their unhealthiness, "monotony, lack of beauty, and antiquated layout on the Spanish grid." Now the destruction of the city made it possible—and urgent—for architects to think past the forms "we are used to contemplating and enduring" and imagine others more in

23 Sargento Cabral barrio, outside Buenos Aires, 1937. CREDIT *REVISTA DE ARQUITECTURA.*

keeping with local ecology and industrial modernity. This was the moment to rebuild San Juan in an entirely different way, and on a new site, adjacent to its former location. Here a powerful and confident state guided by expert planners would create a city that "expressed the grandeur, the technical and artistic efficiency, and the economic strength of the country."[3]

The architects made their case in a ten-page report that included no drawings but established "the organizational and aesthetic advantages of modern urbanism" by invoking a telling precedent: Sargento Cabral, a decade-old Army housing complex outside Buenos Aires. Sargento Cabral was both a landmark in Argentine urbanism and the centerpiece of a military campaign to dignify living conditions for the lower ranks. It was thus a powerful symbol for the regime's larger project: social justice within Catholic and military hierarchy, in a park just outside the cosmopolitan city. Moreover, it had been built by the military engineers under the command of General Pistarini and designed by a team including Fermín Bereterbide, lead author of the San Juan proposal, the pioneering modernist Alberto Prebisch, and his former partner Ernesto Vautier. Bereterbide was already on the San Juan team, and Pistarini now appointed Vautier to lead it.[4]

For architects as well as the military, a new San Juan would be the seed of a new nation. "We should not speak of rebuilding, but rather of a new city," the architects' professional journal declared, "a large-scale 'test' of what will have to be done later in every city in the country."[5] Rebuilding the city would be "a true school of urbanism," and the scope of the work was so great, "there will hardly be an architect or engineer without some connection to the project." This was an opportunity to fundamentally reshape how every Argentine city—and building—was made.[6]

Once the rubble was removed, the architects and their military sponsors assumed, San Juan was a blank slate. But they overlooked the people, institutions, and even buildings that remained, battered but standing. A community was still there, and its assent to the architects' vision was by no means assured. Local caudillos were discredited, but despite confident military claims, they had hardly vanished. Indeed, they would prove quite effective at blocking some projects for social reform—and turning others to their own ends.

The first indication of how the *fuerzas vivas*, the local establishment, would respond was a gathering in the main plaza the day after the quake. Only a few major bodegueros were there: most had left town and would not return for months. But those present saw the need to act swiftly. In formulating their demands, they paid little attention to the horror around them. Burying the dead, healing the wounded, feeding the survivors, housing the homeless: all this went unmentioned. Instead, they concentrated on restoring their own power. From the ruins, they produced a utopia of their own.

When the interior minister arrived by train that afternoon, they presented him with three simple demands. First, the state should guarantee their property, by issuing one hundred fifty million pesos of bonds to compensate them for any losses. Second, it should guarantee their production, by rebuilding private wineries immediately at government expense. Third, it should guarantee their labor supply, by immediately conscripting fifty thousand men for rebuilding. The number was arbitrary and enormous: one paper reported the figure as one hundred thousand men, at a time when there were ninety thousand workers in construction nationwide and only thirty thousand conscripts in the Army.[7]

Claiming to represent all of San Juan, the bodegueros demanded massive state action to secure their individual positions. Their demands were extraordinary, as was their indifference to local workers. By contrast, another group—sanjuaninos living in Buenos Aires—requested only a bank holiday, rebuilding loans, and preference for sanjuanino doctors in the relief effort.[8]

Perhaps the boldness of the bodegueros' demands reflected false confidence, or desperation: they too had loved ones beneath the rubble. Certainly nothing would ever be the same. Importing thousands of workers would inevitably have transformed the province. It is unlikely that, with a day's reflection, any of these notables could have seriously contemplated the idea. But after only a few hours, they demanded it of the highest government officials. They took for granted decisive state action to advance their purposes. They saw nothing unseemly in elevating their private interests above the collective good or, indeed, in equating them with it: the millions of pesos in compensation were to come from "patriotic bonds."

Like the architects, the local elite looked back to the previous decade for a model for state action. During those years, the national state had helped overthrow Cantoni, shored up their power, and funded major infrastructure projects. Most importantly, the state had responded to a deep crisis in the wine industry with a restructuring, funded by "patriotic bonds," that had benefited large bodegueros at everyone else's expense. Facing another catastrophe, they hoped once more to strengthen their hand.

The notables' demands did not prosper at first: the government ignored the request for conscript labor, ruled out compensation, and postponed repairs until after the harvest.[9] The very aggressiveness of the demands certainly provided more fodder for military critiques of the old order. Yet that same aggressiveness ensured that these notables remained the spokesmen for the local elite. Within weeks, as the proposed move became public, this very group would become the main advocates of rebuilding on the same site— while continuing to demand compensation for their losses.[10]

Here was the central conflict of the aftermath: two opposing projects for transformation from above, architects and military reformers versus bodegueros and their allies. The conflict would be framed as "movers" against "keepers," those who wished to move the city to a new site versus those who wanted to keep it where it was. But far more was at stake here than location: this was a fight for the future of the province.

Both projects were rooted in the robust state power forged in the previous decade: the architects hoped to use it to ensure transformation, and the bodegueros to strengthen their position. Both saw rebuilding as a process directed from above—even the architects, whose project was far more inclusive, made little effort to involve the local public. Both swore fealty to the military regime's Catholic, nationalist, and modernizing ideals but understood them differently and pushed for opposing projects in San Juan. Both proclaimed great confidence in the state as a unified actor able to accomplish their desired goal, even as they launched lobbying efforts that laid bare how divided the state actually was.

Since military leaders were committed to a new beginning, they were drawn to the architects' proposal, but with two important limitations. First, for all the official talk of unity, the regime was still divided, as Ramírez's fall confirmed. While officers like Perón advocated an aggressive approach in San Juan, others favored a less ambitious course, out of rivalry with Perón, a desire to cultivate Conservative provincial elites, or a sense that rebuilding the city was ancillary to the military's larger aims. Even Perón himself, seeing his fortunes wax and wane in the coming months, would push for rebuilding without tying himself too tightly to it.

Second, while the weakness of the winery elite suggested this was the moment to take forceful action, the very centrality of wine to the local economy made it difficult to do so. The disaster struck a few weeks before the crucial grape harvest, which accounted for 42 percent of annual wages.[11] However unjust the local structure of power, a successful harvest was key to keeping workers, smallholders, and merchants afloat. Securing the harvest was essential, even if it meant shoring up those the government would later have to confront.

Thus the military was divided on how quickly and how decisively to act. Even though all three state institutions directing relief and reconstruction were aligned with Perón—the provincial administration under Sosa Molina, the Ministry of Public Works under Pistarini, and the Secretariat of Labor itself—they worked in tension as much as in concert. Sosa Molina, in particular, was obliged by the nature of his position and the importance of the harvest to defend bodeguero interests. But he would go further, offering them crucial political support, expressing suspicion of the move, and allowing a surprisingly open debate between movers and keepers.

The three chapters of this section explore this struggle in the six months after the earthquake. Chapter 4 sketches the trajectory of modernism and its rivals in Argentine architecture, tracing how architects came to advocate radical schemes for renewal and what those schemes looked like. Chapter 5 examines how local elites rallied their supporters to battle these schemes, building a counterargument focused on rethinking individual buildings rather than the city or province as a whole. Chapter 6 then turns to state action on the ground, as it restored a provisional normality, winning prestige for the military regime but opening a back door to discredited elites. Here I show how the battle between movers and keepers brought in outside allies, while playing to an initial standstill.

CHAPTER 4   UTOPIAS IN THE DUST

ARCHITECTS' VISIONS FOR THE NEW CITY

Conceived in five days without visiting the site, the Bereterbide and Muzio proposal might seem like a textbook case of architectural hubris. The architects laid out a forceful vision for change, aiming to achieve by fiat in San Juan reforms they had been unable to accomplish by persuasion elsewhere in the country, changes in housing, parks, roads, and zoning. Clearly presented at the outset, this vision remained consistent over the next four months, and multiple visits to San Juan, as the team developed their memo into a set of plans and drawings. This consistency could also be read as proof that the architects were simply following modernist dogma.

But the radical gesture at the heart of the proposal—moving the city to a new site—was a specific response to the challenges of San Juan, not a rote application of modernist precepts. To be sure, the choice of a site and the vision of what to build there were shaped by contemporary ideas in urbanism. But even this apparent flight from history has a history, rooted in the prior course of Argentine architecture, as well as the material constraints, political experience, and reformist drive of the moment.

Understanding this vision for the city, therefore, requires first a brief survey of the urban and professional landscape of the 1930s, the world from which these architects and their projects emerged. In these years, dreams of modernization and the expanding power of the state were reshaping architecture and engineering, even as the professions were torn by intense debates over the scope and future direction of their work. Many of the leading actors in these debates would later produce plans for rebuilding San Juan. Two would produce the projects that would form the baseline for future debate:

the pre-earthquake plan by Guido and Carrasco and the post-earthquake plan by Bereterbide and Vautier.

Design and the State in the Infamous Decade

"The "Infamous Decade," the thirteen years between the coups of 1930 and 1943, was a time of paradox, as the national state lost political legitimacy but expanded its economic and territorial power. Unable to win office legitimately, yet unwilling to abandon the formal trappings of democracy, the rulers during these years stumbled along, first trying to revive the earlier export bonanza by making extraordinary commitments to European powers, then turning inward, looking to a growing domestic market as a way out of the crisis. This was hardly as sharp a rupture as would later be claimed, for exports continued to be crucial and, as already noted, some domestic producers— notably wine and sugar—had already benefited from decades of protection. What changed were the mechanisms, scale, and impact of state intervention. A cadre of young experts reoriented economic policy, increasing the state's fiscal authority and regulatory reach, protecting agricultural producers, and beginning to explicitly promote industry. All these interventions shared a modernizing drive and a persistent bias toward the powerful, and they offered little voice and few benefits for workers, consumers, and small producers.

Like Depression-era governments worldwide, the state launched a broad public works program to alleviate unemployment and jump-start domestic industries like cement. This program was the most obvious sign of greater state power, especially two landmark projects: the reshaping of the national capital and the construction of a national highway network. In Buenos Aires, the appointed mayor launched a frantic building program, cutting short two decades of vibrant debate about urban reform by implementing an array of grand projects: a broad avenue through the center, a web of subway lines underneath, and a ring highway along the municipal border. Downtown there were imposing new official buildings—banks, ministries, and university faculties—and a fitting jewel at the midpoint of the new avenue: an obelisk commemorating the city's four hundredth anniversary in 1936. Left out of this flurry of activity was any attempt to address the city's deep housing crisis or sprawling growth. Spectacular as they were, the grand projects for the capital represented, as the historian Adrián Gorelik has put it, "modernization without reform," an apt characterization of the Conservative governments overall.[1]

The other landmark was the highway system built by the Ministry of Public Works (MOP). This was part of the ministry's expanding control of infrastructure, as it gradually took over much of water, sewer, and electrical provision nationwide. But highways were its model intervention: from 1932 to 1944, the network of paved roads increased by a factor of fifteen, to more than thirty thousand kilometers. The initial idea of a national highway system was to truly integrate the territory, countering the private rail network that funneled traffic to Buenos Aires, but ultimately the highways ended up following rail lines fairly closely.

Centralization was a dominant note in these years, with the strengthening of national institutions, the outward expansion of infrastructure, and the erosion of provincial autonomy. But this process was paradoxical in two ways. First, centralization weakened provincial institutions, but not all provincial actors. Federal intervention was more often invited by local elites than imposed from the center, as in San Juan, and frequently increased the patronage powers of those elites. This was particularly evident in the expansion of infrastructure and the consolidation of scattered local institutions into national universities in the west and northwest.[2] Second, political centralization was accompanied by a kind of cultural federalism. Many public projects were premised on a greater knowledge of the interior, such as oil exploration, road building, and national park construction, and once underway they strengthened the hold of the interior on the national imagination. Even as the provinces were being remade in the image of Buenos Aires, the image of the nation was being remade around an idealized notion of the provinces. The growing prominence of the interior was evident above all in literary essays but also in the rise of folklore within popular music and regional elements in architecture.[3]

State expansion brought new opportunities and institutional power for design; the 1930s was when architects and especially engineers came into their own. During the export boom, foreigners had dominated the design professions: they established the engineering faculty and architecture school, founded the professional associations, and designed and built the bulk of national infrastructure. Yet the immigrant experts who led both professions gradually gave way, first to locals trained abroad, and then, starting in the 1920s, to those born and trained in Argentina. Few of the practioners of these new liberal professions came from humble backgrounds, but even fewer had traditional surnames or great family wealth.[4]

From the outset, engineers were more numerous and institutionally powerful than architects. The engineering faculty in Buenos Aires was already three decades old and had two hundred graduates when the architecture school opened its doors in 1904—as a division of engineering. According to an 1876 law, engineers alone could inspect and certify buildings, which gave an engineer without construction experience greater legal authority than the most seasoned architect. This enabled many engineers to practice as generalists, designing everything from speculative residential buildings to sewage systems. Their range of practice is suggested by the career of Enrique Butty, who was dean of the engineering faculty and briefly rector of the University of Buenos Aires, head of virtually every important technical agency of the state, designer of docks and sewers, and the author of a study of space-time in Einstein and Bergson, the standard Spanish-language textbook on concrete, and a treatise on the profession which argued that "engineers should . . . fully enter into the circles of leadership and government."[5] By the 1930s, engineers headed many industrial companies, all the major construction firms, and a host of state agencies—the state oil company, the roads department, and the sewer authority. By contrast, architects held no leadership posts—even the Architecture Department of the MOP was commanded by an engineer.

The size of the professional associations reflected the differences in power: by 1945, the Center of Argentine Engineers (Centro Argentino de Ingenieros, or CAI) had three thousand members, while the Central Society of Architects (Sociedad Central de Arquitectos, or SCA) had fewer than eight hundred. Engineers were dispersed across the country, broadly influential within the state, and played power-broker roles in several provinces, notably Jujuy and San Juan. Architects were largely concentrated in the capital, weak within the state, and largely gained influence through more powerful patrons. But architects were broadening their horizons: by 1945, two-thirds of the charter members of the SCA were located outside the capital, although primarily in the three provinces with architecture schools.[6]

The national expansion of architectural practice was accompanied by a nationalization of architectural style. During the export boom, an eclectic architecture of cosmopolitan origins had flourished in Buenos Aires and set the pattern for interior cities, even those with few immigrants. But by the 1920s, young architects were growing resentful of their subordinate status, criticizing the earlier eclecticism as emblematic of a rootless national order, and looking for new forms fitting their institutional aspirations. "Faithful image of a people without memory is the architecture that has flooded the country for some time now," the architect Eduardo Sacriste observed in 1943, "a constant doubt, an endless wandering, a not-being." Finding a way to a proper modernity would require architects, in his view, "to dig deep into our earth to find the roots of our tradition."[7] However much this language suggested a conservative return to a mythical past, this was a project that aimed at transformation, at laying claim to a true modernization.[8]

By the late 1930s, Argentine architects could be divided into four broad groups: eclectics, neocolonials, and older and younger generations of modernists. First was the Beaux Arts old guard, who had built much of the modern cityscape in an eclectic mix of (European) historicist styles. Despite its numbers, this group was in decline, producing little in the way of new ideas. Indeed, as early as the First World War, leading Beaux Arts architects already recognized the need for "new directions" more in keeping with the changing culture and innovative materials like concrete.[9]

Two distinct groups of challengers had emerged in the 1920s, each led by recent graduates, each claiming to offer a more rational, modern, and national approach. The neocolonial movement rejected the dominant pastiche of European historicism in favor of designs derived from local tradition. Neocolonial designers like Ángel Guido (a 1921 graduate of the University of Córdoba) took the built patrimony of Spanish colonialism as their starting point and aesthetic model. Naturally, there was considerable debate about which parts of that legacy to stress, and how much hybridity and American variation from Spanish models to acknowledge. Over time, Guido came to defend a pared-down version of the colonial baroque—white plaster walls, red tile roofs, accents in dark carpentry—as the proper vocabulary for architecture in the Americas. Yet for all its insistence on history and locality, this movement was emphatically modern and quite international. Guido drew on German scholarship, published in French, and partly derived his design approach from the California Mission Style. Indeed, the enormously popular neocolonial single-family homes pioneered by Guido would be locally known as "little California chalets."[10]

The other challenge came from early modernists, who denounced historical precedent in favor of adaptation to the present: buildings spare in decoration, functional in design, and modeled on machines. The first Argentine standard-bearers for this international movement were Alberto Prebisch and Ernesto Vautier, who graduated from the University of Buenos Aires in 1921, spent a few years in Europe, then returned to produce a prize-winning design for a new industrial city in Tucumán and proclaim their country ideally positioned to build a different future because "we have no history and we have no tradition."[11] Their primary opponents were the eclectic establishment, but they initially disdained neocolonial advocates as well. Denying the value and even coherence of the vernacular past, they argued that "our era is searching . . . for a classicism, *its* classicism," and only modernism fit the bill.[12]

After the 1930 coup, the early polemics cooled and the positions of the challengers partly converged. Accepting the conservative turn in politics, the modernists pursued a parallel move in aesthetics, shifting from novelty to austerity, and from formal experimentation to spare, white, and purified forms. Prebisch, a son of the Tucumán elite whose brother was the government's chief economic planner, produced two exemplary works in Buenos Aires: a sleek movie theater and the obelisk that was the centerpiece of "modernization without reform."[13] These early modernists now embraced parts of the vernacular past they had earlier disdained as the basis for a supposedly more authentic path to modernization. The most notable example was the Sargento Cabral barrio designed by Prebisch, Vautier, and Bereterbide (a 1919 University of Buenos Aires graduate), which would be deployed in 1944 as a model for a new San Juan. For their part, the neocolonial architects also moved toward common ground, and a kind of dual style emerged, consisting of a stripped-down neocolonial for individual homes and an austere monumentality, alternately modernist or neoclassical in its vocabulary, for larger buildings that demanded grandeur.

After 1936, the major projects in Buenos Aires inspired several interior cities to emulate the capital. Whatever their disappointments in Buenos Aires, many architects hoped to carry out comprehensive projects in the smaller settings of the interior. This was the beginning of a gradual shift from urbanism to city planning, a move from widening avenues and building parks to systematically gathering social data and reshaping every aspect of the city in keeping with the four functions planners saw as essential: circulation, housing, work, and leisure. Ángel Guido and his partner Benito Carrasco were hired by Rosario, Salta, and Tucumán to develop plans, while Mendoza held a competition for its master plan, won by a team led by the early modernists Fermín Bereterbide and Alberto Belgrano Blanco.

More broadly, professional debate expanded from narrower questions of building form to broader issues of planning the city, reforming the countryside, and housing the whole of the population. Many pioneers were active in this debate: Guido, Vautier, and Bereterbide published extensively on planning in these years and undertook important projects. But the most innovative thinking came from a younger generation.

The late thirties saw a rebirth of modernism in Argentina, this time with a distinctly national and regional twist. In 1938, a group of recent architecture graduates began meeting in Buenos Aires to form a local branch of the modernist movement.[14] They called themselves the Grupo Austral, and although their joint body of work would be small, their impact on the future of the profession would be great. Two founding members of Austral had just returned from a year in Paris, working with the leading Swiss French modernist

Le Corbusier on a master plan for Buenos Aires. Now they came back determined to radically remake their city and country and to build a network of alliances with opinion leaders—industrialists, politicians, union leaders—for the task. "Nowadays, the meaning of the word architecture has changed," as their ally Eduardo Sacriste put it in 1945. "It has gained a broader reach, going beyond the bourgeois home and the speculative building . . . [to] be associated with a new term: urbanism. Architecture in everything, urbanism in everything, in the felicitous phrase of Le Corbusier."[15]

With these ideals in mind, the architects of Grupo Austral—Jorge Ferrari Hardoy, Juan Kurchan, Hilario Zalba, Jorge Vivanco, Simón Ungar, and others—set to work. While seeking support from older modernists like Prebisch, Vautier, and Beteterbide, they considered their elders' work timid and constrained and promoted a more comprehensive approach.[16] They produced a range of projects, from the internationally successful butterfly chair to a few buildings in Buenos Aires, but increasingly they focused on work in the interior. Their designs won a series of state-sponsored competitions on rural housing prototypes. Three Austral members addressed the same program as Prebisch and Vautier a decade earlier—a Tucumán sugar mill—but pursued a very different direction, emphasizing that the failings of Argentine architecture were due to "the absence of social content" and that it was only "by turning down the road of the anguished national problems that vainly demand resolution, down the road of problems of land and housing, that we will reach an architecture."[17]

One Austral member went even further. Surveying the history of housing reform in Argentina, Horacio Caminos located the root cause for repeated failures in reformers' narrow perspective: "Every initiative is condemned to fail unless the problem is approached from a holistic viewpoint, keeping in mind factors beyond the four walls of a house." Caminos (and his fellow Austral members) insisted that "the problem of housing is not technical but social," emphasizing that true reform would require increased wages and broader social transformation.[18]

This led him to advocate far-ranging reform instead of patchwork solutions. Anyone who cannot perceive that the world "is at a critical moment, in full liquidation, can hardly grasp the beat of our time, not in art or in architecture," Caminos argued. "Let us not lose time in shoring up a system that is collapsing; let us win time by structuring a new system. Our mission as architects at this moment is not exactly to build, but rather to help to tear down."[19]

Creative as the approach of the Austral modernists to remaking the interior was, more established architects had greater success in winning over interior elites. The bold entry by Austral for the Mendoza competition thus lost out to the more institutionally powerful team led by Fermín Bereterbide, co-designer of the Sargento Cabral barrio. Just to the north in San Juan, the Catholic Conservatives who came to power in 1942 decided to emulate the drive for modernization but avoid the complexities of competition. Thus they directly hired the team they found agreeable: the neocolonial urbanists Angel Guido and Benito Carrasco.

The Guido-Carrasco Plan, 1942

Surveying the city in 1942, Angel Guido and Benito Carrasco were filled with "pathos" at the "ungenerous destiny" of this place of "extraordinary industrial growth" but little civic distinction. Noting the dusty walls, narrow sidewalks, and lack of trees, their "clinical-urbanistic portrait" emphasized the city's lack of comfort, efficiency, and grandeur.[20] They proposed a battery of remedies: an imposing new civic center, a highway around the city perimeter, a beltway of parks, and uniformly neocolonial construction.

At the heart of the city, Guido and Carrasco sensed an absence: the main plaza hardly expressed the prosperity of the province. The engineers envisioned a new monumental center: the province should expropriate the four blocks between the two major plazas, demolish all existing structures, run a broad avenue down the middle, and line it with trees, canals, and impressive new government buildings. Then institutional authority would have a proper setting, an "entrance hall" for the city.

But even with the center strengthened, the city would remain fragmented, divided in two by the "iron belt" of railroad tracks and wineries looping around it. With the railroad beginning to decline and many sidings no longer in use, the urbanists proposed tearing up unused tracks and combining the two separate train stations currently standing on the west edge of the grid into one central station to the northeast, in a new industrial district. Moving the stations and eventually all industry to one area was a first step toward effective zoning. In the meantime, on the land where the stations currently stood, the urbanists proposed a new park, centered on a reflective pool, a gateway from the traditional downtown into the expanding western suburbs.

Removing the rails made it possible to ring the city with a parkway, perhaps with a new campus for the engineering school and a few housing complexes along its length. This was an attempt both to modernize transportation— marking the shift from rail to road—and to carve a green swath across the dusty city. As the former park director for Buenos Aires, Carrasco was particularly critical of the absence of greenery and the "lamentable" failure to dig

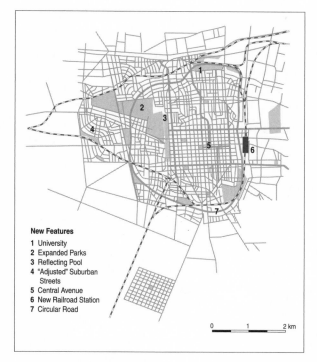

New Features
1 University
2 Expanded Parks
3 Reflecting Pool
4 "Adjusted" Suburban
   Streets
5 Central Avenue
6 New Railroad Station
7 Circular Road

0   1   2 km

Guido-Carrasco plan,
1942

canals or plant trees. For him, trees and canals marked "the real difference between Mendoza and San Juan," and the parkway was a first step toward remedying this deficiency.[21]

The urbanists claimed what would ultimately bring the city together was a unified civic aesthetic. They had a clear idea what this aesthetic should be: to "re-Argentinize" construction, they wanted to make neocolonial design mandatory for all future buildings.[22] This meant rejecting the "impoverished concept of modernization" that had prevailed for a century, with the "invasion of cosmopolitan architecture . . . from Buenos Aires," and returning to the "authentic and noble city dreamt by Spain." Getting back to the roots, the urbanists claimed, would make for a city better adapted to local ecology and better aligned with national tradition.[23]

The urbanists highlighted the benefits of planning and modernization but stressed that their approach was sensitive to context and "more practical than theoretical." Indeed, a desire to avoid conflict was evident throughout. They proposed new trees for only a few locations, hoping that from those beach-heads the city might some day be "invaded" by trees.[24] Similarly, although they regarded the Spanish street grid as a "fundamental defect," they did not attempt major changes in the streets.[25] Beyond the monumental complex and short central avenue, they concentrated their interventions on the periphery where land was easily obtained, like the railroad right-of-way for the parkway.

Despite their rhetoric of local variation, the urbanists mandated the same neocolonial architecture here as everywhere else they worked.[26] While they rejected "exotic imitations of Buenos Aires," their plan echoed the "modernization without reform" of the national capital: monumental buildings and wide avenues in the center and a parkway around the perimeter. And whatever their claims of pragmatism, their plan ultimately required expropriating one-fifth of the city.

The Guido-Carrasco proposal came at a moment of transition in urbanism and planning. While officially described as a "plan regulador," a term suggesting a comprehensive document for governing future urban growth, in substance it was closer to earlier urbanism: a few strategic interventions within an established city fabric. The only specific requirement for the future was that new construction be neocolonial: there was no sense of how the plan would shape growth, only a laundry list of infrastructure projects. While the plan included demographic statistics, these had no impact on the design. Alongside the plan, the Conservative administration had undertaken several complementary initiatives: there was the new city hall built by federal funds, anchoring one end of the proposed boulevard, and two neighborhoods of worker housing, well outside the four avenues. But the plan had no specifics on housing or zoning.

Limited as the plan was, many property owners still rejected it as an indulgent folly. Expropriations were especially controversial: the plan did not specify the mechanism or cost for carrying them out, offering only the vague idea of recovering any investment by reselling leftover parcels at higher prices. While well established elsewhere, this method of funding urban reforms was untested in Argentina, much less San Juan, and threatening to a local elite deeply skeptical of state action.

The Graffigna Conservatives rammed the plan through the provincial legislature before the 1943 coup, establishing an Office of Urbanism to carry it out. But these measures were easily reversed. The new expropriation law accompanying the plan was expansive in theory, covering any project "that aims to achieve a material or spiritual satisfaction for the community," but minimally funded in practice.[27] The director of the impressive-sounding Office of Urbanism was also its sole employee. When the Conservatives' rivals came to power locally after the 1943 coup, they quickly scrapped the Guido-Carrasco plan.

The most telling indication of the plan's limits came in January 1944. In the plan, Guido and Carrasco had addressed the city's history but made no mention of the 1894 earthquake. They mandated white walls and red roofs but dismissed anti-seismic design as "not crucial . . . at this time."[28] Just after the earthquake, Carrasco published newspaper articles to remind the public that "San Juan already has an indispensable instrument" for rebuilding, a plan which foresaw everything and "left nothing free to the improvisation that has caused the irreparable errors in most of our cities."[29] Such claims to foresight rang hollow among the ruins.

From the standpoint of the military regime, the plan had two further drawbacks. First, while Guido was an ally, Carrasco had signed a September 1943 manifesto against military rule, making him an unlikely candidate for a politically important project. Second, and more importantly, what had seemed bold before the earthquake now seemed timid. The military wanted a more comprehensive rethinking.

Yet the very features that now made the Guido-Carrasco plan less attractive to national leaders made it more appealing to local elites. Here was a vision for how to rebuild, as a "garden city," without moving. A broad range of local elites, including several previous opponents, would soon embrace the Guido-Carrasco plan.

The Bereterbide-Vautier Plan, 1944

Rather than settle for piecemeal improvements, Bereterbide and Muzio argued six days after the earthquake, this was the moment to pursue comprehensive solutions. Instead of breathing new life into old errors, the architects proposed a break: the city in ruins should be abandoned. San Juan should be rebuilt in a new way and on a new site.

From the initial memo in January to the presentation drawings in June, the team expanded but the core ideas remained consistent. The two primary designers, Bereterbide and Vautier, were accomplished professionals with many built works. They shared an outlook on housing and city planning, as reflected in their work together on Sargento Cabral or a 1933 pamphlet for a Buenos Aires master plan titled *What Is Urbanism?*[30] Most of the ideas came from Bereterbide, as later publications and private papers make clear, which is not surprising, as he had twenty years of housing projects for clients ranging from a Socialist housing cooperative and the city of Buenos Aires to the Catholic Church and of course the Army. Willing to work with anyone, Bereterbide also had a utopian side: he was a Socialist, an Esperanto enthusiast, and the author of many articles in technical publications sharply critiquing property rights. Beyond his buildings, he had extensive, if dispiriting, experience in city planning: he had worked for a decade on a new Buenos Aires building code, only to see his most important ideas dropped, and his team had won the Mendoza master plan competition, only to see their proposals ignored and sidelined.

The radical approach to rebuilding San Juan emerged from the frustrations of experience rather than the fantasies of ideology. Bereterbide and Vautier were not repudiating the Guido and Carrasco plan but taking it much further, building its fragmentary insights into a systematic approach, turning the "garden city" from a vague slogan into a fundamental organizing principle.

Modernist architects had long criticized the dense building, tiny lots, narrow streets, and absence of greenery of cities like San Juan. Now that these flaws had proven deadly, the architects argued for broader streets, larger lots, more dispersed homes, and far more trees and parks.

Carrying out such reforms would require expropriating some or all of every lot in the city.[31] This promised to be difficult, in operational, political, and financial terms. The shoddy and incomplete property register made it particularly challenging. The precedent of Guido and Carrasco was not encouraging: limited as their proposal was, it still required significant expropriations, which sparked enough resistance to sink it. But the most important barrier was financial. Forty years earlier, the Supreme Court had set strict limits on public expropriations of land, requiring separate legal action for each property owner with the purchase price only set at the close of the trial. This ruling had encouraged speculation and hampered major projects, largely relegating public action to cities' undeveloped fringes.[32] Here it ensured that rebuilding could only proceed at great expense, and after the resolution of over four thousand individual cases. Expropriations would cost far more than existing infrastructure was worth.

This was why Bereterbide had long been suspicious of "absolute" property rights. Property was everywhere a collective artifact, "the result of the labor of all," he argued, and in San Juan "this affirmation becomes categorical, since it is only due to hydraulic works carried out by the government . . . that the region can be inhabited at all."[33] Yet the benefits of public action were "almost always absorbed by a particular owner," who then limited further public action. For this reason, he insisted, "the value of land is not a constructive, but a disruptive value."[34]

The architects called for a different approach. Instead of expropriating thousands of small parcels across the city, the state should purchase a few large parcels just outside it. This rural land would be cheaper and simpler to obtain,

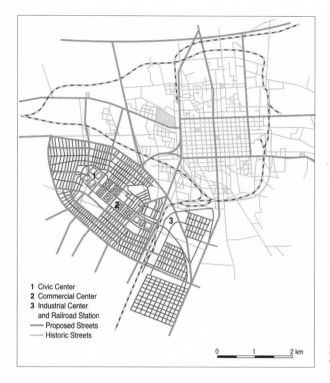

1 Civic Center
2 Commercial Center
3 Industrial Center
   and Railroad Station
—— Proposed Streets
—— Historic Streets

0   1   2 km

Bereterbide-
Vautier plan, 1944

and with fewer constraints, architects could build a more humane, equitable, and enduring city. The new city would have decent housing for all, not just the few who owned property.

This scheme did not leave behind property owners in the old city: each would be issued a voucher to purchase a comparable plot in the new city. This "swap" would avoid expropriation proceedings and, when complete, would leave the old city in the hands of the state, which could then clear the rubble, restore the monuments, and turn the ruins into a park.[35]

While the architects did not mean to overturn the political order, their proposal deeply alarmed local elites. Architects were convinced that property would be more valuable and secure in the new city than the old and thought they could convince property owners as well. Thus their first memo dwelt on the virtues of "facilitating" as opposed to "mandating" a swap, and as opposition emerged, Bereterbide worked hard to win over local elites, writing long solicitous letters and passing along design drawings. Yet this diplomacy could not hide the threat the move posed to the power of the propertied. After all, they owned property not simply for shelter but as a sign and guarantee of their social power. The swift and uniform construction of a new city would disrupt that power, and the architects' proposals contained no guarantees that it would be preserved. Crucially, the explanations of the swap highlighted how it would work for owner-occupied homes—but not for rentals, the majority of the housing stock.[36]

By moving the city, the architects hoped to outflank entrenched property relations and produce a demonstration effect for the nation. As I will show, they were thinking about how the rebuilt city could model new approaches to the design of houses, institutional buildings, and neighborhoods. But they were after something more. Because rebuilding San Juan required rethinking how *everything* was put together, from individual houses to the region as a whole, it offered an exceptional opportunity to put architects' full set of tools to use. They hoped the design approaches and legal powers employed in rebuilding one province might become standard practice nationwide. This would be a new regulatory regime for building, property, and zoning, with architect-planners as the key experts.

Considering this, it is easy to understand why the architects downplayed the geological argument for moving the city. The city was built on unsettled alluvial soil ten meters below the level of the river, although other nearby settlements stood on firmer soil well above the river. The earthquake cut a swath of destruction across the central valley, but the low-lying areas of the capital suffered the worst destruction, while several of the hamlets on higher ground were virtually unaffected. Moving to new ground had an intuitive appeal as a baseline defense against earthquakes: after all, this was what Mendoza had done after 1861, and what San Juan had failed to do after 1894. The architects did not highlight this argument, partly because they had no geological data when they made their first proposal.

But there was more to their reticence. As advocates of a bold vision, they wanted to make an active case based on the virtues of their future city, rather than offering a passive case based on the quality of the soil. As Bereterbide put it, a new site made it possible to "raise up a city rationally planned and harmoniously built . . . on ground more apt for foundations and for plantings, with a better climate, a healthier soil, better defended from floods . . . a garden city where life unfolds within order, in the greatest adaptation to varied functions, and permanent surroundings of nature and beautiful views." The social and ecological benefits of the new city, and the precedent it would set, were far more important—and far more conclusive—than the geology.[37]

In presentation drawings, the architects clothed the new city in tradition. The city was laid out in keeping with modernist principles, but its buildings suggested a deeper continuity. Like Sargento Cabral ten years earlier, this was

24 Government center, Bereterbide-Vautier plan for San Juan, 1944. CREDIT AGN.

an exercise in unified neocolonial design—a radical extension of the timid ideas of Guido and Carrasco. This was a pragmatic choice, a concession to the imagined taste of military officials, local elites, and the broader public. The architects chose to downplay their own modernist preferences, offering nothing of the glass-and-steel towers they were designing for other clients at the same time.[38] The accompanying text explained that this formal unity was only provisional, and the actual buildings would be in a variety of styles. But the grand drawings showed neocolonial buildings, and architects clearly expected lay audiences to take this as a core attribute of the city. By defusing stylistic controversy, the architects hoped to gain room to maneuver on the issues they regarded as crucial, which were social and economic.[39]

The common aesthetic also held the plan together. The central idea was to implement functional zoning throughout the city, physically and conceptually separating administrative, commercial, industrial, and residential areas while building a new road system and park network to link them together. In drawings, the new city was an oblong shape running from northwest to southeast on the outer edge of the former city. Public activities would be concentrated in a sequence of building complexes arrayed down the central spine of the new city; first was government, followed by religion, then banks, and finally commerce and entertainment, with a new train station sited where the existing tracks crossed the new downtown. Across the train tracks stood the industrial district, where bodegas, factories, and warehouses would be located, with easy access to transport and each other. On either side of the spine all down the city's length were residential neighborhoods, planned on a new model. The idea was to build the neighborhoods closest to the old city first, so as to quickly create a continuous urban fabric, and then expand outward.

Instead of the scattered parks proposed by Guido and Carrasco, this plan envisioned a network of tree-lined canals down every street, shade woven into the fabric of the future city. Both the city center and the residential neighborhoods were largely pedestrian spaces, with vehicles limited to the internal garages in the center and the boulevards on its edge. Instead of a few individual boulevards, this scheme imagined an entirely new road system, hierarchically organized, in keeping with the broad professional consensus among architects and engineers about separating pedestrian and vehicle traffic. Nearly all vehicles would travel on the park boulevards; cars would be limited from smaller streets; pedestrians would travel on a parallel network of public walkways.

The architects aimed, in Bereterbide's phrase, "to create the city of the present where the natural blends with the urban . . . where one moves continuously through color and freshness surrounded by buildings that are simple, varied, and harmonious." But while tied together by roads, trees, canals, and "harmonious" architecture, the two major areas of the city—downtown and the neighborhoods—were designed in distinct ways. Bereterbide and Vautier prescribed density for downtown, but advocated dispersal and decentralization for the neighborhoods.[40]

In modernist planning, the characteristic move was to reverse previous figure-ground relationships: where previously low buildings had dominated the city block and left no open space, typically modernist buildings were tall and had small footprints, leaving much of the block open—the strategy of the tower in the park. In the city center, Bereterbide and Vautier pursued a different approach. Recognizing the intensity of sun and wind, they made sheltered spaces a central motif, imagining the core as a series of low buildings surrounded by covered walkways, bordered by canals, and occupying the entire perimeter of each block. They designed the city center not as a series of towers in an open undifferentiated space crossed by highways, as many later modernist designs would, but rather as a series of distinct public spaces marked off by buildings and filled with vegetation, spaces whose "exclusive owner is the pedestrian."[41]

Bereterbide and Vautier shared the general modernist suspicion of mixed functions as "disorder" and therefore separated bank offices from churches, and movie theaters from government buildings, a stance that would finally undermine much of what made the central plaza vibrant. But they did recognize much of what made the plaza lively—its intimate scale, sequence of spaces, and temperate surroundings—and proposed expanding these across a broader stretch of the central city. Rather than simply producing one monumental complex, they proposed a broader rethinking of civic space.

In their drawings, the buildings and public spaces that showed the greatest care and variety were government offices and centers: this is both understandable and revealing. Only state offices were granted iconic power; banks and commercial buildings were depicted as generic block-sized buildings. This was because these early drawings were based only on the estimated size of buildings, but it suggested the minimum level to which design could fall for a functional city.

The city center was surrounded by an outer ring of housing. These residential areas were to be rebuilt as "neighborhood units," drawing on a major concept from Anglo-American planning. While Guido and Carrasco had allowed that new approaches to housing and neighborhoods might be tried out on the periphery, Bereterbide and Vautier made such approaches central to their project. Each neighborhood would be a cluster of two to four thousand residents, with a civic center containing a school, plaza, church, corner stores, and playing fields. Instead of being built up to the sidewalk, these houses would stand alone in a garden, set back from the street and from each other. Unlike previous homes, they would be anti-seismic and, the architects assumed, largely built from concrete. In its emphasis on individual homes and a reinvented street bordered by trees and irrigation canals, this scheme revealed an affinity with Anglo-American suburbs.[42]

The architects envisioned housing for all funded by generous official subsidies but had worked out few details—only two overall principles. First, nearly everything would be freestanding individual homes: there would be no towers, at most a few apartment buildings in between residential and commercial areas. This was a deliberate attempt to sidestep bitter and recurring fights among housing reformers, which had pitted Socialist and modernist advocates of collective apartment buildings, like Bereterbide, against Catholic defenders of single-family homes. Although Bereterbide was co-designer of the leading collective housing project in the country, he and Vautier chose to respect Catholic and military preferences. Second, despite the project's egalitarian goals, not all housing was equal. At least one "neighborhood unit" was reserved

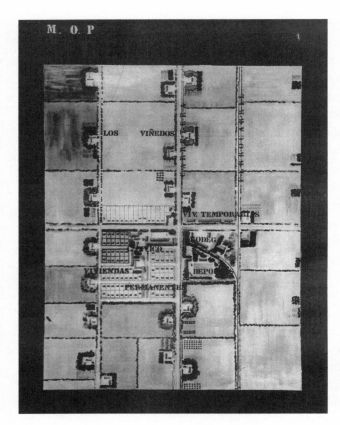

25 New cooperative winery, Bereterbide-Vautier plan for San Juan, 1944.
CREDIT AGN.

for workers—and it was next to the industrial district, across the tracks from the rest of the city. Overall, their rough budget set two categories of housing: about 20 percent for "the wealthy, the middle-class, and their servants," and the remainder for sanjuaninos of "modest condition." While the distinctions would be far less sharply drawn than before, still the architects planned to spend nearly three times as much per person on the better housing.[43]

To some extent, "neighborhood units" simply reproduced practices of existing neighborhoods: the central role envisioned for school, parish, and plaza in the new neighborhoods paralleled the role each played in the four towns absorbed into San Juan. In formalizing these practices and designing for them, of course, the architects ran the danger of misunderstanding what made them important. Here was another sign of a larger problem: the architects recognized much of what was appealing about the former order, and tried to incorporate it into their design, but had difficulty in placing their project within a locally recognizable world. They wanted to make the old city into a park, and to connect the new city to the surviving settlements alongside it, but offered no specifics for either, only a comment about these "very mediocre suburbs" on the margin of one drawing. Still, in a broader sense, "neighborhood units" represented a decentralization of power, resources, and institutions, a dramatic change for this highly centralized city and province.

Decentralization was a key theme in the architects' project, both within the city itself and across the central valley. Their approach to designing new city neighborhoods was modular and could easily be applied elsewhere in the province. Indeed, as they noted, "The construction problem in San Juan is the problem of the entire region. Every town must be rebuilt and this is a unique opportunity to do it in an unbeatable way: the next quake will find garden cities . . . of houses that will never collapse again."[44]

Rethinking the city's physical location also meant rethinking its economic and political place within the province. Proposals to move the city went hand in hand with proposals to reshape the countryside. Their scheme proposed to weaken the hold of large wineries, build new villages around smaller coopera-tive wineries and complementary industries, and diversify and modernize the local economy. By April, the architects had divided their proposal into two components: a "minimum plan" to rebuild the city alone and a "maximum plan" to rebuild the region as a whole, replacing most existing housing in the countryside and founding dozens of new agro-industrial towns. The further the team advanced in their design, the more it became evident that, regardless of their efforts to assuage local fears, their proposal for a new site already was a proposal for remaking the region, as well as remaking economic and political power.[45]

The local establishment did not welcome the move. Winery owners had made their priorities for the future quite clear the day after the earthquake, by demanding fifty thousand workers and hundreds of millions of pesos in compensation. They wanted rebuilding to strengthen their control, not undermine it. Thus opposition to the move emerged as soon as rumors started to circulate, but this did not coalesce into organized resistance until February, one month after the earthquake, when Public Works Minister Pistarini came to survey the relief effort and set a future course. In response, the same winery owners who had demanded compensation formed a Commission for Restoration of the Province to advocate rebuilding on the same site—and still more funds for themselves.

In the intense debate about the future city around the time of Pistarini's visit, the usually fractious establishment came together to oppose the move and propose an alternative. "After the initial shock," one power broker noted later, "no resident could avoid asking himself about rebuilding."[1] But it was during Pistarini's visit when individual dreams and private conversations turned into public discussions and institutional advocacy. This early debate was somewhat hollow, as the fabric of civic life was deeply frayed by the absences of the dead, the wounded, the evacuated, and many familiar settings and institutions. Even the lively local press would not return to print for another month. Thus, most debate took the form of lobbying efforts by the powerful and polemical articles published elsewhere, in regional and national newspapers.

One striking aspect of the debate in 1944 was how strongly the major alternatives echoed those of 1894: once again, the choice was between "movers" and "keepers," between striking out for a new site or trying to build better on the same one. Considering that the current tragedy was partly attributable to the fact that rebuilding on the old site in 1894 had ultimately also meant rebuilding with the old techniques, this time around the defenders of the status quo ante had to prove a real commitment to changing how the city was built. In order to defend the old site, as I will show, they would have to attack the old building techniques in adobe and embrace new techniques in reinforced concrete with particular fervor.

Movers

When Pistarini arrived on 15 February, he had just gained full control of reconstruction. In the administrative free-for-all of the previous weeks, Perón first laid claim to rebuilding, only to be rebuffed by the president, then Sosa Molina asserted provincial primacy and even named an advisory council, only to have the president vest final authority in Pistarini. But Pistarini, who would become a close ally of Perón, had not made any final decisions yet. The Bereterbide-Vautier team was working for him, but so far their formal charge was only to weigh the arguments for and against the move, make a recommendation, and, if they decided for the move, prepare a detailed plan. Pistarini wanted to undertake an ambitious project, but he was keeping his options open. As the early frenzy of demolition and repairs faded, he arrived with his top advisors and the architectural team to determine the next step.

On taking charge of the MOP at the beginning of 1944, Pistarini had declared his intention to use this core agency of the liberal state to implement the social program of integralist Catholicism. An active participant in the 1930 coup, Pistarini had been a leading figure in "Catholicizing" the army afterward, working closely with lay activists and Church officials and taking such symbolically powerful actions as personally leading a military delegation to Rome to celebrate when Pope Pius XII took office. Sympathetic to the Axis—and once photographed giving a Nazi salute at a public rally—Pistarini had spent the 1930s commanding the military engineers and leading a weapons-buying mission in Germany.[2] For the MOP, he had recruited Catholic engineers from the military, like his second-in-command Colonel Joaquín Saurí, and Catholic reformers from the ranks of lay activists, including the editor of the newspaper of the Buenos Aires archdiocese, and from the cluster of economists and engineers gathered around Alejandro Bunge.[3]

These groups aimed to promote "social justice" through industrialization, using the tools of modernity to recreate an organic solidarity they found in the past. For a sense of this vision, consider a speech titled "National Income," delivered in 1944 to the Catholic engineering association by Emilio Llorens, a Bunge disciple who served with Colonel Saurí on the board of the Industrial Bank just established by the government. Llorens portrayed "social justice" as an essential component of the economic as well as the moral development of the nation, defining it in a simple but revealing way: "increasing the living standards of the people, giving them the capacity to consume . . . in order to achieve a dignified and appropriate life." For Llorens, "the satisfaction of human needs is the determinant of the entire economic process. Production should be subordinated to this, and not the reverse, as in liberal economies." This speech was remarkably anticapitalist, given that the association was funded by the largest industrialists.[4] But it was consistent with the broader project the Catholic paper *El Pueblo* set out just before the earthquake: the state should act "with all its force and capability in defense of those trapped beneath the tyrannical and unjust rule of wealth," which "our present anti-Christian order gives such supremacy."[5]

For Pistarini, the ministry should become "the best boss"; instead of emulating the policies of large private corporations, it would model for all employers "an ever-more Christian understanding of the relations between Capital and Labor." The MOP began to issue new regulations on wages, working conditions, and social welfare, reshaping the practices of private contractors as well as the state itself. Pistarini undertook an expansive social agenda, raising the minimum wage for MOP laborers by a third, establishing a family supplement for workers with children, declaring paid summer vacation "a social necessity," and creating the first employee vacation colonies. Under Pistarini, the MOP built housing projects for employees (and later for the public) with an eye, as an official later put it, "to a comprehensive approach . . . by pointing lives down the correct path of morality and proper customs and inculcating in parents and children a true sense of home." With eighty thousand workers under its purview, the MOP was the largest employer in the country, and these initiatives had a sizable impact. As an official publication declared, these measures were "inspired in concepts of true social justice" and designed to overcome an existing poverty that was "incompatible with the progress achieved in our country . . . and with the formation of the future morality of the working class."[6]

Announcing "a ministry of works not of papers, of technical experts not paper shufflers," Pistarini launched many projects. One key objective was transforming the country's economic geography by industrializing the interior. This project was tied to a changed place for labor—while the minimum daily wage rose from 3.6 to 4.8 pesos in the interior, it held steady at 6.4 pesos in more developed areas.[7] Yet while his overall direction was clear, its implications for San Juan were not. Did the ruined city demand complete rethinking —or a swift rebuilding? That was why he was returning to the city now.

From the beginning, there was significant local support for the move, although it would remain a minority position among the elite. Enévaro Rossi, a leader among the half-dozen local architects, had built homes for much of the establishment, including the last Conservative governor. After the earthquake, every one of his forty buildings was still standing. Even so, he wrote colleagues abroad for technical advice on how to plan a move, carry out expropriations, and finance rebuilding. If the rebuilt city was to be "modern," he noted, it "could not be very well set up in the same place."[8] Calling the idea of rebuilding atop the ruins "a colossal error," a local nationalist insisted the city needed a "new foundation."[9] Another local argued that "vested interests on the current site should be subordinated to antiseismic security," and in light of the city's proven vulnerability and sunken location, the state should "found a new city of San Juan."[10]

"The primitive San Juan with its fragrance of provincial nobility, encased in old sun-warmed houses, is dead forever," wrote Odin Gómez Lucero, one of the finest chroniclers of the "city of statues." Now came "the age of modernism": wide streets, trees, plazas, and parks throughout, a moment when "the entire province should be comprehensively rebuilt."[11] A sanjuanino scholar living in Buenos Aires, Juan Rómulo Fernández, argued that rebuilding on the same site would require extensive investment, but raising the city "out of the pit where sixteenth-century Spaniards established it" could produce "one of the most beautiful cities in America."[12]

Even as they recognized the need for radical reinvention, most advocates of the move, like Gómez Lucero and Fernández, argued that this represented a deep continuity with the local tradition of innovation embodied in figures like Sarmiento. Federal prosecutor Octavio Gil, the son of a governor and president of the exclusive Club Social, generally defended "conserving the institutions of the past, which are the leaven of the race, [and] only transforming them incrementally, when the needs of life demand it." But he was also convinced that old San Juan was already gone forever, courtesy of Cantoni if not the earthquake, and that tradition could only be preserved through renewal.[13]

Six months earlier, Gil and a handful of other descendants of traditional families—del Carril, Mallea, Albarracín—had founded a club for "moral, cultural, economic improvement" called "Amigos Sanjuaninos." They now swung into action in support of reform, issuing an extensive statement just after Pistarini's arrival. The group advocated a census of victims, government-funded neighborhood relief and rebuilding committees, cheap long-term credit, extensive construction of emergency shelter, and expanded schools and social services. They called for the government to take over all medical care in San Juan, using the province as a testing ground for a reform widely debated in national medical circles. Their focus on popular needs contrasted sharply with the demands of the establishment, but lined up closely with the agenda of Perón's STP.[14]

The "current location is not the most convenient" site for rebuilding, the club insisted, because the subsoil is subject to flooding, "filled with cesspools, . . . the lowest point in the valley, . . . and the least appropriate for the foundations of buildings, even if they are anti-seismic." The surviving buildings, pavement, and water lines in the city were of marginal value relative to the cost of demolition and removal. A complete expropriation of the old city followed by an auction of lots in a new location would make possible dignified housing for all. But rebuilding on the same site would make it impossible to build a "modern" city and squander the opportunity to place San Juan "in a place of privilege among all the cities of the Republic." Therefore they called on the government to expropriate the entire city and rebuild it elsewhere. In short, this club drawn from traditional families embraced the Bereterbide-Vautier plan as the path forward for San Juan.[15]

While recognizing the need for "mobilizing the civil element," however, this group of notables lacked a popular base or organizing drive of its own. Distanced from labor or Cantonista groups, they advocated their cause in lobbying and a widely-read newsletter.[16]

Keepers

Opponents of the move came together quickly and organically, building from specific initial demands into a general defense of property and privilege. Given the divided history of the elite, this unity was noteworthy. Within the keepers, there were two distinct strands which broadly paralleled earlier responses to the Guido and Carrasco plan: Graffigna Conservatives favored a powerful role for the state in reforming the city along their preferred lines, while Maurín Conservatives, most Radicals, and even Socialists were opposed, often quite resolutely, to the expansion of state power or any accompanying reforms.

The first published ideas for a future city came from a provincial judge, Pablo Ramella, who laid out his thinking in several articles in national papers, starting eight days after the quake. An imaginative Catholic intellectual and legal thinker, Ramella was an ally of the Graffigna Conservatives but also a sharp social critic. He had long been interested in remaking the city and was close to Costantino Prego, the head (and sole employee) of the Office of Urbanism charged with implementing the Guido and Carrasco plan.

Ramella agreed with the architects on several key points regarding rebuilding. Like them, he condemned past neglect and corruption, finding an institutional cause for the city's collapse. He also saw opportunity in the tragedy: now that a force of nature had overcome "the unjustified resistance" to the Guido and Carrasco plan, the Conservative counterreform could finally go forward. The existing master plan could be the basis of a restored city, built under expert supervision, with anti-seismic construction on broader streets and larger lots. This last point was crucial: Ramella opposed moving the city but stressed that property lines would need to be redrawn to prevent future collapses, ensure greater access to light and air, and allow for more gardens. Like the architects, he proposed a swap, with the state expropriating every lot and then giving owners a voucher to purchase a redrawn lot in the same area of the city. This meant some owners would not be able to rebuild on the same site—indeed, if lots became larger, some could not rebuild within the previous city limits at all—but Ramella argued that this was necessary for safety and health.[17] All in all, Judge Ramella's vision was distinctly reformist, particularly in its critique of the past, respect for expertise, and willingness to reshape property relations.

But it also contained the core of a Conservative counterproposal: instead of reimagining the city, just make the buildings stronger. This was the other strand of thinking among opponents of the move, and it quickly became dominant. First came a statement from local professionals—the Center of Engineers, Architects and Surveyors—calling for rebuilding on the same site and again demanding 150 million pesos for property losses. Even though the finance minister had already rejected the possibility of compensation, the engineers insisted, adding requests for subsidized loans and building materials. There was no discussion of reallocating property or rethinking the city, simply a demand for funds and local control. All the state needed to do was "set the line": widen the streets, increase building setbacks, and get out of the way. There was however a first gesture on behalf of the poor majority, small but quite revealing—the suggestion that emergency shelter might later be reused as workers' housing.[18]

With the local engineers opting for the minimal approach, and the opposition unifying behind them, Ramella quickly retreated from rethinking the city as a whole to simply strengthening its individual buildings. In an article published on the day Pistarini arrived, he condemned those who "wish to wipe away everything existing" and urged officials to discard aggressive proposals for reform, "lest the ideal city impede building the real city."[19] Soon he would be denouncing the property swap as a violation of rights—omitting that he had proposed the same thing himself—and falsely asserting that the proposed new site was more than fifty kilometers away. Claiming that architects and officials "want to complicate something that is not complicated at all," he too would argue that all that was really required was wider streets and a "severe building code."[20]

By this time, the major winemakers had formed the Commission for Restoration to lobby against moving the city.[21] Under the leadership of the wealthy industrialist Bartolomé del Bono and former vice governor Horacio Videla, the Commission aimed to rally the propertied against the move, and thus it included at least token representatives from nearly every locally powerful group—except, naturally, for labor and the Cantonistas. With dissident voices excluded, the fractious local establishment was brought to the table but also firmly brought to heel. Del Bono was chosen to lead the Commission, instead of the more divisive Santiago Graffigna. But Graffigna remained the strongman of the Catholic Conservatives, and the leaders and most members of the Commission were his allies.[22]

"Every corner of this present city," the Commission declared, "evokes a history written and lived over nearly four centuries which cannot be destroyed without harming respectable feelings." They demanded that the city be rebuilt on its previous site, making their case first to Pistarini, then to officials in Buenos Aires, and finally to the broader public through newspaper editorials and a published pamphlet.[23] The Commission clearly did not conjure up their ties to the spirit of the place out of nothing. The city and province were still physically and symbolically centered on the plaza laid out by the Spanish conquerors; a new site meant reimagining this urban world. However hollow their invocation of tradition, the Commission did speak to a pervasive sense of loss and disorientation. If disasters intensify "the importance of place" for even the propertyless and excluded, as scholars have noted, then their impact is that much more emphatic for the landed and powerful. As one study of reconstruction plans elsewhere has observed, "There already is a plan for reconstruction, indelibly stamped in the perception of each resident—the plan of the pre-disaster city." This was why the Commission was able to build broad support across the otherwise divided local elite.[24]

According to the Commission, the city already was in the best possible location. Since the entire province was subject to seismic activity, they claimed that it was all equally vulnerable to earthquakes—ignoring the variable impact of soil conditions and fault lines. Any site outside the central valley had a "limited future," they argued, and any alternative site inside the valley would be "on the ethnographic and economic periphery." Returning, tautologically, to the importance of San Juan as the geographic and economic center of the province, they finally came to the basis of their resistance to the move: it would be a "great injustice" for "property owners who paid from 20 to 150 pesos per square meter for property that would become nearly worthless."[25] Moving the city without a full expropriation at a fair price would mean "a new economic earthquake," as Commission leader Horacio Videla wrote to the architect Bereterbide. "Progress should come, but not at the cost of justice," commented Videla, and thinking this way was not "private egoism" but "the legitimate defense of very respectable interests."[26]

The power of the wineries was intimately tied to the value of urban property. All the wineries bought grapes from growers with money borrowed against the collateral of urban property, and this greater access to credit was a decisive component of their market power. As one architect later observed, "When the city ceased to exist, the system was interrupted. Collateral disappeared . . . The powerful tried to maintain the system, and the best way to do that was by denying the earthquake. Keep everything as it was."[27]

Taking a pragmatic tack, the Commission insisted that the city could easily be rebuilt on its present site in accord with modern urbanism. Since basic infrastructure was already in place, they claimed, a move would needlessly squander the fifteen million pesos of recent road, sewer, and water work. Moreover, since nearly every building was destroyed or beyond repair, the state could carry out any necessary expropriations for little money. Even the "indemnization" would not cost much, as it should only allow claims where there was proof of a "real loss of economic value." Of course, however little this cost, the state should pay, because the recovery of the province demanded it. As in the 1930s, the state should intervene to secure the property of the powerful.[28]

On the one hand, the Del Bono Commission argued that rebuilding would be easy: everything had been destroyed, so expropriations would be cheap. On the other hand, they argued that if expropriations were cheap, this would be a grave injustice for "very respectable interests." In either case, the only sum they specified was not for expropriations but for "indemnization" for losses— without any property changing hands. The contradictions in the argument are at first puzzling, perhaps remnants of rival positions within the elite.

But there was a reason to favor compensation over expropriation, as the Del Bono Commission would later acknowledge: the property registry was full of "grave financial irregularities," many perpetrated by the Commission leaders. Both the assessed values and tax rates were dramatically raised in Cantoni's last administration, and then slashed to virtually nothing by Conservatives. For example, when Videla was president of the Club Social, its assessed value dropped from one million to fifty thousand pesos. The powerful now had to recognize the fraud, lest their property be expropriated at the false value they had declared to evade taxes.[29]

This was why they emphasized compensation. Government officials thought this was a petty defensive tactic, but it was actually an offensive strategy.[30] If aid were distributed according to the size of losses rather than need or suffering, it would overwhelmingly go to the propertied. At the same time, "indemnizations" would give them greater liquidity than anyone else during the rebuilding: the payment for a lost grape shipment could be used to purchase property or build rental housing.

To keep their own options open, the propertied needed to shut down debate over rebuilding. While some Del Bono Commission members favored broader reforms, they only put forward the minimal program everyone agreed to. Any problems could be resolved by widening the streets and requiring all new buildings to be anti-seismic, they argued, and there was thus no need to rethink the larger economy of the province or to consider rebuilding elsewhere. All the government needed to do was compensate the wealthy, set new street widths, mandate anti-seismic building, and step out of the way.

A Brief Reprieve

Pistarini was a leading national advocate of the Catholic integralist program, but in San Juan, local Catholic leaders were arrayed against him. At the same time, those who stood to benefit from his authoritarian vision of social justice were absent, silent, or divided. The dispersal of the evacuation, the desperation of the aftermath, and the flattened nature of public life under curfew meant that the organizations that had channeled popular demands for change were at their weakest precisely when they were needed the most. Neither the battered Cantonista machine nor the handful of unions could mount much of a challenge to the establishment, or even offer support for military visions of transformation. Newer pro-military groups, like Amigos Sanjuaninos, remained isolated and lacked a popular base.

This partly suited Pistarini's vision of social change: like many other officers, he firmly believed in reforms imposed from above and was less concerned with finding support beforehand than with consolidating it afterward. This was why the military largely kept its distance from the Cantonis: few leading officials saw a need for support from such figures, and those like Perón who might see the need were more interested in building a new movement than in allying with existing ones. The initiative, in any case, would come from the military.

For all his enthusiasm for dramatic action, Pistarini had ample reasons for caution. First, there was little to be gained technically by forcing the move now: immediate needs were more pressing in any case, and it would take time to get rebuilding underway, even if he decreed the move immediately. Second, there was even less to be gained politically: the Catholic establishment opposed the move but supported the military more generally, and at a moment of intense struggles within the regime, Pistarini and Perón were reluctant to alienate any local faction by pushing too forcefully for a move or by striking an alliance with a polarizing figure like Cantoni. Third, Pistarini had not entirely made up his own mind: his entourage for the trip included not only the Bereterbide and Vautier team officially assigned to work on the move but also his personal friend Ángel Guido. Although formally invited only to consult on the restoration of Sarmiento's home, Guido brought and presented a copy of his own plan, finding locals far more receptive than before.[31]

When Pistarini met with opinion leaders on 14 February, many supported the Del Bono Commission. The only open advocate of the move was Federico Cantoni, whose influence in this group was obviously limited.[32] Pistarini tried to find common ground, recognizing that everyone wanted to keep "their patio and fig tree"—an apt phrase for the attachment to place many felt—but insisting that kind of intimate space could be just as easily created on a new site as on the old.[33] Pistarini favored the move, but he made clear he would not impose a solution yet.

Instead, he focused on the more immediate challenges of bringing in the harvest and putting up emergency housing, and allowed the debate about rebuilding the city to continue. On returning to Buenos Aires, he announced that "the project for definitive reconstruction of San Juan and nearby locations will temporarily . . . give way to the urgent work" of building five thousand homes before winter, "hopefully by April," to house the population during the "two years" it would take to fully rebuild.[34]

This hardly stopped the architects: on the contrary, this was the point, after extensive on-site research, when the team fully fleshed out their project. But this work took place out of the public eye, as government efforts and larger debate refocused on the pressing question of emergency shelter.

Meanwhile, this reprieve offered the keepers time to sharpen their own argument. Against the move, they could argue from history and tradition and play on local attachments to place to bring a sizable part of the province to their side. This argument had some force and likely won them broader support than they initially had.

But state planners and modernist architects also spoke of a city of new houses for all. This was a harder claim to combat. The sense of attachment to the ruined city could be marshaled in favor of rebuilding on the same site, but not in favor of rebuilding the same homes. The memory of collapsing walls was too fresh. To secure their position the keepers had to imagine a credible future for the city, which clearly meant rethinking how houses were built. Rather than rejecting the architects' vision completely, they would isolate a small piece of it and make that their own.

Thus, after years of largely ignoring housing, the winery elite now stressed that a simple technical solution was at hand. When the architects argued for a broad rethinking, they pushed for a narrow retooling. The core of their argument was the attack on adobe.

"This Superstition of Adobe"

Why did the 1944 earthquake level San Juan? "It would seem as if the experience of earlier quakes did not survive in the memory of the population," one geologist remarked, as "there is the deep-rooted belief that adobe buildings are the most resistant to earthquakes."[35] This belief extended even to the national newspaper of record, which on the night of the catastrophe claimed that adobe was "the most appropriate material in areas subject to seismic movements."[36] By the morning, nearly every adobe building in the city had collapsed.

"This superstition of adobe has been destroyed by the earthquake," Judge Ramella wrote.[37] Weeks later, a commission of geologists and engineers reported that "the earthquake caused destruction out of all proportion to its intensity . . . due to the terrible quality of most buildings, made out of adobe." Indeed, the commission declared adobe "the worst imaginable material for seismic zones."[38] Considering "strategic necessity, building aesthetics, and security against earthquakes," one military officer declared, "adobe must disappear."[39]

Nearly everything in the province was built from earth, but as already seen, it was not all built in the same way: while most buildings within the city were constructed with heavy walls of solid adobe bricks, some homes inside the city and most outside were lighter structures fashioned from quincha, cane and twigs smeared with a mixture of mud and excrement. Solid adobe structures had been valued as traditional and secure, but quincha ranchos had been disdained as frail, filthy, and backward. The need to abolish quincha ranchos was a recurring theme in local reformist discourse, though little had been done to replace them or improve the lives of their inhabitants. Thus far, the condemnation of quincha had been more successful at marking the unworthiness of those homes and those who lived in them than at producing any improvements. But the discourse was solidly established, in the end more solidly than the houses it regarded as sources of virtue. And after those supposedly solid constructions of the city came down in the earthquake, this familiar line of argument was deployed to new ends.

Looking at the rubble, many locals repudiated what they had long accepted as natural, condemning "this superstition of adobe" like Judge Ramella. In the following months, this visceral response was reinforced by the technical analysis of outside experts examining building collapses, who focused largely on the first type of adobe construction, the heavier houses with load-bearing walls most common within city limits.

The failure of these adobe houses, visiting experts concluded, was due to the weaknesses of the material and the lack of structural reinforcement, irregular layout, and high heavy roofs in most buildings. The basic problem was that adobe withstood compression well but tension or lateral force hardly at all. This meant that these houses were extremely deformable: one part of a structure would resist any given force quite well, while another would give way almost immediately. This weakness was compounded by the absence of any reinforcement or ties holding the whole together. Most houses were sprawling, irregular affairs, built a few rooms at a time, strung along long hallways and interior patios. The more spread-out the floor plan, the more likely the building was to break apart in a quake. The high ceilings and heavy roofs that shielded from the intense climate also played a role. The higher center of gravity meant houses were more likely to move, and with the roof resting unsecured on the walls, any shifting was likely to knock the roof off and bring the walls down. Pulled apart in quakes, walls broke free and simply collapsed.[40]

The expert solution was fixity and unity instead of movement and fragmentation. Future homes should be compact, symmetrical, and structurally rigid. Above all, they should not be made of adobe.

There was one striking counterpoint to this analysis, though it was largely ignored at the time. Those quincha shacks long regarded as backward, which "even when new . . . give a feeling of immediate collapse and maximum insecurity," had turned out to be far more secure than the homes of their betters. "None of these houses was knocked down by the quake," one geologist noted, thanks to their flexible construction, light roof, and low center of gravity.[41] But this lesson was lost on locals. Quincha shacks could not be a model of anything. Any project for the future had to rest on solidity, and since solid building in adobe was flawed, adobe had to be discarded—and the possibilities of quincha ignored.[42]

Newspapers and locals alike passed lightly over the technical analysis of why adobe structures failed and instead launched an intense attack on adobe as a material. They were not concerned with how to build safely in adobe; they wanted to stop anyone from building in adobe at all. But they repudiated the past in terms drawn directly from the past. Ignoring the structural virtues of quincha ranchos the earthquake had revealed, newspapers instead revived the familiar attacks on quincha and expanded them to cover all adobe.[43]

The campaign against adobe quickly won broad support in San Juan, particularly among the elite, but the temporary closure of local newspapers meant that its arguments were most fully spelled out elsewhere, especially in the Mendoza daily *Los Andes*.[44] As already seen, Mendoza was similar to San Juan in its ecology, soil, and buildings, and thus in its seismic vulnerabilities. In early February, the professional association of architects and engineers in Mendoza threw down the gauntlet: "Popular belief has always held that adobe constructions, because of their greater 'elasticity,' were more adequate for resisting seismic motion. Because it is so widespread and deeply rooted ... this belief must be destroyed with an intense and prolonged campaign. New construction, without exception, whatever its location, must be in keeping with anti-seismic expertise."[45]

"We live in a city of mud," *Los Andes* declared, constantly threatened by failings of hygiene and safety.[46] In the past, the paper had undertaken sporadic campaigns against quincha shacks, viewing vernacular housing as a measure of popular backwardness and an infectious threat to the social order. But now it shifted the blame, portraying adobe as a sign of government indifference and social injustice. Just as the government defended citizens against disease, so "the State should rise up with all its force to defend the lives of its inhabitants in their habitations."[47] Abolishing adobe was a step toward building a new nation: "The future Argentina will not be forged in adobe ranches where mothers are ashamed of their misery, but in dignified and safe homes ... which display the strength of their children in a clean frame."[48] The call to replace shame with dignity was a crucial shift. Ideas of dignity had always been at the center of cultural discourse about housing, of course, but instead of being won through individual action, dignity was here to be created by broad state intervention. A month after the earthquake, new adobe construction was banned in the city of Mendoza.[49]

The critique of adobe could be the vehicle for a particularly powerful repudiation of the past. It was not difficult to make adobe the central example of the fragile, unjust, and inadequate arrangements that had anchored local social life prior to the earthquake. The failure of the state to do anything to ensure the safety of its citizens' homes was emblematic of its broader failures. The proof of a new moment and new social compact would be in the resilience of the houses. This was the line of argument advanced in Mendoza, and also embraced by various groups in San Juan.

At the same time, this repudiation could just as easily be used to avoid a serious reckoning with the past. By blaming the tragedy on a building material, local elites could turn attention away from questions of power. Rather than presenting adobe as emblematic of a broader pattern of corrupt short-sightedness, they could isolate it as a single fatal flaw, easily remedied by technical means.

The Certainty of Concrete

From early on, the movers placed less weight on the geological advantages of a new site than on the disadvantages of the old: its proven instability, poor soil quality, and thousands of cesspools. For their part, the keepers defended the old site with confidence, insisting that it was just as stable as anywhere else in the province. Both groups did agree, however, that the question could only be settled by geologists. In the months after the disaster, many geologists came to assess the earthquake's causes and impact and to suggest how to protect against future recurrences.

The most prominent team was sent by a quasi-governmental body dedicated to promoting industrialization.[50] Their agenda was clear, as they were charged not only with surveying the soil to determine suitable sites for construction but also with surveying mineral deposits with an eye to establishing a cement plant.[51] Given this double mission, it was hardly a surprise when they concluded that moving the city was unnecessary but new construction techniques were essential.[52]

Whatever bias this team might have, all other geologists reached similar conclusions. They were not arguing that soil conditions were irrelevant. On the contrary, all highlighted how similar structures on different terrain behaved quite differently, and several noted the particularly unstable nature of the alluvial soil beneath the city. Both points undercut the notion that the whole province faced equal seismic risk.[53] But while the geologists recognized that there were great variations, they emphasized that the limited knowledge of local soils and the even more limited knowledge of the behavior of those soils during seismic motion made it impossible to predict precisely where it was safest to build. Moreover, several areas that clearly were safe in geological terms were unacceptable for other reasons—lack of water, infertile soil, or simple physical isolation.[54] All this was an impetus to further study, but also a call for caution. For the geologists, improved structures were more likely to save lives than improved locations and therefore, as one closed his report, they left "the problem of the future of the city of San Juan to the engineers, especially those who specialize in the design and construction of reinforced concrete."[55]

After years of ignoring earthquakes, local elites now embraced the need for anti-seismic building. Rebuilding on the old site was perfectly safe, many argued, provided all houses were anti-seismic. Some, like Judge Ramella, recognized a need for adjustments to streets and property lines, although they grew quieter over time. This was a technical matter, not a larger social issue. Only two things were needed to make the city safe: expertise and concrete. Having denounced "this superstition of adobe," Judge Ramella insisted that all future construction be entrusted to experts, "not builders without technical knowledge or homeowners themselves."[56] Outside professionals agreed; one geologist flatly decreed that "it is within the power of builders, architects and engineers, to erase earthquakes from the list of human scourges, if they wish it."[57]

Advocates of concrete had a clear model in mind, as a local engineer suggested ten days after the quake. Irregular, disorderly, and "superstitious" adobe would give way to regular, ordered, and rational concrete. Set off from its neighbors, rigidly guarded against the threats of nature, each house in the future San Juan was to be a miniature fortress.[58]

The dream of a concrete city was appealing for several reasons. First, reinforced concrete was a sign of modernity. Though relatively new, the concrete industry in Argentina was dynamic, already the fifth largest in the world.[59] Here as elsewhere, the industry was a consistent backer of cutting-edge architecture. The most innovative buildings were made with concrete, as were the new roads and dams, the physical infrastructure of the expanding state. Thus the material was powerfully connected to social progress.

Second, concrete could also be tied to tradition. Most construction in Argentina used load-bearing walls, in masonry or adobe, and local notions of what constituted a proper house were based on solid structures made of such materials. In local speech, to say something was made with "material" meant that it was made with stone or brick. Concrete could easily supplant masonry in this role, while building in wood or steel would require different designs and techniques and yield different outcomes. Thus reinforced concrete could speak to historically well-established ideas of home even as it signaled a dramatic break with local history.

Finally, reinforced concrete seemed especially appropriate for anti-seismic design, in the approach pioneered by the Japanese and publicized by North Americans. The central question was "flexibility versus rigidity," and as a North American engineer had put it, "the utmost practicable structural rigidity is desirable."[60] While the technical reasoning behind this argument was lost on most locals, solidity and stiffness had a clear visceral appeal and also fit well with the other cultural virtues of concrete.[61]

All three lines of argument—modernity, solidity, and anti-seismic strength—converged on the vision of a future city of free-standing boxes of concrete. Compelling as this vision was, it did contain some striking paradoxes and contradictions. Most obviously, this concrete vision, with its powerful symbolic links to the modernist project, was here being deployed precisely to oppose modernist architects. A construction technique closely tied to the comprehensive rethinking of the city as a whole was being used exactly to avoid such a comprehensive rethinking. This move had a certain tactical brilliance and provided a compelling portrait of the future to a group primarily concerned with preserving the privileges of the past. But however clever the local elite were in appropriating the trappings of modernity, they still had to address the changes this way of building would bring.

Only with a major social transformation could this seemingly technical solution be fully achieved: rebuilding everything in concrete was a more radical idea than its proponents seemed to realize. In the Japanese and North American examples local advocates drew upon, the expense of anti-seismic techniques in reinforced concrete meant they were largely reserved for major multistory buildings, while most construction employed materials like wood. Here, by contrast, local leaders were proposing to fashion every structure in the entire city from reinforced concrete, the first time such an ambitious project had been attempted.

While concrete was less expensive than many more refined materials, it was far more expensive than the mud, cane, and straw previously used for most local construction. Moreover, only reinforced concrete, that is, concrete poured over a framework of steel rods, would work as advertised—without reinforcement, concrete is vulnerable to tension and shear forces like adobe—and because Argentina did not produce steel, this would be costly. As the geologists recognized, concrete was "too expensive . . . for the modest inhabitants of these areas."[62] Simply requiring concrete for new construction would guarantee little: a rigorously enforced ban on adobe would leave most of the province homeless, while a flexibly observed ban would ensure most building took place outside the city or outside the law. This challenge could force advocates to think more expansively: for one outside architect, the need for subsidies for anti-seismic construction was the starting point for justifying a far larger state role in housing overall.[63] But the local advocates of concrete took no such stance and made no mention of subsidies for the poor.

There was also the question of expertise. As one geologist noted, the collapsed buildings testified to a constant drive "to save on the costs of materials and the fees of qualified experts." Having ignored technical authority before, local elites now claimed to embrace it.[64] Yet this acceptance was shallow: the Del Bono Commission listened only to the experts who agreed with them, and the local press soon began disparaging critics as absurd dreamers unworthy of any respect. None of this was a particularly promising start for the kind of strong, independent supervising authority this vast construction project required.

In a province that had never had a building code, making every building anti-seismic was no simple task. Establishing mandatory anti-seismic standards might be easy in theory, an architect observed, but "their full implementation in a city constitutes not just a sum of individual matters but a truly collective problem."[65] Every aspect of construction needed to be controlled, from cement production to building design to final execution. This was a major change in governance, for the state itself and for the experts it would employ. It was unlikely that the province's sixty engineers and architects would be enough to carry it out. It was also a major change in construction technique, which would require training or importing large numbers of workers.

Finally, there was the question of supply. While geologists waxed enthusiastic about building a cement plant, stressing that raw materials were nearby and the guaranteed market for production would make it attractive to private investors or the state, the province lacked cheap electrical power. The best way to obtain this was to build a hydroelectric dam, which would bring power to many besides the cement plant and promote the creation of new industries. Each of these initiatives—industrialization, economic diversification, extensive public works—were the sort of expansion and rethinking the architects and military leaders were calling for, and the local elite were determined to resist. The broader possibilities such projects would create were exactly why they were embraced by the modernist architects, as part of their attempt to diversify the local economy and weaken the power of grape monoculture. Here again, actually implementing the concrete solution threatened to generate precisely the kinds of changes the local elite opposed.

Ultimately, the connection between reinforced concrete and modernist planning was more than symbolic. Rebuilding in concrete would set into motion many of the same processes as modernist planning, rendering the local attempt to bury planning in concrete partly self-defeating. Many in the local establishment were blind to this dynamic; others were confident they could overcome it; and still others, recognizing this danger from the beginning, clearly regarded the argument for concrete as a gambit to be discarded as soon as the ambitious plans for moving the city were defeated.

CHAPTER 6 LOOKING FOR ORDER AMONG THE RUINS

When Public Works Minister Pistarini arrived on 14 February, provisional order had been established: soldiers were standing watch and distributing food, while workers cleared the rubble. But orderly food lines hardly constituted full recovery, and the three thousand demolition workers were, a reporter noted, about "the only expression of activity in San Juan."[1] With tens of thousands still homeless, providing work and shelter seemed more urgent than deciding the shape of the future city. Pistarini thus tabled the move for the moment, concentrating instead on bringing in the grape harvest and building emergency housing.

During the six months after the earthquake, the state acted decisively to restore order, powerfully shaping the contours of the future city. The MOP under Pistarini and the provincial administration under Sosa Molina played particularly important roles, working together but also at cross-purposes. The most important steps in this were the MOP's scramble to build emergency housing and the provincial government's stabilization of the community. But even as a provisional order emerged, the debate about where and how to rebuild grew more intense, moving from local meetings and backroom lobbying to the national press and professional journals and leading to the ambiguous solution of June 1944, with the apparent triumph of local resistance but also the expansion of national authority. This exploration of government actions and local responses begins with the city as Pistarini found it, one month after the disaster.

An Uneasy Calm

San Juan remained deeply unsettled: since the quake, there had been sixty major aftershocks and countless tremors, more rain than in the previous thirty months combined, and two days of devastating hail.[2] There was little comfort even for those who had found shelter in shacks or tents: "one turns over, sweats, weeps, thinks of winter, prays, fights off the raindrops" while listening to "the whistles of police, the galloping of patrols, and the gunshots of soldiers scaring off thieves or warning of a collapsing wall."[3] "There was a lot of theft," a priest later recalled, by outsiders and locals alike.[4] After the evacuation, things began to disappear from unoccupied homes. A Cantonista butcher dropped in on a friend and discovered "beautiful furniture and a new refrigerator" in a shack without electricity. And not all the theft was small-scale. Among the elite, "whoever had a daughter had a piano," the son of the industrialist Bartolomé del Bono observed, and those pianos were systematically taken.[5] Even the forces of order played a role in the clandestine redistribution of wealth: the authority to move around freely and requisition any necessary supplies tempted many, from the garrison commander's wife who helped herself to high-quality nylon stockings and a major who plundered a jewelry store down to draftees who pocketed valuables.[6]

A few days after Pistarini's visit, when another nighttime aftershock drove many outside, a Conservative journalist pounded out a dispatch shot through with uncertainty and fear:

> "There can be no tranquility, no calmness of nerves when one fears a tremor at every moment, when one has to leave the doors open at night to escape quickly if a tremor comes, and when one is exposed to disagreeable nocturnal visitors who wander into certain houses to take what is not theirs, as happened at our farm a few nights ago. . . . We have very present in our memories and our hearts the more than fifty thousand people—the whole of the people, we could say—who are living outdoors, largely the poor and the modest. They are used to all kinds of suffering, but not to this: to see oneself die of terror, whipped by the frequent rains and the Andean winds that burn through already weak bodies . . . or the cold that leaves shivering children with no cover and no protection but the shriveled bodies of their mothers. We are not exaggerating this somber portrait of San Juan. No: we have already said it is impossible to fully describe this reality."[7]

This account underscored the tragedy's divisive impact: the wealthy had found shelter in the countryside or away from the province, but the poor—or "the whole of the people, we could say"—were uprooted and still largely unprotected. The newspaperman was thinking of the poor out of sympathy, certainly, but also because at any moment they might become "disagreeable nocturnal visitors."

26 Life under the trees, 1944. CREDIT AGN.

The wandering poor posed another threat to the powerful: they might simply leave. Over twenty thousand already had. Citing lessons of the 1939 quake in Chile, a Rosario engineer recommended the state provide shelter as soon as possible, before losing much of the local workforce for good. Property would eventually bring the middle class back, he wrote, but "when the humble march off, they take everything they have . . . set up in a new place, adapt themselves . . . return to normal life, and later resist return."[8] Some employers already noted a labor shortage.[9]

In San Juan, the earthquake and evacuation radicalized an existing crisis. During the agricultural collapse and rural exodus of the previous decade, reformers and landowners had debated how to keep rural workers on the land, with improved housing often recommended but never built. Now the swift provision of housing and work for the poor had become essential for the survival of the province as a whole.

The Provisional City

After Pistarini's February visit, with basic order restored and the grape harvest underway, government officials turned to housing. The MOP, by now the province's largest employer, launched a major housing project, the first of many to come across the nation. In two months, the state erected homes for

27 Assembling emergency structures, 1944. CREDIT AGN.

thirty-five thousand, almost all outside the four avenues, a provisional city surrounding the shattered core.

The MOP put up three kinds of shelter: emergency "structures," masonry homes, and wooden huts. First, three thousand "structures" went up in fourteen barrios. These housed the most families and had the greatest symbolic impact. The design came from MOP staff, but its stripped-down take on vernacular form and aggressive use of experimental materials were rooted in architects' prototypes for recent government competitions.[10] In formal terms, the design began with the traditional rancho, with its slanted roof and shaded front porch, then added rooms, glass windows, and (sometimes) concrete floors. Instead of being framed in logs and covered in quincha, these structures were built with machined lumber and covered with panels of fibercement, a new industrial cladding made from a thin layer of cement poured over a web of asbestos fibers. The MOP claimed the houses offered "superior comfort and security," and they undoubtedly were an improvement over most housing destroyed in the earthquake.[11]

The fourteen barrios were fragments of state order in a ruined landscape. They were laid out in a strict geometry and named for the heroes of the moment: leading government officials, like Pistarini and Perón, and the fallen volunteers of the relief effort, especially the doctors, nurses, and aviators killed in the tragic plane crash of January 1944.[12] But for all the order in their naming, the barrios were sited haphazardly. Despite all the talk of expropria-

28 Emergency barrio, 1944. CREDIT AGN.

tion, the state was reluctant to permanently seize land for temporary projects, so these went up wherever sites were available, on railroad properties, government holdings, and donations—including one plot given by Federico Cantoni.[13]

This produced marked differences between barrios. Because land was in short supply, the larger sites were packed with as many houses as possible. Nearly half of all units were in the three largest barrios: Captain Lazo (1,020 units), 4 June (363 units), and General Pistarini (240 units). From the beginning, these larger barrios had neighborhood institutions like schools, churches, and clinics. But they also had small units, with at most two bedrooms, no electricity, and no individual bathrooms—there were collective latrines instead. Their size and uniformity gave these barrios the air of a military encampment.

By contrast, in the eleven smaller barrios, houses had three or four bedrooms, electricity, and often indoor plumbing. The smaller barrios generally lacked schools or clinics, but their more intimate scale and connection with surrounding neighborhoods meant they were less of a rupture with previous ways of living. These distinctions did not matter at first, when any shelter was welcome, but later they would loom large.

Second, the government built five hundred permanent homes, generally in masonry. Many were dispersed in twenty-three small projects for employees of national agencies, but most were in the two larger projects begun under the Conservatives. Started before the earthquake as modest "workers' housing" far from the city center, the nearly three hundred homes in the Rivadavia

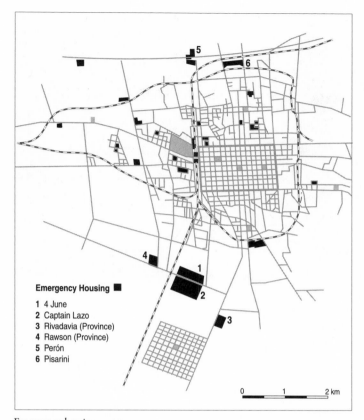

Emergency barrios, 1944

and Rawson barrios were completed afterward as islands of relative luxury and safety.[14]

Third, the government provided property owners with three thousand small wooden huts. These had been developed in the 1930s to house the transient workforce of the Road Department. Right after the quake, the MOP erected a cluster of sixty as an experiment.[15] These few huts were grouped together; the rest went up on the recipient's land, often behind a ruined home, enabling many to stay put while awaiting rebuilding. While three hundred were placed within the four avenues, most were out in the suburbs, especially Concepción to the north and Desamparados to the west. Tiny and often hidden behind ruins, these structures had little symbolic visibility and did not prompt controversy, because they allowed residents to remain in place.[16]

Finally, outside the city, the provincial administration took the lead. The MOP provided two thousand units and a roving assembly crew, but local

29 Workers' housing, Rivadavia barrio, 1944. CREDIT AGN.

authorities decided where to put them. These were mostly fibercement structures, but outside the capital, they almost always went up alone, like the wooden huts, without poured floors, neighboring structures, or surrounding infrastructure.

Whatever its design, the MOP emphasized, all emergency housing was "anti-seismic," unlike the "dangerous local houses of adobe and cane." Rather than following local patterns, the MOP brought new designs, materials, and even workers from elsewhere. This was another indication that industrial production and a powerful state would shape the future city. In part this was a matter of expediency: skilled labor, industrial materials like fibercement, and proven designs like the Road Department huts enabled the MOP to build more quickly than local workers and traditional approaches. It also expanded the market for novel building materials, and thus for new industrial firms.

But this strategy reflected more than a desire for speed, control, and modernity: the MOP was also consciously trying to leave local labor and materials for the harvest and private rebuilding. The government knew that it could not provide for every survivor, and it encouraged those who could build their own housing to do so. "Speaking ill of adobe is easy," a journalist noted, but "replacing it will be hard."[17] MOP officials saw adobe as "dangerous" in the long term, but they knew it was essential in the short term: whatever its failings, this was the only material local workers knew how to build with. Thus the MOP made everything recovered from demolition available to

30 Road Department huts, Enfermera Medina barrio, 1944. CREDIT AGN.

builders and provided technical guidance to repair nearly a thousand houses. Adobe mansions might be banned, but some adobe shacks seemed unavoidable, at least for now. No one saw fit to rebuke a local official out in the countryside when he ended his request to supervisors for more "anti-seismic" structures with the vow that "with adobe bricks, cane, nails, and our own effort, we people of Chimbas will help the government and ourselves . . . and erase the memories of tragic days."[18]

Here was another paradox of the aftermath: the return of adobe just as it was being denounced and outlawed. The orderly rows of state-built housing were flanked by the disorderly improvisations of locals. While waiting for the government, thousands put up quincha shacks wherever they could: in fields, along roads, and behind collapsed homes. By force of necessity, the "symbol of rural backwardness" now returned to the city center.[19] To be sure, very few of those building the shacks saw them as a permanent alternative. A handful saw promise in the unexpected return of the rancho, and some tried to fashion resilient structures out of adobe brick, but these minor experiments would be largely overlooked.[20] Most shacks were fragile affairs and were readily abandoned when something better came along.

Overall, the emergency housing effort was an impressive success: in sixty days, the MOP put up over 8,500 homes, more than an average year of construction in Buenos Aires.[21] The ministry raised emergency quarters for every civic purpose: government offices, clinics, and schools, chapels in the barrios

31 Interventor Sosa Molina visits improvised quincha structure, 1944. CREDIT AGN.

and a fibercement cathedral on the main plaza.[22] Beyond clearing the rubble, the ministry planted 22,000 trees and doubled the installed length of water and sewer pipes.[23] All told, the MOP spent 22 million pesos in San Juan, nearly double the entire provincial budget for the previous year.[24]

For the government, this was the initial step toward a more just, ordered, and industrial future, a first installment of the New Argentina. The emergency shelter campaign was extensively promoted in daily papers, newsreels, and finally a glossy official report. Claiming that "family life has returned to its normal rhythm," the report offered as evidence photographs of a small garden in front of one emergency home and a dog sunning itself across from another.[25] But its core message was conveyed by the opening page, which portrayed two hands reaching out over the ruins to offer a finished emergency home.

Back in Buenos Aires, Perón opened an exhibit on government solutions for the housing crisis. The exhibit was intended as a call to action, much like the relief effort in San Juan—indeed, the architects who designed the exhibit also created an installation and film on the relief effort. Drawing three-quarters of a million visitors over a month, the housing exhibit featured materials on the high cost and inadequate conditions of most housing in the republic, plans and drawings for a model project already underway in Buenos Aires, and slogans like "Urbanists and not speculators should make the

32 Frontispiece of MOP report on San Juan, 1944. CREDIT AGN.

neighborhoods of the future."[26] Perón promised to do everything necessary to build the hundred thousand homes the country required, and emergency housing in San Juan gave this promise credibility.[27]

Provided free of cost to all who needed it, emergency housing represented a dramatic step forward for a state that had built housing rarely and at great cost to users. However temporary, it was the beginning of an enduring state commitment to housing as a right. During the liberal era, a house was conceived of as a prize for those possessing resources and also as a machine for integration, a device to encourage saving, discipline, and order among workers. At its most egalitarian, this liberal approach also recognized housing as a need. But it fundamentally saw housing as a device for achieving political and social legitimacy—and thus for the exclusion of those who did not achieve it. This vision of housing encapsulated the social injustice that Perón said he would bring to an end.

Beginning in San Juan, Perón offered a vision of social justice which made shelter a fundamental right. Consider the words of the head of the national housing office established by Perón, inaugurating the military government's first permanent housing development in June 1944: "This experimental citadel will be the vanguard of the new days to come, days anxious for redemption, for justice, for . . . a life that is better, fuller, more completely Christian . . . it is the firm anticipation of a reality on the march . . . Nothing can stop us from carrying out our plan to give every Argentine the proper shelter to which his dignity as a human being gives him the right."[28] Few statements more richly expressed the shift in discourse on housing or more clearly showed how much this shift was shaped by Catholic and military thinking.

Perón himself stated in August 1944: "A home is not a prize for the man who possesses resources, but an elemental right of the man of the people." By turning housing from a sign of respectability into a right of citizenship, Perón was changing the meaning not only of housing but also of citizenship itself. Thanks to the military regime, Perón claimed, "Every Argentine of our generation will be able to say with pride to his children, in his will, 'This house that I give you is a piece of the New Argentina'"—a phrase that echoed the powerful drawing that opened the MOP report on San Juan.[29]

A Fragile Restoration

Dramatic as the emergency shelter effort was, it was only one component of the broader revival of local social life. While the larger agenda was set by the MOP under Pistarini and the STP under Perón, its local implementation was in the hands of the provincial administration under Sosa Molina. The MOP built houses, but the province allocated them; the STP provided relief, but the province distributed it. This division of labor became significant as Sosa Molina, while remaining a national ally of Pistarini and Perón, charted a provincial course at odds with radical transformation. The divergence was sharpest precisely on the key issues of who should receive shelter and where the city should rebuild.

Sosa Molina took office as interventor on 30 January with a promise of redemption: "purified by suffering, a new San Juan will emerge from this catastrophe." The relief effort was the starting point, and Sosa Molina lavished praise on military, medical, governmental, and even civic leaders. Such celebration of reconstituted authority was common among military officials, but Sosa Molina's explicit commendation of the local *fuerzas vivas* (establishment) was not. Most military officials stressed the complicity of the fuerzas vivas in the collapsed order, not their contribution to the new one. Even more striking was who Sosa Molina did not praise: he offered no recognition for the soldiers who had rescued victims, the railroad workers who had brought relief, or the common folk of San Juan, whose stoicism was so praised by other officials.[30]

Sosa Molina was portly, severe, and energetic; born into a military family in Mendoza, he had made his way up the ranks, and across the country, before assuming the regional command in his native province. Like other garrison commanders, he had built strong ties with Conservatives and especially Catholic activists—his were so strong he did not remove the Conservative administration in Mendoza until three days after the military took power in 1943.[31] He was committed to building a more just society, but above all to building a more stable one, drawing on the morality and hierarchy of institutions like the Army and the Church.

In the relief effort, Sosa Molina saw a reflection of his social ideal: a strong state and a proper elite acting together to protect the weak and defend the respectable. Crucially, the fuerzas vivas were the only locals Sosa Molina saw as active participants in this—rather than as passive victims. Casting about for allies in San Juan, Sosa Molina was naturally drawn to those whose ideals were closest to his, the Graffigna Conservatives.[32]

Thus the fuerzas vivas came to exert decisive influence just when they seemed most radically discredited. Sosa Molina named outsiders as ministers, but he left Graffigna clients in place within the administration, elevated the head of Catholic Action to chief justice of the provincial courts, and named as his chief of staff a young Catholic lawyer from a prominent Conservative clan, Jose Amadeo Conte-Grand.

Conservatives had many opportunistic reasons to ally with Sosa Molina. For starters, such tactical alignments with national power had been their governing strategy for decades. This time, moreover, they had reason to fear the regime might actually deliver on its promises of change: after failing for twenty years to drive Cantoni from the provincial stage, Conservatives were alarmed to hear regime officials echoing his words. Most importantly, moving the city represented an existential threat to their power, one that they had to counter by whatever means available. Since there was no space for political action outside the regime, they sought allies within.

There were also affirmative reasons to join Sosa Molina. "If there is one thing evident in the physical and moral world, it is the existence of an order," Judge Ramella wrote at the time. "Order means relations of interdependence and hierarchy, and liberalism is the opposite of all that," Ramella held, "an elastic and shifting idea . . . incapable of setting a course for society." By failing to recognize God and follow his precepts, liberal governments "had permitted . . . plutocratic injustice to rule over inert and impoverished justice."[33]

Profoundly critical of the liberal order they had helped to corrupt, provincial Conservatives had been looking to uproot liberalism for good, and the military's program for authoritarian renewal seemed promising.

Because provincial oligarchs claimed to oppose liberalism, they even welcomed denunciations of the liberal oligarchy, which they identified above all with Buenos Aires. Indeed, the province's largest industrialists did not see themselves as capitalists, claiming that a business which provides for its workers "is not capitalist, since its capital carries out a useful social function."[34] Capitalism, for them, was a term of invective to denounce the moral failings of monopolists, not an analytic category to describe the property regime they presided over. Following this reasoning, the Graffigna newspaper argued that San Juan's wealthy were so virtuous and small property owners so numerous that "capitalism doesn't exist here, at least as a local phenomenon."[35] By exempting themselves from the larger critique of liberalism, they hoped to exempt themselves from military reforms. Instead, they hoped these reforms would restore the natural order, in which they would naturally play a leading role. This course of action might do more than preserve their power; it might win them a new legitimacy.

The Catholic paper argued for "complete . . . restoration of San Juan, but tied to high aspirations of social justice, of the recognition of the right to a better life for the working masses." As the province was rebuilt, not only the rubble but also "the still-dominant privileges of class must disappear as much as possible," along with "the factors that generate a state of misery for workers and a prize of opulence for the lazy, and for those best fortified for the struggle for existence." In its erratic reasoning, this statement encapsulated the ambiguities of the Catholic program, forcefully insisting that "privileges . . . must disappear" only to immediately add a measly "as much as possible," veering from sharp attacks on "the state of misery for workers" to backhanded praise for "those best fortified for the struggle for existence," which casually invoked a concept from the positivist liberalism they wanted to overturn.[36]

Even if the Graffigna Conservatives were the greatest beneficiaries of prior injustice, Sosa Molina was glad to work with them, because they agreed with his overall critique. Local Conservatives, in turn, saw joining his administration as a means to preserve and also legitimate their power, to undertake needed reforms while blunting their threat.

Sosa Molina saw his mission as restoring a lost order, using a strong state to bring political rectitude, economic development, and social justice. As his minister of government stressed, the provincial economy was strong but "the bulk of the population lives in . . . great poverty." While attributing poverty partly to drinking, illness, and "the indolent nature of the criollo," the minister, a Catholic Conservative from Mendoza, also recognized structural causes: the absence of alternatives within the grape zone and poor "working conditions" outside it. Public works were the cure: an expanded network of canals, roads, and electrical lines.[37] Sosa Molina intended this expansion to diversify the economy of the province as a whole—by promoting mining and industry—and of the central valley in particular—by supporting alternatives to grape monoculture. While advocating cooperative wineries, he otherwise had little to say about power within the grape zone, the central political issue for a generation—and referred to labor only in passing. Strikingly, he viewed the present dominance of grape monoculture and the limits of irrigation as natural phenomena, rather than the product of specific decisions benefiting identifiable actors—namely, the largest wineries, his new allies.

Sosa Molina aimed to reshape this society from above, not to rethink it altogether, and trusted in the demonstration effects of setting a new moral standard. Thus he preferred to issue blanket denunciations and hope for a moral renewal rather than building a constituency for broad reform. Down the road, as we will see, his actions would indeed contribute to a transformation. But in the short term, they primarily shored up the powerful, especially Graffigna Conservatives. This is evident in five key policy areas: the embrace of the Church, the expansion of social assistance, the regulation of the harvest, the distribution of emergency housing, and the debate over where to rebuild.

From the start, Sosa Molina aligned himself with the Church and tried to meet its long-standing demands. He introduced religious instruction into public schools, directed rebuilding subsidies to Catholic institutions, and made sure every new emergency construction was blessed by a priest, and often by the archbishop himself. These actions were especially helpful to strengthening the Church, which was on the defensive due to the questioning of the archbishop and the dispersion of so many of the faithful after the quake. Clergy and lay activists were trying to reassert the centrality of the Church in local life. In the subdued ceremonies for Holy Week, the Benedictine prior received and blessed an urn containing the ashes of those cremated in the common grave. In the weeks afterwards, the first of many processions following sacred images through the ruined city set out from the one church that had survived, the concrete chapel at Don Bosco school. These piecemeal rededications to a sacred purpose built up to the consecration of the entire province to the Sacred Heart of Mary, in a downtown ceremony on the patriotic holiday of 25 May. The archbishop challenged sanjuaninos to raise up each fallen church and to build a new Votive Temple, as a confirmation of

33 Procession of Catholic women, San Juan, winter 1944. CREDIT JOSÉ MAZUELOS FRÍAS, COURTESY LEOPOLDO MAZUELOS.

the province's return to the godly path and a guarantee against future wrath, or as he later put it, a "lightning rod for Divine Justice."[38]

The provincial state dramatically expanded under Sosa Molina, along the lines suggested by the Catholic social agenda. This expansion meant greater aid for the poor, but also state posts for the powerful. In public health, for example, Sosa Molina addressed the increased demand for medical care and the weakened position of many professionals by bringing almost half the province's doctors and dentists onto the government payroll, augmenting hospital staff and establishing new clinics in emergency barrios and remote towns.[39] He established a school of social work, an agency for children, and two residential schools for orphans and invalids. When free food distribution ended, he launched targeted aid programs coordinated by the province's first social workers. Convinced that illegitimacy itself caused poverty, he set up a roving civil registry office to make it easier for the poor to marry and record their children's births. All these initiatives aimed to document social conditions and make them visible to the state, as in a proposed master file of social data. Deeply paternalistic in conception and execution, these reforms none-theless marked a shift in the local state's relationship with the poor.[40]

Saving the Harvest

The most important changes came with the grape harvest. Everything else was in ruins, but with grapes on the vine and most wineries able to process them, the harvest had to go forward. Forty percent of the wineries were damaged, and their owners were on the defensive, but the military did not confront them directly. With no other work to be found, harvest wages, always impor-tant to the poor, were absolutely crucial. Grape chemistry dictated the timing; the harvest had to begin by March, so ambitious reforms had to wait. Even those who thought the province needed a radical remaking understood the need to secure the harvest first. The government might not grant the massive subsidies bodegueros had demanded, but it could not afford to abandon them.

Thus the first weeks after the quake brought stern calls for renewal and solicitous meetings with familiar power brokers. As before, the thirty-one largest bodegueros spoke for the industry as a whole; Graffigna allies domi-nated an official committee to supervise repairs and the harvest.[41] The maxi-mum demands were ignored, but their interests were still protected. For example, even though the state winery, the largest building in the province, had suffered relatively light damage and could easily process one-third of the entire provincial harvest, the authorities made little use of it, failing even to repair its official scale.[42] Instead, they concentrated public repair efforts on the largest and most capitalized private wineries, starting with Graffigna.[43] They also obliged Mendoza wineries to purchase the wine their San Juan counter-parts had in storage. This move provided local wineries with immediate capi-tal, freed their facilities for needed repairs, and, by otherwise occupying their Mendoza competitors, effectively ensured that they remained the sole buyers for local growers.[44]

The state did set grape prices, but bodegueros retained the upper hand.[45] Negotiations began with state officials arguing that grapes in San Juan de-served a significantly higher price than in Mendoza, because of their higher alcohol content, but bodegueros stood firm, official efforts to organize viña-teros faltered, and Sosa Molina set the price by decree—just above the level in Mendoza, but below the government's opening position.[46] Even then, bode-gueros dragged their feet, refusing to buy from some producers or to pay above the minimum for better grapes.

Two weeks after setting the price, Sosa Molina reconvened the harvest committee under a new leader, Ruperto Godoy, Perón's delegate in San Juan, who forced wineries to buy more at higher prices.[47] While the provincial administration had been offering the wineries concessions and halfheartedly trying to organize growers, Perón's STP had begun asserting regulatory power and organizing workers. Granted the legal authority to oversee grape sales, the STP required formal written contracts and fixed timetables for payment: these were dangerous precedents for winery owners used to buying grapes by oral agreement and driving down prices and stretching out payments as they wished. Until recently, state regulation had favored bodegueros and been carried out by their allies, from the provincial administration to the Wine Board. Now they were subject to the scrutiny of a powerful new state actor. Meanwhile, Godoy established a labor pool to connect employers with suddenly scarce workers and used it to reshape the labor market, standardizing conditions and raising wages industry-wide. By April, the labor pool numbered over seven thousand workers.[48] Bodegueros and growers were soon complaining that the "absenteeism" produced by the provision of food to survivors, the standards set by the labor pool, and the high wages available in demolition meant they had to pay pickers up to eight pesos a day. Their claims were exaggerated, as the government had cut off food precisely to avoid such "absenteeism" and wages rose less than they claimed.[49] But their protest was significant: although there were no official regulations on agricultural labor, changing conditions and official attention to harvest workers were having an impact.[50] Sosa Molina saved the wineries, but he hardly handed them an unqualified victory. Their industry was being rebuilt, but their maximum demands had been rejected, and the government had vastly increased its control over their key inputs, grapes and labor.

Allocating Homes

The outcome was similar in emergency housing. The first barrios were ready in early April, as the harvest was winding down and winter coming on. After urging evacuees to stay away, the interior ministry now offered passage and shelter back home.[51] The fruits of the massive emergency effort were now going to be portioned out.[52] This task fell to political appointees tied into local networks.

The government never intended to provide emergency housing for all. From early on, the authorities urged the "more or less wealthy" to rebuild on their own, and the MOP deliberately used outside labor and materials to stay out of their way.[53] When the two Conservative papers returned to print in March, they also insisted that the wealthy should rebuild themselves. Moreover, those who could not yet rebuild could always request a wooden hut for their property. In theory, that was all the wealthy needed.

The barrios were intended primarily for the poor.[54] From this egalitarian seed, a citizenry united by common suffering and dignified by state action would forge a different future. "There are no social classes anymore," the Graffigna paper declared, "and out of the provisional barrios a new society will emerge, an aristocracy of the earthquake."[55] As the barrios neared completion, one provincial minister proposed charging rent, on a sliding scale, to generate funds for neighborhood groups, routine maintenance, and eventual improvements. By making the wealthy pay more, he hoped to reinforce an egalitarian commitment to the barrios—and perhaps encourage those with resources to build their own homes elsewhere.

But the exhortations had little effect and the rent proposal was discarded. Even as the state challenged class divisions by building housing for all, it partly reaffirmed them in the way it distributed those houses. Every day the administration released a list of the names, professions, and family size of those receiving housing, and a clear pattern began to emerge: the masonry homes originally intended for workers went to the wealthy, the emergency structures in the smaller projects to the middle class, and the more austere buildings in the largest barrios to workers. On 19 April, for example, a list of the names and professions—mostly teachers and clerks—of those assigned to the smaller barrios was followed by a comment that "day laborers, small farmers, and those of modest means predominate" among those assigned to the 4 June barrio, none of whom were identified by name.[56] Five days earlier, a "piano teacher, clerk, tailor, merchant, dentist, lawyer, doctor, and engineer" received houses in two smaller barrios.[57] The official goal of social justice did not require all housing to be equal, of course, and the repeated insistence on proper hierarchy suggested it would not be; white-collar state employees received better housing than their blue-collar counterparts. But the divisions within emergency housing were blatant.

Facing pages of the same newspaper featured an editorial calling for a new beginning, an article denouncing the powerful for exploiting their position, and another article showing how such exploitation was benefiting the papers' own allies.[58] In April, just as most housing was being assigned, an investigation uncovered that provincial employees had been pocketing some aid themselves and diverting even more to select members of the elite. Nineteen workers were fired, and the provincial minister of public works resigned.[59] Because each of the overlapping patronage networks had benefited from these arrangements, except for the Cantonistas, each Conservative newspaper attacked the other

34 Interventor Sosa Molina in Captain Lazo Barrio, 1944. CREDIT AGN.

to deflect attention from itself. The Graffigna paper declared "the absence of scruples repeatedly demonstrated by certain of the wealthy has caused great moral harm to society and wounded the feelings of the humble folk, where . . . class hatred is latent and ready to develop with abuse and injustice."[60] The papers kept the specifics vague; both simply asserted their own virtues for having stayed and struggled for the city. Here too their fight against the move seemed to offer some redemption.

To be sure, most emergency housing did go to the poor, and it certainly represented a dramatic improvement in their living conditions. Most of the barrios had a strongly egalitarian ethos, and when the school chief for the province wrote a short anecdotal history of the tragedy and aftermath, his central image of recovery was the story of a worker finding a job in demolition and a home in an emergency barrio.[61] Sosa Molina, for his part, saw this as only the first step, and commissioned another barrio of "workers' housing," using the same blueprints as the first two, and the provision of more emergency structures as an act of "great social transcendence" in "raising living standards."[62] But even as emergency housing advanced the egalitarian vision of national officials, it also reinforced the parochial power of local elites.

The Sacriste Team: An Alternate View

Finally, consider Sosa Molina's stance on reconstruction, and particularly his response to the report by the architectural team working for the province. In the week after the earthquake, as already seen, two separate teams of architects were recruited to plot a future for San Juan: the Bereterbide-Vautier team stationed in Buenos Aires and a second team of three young modernists— Eduardo Sacriste, Hilario Zalba, and Horacio Caminos—brought directly to San Juan by the provincial minister of public works.[63] All three were recent graduates of the University of Buenos Aires (Sacriste in 1931, the others in 1938), with close ties to the Austral group and recently completed pilot projects: an improved hut for road construction workers (Zalba), a rural school in Buenos Aires province (Sacriste), and an emergency housing plan for Tucumán province (Caminos). In San Juan, they were tasked with guiding repair work while thinking through the larger implications of reconstruction. Working in the shadow of the larger national team they knew would prevail, they issued a report in March 1944 that argued powerfully for structural transformation.

Sharply critical of emergency aid so far, they saw "no indications . . . that harshly castigated neighborhoods . . . are receiving effective help from the authorities." They placed the blame partly on poor coordination between government agencies, and partly on centralized power within those agencies. According to the architects, the effort to build emergency shelter was proceeding slowly and taking the wrong path. Although open to novel techniques and materials, they argued that abandoning adobe was a mistake—and Sacriste went on to offer an eloquent defense of this "noble material" in the leading professional journal. But their most striking observations were about rebuilding as a whole.[64]

"What must emerge as a result of the earthquake is not a new city, but a new structure for the entire province," they argued. Two months of intensive research had convinced them that the province's economic potential was "enormously superior" to present production. To unleash this potential, they proposed a far-ranging program: dams and canals to generate electricity and triple the amount of irrigated land, from 70,000 to 200,000 hectares; a broad shift from grape "monoculture to polyculture"; the industrialization of agricultural production; and the expansion of mining. The main idea was to move the wineries away from the "ring of iron" around the capital, and out to where grapes were actually grown. Rebuilt as the center of small towns, wineries complemented by new agro-industry could provide year-round work for the currently "semi-nomadic" majority of the population. For the architects, the centralized domination of the wineries was the major cause of the decline of the rest of the province, and the uprooting and instability that had produced persistently high levels of inequality and disease. With so many wineries damaged and requiring government assistance to rebuild, this was a signal opportunity to reshape the economic and political structure of the province.[65]

The Sacriste team shared many broader ideas with the movers, but they deliberately avoided taking a position on moving the city. Instead, they shifted attention to the province as a whole, arguing that regional planning meant taking the province's political economy as a starting point for planning the future. Insisting that rebuilding was a project for the entire province, the Sacriste team argued that new social arrangements should be designed before new buildings. They also recommended that whatever approach was chosen, rebuilding should be implemented by a single government body, based in San Juan and responsible for both relief and reconstruction.

Not surprisingly, Sosa Molina was incensed at the criticism of the military and the relief effort. The architects offered the most coherent argument yet for the policies he supported—to decentralize, diversify, and industrialize the provincial economy—but he rejected the report and summarily dismissed them. When Sacriste gave the report to a journalist from *La Acción*, which printed it in full, an angry Sosa Molina arrested the architects and had them expelled from the province—although, revealingly, he declined to take action against the paper.[66]

Movers versus Keepers Revisited:
The Press, the Engineers, and the Architects

In March, the two Conservative newspapers returned to print, and soon after, the two radio stations went back on the air. For the first time in decades, Conservatives controlled all local media—the Cantonista paper would not appear regularly for a year—and could mount a unified campaign against the move. Dozens of businesses, professional associations, and civic groups lined up behind the Del Bono Commission.[67] Sosa Molina remained neutral: elsewhere, the government was censoring and even shutting down newspapers, but he allowed the local press to oppose the move in strident terms.[68]

"Who are the enemies of the old city in disgrace?," the Conservative leader Horacio Videla asked: "The urbanists, who are confronted with a flattened city, but think they are facing an academic problem."[69] Nearly every day, editorials mocked the promise of bold renewal and the very idea of expert knowledge, offering instead their own pragmatism, history, and rootedness. The Conservative press equated geology with astrology, asserted that the Spanish conquerors understood the soil better than contemporary scientists, and insisted that "it cannot be demonstrated that this site is more seismic than any other in the province."[70] *La Acción* published the Sacriste report but ignored its analysis, choosing to highlight only the point that rebuilding should be controlled from San Juan. "One need not be an architect to build a city, and on the contrary, it would be better not to be one," one editorial maintained.[71] "We reject their marvelous fantasies altogether," another declared.[72] The newspapers praised anti-seismic construction without explaining it, offering it up as a magical solution and ignoring the arguments of its proponents when they did not coincide with their own.

The keepers agreed on concrete, but disagreed on much else. *La Acción*, the Maurín paper, claimed all that was needed was wider streets and an antiseismic building code.[73] The Graffigna paper, *Tribuna*, spoke of broader reforms. Failing to rethink the city would be "unforgivable" and "true myopia," according to Videla, the secretary of the Del Bono Commission, who called for new zoning, parks, and wide streets lined by trees and canals. He also recognized the need to redraw property lines. Buildings should be anti-seismic in structure and neocolonial in form. Videla dwelt at length on actions inside the four avenues, then remarked in passing that outside the traditional core, "urbanist initiative can freely plan radial streets and a garden city."[74] This exposed the true basis of his opposition to the move, which was property, as he acknowledged in public statements and private letters. If he were so worried about the ominous "urbanists," he would have offered some protection to those living outside the four avenues, the majority of the province. But his core commitment was to defend the property of the powerful, not to fend off modernist architecture.

These disagreements among keepers were far less important than their fundamental agreement to oppose the move and offer concrete as the solution. No one pushed this argument harder than local engineers. The March meeting of the local engineering association, the first since the disaster, was a farewell to the Sacriste team, with speeches by everyone from the architects themselves to the MOP chief engineer they criticized, and a final view of reconstruction from the association president, Carlos Macchi.[75] "Never have Argentine professionals faced a problem of such interest and magnitude," he observed, then he presented a minimum program for this maximum problem: wider streets and a proper building code.[76] Given that bodegueros were the largest clients of most engineers and that many leading engineers were themselves bodegueros—starting with Graffigna—it was hardly surprising that local engineers embraced the bodeguero position and successfully convinced their national association to intervene.

"The work to be done is undoubtedly enormous," the national engineering association, the CAI, acknowledged in a late March report on San Juan. But like their local affiliates, they insisted this work should follow cautious and narrow objectives.[77] This restraint, in such contrast with the boldness of the architects, was due to engineers' preference for clearly bounded technical solutions, their close identification with the previous establishment, and their increasingly strained relationship with the regime.

The CAI had supported the 1943 coup at first, welcoming the repression of unions (especially in construction) and hoping the military would promote industrialization. Shortly after the military took power, the CAI published a book calling for the systematic planning of public works and praising "the total planner, the high-flying statesman" who could use the power of the state to remake a country where "everything remains to be done."[78]

But their enthusiasm quickly cooled. While military leaders did embrace industrialization, they also sent Catholic outsiders to take over the universities where engineers taught and military officers to meddle in the state agencies where engineers worked. The military denunciations of the "oligarchy" grated on the engineers who had faithfully served that order, and grandiose military projects threatened to choke off a private construction boom. As the military bias for the Axis became clearer, the overwhelmingly pro-Allied engineers grew more distant.[79] In December 1943, they elected as CAI president one of the authors of an October call for restoring constitutional rule. While many leading engineers did support the government, including the lead author of the CAI report on San Juan, Raúl Martínez Vivot, a patrician who had held several official posts, even they felt that engineers needed to reassert their authority.

The CAI flatly rejected moving the city, asserting that the whole province was a seismic zone. Rebuilding was "a matter of regulation": the state role was to set a building code and ensure that property owners could follow it.[80] The engineers did believe decisive state action was required: owners would rebuild most homes, but the state would have to organize and perhaps finance the whole process. Like Judge Ramella, the engineers favored expropriating the entire city and repartitioning it into wider streets and more regular lots. They also suggested the state become the central provider of building materials, to guarantee supplies and avoid speculation. Most remarkably, they insisted the state should intervene forcefully in the labor market—to hold down wages. They worried that labor scarcity might lead employers to bid wages up, drawing workers toward "property owners with the most resources" and making it harder for smaller property owners to rebuild. Of course, this was a natural outcome of an approach premised on favoring the wealthy. It is revealing that engineers ignored both the larger question of how homes would be built for those without property—the majority of the province—and the important point that higher wages might in fact make it easier for laborers to build something for themselves. Seeing reconstruction as "a matter of regulation" meant adopting a systematic bias in favor of the propertied.

While focused on long-term reconstruction, the CAI report did devote some attention to temporary housing. Surprisingly, engineers who had led the effort to develop new materials and industrialize construction declined to experiment in San Juan, instead endorsing "wood as the principal material" for emergency housing along with "the typical straw, cane, and adobe."[81] At first glance, this might seem flexible and practical, perhaps employing more workers and yielding quicker results than new materials and techniques. But this practicality was an illusion: wood was in short supply, as the CAI report lead author knew well after spending four years on the rationing board, and the safety of structures of "typical" materials was very much in dispute.[82] Indeed, the engineers endorsing "typical" materials for the poor were the same ones leading the charge against adobe and codifying anti-seismic standards. In this light, their stance reflected not flexibility but indifference. Rather than placing housing for the poor at the center of a rebuilding project, the engineers regarded it as a side gesture, unworthy of serious consideration.[83] Reform was only possible within "local possibilities"—that is, after the established powers had been secured.[84]

The engineers' forceful opposition to the move caught the architects off guard, and they scrambled to respond. "Silent until now in public declarations," the SCA issued a statement, insisting on its "natural and indisputable authority" over the matter.[85] The SCA claimed its intervention was prompted by colleagues working in San Juan, a casual comment which revealed how intertwined rebuilding, the SCA, and the military regime had become, as these were the same architects, reporting to Perón, who had planned the housing exhibit and the documentary film on relief. Thanks to Perón and Pistarini, the architects had made great institutional progress in a short time: old laws restricting professional exercise had been lifted, and architects were now mayors of important cities, deans of major faculties, and for the first time, leading the MOP Architecture Department. In short, the government "had opened up paths which had been blocked by routine, ignorance, and misunderstanding."[86] Beyond institutional gains, architects also had a chance to pursue the visions of comprehensive planning and popular housing that had become increasingly vital to the profession.[87]

Thus, the SCA presented the new San Juan as the "cornerstone of national planning." This was the moment to reimagine the city, to break the traditional mold. No one should "squander" the opportunity "out of sloth, ignorance, routine, or . . . most damning, self-interest."[88] The SCA presented its program for modernization in the Catholic nationalist rhetoric of the regime, in keeping with the convictions of some influential architects and the tactical calculations of others.[89] If reconstruction was done properly, the architects argued, the country would remember the tragedy "as a divine sign of redemption that opened our eyes" to the importance of housing, "a problem that threatens the very essence of our social organization." Reconstruction was the first step toward a New Argentina, "where no man, woman or child lacks a home to return to." This dramatically contrasted with the engineers' emphasis on rebuilding the homes of the wealthy.[90]

As "an immense park with buildings," the new San Juan would be a rebuke and example to other cities. Echoing Bereterbide, the architects argued that trying to rebuild on the same site would be costly, slow, and litigious, while a property swap would be "more just, rapid and simple," as well as less expensive, leaving greater resources for housing, parks, and social services. According to the architects, once the full evidence for the move was made public, even the most intransigent opponents would welcome it. The SCA failed to appreciate that, with architects making casual references to the "artificially overvalued lands of the old city," such conversions were unlikely.[91]

This defense was still framed in the terms set by Bereterbide and Vautier. There was no discussion of emergency housing, no specifics on what to do outside the capital, and, most remarkably, no mention of anti-seismic design. The SCA assumed that all new housing would be anti-seismic, and most likely built from reinforced concrete. But the architects offered no specifics on how it would be built or guarantee locals' safety. Providing housing for all was the core of the architects' vision, which made rebuilding a "cornerstone of national planning" rather than a "matter of regulation." But the architects conceded this key point. Rather than insisting that treating rebuilding as "a matter of regulation" meant leaving to chance the shelter of most of the province, the SCA simply accepted the engineers' ideas for regulation while calling for a broader vision.

Outside of the province and professional elites, the national debate over rebuilding was less polarized and unfolded in surprising ways. *La Nación,* the major Buenos Aires paper, naturally opposed the move, claiming that advocates ignored "science, tradition, or equity" and asserting, remarkably enough, that "no one could prove" the current site was vulnerable to earthquakes. More surprisingly, the Catholic paper *El Pueblo,* which was directed by Pistarini's lead advisor, was also cool to the move: it did not take an editorial stance, but every signed article it published favored rebuilding on the same site.[92]

The most important establishment paper, *La Prensa,* was committed to defending property rights and suspicious of state planning—later in 1944 it denounced industrial policy as rule by a "soviet of engineers"—yet its editorials returned again and again to the forgotten lessons of 1894 and the need to make a break.[93] Describing local resistance as "motivated exclusively by personal interest," the paper rejected "pragmatic short-term concessions" and declared anything short of a bold solution "inexcusable."[94] The paper later qualified this stance by claiming that the move could only be authorized by an elected local legislature, an indirect attack on military rule. But even then it insisted that the debate should involve only "respectable men, utterly unaffected by local interests," and called the move absolutely necessary.[95]

Crítica, which was close to Perón, published editorials strongly favoring the move. Reporters interviewed everyone from the SCA president to José Pastor, editor of the professional journal and author of the statement on San Juan. Pastor argued that rebuilding on the current outline would mean "a sad repetition of the drama of Buenos Aires and Rosario . . . a true babel of architectural "tastes," a display case of dividing walls, a mortal danger for children, a nightmare for traffic, and an infernal concert of noise." For Pastor, the move enabled a new urban future that was "social and not commercial, humane and not mercantile."[96] A week later, an editorial argued for building a "new, modern and young city," reflecting the best aspirations of the republic and "dignifying the Argentine family."[97]

This national advocacy for the move only reached San Juan indirectly, through the six bulletins the reform club *Amigos Sanjuaninos* published between February and May, which included articles favoring the move from locals, editorials from the national papers, and statements from the SCA. "We have never declared ourselves 'movers,'" the club stated in early May, "not because we are afraid to assume a clear position . . . but because we believe we should leave geologists, engineers, architects, urbanists, and hygienists to study the question serenely and without pressures and let the national government find a solution since this is not a task for the laity but for experts and statesmen."[98] As this comment suggests, neither the government nor local supporters considered winning mass support within San Juan as a necessary first step toward rebuilding on a new site. Indeed, after their large-scale publicity efforts for relief and housing, officials had apparently assumed the new city would triumph without effort. The plan's specifics only began circulating outside government and professional circles in late April. It was only at this point that the military authorities became forceful advocates of the move.

But they had not built a movement for raising the city on a new site, only recruited a cluster of friendly notables. Those with property were alarmed at the possibility of losing it, but those without were not yet inspired by the hope of winning it. Any official support was hamstrung by Sosa Molina, while the architects themselves fruitlessly cultivated opinion leaders like Videla instead of making their proposals to a larger audience. By the time they did, the window for winning mass support, local or national, had nearly closed.

A New Nation on Display, A New Framework for Rebuilding

In early May, General Edelmiro Farrell, who had replaced Ramírez as president three months earlier, traveled to San Juan "to get in touch with the people."[99] The local papers laid out the case against the move and published long lists of supporters including Conservatives, Radicals, Socialists, and, by now, even a few Cantonistas.[100] But if opposition was the dominant opinion of the elite, it was hardly the unanimous opinion of the province: those lists included no unions and few popular organizations. Indeed, in canvassing opinion, local newspapers dismissed any supporters of the move as illegitimate, since the poor had been "seduced" by the "aroma of bucolic gardens" and the "mirror-play of styles." "Of course those who own nothing . . . and have no spiritual sensibility" favor the move, *La Acción* commented the day of the visit.[101]

Farrell brought a welcome surprise. He had not decided where to rebuild, but he was reassigning the task: the MOP would cede control to a new authority, nationally funded but based in San Juan. What the authority would look like was up to Interventor Sosa Molina, who had a month to draft a proposal. Finally given a voice in rebuilding, local elites were jubilant.[102]

This concession to local resistance was also the outcome of regime infighting. Since the fall of Ramírez, Interior Minister Luis Perlinger had emerged as Perón's main rival; he annexed to his portfolio first the aid collection and now, since Sosa Molina reported to him, rebuilding as well.[103] Farrell's visit was designed to recapture the initiative.[104] After San Juan, Farrell launched a second aid campaign, to help the impoverished neighboring provinces. "If the work required to restore what the quake destroyed is great," he declared, then even more is required "where geological events have destroyed nothing because man has built very little." The average citizen still "knows little of the dramatic reality of the interior of the Republic," but Farrell claimed that the challenge of the earthquake and the inspiration of the regime were leading citizens to look inward, and think differently.[105]

Within San Juan, this looked like a triumph of the fuerzas vivas. Sosa Molina designed a Reconstruction Council with local staff but national funds. To the Del Bono Commission, this was the "perfect" arrangement, as Judge Ramella later put it, and blunted any real danger of a move.[106] While Sosa Molina had remained technically neutral on the move, he had often signaled his support for "keepers," and after sending his proposal to Buenos Aires, he put the Guido and Carrasco plan on display in his office.[107]

No wonder that when Sosa Molina left a few months later, local elites praised him for laying "the cornerstone of the new San Juan." He had arrived in the midst of "chaos," but left with order reestablished, wounds healed, and collective morale on the mend. The keynote speaker at his farewell banquet lauded his work in securing food and shelter for all, guaranteeing a permanent solution for "popular housing," and ensuring that "workers receive the salary demanded by their dignity as persons, whose rights and responsibilities . . . it is impious and hateful to deny." He thanked Sosa Molina for reviving commerce, charting a bold future, and, above all, for creating the Reconstruction Council. While the description seemed drawn from Sosa Molina's own press releases, it came from an even more revealing source, the Conservative leader Santiago Graffigna.[108]

Yet for all the bodeguero celebration, the move was not dead. On returning to Buenos Aires, President Farrell declared flatly that "the city should rise somewhere else, on firmer soil."[109] The Bereterbide and Vautier proposal might have been shelved, but it was prominently displayed at the official expo. In June 1944, to commemorate one year in power, the military regime mounted an exhibition of its accomplishments that covered several blocks in the center of Buenos Aires. Designed by a team of architects under Perón, including a former SCA president, the expo was another step in the profession's alliance with the military regime.[110] It presented a cornucopia of projects, from educational reforms to the first Argentine-made tank, but gave pride of place to the first proof of the regime's "social justice": relief for San Juan and the follow-up campaign for the Northwest. The entrance to the exposition was flanked by three emergency houses from San Juan. Entry was free, but donations were accepted to aid the Northwest.[111]

"It is not enough to clear away the mess we were standing upon," one nationalist author declared at the time, "we must build a new fatherland."[112] The new San Juan was a centerpiece of the exposition, with a full range of drawings and plans on display. Lead architect Ernesto Vautier and team member Carmen Renard both gave public talks. Since their proposal had apparently been shelved, their tone was more elegiac than inspirational. Renard dwelled on how shifting soil, hidden cesspools, and confused property demarcations would make rebuilding treacherous. Failing to expropriate the entire city, she warned, would guarantee four thousand lawsuits over boundaries.[113] Vautier opened by invoking a woman who had survived both the 1894 and 1944 earthquakes and told Farrell on his visit: "Sir, the holy book says that new wine should not be put in old skins. Do what the holy book says, and rebuild San Juan on virgin land."[114] For Vautier, the fuerzas vivas had temporarily thwarted this popular will, "just another episode in the struggle . . . between egotism and fruitful cooperation." But he was confident an expansive vision of rebuilding would triumph, not to impose "a bastardized little Buenos Aires" on the ruins but rather to plan "for San Juan" for the first time:

> Our desire is that the passions which so perturbed the serenity necessary to study the problem might grow quiet, so that we might all turn to the problem itself, which is not only a problem of San Juan, but a problem of the whole nation and the well-being of her children. Let us not forget. San Juan has suffered a painful blow with the quake, but that pain has only added to the pain the most humble of that land have borne for years. The quake was only an incident. We must aim our spirits beyond it.

Vautier failed to grasp that an ambitious program for rebuilding required harnessing passion, not pushing it aside. But he clearly gauged the stakes and the cost of failure. Trying to rebuild on the same site, he predicted, would be an enormous frustration for all.[115]

For Pistarini, losing control of rebuilding was only a temporary setback. Instead of the provinces, he turned to the outskirts of the capital city. Expropriating five times the area proposed for San Juan, Pistarini began the Ezeiza project on the southern edge of Buenos Aires, eventually building an international airport, access highway, park belt, and a model city of fifty thousand.[116]

Meanwhile, the Reconstruction Council was set up along more centralist lines than Sosa Molina had envisaged. Perlinger's civilian advisors granted representation to local elites but retained the ultimate authority for Buenos Aires.[117] This institutional arrangement would prove more enduring than Perlinger. He inaugurated the anniversary expo in June, but within a month, he lost a contest for the vice presidency to Perón and left the government. Perón was now the most powerful figure in the regime, ready to carry out a broad program of social reform.[118]

The first proposal for remaking San Juan—the Bereterbide plan—had been defeated. But a new authority was now in charge, and despite the best efforts of local Conservatives, it remained committed to radical transformation. The new authority took the Bereterbide plan not as a false start but as a first draft. The struggle for the future city had only begun.

PART 3

FROM LEADING CASE TO EXEMPLARY FAILURE, MID-1944 TO MID-1946

Eight months after the earthquake, Perón finally came to San Juan. It was early spring, after a hard winter, and he was received as a hero. There were crowds at every stop: his arrival at the airstrip, a ceremony honoring the dead at a convent, a visit to the emergency barrios, and a rousing speech at the stadium. Prominent locals lauded his efforts on the province's behalf. Confident that "cross and sword have always advanced together," the convent prior thanked Perón for "all the good your full hands poured out." At the stadium, a leading viñatero praised the "opportune" raising of emergency barrios and the success of the harvest despite great adversity, emphasizing that "the people who proved themselves capable of such effort now await the instructions of their ruler." The viñatero stressed local resilience, but he was clearly grateful for military action, and looking to Perón to shape rebuilding.[1]

Beyond the provision of aid, others hailed the emergence of an ambitious social vision. "For the first time in the history of our country," union leader Ramón Tejada exulted, "labor laws are . . . not a dead letter, but a reality." The speaker lineup at the stadium was suggestive: there were two establishment figures, but five labor representatives—Tejada, Perón's delegate Ruperto Godoy, and three rank-and-file workers. Rebuilding promised to change the social order, as well as the physical city.[2]

"The Secretaría de Trabajo y Previsión was born when San Juan was destroyed," Perón told the stadium crowd, placing relief for survivors at the origin of his campaign for social justice. "We are not fighting for the good of four or five of the privileged," he said, "but to remedy all the ills that affect the whole of the population . . . to look out for the common good, which is the good of the poor, because the rich look out for themselves." This meant shifting the balance of power, dignifying labor and "humanizing capital." To make his case, Perón pointed to successes so far, and audiences were largely persuaded. Perón's visit came only three months after he had become vice president and de facto leader of the military regime, and promised greater resources and attention for rebuilding. The proof would be in the results: as the slogan hung outside STP headquarters put it, "Deeds not words, achievements not promises." But Perón already saw the transformation as irreversible: "The victories we have won and keep on winning" had so marked "the consciousness . . . of *criollo* workers . . . that no force on earth will be capable of removing a single brick from the social edifice we are constructing."[3]

The first step toward building a New Argentina was rebuilding the city in ruins. That was "the truth of this hour": prosperity, dignity, and, above all and "as soon as possible, reconstruction." In another speech two weeks earlier, Perón had promised that "every Argentine" would be able to give a home to his children, as "a piece of the New Argentina." Now he simply had to fulfill this commitment in the place where it was most needed.[4]

But the record so far, for all its promise, was more uneven than Perón acknowledged. Nearly half of the city had not yet returned.[5] Perón's leadership drew praise, but he was late in coming to the destroyed city; the relief effort began strong but faltered over the winter; emergency homes were much appreciated but insufficient in number and perhaps inappropriate in design. The evident gratitude hid the beginnings of discontent, which surfaced in one telling moment during the visit. Perón was greeting children, asking what their names were and if they were happy, when one burst out, "My name is Luis, there are twelve of us, and we have no mother!" Perón was stunned but quickly turned consoling, patting the boy on the head and assuring the crowd that he had twenty warehouses of goods he would dispatch immediately. The aid was welcome, and no one published any criticism at the time.[6] But as many recalled later, it was striking that the goods were in the warehouses and not where they were needed. Indeed, nine months after the disaster, despite evident need, less than a third of the money collected for relief had been spent—the rest was languishing in government accounts. This was a sign, first, that San Juan had lost importance during months of political infighting, and second, and more importantly, that officials were still unsure of how to proceed. As I will show, these dissonant notes pointed toward larger frustrations to come.

This section of the book explores the shifting relationship between rebuilding the city and building a New Argentina over the tumultuous period from July 1944 to June 1946. This is the period when Peronism properly speaking emerged, the mass movement with a labor base that would transform the country. It was also when San Juan went from leading case for ambitious reforms to exemplary failure. It can be divided into three periods.

First, after July 1944, Perón launched a battery of social reforms—especially labor reforms—which won him surprisingly strong popular support, even as the military regime saw its power and credibility erode as the Second World War came to a close.

Second was the emergence, consolidation, and seeming triumph of a wide-ranging opposition to the military regime and especially to Perón. In May 1945, a combative new U.S. ambassador arrived and launched a campaign to overthrow the "Nazi-fascist" regime. On 15 June, the leading Buenos Aires economic interests issued the "Manifesto of the Fuerzas Vivas," which decried the "climate of distrust, provocation and rebelliousness" created by social reforms and called for their immediate repeal and "the prompt return of the rule of law."[7] Perón's attempts to mollify the opposition only served to embolden them, forging a broad front that now included most of the social and economic establishment and every political party from the Communists to the Conservatives. A month of opposition street protests culminated in the two-hundred-thousand-strong "March for Freedom and the Constitution" on 19 September, and Perón's removal and arrest by his military rivals on 9 October.

Third, just as the opposition triumph seemed assured, Perón found unexpected support from workers, as hundreds of thousands filled Buenos Aires on 17 October and forced his release. This was the decisive confirmation of Perón's ties to labor. It also marked labor's decisive break with the left, as Socialists and Communists attacked workers who supported Perón as foolish and barbaric. After Perón's release, the campaign began for democratic elections in February 1946, which pitted Perón as the candidate of the newly formed Labor Party against an alliance called the Unión Democrática which included nearly every existing political party.

The next three chapters view these three national moments from the standpoint of San Juan. Chapter 7 examines Perón's drive for reform in San Juan, highlighting the success of labor organizing and the failure of rebuilding by focusing closely on the new Reconstruction Council and the three teams of architects it employed from July 1944 to July 1945. Chapter 8 details the emergence of a vibrant opposition, based in the propertied classes and employing the political language of liberalism, which made the failure to rebuild into a central argument against not only official plans but the military regime as a whole. Chapter 9 explores Perón's counterattack, with unexpected success nationally but dispiriting consequences for San Juan, showing how the failure of reconstruction became a central symbol for opposition politics in the 1946 election, even as the broader debate about the future of the province was largely brushed aside.

I have stressed the importance of San Juan in the making of Peronism. But here, just as Perón gained national control, the rebuilding of San Juan began to falter. This was when the project to rebuild San Juan took its most radical turn, but also the moment when the project began to slip in importance, as local rebuilding became increasingly disconnected from the national rebuilding it had modeled. Peronism was beginning to reveal its limits.

CHAPTER 7 DIVERGING PATHS OF REFORM

ARCHITECTS, LABOR, AND THE RECONSTRUCTION COUNCIL

After winning control of the government in July 1944, Perón pushed force-fully for social reform. In San Juan, this effort had two intertwined strands: the rise of labor, a familiar theme in studies of Peronism, and the struggle to rebuild, a theme first examined here.

Once again, three state agencies were key: the Secretariat of Labor, the provincial administration, and the new Reconstruction Council. The first was a dynamo of activity, and with government support, unions increased dramatically in size and power, becoming major players in local politics for the first time. Particularly after Perón's visit, government reforms and labor mobilization provided concrete evidence of the social changes on the way. In this respect, San Juan followed the national pattern.

By contrast, the provincial administration became a dead weight: in August 1944, Sosa Molina was replaced by Colonel Juan Berreta, the local garrison commander, who was distant from regime leaders but intimate with the propertied classes—especially Graffigna Conservatives. Across many policy areas, and most critically in housing, the drive of prior months slowed to a crawl. This lethargy clothed in dreamy rhetoric is well captured in the activities of Judge Pablo Ramella, a Graffigna ally: after the quake, his case load had dropped, so he finished his work quickly every morning, walked home through the rubble, then spent the afternoons writing a dense theoretical work setting out his views on "The Structure of the State."[1]

The most decisive agency for reviving San Juan was the Reconstruction Council. The agency was led by a military officer and staffed by experts, many from outside the province. But its actions were to be guided, as its name suggested, by a council composed of prominent locals. Thus the agency had considerable institutional power and became an important space for debate over how that power should be used.

After briefly examining the trajectory of the new agency, I turn to the three architectural teams and their progressively less radical schemes for the future city. The first team, led by Jorge Ferrari Hardoy, undertook the most ambitious attempt at modernist urban planning yet in Latin America. Carefully rethinking local geography and economy, they produced a new city plan that was also a broader scheme for development. But their plan was stymied by institutional conflicts: the head of the Reconstruction Council alienated local elites, isolated the architects, and failed to settle on a strategy, leading to the architects' dismissal and the agency's reorganization around the first anniversary of the earthquake.

By this point, many locals had become disenchanted with emergency housing, the Reconstruction Council, and increasingly with the military regime. The following two architectural teams, under Julio Villalobos and Carlos Mendióroz, pursued less imaginative and more constrained designs. Both turned modernist forms to conservative ends, retaining the idea of regional planning even as they largely abandoned the effort to transform the province. Both claimed to be pragmatic but failed to either persuade local elites or connect with the broader appeal of Perón's increasingly powerful social project, based on the mobilization of labor.

The Reconstruction Council

Three weeks before Perón's visit, the president of the new Reconstruction Council, Colonel Julio Hennekens, gave his first interview to the local press. He chose to make his case not to the usual journalists but rather to an outsider, the labor leader Ramón Tejada. The symbolism was clear: this was not business as usual but a new kind of politics, advanced by an alliance of soldiers, workers, and reformers. For the colonel, the fundamental principle of rebuilding was to "place the interest of the majority . . . above the interests of individuals," and thus to favor "the middle class and workers," who either never had their own home or "lacked the means to rebuild what they have lost." This meant "rebuilding one or more cities of lovely, comfortable, and appropriate homes," of course, but for Hennekens rebuilding also required "the creation of new industries that take advantage of the enormous wealth of resources in the province" and generate "permanent year-round jobs," in contrast to the seasonal employment of the wine industry. In short, he sketched out an ambitious agenda to industrialize the province, diversify its economy, and provide homes for all. As Perón had underscored on his visit, rebuilding the city was a first step to rebuilding the country, and the new Reconstruction Council was at the center of this effort.[2]

For the fuerzas vivas, these ambitions confirmed an unwelcome trend. They had initially seen the Reconstruction Council as their instrument; and, courtesy of Sosa Molina, establishment figures were named to eight of the Council's twelve seats.[3] But even as the government appointed their allies, it had narrowed the Council's deliberative role and granted more power to its president.[4] The decree establishing the Reconstruction Council banned the sale of property or permanent repair of damaged buildings. Moreover, it gave the agency a broad mandate to "decide the location of the city," produce a master plan, expropriate land, and carry out construction—and even included provisions to "swap" existing lots for new ones, with the forced expropriation of those who refused.[5] The closer the fuerzas vivas looked, the less of a triumph this seemed.

Hennekens's long delay in convening the new Council only deepened their unease. He was appointed in June but did not reach San Juan until August—held up first by the fall of the minister who had chosen him, Perlinger, and then by hiring staff and planning.[6] When he finally did arrive, the Del Bono Commission greeted him with a detailed letter rejecting swaps, arguing for minimal expropriations, and declaring once more against a move.[7] They would admit no restrictions on property, saw little need for planning, and wanted the state simply to get out of the way.[8]

But Hennekens clearly was going to pursue his own course. He was a soldier first and foremost, and he had come to remake the province. He had drive, but not much cunning. His communication model was the chain of command; he regarded debate as confusing, alliances as distractions, and decree as the most effective technique of rule. For eight years, he had directed military construction, supervising projects with clear objectives, narrow scope, and no civilian consultation. Now he seemed to think he could rebuild a city just as he had built barracks. Soon Reconstruction would become a kind of parallel provincial administration, one far less amenable to Conservatives.

Before leaving Buenos Aires, and without consulting the new Council, he hired a design team. He chose the core members of the former Grupo Austral, the young modernist architects Jorge Ferrari Hardoy, Jorge Vivanco, Simón Ungar, Alberto Le Pera, and Samuel Oliver. From the beginning, he entrusted team leader Ferrari Hardoy with key tasks like lining up concrete suppliers and recruiting a scientific advisory board. Placing his trust in avant-garde architects showed his determination to do something new, even if he was unsure exactly what.

Radical Modernism: Ferrari Hardoy Team, 1944

A week after they were hired in Buenos Aires, the new architectural team was in San Juan. The first thing they did on arriving was draft a communiqué to the population. They already had a good sense of the challenges ahead, as all had closely followed the rebuilding debate so far, and several had visited San Juan on their own and spoken with architects from the first two teams.[9] They saw reconstruction as an opportunity to remake the structure of the province, not simply to provide structures to inhabit. They firmly believed rebuilding would only succeed if it involved the population and was directed from San Juan. Explaining their purpose and securing popular support was therefore "their first duty."[10]

"We are at a critical moment in history," Ferrari Hardoy wrote, as "one civilization comes to an end, making way for another." The fallen city was the material expression of a way of life four centuries in the making. "The quake has destroyed this form," Ferrari Hardoy argued, but left "the spirit of the city, our starting point." To embody that spirit, each resident must understand she is not simply securing her property, but refounding the city: "Every street, every house that is built now will and must represent many years of history."[11]

The team had a clear idea of what should not be done: "whether the city stays or moves, the current property layout cannot be kept." Reducing planning to a matter of street lines would impoverish the future city without accelerating its construction. On the contrary, considering the lack of materials and technical resources, such an approach would guarantee "speculation, theft and disorganization." Thus planning was crucial, as well as a strong guiding role for the Reconstruction Council, even if most rebuilding would be done by private means.[12]

Before carrying out this radical renovation, the architects felt, Reconstruction needed to gain credibility by addressing immediate needs. Encouraged by initial discussions with Hennekens, they proposed actions to win local trust and support: get schools functioning quickly, establish a registry for demolition requests, grant temporary construction permits, and draft a building code, including a quick determination of which areas would not be affected by rebuilding and could therefore begin permanent construction.[13]

Emergency barrios were the highest priority. To improve them, the Council should act quickly to ensure the provision of electricity, running water, and adequate sanitary installations, and more generally establish resident associations to improve communication and local resolution of problems. Ultimately, Reconstruction should allow residents greater freedom to improve houses, by planting gardens, for example, or coating fibercement roofs with a thin layer of mud to counteract the heat. By taking pragmatic action to demonstrate capacity, Reconstruction could win support for its broader project.

This opening gesture stands in contrast to the usual rhetoric of architectural vanguards, and also to their own earlier ideas. Five years before, the Austral group had praised fibercement as an excellent material and decreed that "large industry should take care of the needs of rural housing"; now they were rethinking their confidence in top-down technical solutions.[14] These actions were hardly signs of the doctrinaire modernism local elites (and later critics) ascribed to the architects.

There is a simple reason why these pragmatic beginnings are not well known: Hennekens changed his mind and did not issue the communiqué. Rather than building credibility by helping the population, Hennekens pulled the Reconstruction Council into itself. He reassigned the architects away from emergency housing, either to avoid a turf battle with the provincial government or to speed progress on a rebuilding plan. This choice was revealing of his future direction: by failing to confront the provincial administration, he effectively left everyday urban management in the hands of Conservatives. This decision distanced the architects from locals, making it easier for Conservatives to discredit them as foolish outsiders.

Of course, while the architects were far more thoughtful about political strategy and local needs than their avant-garde commitments might suggest, they still had those avant-garde commitments. They aimed for a radical transformation of city and province, going well beyond any of the earlier proposals. Their work in San Juan drew on earlier plans, developed in collaboration with the Swiss modernist Le Corbusier, for Buenos Aires and for Mendoza. As in those earlier cases, they were applying to this local reality the major tenets of modernist urbanism, set down in the CIAM Athens Charter. But as their communiqué suggests, and recent scholarly work on modernism has emphasized, there was much room for adaptation within modernist urbanism, and their project for San Juan would prove deeply researched and carefully integrated into the local social and geographic world. Indeed, their plan sparked resistance not because of how poorly they understood what was necessary to transform the province but because of how well they understood it.[15]

The plan emerged out of detailed research over the last half of 1944. For the first two months, the team was simply tasked with determining whether to move the city. On 3 October they recommended rebuilding on the same site and offered an outline plan, which Hennekens approved, and then they produced a more detailed plan by the end of November.[16] From the beginning, the team was convinced that political resistance made moving the city impossible. Instead, they advocated expropriating, redrawing, and reallocating all property. This was in keeping with what the more reform-minded keepers had previously supported, although that support would prove fragile. By taking the move itself off the table, however, they hoped to win backing for a range of other bold reforms and a rebuilding program that was in several respects more radical than the Bereterbide plan.

While the original drawings themselves have not survived, archival documentation and later renderings made by the team clearly show the evolution of the project. Their working style contrasted with the Bereterbide team in three ways: first, they attempted to apply modernist principles more consistently; second, their presence in San Juan produced far more detailed knowledge of local conditions and stronger connections with local actors; and third, their proposal therefore was a more sustained effort at urban and regional planning, really the first such attempt in Argentina. The notes the Bereterbide team developed from single conversations or brief visits contrast sharply with the archive of materials gathered by the Ferrari Hardoy team, which included everything from careful historical maps of the canal system and aerial photography of the valley to lists of everyone who owned more than six properties in the city.[17]

Like earlier teams, the Ferrari Hardoy team thought rebuilding should start with the valley and only then address the city. But they took the idea much further, proposing a broad restructuring of the economy and ecology of the valley. They worked out the details in close consultation with local leaders, particularly with the engineer, hydrologist, and mining official Juan Victoria. Incorporating the ideas developed by Enrique Zuleta, the head of the water department, they proposed the first expansion in fifty years of the canal system, in a project explicitly modeled on the Tennessee Valley Authority. This project included building a new canal, to open new terrain to irrigation; expanding and sealing existing ones, to reduce the water lost to leakage and evaporation; building small generators along the canals, to increase electricity; and building several dams upriver, in the mountains. The dams in particular were key to regularizing water flow, expanding arable land, and dramatically increasing electricity production for mining and industry.[18]

This was important to breaking the coercive power of grape monoculture. With more arable land, local agriculture could be diversified, production industrialized, and landless workers resettled in cooperative towns across the countryside. As already seen, rural depopulation was particularly pronounced in San Juan, and directly tied to bodeguero efforts to create a seasonal workforce for the vineyards.

By destroying both the wineries and the city, the earthquake offered an exceptional opportunity to reshape the industry and the province. Both earlier rebuilding proposals had mentioned decentralization, but the Ferrari Hardoy team now carried it into design. Six years earlier, the team members had argued that a new architecture would emerge only from confronting rural injustice. Now they called for relocating private wineries and establishing cooperative wineries in new areas of cultivation, spreading industry and the working population out across the valley. They proposed a dozen new settlements across the valley, some in new locations close to expanding cultivation, and others on the site of towns destroyed by the quake. This challenge to the spatial order coincided with a powerful challenge to the social order—the rural labor unions being organized in these same months. From the standpoint of the wineries, this convergence was threatening, as we will see.

Consistent with their overall vision, the team called for opening the city to the landscape. For generations, the city had been built in opposition to the countryside, with walled houses, the four avenues, and the "ring of iron" serving as barriers against the surrounding valley. Now the barriers would be eliminated. The "ring of iron" would be pulled up, the two stations merged and moved to the east side of the city. At the western edge of the grid, in the space left by the railroad stations, the new city center would rise. Set in a park, this center would tie together the old core and the higher ground to the west.

Following the modernist call, the Ferrari Hardoy team designed a downtown of free-standing buildings, set in the dense planting of trees made possible by irrigation canals. Instead of the imaginary colonial citadel of Bereterbide and Vautier, this was a modern oasis at the foot of the Andes. The existing blocks of the city grid were regrouped into "superblocks." Each had a park and public walkway running through its center and vehicle traffic at its periphery; for each cluster of superblocks, there would be a neighborhood center with school, market, parish, and civic facilities, as in the Bereterbide scheme. In splitting walkways from highways, and turning the old continuous street fronts into a series of free-standing homes, this plan followed modernist ideas more closely. But it hardly followed them slavishly: despite the modernist enthusiasm for towers, nearly every proposed building was low, generally single-story and single-family, allowing for private gardens and preserving the intimate scale of the old city. The only place where the plan envisioned taller buildings was in the new center, as offices and a few apartment buildings.

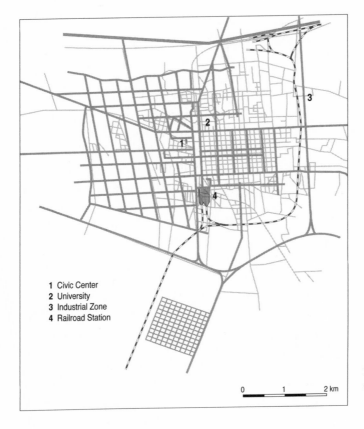

1 Civic Center
2 University
3 Industrial Zone
4 Railroad Station

0   1   2 km

Ferrari Hardoy
team plan,
1944

From the moment they arrived, the architects drew familiar attacks in the local press. San Juan could not afford extravagance, according to the newspaper run by the Graffignas, owners of the province's most renowned mansions. The papers drew a contrast between exuberant outsiders, "urbanists of the literary class" who purveyed a "marvelous series of banalities," and pragmatic locals, "interpreters of the people" who knew what it meant to "found cities."[19] Horacio Videla, the secretary of the Del Bono Commission, later described how "a swarm of bearded faces with pipes and berets descended upon the city . . . come to give free rein to their impossible imaginings."[20] Conservatives mocked the ambition, age, and even facial hair of the architects, these "young experts who have popped fresh out of the university oven, to slay the very memory of [city founder] don Juan Jufré, and then build for us, on little maps of Zonda or Villa Krause, a fantastic and mythical garden city just like in children's weekly comics."[21]

The point was always to make locals the voice of reason: "We would exchange all the Babylonian gardens and Venetian aquatic mirrors of 1970 for a discreet number of decorous, modest, clean, and secure houses we san-juaninos could build in 1945."[22] The architects were hardly proposing "Babylonian gardens" or "Venetian aquatic mirrors," as the journalists were well aware. Indeed, however limited the official communications of the architects, elite journalists were well informed about architectural proposals, as their correspondence, internal evidence from press critiques, and Reconstruction Council documentation all confirm. Therefore one can only read the attack on "Babylonian gardens" as an attempt to trivialize work the journalists knew to be ambitious, to discredit a comprehensive proposal for reshaping the province by reducing it to a minor matter of exotic decoration.

To bodegueros, the comprehensive nature of the proposal was exactly what made it a threat: it would reshape the city and the valley and potentially change the balance of power between them. The danger was not just what it proposed for urban property but also what it proposed for the countryside. The bodegueros were hardly against expanding canals or building wineries near new areas of cultivation. Indeed, Bartolomé Del Bono had pioneered this by establishing his own massive complex on the far southeastern edge of the grape zone. But bodegueros were determined to control the process and reap the benefits. All this talk of cooperative wineries, labor unions, and economic diversification was deeply alarming, because it would constrain and ultimately undermine their power.

Mockery and disdain was therefore the key establishment strategy, dis-qualifying designers as outsiders and fools. By stressing that the architects were concerned exclusively with designing unnecessary buildings, the Conservative press denied legitimacy to their planning and blocked its challenge. And this strategy only benefited from the silence, distance, and glacial pace of the Reconstruction Council itself.

The Rise of Labor

Even as rebuilding was losing steam, labor organizing was taking off. This built on the preparatory work of the previous year. From October 1943, when he took over the STP, Perón had brought labor to the center of national political debate, consulted extensively with union leaders, and greatly expanded the state bureaucracy. But until May 1944, his only visible accomplishment was the San Juan relief campaign. Indeed, during this whole period, Perón focused his energies primarily on securing power within the regime and winning civilian allies outside it. It was only in April 1944, with the collapse of his nego-tiations with civilian politicians, the threatening advance of Interior Minister

Perlinger, and the growing restlessness of the unions that Perón shifted direction. Looking for allies, he turned to workers, a momentous decision.[23]

With a generous budget, a zeal for organizing, and an ambition to make new law, the STP set out to reshape workplaces nationwide. Veteran union leaders became important government allies; new unions were formed nationwide. The STP pushed employers to recognize unions and sign contracts: there were 27 contracts in the first half of 1944, but 508 in the second half.[24] Wages, benefits, and working conditions improved dramatically, first in sectors represented by established unions, like railroad workers, but soon in sectors organized weakly if at all, such as meatpackers and sugar workers. The specific proposals often came from veteran union leaders, and the energy obviously came from workers themselves, but Perón made the changes possible and thus won the credit. By the end of 1944, one union leader would observe that labor had accomplished in months "what it had been unable to do in twenty years."[25]

In San Juan, this began shortly after the quake, as Perón's delegate Ruperto Godoy started enforcing labor laws and used the hiring pool to raise wages.[26] Soon Godoy was calling businesses to the bargaining table through daily notices in the newspaper, and the chamber of commerce was howling at his application of such "intensified rigor" when "life was so precarious."[27] But organizing proceeded more slowly. When Perón visited in September, workers were on the podium, but their coordinating council, the Federación Obrera Sanjuanina (FOS), comprised only a half-dozen unions with a few hundred active members, largely in more skilled and urban sectors. In October, when the province's first social workers began conducting surveys, they found some laborers were earning only one peso a day.[28]

The dramatic changes followed Perón's visit. Unions in the wineries expanded to represent all permanent workers, not just the skilled barrel-makers, and won a new government-set wage scale.[29] Dozens of other unions formed in the city, from meat-cutters to waiters. In the countryside, the October 1944 Rural Workers Statute laid out specific standards for wages, working conditions, and labor representation. While moderate in intent, the statute proved quite radical in impact, as even limited official support for unions, rights, and wage demands had a transformative effect.[30] New unions were formed in the vineyards and orchards, and rural labor found a political voice for the first time since Cantoni's overthrow. Just before Christmas 1944, the leader of a new rural union in Las Casuarinas, the municipality dominated by the Del Bono winery, rode to Buenos Aires on his bicycle—over a thousand kilometers—to personally thank Perón.[31] The winery owners took note, and early *Tribuna* editorials praising Perón's reforms began to give way to complaints about "lazy" workers and excessive compensation—at four pesos a day.[32] By June 1945, nine months after Perón's visit, labor was a far more formidable actor, as the six unions with a few hundred active members had grown into more than fifty organizations representing twelve thousand workers.[33]

The Socialist railroad worker Ramón Tejada, who had led the FOS for nearly a decade, became a key local ally for Perón. He was the only local on the new Reconstruction Council not aligned with the Graffigna Conservatives. As a Socialist and as a labor leader, he was deeply suspicious of the Cantonis, whom he saw as authoritarian figures who had enticed workers away from their true home in the enlightened left and properly constituted unions. Tejada and his allies embraced Perón's cause not only for the social gains it offered workers but also for the political gains it offered the province, a new order free of Conservatives and Cantonistas. The true test of this new order, however, would be the new city that emerged from it.

The Troubles of Emergency Barrios

The landmark emergency effort to house the province had been the first installment on Perón's overall social project. But when the MOP withdrew in May, turning emergency housing over to the province, the effort stalled. The STP launched reforms, and Reconstruction planned even more ambitious ones, but the province dithered and did little to improve existing emergency housing or provide more. As a result, by late 1944, the neglect of the provincial administration was beginning to undermine emergency housing—and the credibility it had won the regime.

There were three basic problems. First, despite their modern appearance and structural stability, emergency structures had serious drawbacks. Fiber-cement was certainly lighter and cleaner than adobe, and perhaps—as trade advertisements claimed—more "anti-seismic" as well.[34] But it proved poorly adapted to the local climate—freezing in winter, scorching in summer, hardly the comfortable shelter the government had promised.

As early as July, satirical poems in the press called attention to how poorly emergency housing was withstanding the winter.[35] This was the first thing the Ferrari Hardoy team wanted to tackle on arrival in August. But they were given another assignment, and the province did nothing. It was only in December that the province hired a local engineer to coat the houses in reflective paint, to moderate the extremes of temperature.[36] A better solution would have been to use local materials from the start, as the Mendoza paper noted, pointing to the success of emergency housing outside the capital, where strong wooden frames (and fibercement roofs) were often combined with adobe infill walls to create homes that were seismically sound but climatically appropriate.[37]

Second, for all its ambitions, the initial effort had fallen short of the province's needs. The infrastructure in the barrios, especially the larger ones, was quickly overloaded, and few improvements were forthcoming. Moreover, many still needed shelter, particularly in rural communities across the central valley. Hennekens obtained two thousand more wooden structures, but the province was slow to distribute them. A reporter traveling in the countryside was approached by a frustrated rural worker who, seeing him as a generic figure of authority, asked, "Sir, are you going to bring my structure now?"[38] One letter to the authorities asking for emergency shelter noted the long delays and endless promises from provincial officials, and the building materials rotting in the sun at the local train station. "This is the voice of the fatherland reaching your office," the author wrote, urging action because frustrations were only serving to "discredit" the local administration.[39] A worker from the capital sent the provincial minister a handwritten note requesting a slot in the barrio near his former home. He complained that lower-level officials refused to accept his application unless it came on specially stamped paper, which he could not afford, and he tried to get around the requirement by writing higher-level officials on the letterhead of the "Juan Pistarini" Circle of Catholic Workers. In this case, the worker's path was blocked by provincial bureaucrats, all Conservative holdovers, but he made his appeal through an institution with national ties, the reformist church group (close to Perón) whose local chapter was named for a government minister and located in Captain Lazo, one of the two large barrios.[40] Ultimately, the stream of complaints and evident inadequacies of the provincial housing office led the interventor to fire all its employees, but even this drastic step did not produce much improvement.[41]

Third, the forced intimacy and "social heterogeneity" of the barrios was deeply upsetting to respectable San Juan. "The earthquake leveled all the classes, at least in the external form of daily dress," *La Acción* noted in late 1944, "and both the rich and the poor had to use their wits to find a bed and a roof." But while the initial effort to provide emergency housing had been good, there persisted

> problems of a moral and a material order. Although certain projects have brought together families of more or less the same cultural level, the heterogeneity in others has created bothersome situations . . . since differences

in education . . . bring moral suffering for those who knew a peaceful home life, without outside interference . . . The authorities should facilitate . . . the restitution of families to their own homes. Life in the emergency projects is not a joy for all.[42]

It was certainly true, as one paper put it, that "emergency barrios have a social hierarchy: there are aristocratic barrios, middle-class barrios, and popular barrios."[43] As already seen, many of the well-connected were in smaller barrios closer to the center, with families of "more or less the same cultural level." But even so, many respectable sanjuaninos found themselves living outside the four avenues and among the poor, in barrios that caused them "moral suffering." The domestic space of respectable San Juan had been shattered, and many longed to restore the sense of security, and of power, of their own home.

There was thus an emerging cultural conflict over class and sociability in the emergency barrios. While this conflict would be expressed in various ways over the coming years, popular entertainment was a consistent lightning rod, especially the open-air dance halls that proliferated in the emergency barrios. For the poor, these dance halls, and the emergency barrios more generally, were a space of relative freedom. For all its faults, emergency housing was often an improvement over their previous shelter—that is why there were so many demands for the government to build more. This was especially true because rent was free, while wages were rising. After losing homes and even loved ones, and being torn out of their social networks, the poor found some security in the barrios and even the opportunity to forge new social ties, in sports, dance halls, and new organizations, like the workers' circle in Barrio Lazo.

From early on, their respectable neighbors found this freedom threatening, a sign of incipient moral decay. This was partly because of sheer proximity, which meant that, as one resident put it, dancers' "exercise of this more or less philharmonic freedom evidently conflicts with the freedom to sleep."[44] It was also because respectable San Juan associated dance halls with prostitution. But above all it represented the collapse of social distance, the supposed relaxation of moral discipline, and the "visible perversion of our customs," in short, a kind of popular insolence, which prompted a long stream of complaints from scandalized priests, dour patricians, and self-proclaimed reformers.[45]

Of course, there were emergency chapels in many barrios, as well as Catholic lay organizations. The archbishop said Christmas mass in the largest barrio, and the government distributed pastries and cider to the residents of all the barrios.[46] But as the conflicts over sociability suggested, these new communities were developing in ways that were difficult for local, clerical, or national elites to control.

Thus, as the first anniversary of the earthquake approached, respectable San Juan was increasingly uneasy about the emergency barrios. This frustration was the product of both their failures—the inappropriate materials, insufficient infrastructure, inadequate amounts—and their limited successes, especially in providing a stable home for changing popular sectors. "Business is booming and there are cinemas: but how can we live on the sizzling grill of [Barrio] Lazo or Bardiani, or in those other muddy constructions, teeming with bugs, spiders, and worms?" the Catholic paper summed up. "We are spending this Christmas Eve like the Holy Family, in homes that are not much more convenient than the stable where the Son of God was born."[47]

The First Anniversary: Confrontation and Retreat

As tensions rose, Reconstruction Council President Hennekens stumbled in October into two major confrontations, first with his architectural team, and then with the Council as a whole. On 3 October, the Ferrari Hardoy team presented him with two options for rebuilding. They recommended rebuilding on the same site, but only after expropriating and reallocating all properties. He agreed with their recommendation but apparently also began to doubt his reliance on them. Soon he brought in two older professionals: Julio Villalobos, who became chief architect, and Alberto Belgrano Blanco, who became a design consultant and the state banks' representative on the Reconstruction Council. As the new arrivals began exploring other approaches, Hennekens told the Ferrari Hardoy team to produce a full plan by the end of November.[48]

On 6 October, Hennekens called the first meeting of the Reconstruction Council. Waiting five months after his appointment to convene the Council certainly had not won him the confidence of the fuerzas vivas, and neither did his decision to devote the first meeting to the most controversial issue possible: whether to move the city. Since Hennekens had just approved the Ferrari Hardoy approach, which ruled out a move, it was not clear why he would raise the question with the Council as a whole. Perhaps he was trying to scare the fuerzas vivas into embracing the Ferrari Hardoy plan as a more palatable alternative. But if his aim was to produce consensus in the first meeting, he picked a poor starting point, and instead of welcoming his ideas, all eight locals on the Council voted them down. Defeated in his first try, Hennekens had the national government increase his powers by decree and declined to call another general meeting for months.[49] Even after running into strong opposition on the Council, however, he showed little interest and less ability in cultivating other allies or bringing the broader public into the debate.

By the time the Ferrari Hardoy team presented their plan, Hennekens was under pressure to deliver and increasingly unsure how to do so. He had evidently been listening to Villalobos and Belgrano Blanco, both skilled bureaucratic infighters. When Hennekens met with the Ferrari Hardoy team at the beginning of December, he accused them of generating "worthless" designs, "copying" materials which they had produced, showing "insubordination" for pursuing an approach he had approved, and stealing from Villalobos ideas they had proposed before he was hired. After first subjecting them to a long interrogation about their use of drafting supplies, Hennekens fired them by decree.[50] Without evidence from inside Reconstruction, it is hard to establish why Hennekens took this step. Perhaps he had decided over the past two months to pursue a more conciliatory course, like the proposal from Villalobos and Belgrano Blanco, which closely followed the pre-quake Guido Carrasco scheme. Or perhaps he had decided to pursue a more radical course, as suggested by alternatives Villalobos also worked on, which called for rebuilding on the same site but then building a new capital elsewhere in the province.[51] In either case, the Ferrari Hardoy team's resolve and consistent calls for local participation contrasted with his own wavering, isolation, and highhandedness, further undermining his eroding authority.

Two weeks after firing the architects, Hennekens called a meeting of the Reconstruction Council. The press had not reported the firing, although the fuerzas vivas were aware of it, because the architects had asked the local engineers to intervene on their behalf.[52] The fuerzas vivas were dissatisfied with the glacial progress and opaque decision making of Reconstruction. They may also have sensed a weakness. In any case, the meeting quickly degenerated into scandal, as ten of the twelve Council members first voted against Hennekens and then resigned. Instead of using the Council to divide the elite and build local support, he had managed to discredit himself and unify locals against him.[53]

The mass resignation forced the government's hand, and both Hennekens and Interventor Berreta were recalled to Buenos Aires for consultations. Just before the first anniversary of the earthquake, Interventor Berreta tried to buy time by making his first radio address to the province. He invoked Perón's maxim that "doing is better than saying and delivering is better than promising," announced that "battle has been joined against moral, physical, and material misery," and declared that the city would "be rebuilt in the short term"—or at least its location would be determined, since rebuilding, "by the magnitude of the work, is not something that can be resolved from one day to the next." Most notably, he called for patience and solidarity with government efforts, "especially from the groups in power here, who far from collaborating, have delayed in a certain sense the work of all and for all."[54] Even in his attempt at confrontation, he was timid. As one critic noted, "there was an extra 's' in his speech," because there is only one group resisting, "the very group whose praises he has always sung"—several of whom were in his office when he gave the speech.[55]

Two days later, on the anniversary itself, the national authorities dropped a bombshell: the city would be rebuilt on the same site, and the Reconstruction Council dissolved. The overjoyed local papers declared that it was high time to abandon "an impossible fantasy," give up on architects and plans, and simply set the streetline.[56]

Yet the fuerzas vivas' triumph was fleeting: within weeks, the dissolved organization was back, now called Reconstruction of San Juan, with Hennekens as its leader, a much smaller board, and expanded legal powers. The only local left on the board was the union leader Tejada.[57]

Still, military leaders refused to learn the clear lesson of the past year. Between the intransigence of elites and the confused authoritarianism of Hennekens, the opportunity for a fundamental transformation was slipping away. Instead of opening up the Council to a wider range of groups, they shut it down. The admonishment of Berreta amounted to nothing, and Conservatives continued to dominate provincial institutions. The coming year would demonstrate both the resilience of elite power and, once given a chance, the countervailing force of popular mobilization. But by that point, much of the promise of rebuilding would have been lost.

Back in Buenos Aires, Ferrari Hardoy and his team penned a series of letters to raise public awareness, and while they ultimately decided not to send any, the drafts offer a sharp take of where things stood one year after the quake. First of all, Ferrari Hardoy wrote, "let's put things as clearly as possible." He offered up a series of ideas for improving conditions immediately. But beyond specifics, what the government, the city, the people needed to do was create "a great communal feeling, of enterprise, of confidence—let popular inventiveness manifest itself." Ferrari Hardoy was increasingly convinced that transformation would require mobilization, as locals took ownership of the project and a more unified, effective, and decisive leadership carried it forward. He stressed that this should be the government's main priority: "The governor and the official responsible for reconstruction should be one and the same person, because in San Juan there is no other problem but reconstruction." Above all, Ferrari Hardoy wanted to underscore that rebuilding the city was not a "minor issue" for the nation but an "indispensable" test of politics, solidarity, and technical capacity. Downplaying rebuilding, overlooking the problems it had brought to light, was a sign of division and weakness. For Ferrari Hardoy, the alternatives were clear: "either we are a healthy, creative, and unified people, or San Juan will be our tombstone."[58]

Fixed Ideas: Villalobos Team, Early 1945

The official decision ended any possibility of moving the city. But it hardly resolved the underlying fight over property, which sharpened after Julio Villalobos took over design. Moreover, once Hennekens's control of Reconstruction was confirmed, he tried another tack: he told Villalobos to develop plans for rebuilding San Juan on the same site—and for founding a new provincial capital to the south.[59]

Villalobos was an "odd bird," as one magazine put it, a designer who preached the primacy of the economic.[60] In the August 1944 article on rebuilding that brought him to Hennekens's attention, he had insisted that "the architectural solution is a consequence of the economic solution" and criticized earlier plans for supposedly overemphasizing aesthetics.[61] While strongly interested in regional planning, particularly after visiting and writing about the projects of the Tennessee Valley Authority, he advocated a more circumscribed role for government.[62] In his view, "genuine planning" should aim "not to cramp individual initiative . . . but to facilitate it": government should not focus on building houses for locals but on making it possible for locals to rebuild for themselves.[63]

While Villalobos praised "individual initiative," he did envision a central—and controversial—role for government. For he was convinced that "there can be no dynamic planning worthy of the name unless the land is under public ownership," and he dedicated himself to promoting the expropriation of the entire city of San Juan.[64] Villalobos was the son of a social reformer who, convinced that private ownership of land was an "abominable—although generally unconscious—theft," had tenaciously pursued its abolition. His reform proposal was derived from the North American radical Henry George: the state would purchase all existing land at current value, and then auction off lifelong leases to work it. When a leaseholder died, his heirs would be compensated for improvements, and the land would revert to the state to be leased again. Advocates claimed this reform would end speculation, democratize access to land, and eliminate the power of landlords as a governing force in society. But they also insisted, in sharp contradiction to their overall argument, that this reform was mild and limited, and current landowners would welcome it, because they would receive market prices for their property.[65]

From his first articles on San Juan, Villalobos mocked the timidity of the proposed property swap and advocated his father's more radical ideas instead. He was convinced that once the land was under public ownership, the basic problems could be "resolved at once" by "rational physical-demographic planning" and all other difficulties would quickly "disappear" due to "the spontaneous play of the activities of society."[66]

Villalobos did do some physical planning: he explored possible locations for highways, railroad stations, and the complex of new government offices, as well as refining a superblock scheme for the city center.[67] But the heart of his proposal remained the call for public ownership, a source of endless resistance that he defended with messianic certainty. He won little support inside the agency or outside it: a year later, the local press singled him out for his particular "antipathy to all things sanjuanino."[68] Unwilling to abandon his idée fixe, and unable to advance beyond a generic vision for the city, he eventually lost even Hennekens.

Meanwhile, as Reconstruction remained silent, its critics grew bold.[69] The lack of any visible progress or even plans weighed particularly heavily on the one Reconstruction board member with broader political credibility, the labor leader Ramón Tejada. The labor federation he led had already insisted, the year before, that local workers play a major role in rebuilding.[70] Now Tejada found himself whipsawed between the dynamic advance of social reforms decreed from Buenos Aires and the mysterious standstill of rebuilding in San Juan, between the success of unions and the discredit of the agency. As the second harvest since the earthquake wound down, leaving fifteen thousand workers unemployed but nothing built, Tejada began organizing a large public demonstration.

Here was a clear indication of the morass rebuilding had sunk into: one of the five members of the Reconstruction board had to organize a mass meeting to force the agency—and its superiors—to act. Tejada was one of the few locals with access to national officials, and most workers supported rebuilding as much as they supported Perón, so the meeting went forward, spearheaded by labor but also backed by the Del Bono Commission. The wineries gave their workers the day off and provided free transportation.[71]

Yet even a vibrant demonstration on 1 April and the impending unemployment of fifteen thousand harvest workers did not produce immediate action. Berreta and Hennekens were out of town for the demonstration, recalled to Buenos Aires, and the minister who attended in their stead claimed, amazingly, that planning was complete and the building code approved, but nothing could be done because of a shortage of materials.[72] Shortly afterward, Villalobos finally resigned.[73] Hennekens was in a tight spot: fifteen months after the disaster, the city was in ruins, the political situation was souring, and he had no project for rebuilding. His few local allies could not help him, and after the misadventures so far, there were few professionals, locally or nationally, who might still trust him. But he needed a plan, and fast.

Limits of Pragmatism: Mendióroz Team, Mid-1945

The solution came from the leadership of the architectural profession. After the 1943 coup, as already seen, the ideological convictions of a few architects, and the institutional interests of many more, had led the professional leadership to ally with the military regime, gaining long-sought reforms, appointments to important posts, and government attention to such architectural priorities as planning and housing. The Catholic nationalists who led the profession were the greatest beneficiaries of this alliance, as they won several government posts and were broadly friendly to the regime's overall ideological project. Thus as the tide began to shift, in the middle of 1945, they were especially eager to shore up the regime and the profession. An architectural team led by the Catholic nationalist Carlos Mendióroz, who had held major university posts under the military and now led the planning department of the city of Buenos Aires, eagerly accepted Hennekens's call for help in May 1945.[74]

A year earlier, when Mendióroz was named dean of engineering at the University of Buenos Aires, he had praised the "gigantic effort at national recuperation" underway, which meant professionals could dedicate themselves to producing knowledge for the whole of the country, and "not for the benefit of the few and the suffering of the many." This could also shift the regional balance of power—since, as Mendióroz claimed to have learned at his previous post in Tucumán, "the country lives, thinks, and creates beyond Buenos Aires."[75]

One year after this declaration of federalist intent, Mendióroz led the team producing the most centralist scheme yet for San Juan. Produced far away and in record time, the Mendióroz plan was naturally short on detail and locally unknown: the national authorities approved it on 28 June, Hennekens announced it on 6 July, and local and national papers published a one-page summary in early August.[76] The Mendióroz scheme exemplified the contradictions of elitist nationalists. Convinced that the interior could only be redeemed by repudiating liberalism, and that liberalism could only be

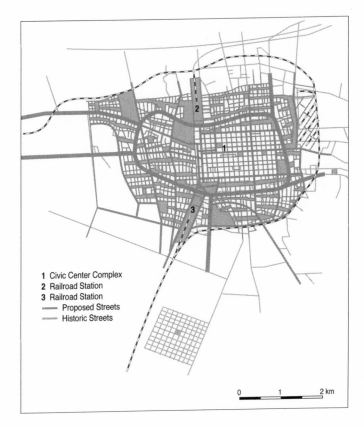

1 Civic Center Complex
2 Railroad Station
3 Railroad Station
— Proposed Streets
— Historic Streets

0   1   2 km

Mendióroz
team plan,
1946

overcome by an iron hand, Mendióroz, like other nationalists, was trapped in the structural contradiction of trying to revive the periphery through greater centralism. While they placed great rhetorical emphasis on roots, they were remarkably distant and indifferent toward the concrete experiences of local communities.

The plan aimed to pacify local elites. According to the Mendióroz team, previous schemes had failed to adjust "planning to the network of respectable economic interests so seriously affected by the seismic catastrophe." This was a time for pragmatism and respect, the architects claimed, not dogmatic utopian schemes.[77] When the team visited in May, Mendióroz recalled, "the city presented an incredible scene of moral recovery . . . hotels, theaters, cinemas, cafes, restaurants, even traffic: in short, social life as a whole had recovered an almost-normal rhythm and not even by force . . . could the people be moved away and established elsewhere."[78] Thus the team concluded that rebuilding on the same site and the same streets was the only possibility. They backed up this conclusion with all the familiar arguments of the Del Bono Commission, from the "intact" sewers to the geologists' studies. They even believed, as Hennekens declared in late May, that property owners inside the four avenues would be able to rebuild on their old lots virtually without restrictions.[79]

Instead of confronting power, the team chose to reaffirm it. Their scheme spoke of "fundamental remodeling" but broadly followed establishment demands. The architects admitted that the plan was "not as innovative as those who only admit theoretically perfect urban structures and systems might wish" but claimed that it was well adapted to local ways of life. There would be wider streets and sidewalks, lined by trees and canals, and a ring road circling the city. Within the four avenues, they abandoned superblocks or neighborhood units and focused instead on official buildings. They left most rail lines in place but moved the two stations outward.

They did make one major change within the four avenues: judging that the city was expanding westward, they proposed a new government complex on the western edge of the grid. Instead of railyards, the area would hold a new seat of government and a new cathedral beside it. A wide avenue would run four blocks east, lined by office buildings and ending at the Plaza Laprida and a new home for the legislature. The courts would rise next to Plaza Aberastain, on the east side. But only the banks and city hall would remain on the main plaza. This was an important shift: after fighting hard to preserve the world of the Plaza 25 de Mayo, elites would hardly welcome emptying the plaza of its civic and religious functions.

Outside the four avenues, the team was more ambitious, erasing existing buildings and property lines and respecting only the existing tree-lined roads into town. They planned an industrial district and workers' housing to the northeast, and new neighborhoods to the south and west. Every previous plan had proposed some kind of industrial district, but while the modernists had seen this as part of a broader program to redistribute the wine industry across the province, the Mendióroz plan simply made it a centralized cluster of wineries. The housing projects were more adventurous, proposing rows of homes along cul-de-sacs with parks woven between them.

Their boldest action was to declare four areas "not rebuildable." Two were suburbs of San Juan—Concepción to the north and Santa Lucía to the east—and two were the towns that together formed Caucete, the province's second city. For these peripheral areas, the team deployed the same arguments against rebuilding—poor soil conditions, seismic threat, chaotic street layouts, absence of parks and public space—they had rejected for the city core. Planning had to respect the wealthy and the center, but not the poor and the periphery.

The striking difference underscored the centrality of political expediency in shaping the scheme, no matter how inexpedient the scheme ultimately proved to be.

The attempt at pragmatism would fail spectacularly. Instead of placating critics, the Mendióroz scheme served to galvanize them, turning simmering resentments of Reconstruction and Perón into open protest. Part of the problem was the abstract quality of the drawings in the papers; many locals were infuriated that planning had advanced so little in so many months. The drawings made sense to planners but not to locals, and they were not accompanied by any street-level views of recognizable buildings. After all, the Mendióroz team had been working on the project for six weeks. While they would eventually produce detailed drawings and models, in August this was probably all they had.

Two aspects of the plan proved especially controversial. First, the city might be rebuilt on the same site, but the wider streets, ring road, monumental complex, new parks, and other buildings all demanded land. In the end, this more pragmatic plan still required the expropriation of nearly a quarter of the city center. Other architects would denounce the Mendióroz plan for doing too little, but locals still saw it as a threat to property.

Second, ruling whole neighborhoods "not rebuildable" alienated former residents of those neighborhoods and undermined the architects' claim to pragmatism. If the rest of the city could rebuild, why were those neighborhoods singled out? The architects may have wanted to favor the periphery in their planning, as their most ambitious work was done outside the four avenues. But they pursued this goal so clumsily that the areas which had received the most design attention, the "not rebuildable" neighborhoods, were precisely where they would face the greatest resistance.

The next chapter will take up the mobilization against Reconstruction, and against Perón, that began just as the Mendióroz plan was announced. But first, we should consider why labor reform succeeded but urban reform sputtered out in this decisive year.

Hennekens's errors compounded the inherent difficulties of overcoming entrenched power. With the fuerzas vivas holding a majority on the Council, conflict was difficult to avoid. But Hennekens made no sustained attempt to broaden representation on the Council or to cultivate the support of groups outside the fuerzas vivas. Instead, when the conflict grew too sharp, he simply shut the Council down, making it an appendage of the agency it was supposed to supervise, ensuring a permanent majority for his own ideas. Throughout, he showed remarkably little interest in mobilizing support—even his ally

Tejada had to mobilize against him, with the 1 April 1945 rally for rebuilding. The inward orientation of Reconstruction stood in sharp contrast with the outward orientation of the STP, which greatly expanded its reach and credibility in the same months. If Reconstruction had begun by improving emergency housing, as the Ferrari Hardoy team suggested, it might have gained similar legitimacy to the STP.

While Hennekens bears much of the blame, the problem went beyond his personal failings. Taking rebuilding away from the Public Works Ministry had meant removing it from the only agency with expertise in managing large-scale building projects. The interior minister at the time later admitted that "this problem has nothing to do with the Interior Ministry"; while there were "very special reasons" why the change had been made, "the ministry that should take charge is Public Works."[80] The Interior Ministry not only lacked the technical capacity to guide the process, it apparently lacked the political capacity as well, as evident in its failure to coordinate the efforts of the two local bureaucracies that reported to it, Reconstruction and the provincial administration. The Interior Ministry seemed more concerned with containing dissent than with advancing social reforms: the STP was dynamic not only because labor had higher political priority but also because it was a more effective bureaucracy better able to win and channel popular support.

In practice, weak supervision gave Hennekens free rein, but he proved clumsy in local circles and irrelevant in national ones. Above all, he failed to persuade locals of the vitality of the connection he suggested when he arrived, between building a new citizenship and building a new San Juan.

It would be easy to portray this, as local elites later did, as deliberate neglect on Perón's part, or, as some embittered architects later did, as a failure to take rebuilding seriously. It would be equally easy to assume that labor was always Perón's priority, and rebuilding a sideshow. But, as many studies have shown, the ultimate centrality of labor to Perón's coalition was not clear from the outset. It is not that labor was always destined to be the backbone of his movement but rather that it took on that role as attempts to win over other groups failed.[81] More generally, projecting later outcomes back to the origins of Peronism radically simplifies the dynamism of these years and fails to grasp how the movement changed as it consolidated.

For many months after the earthquake, as I have shown, the national government was strongly committed to building a fundamentally different future for San Juan. This meant venturing into new territory, as there was no national precedent for such a wide-ranging attempt to remake a city (or province). The competing projects, shifting priorities, and intense conflicts of the two years after the quake underscore both how deep this commitment ran and how uncertain officials were about how to fulfill it. The conflicts were not a sign of the abandonment of San Juan but rather of the sustained and even intensified attempt to transform it.[82] When this commitment later turned in a different direction, this was a product of specific defeats, not an expression of prior strategy.

Far from a narrow technical matter, rebuilding was the central challenge facing any political vision for a future San Juan. In this province, fully achieving the social reforms Perón advocated required the broader transformation of rebuilding. At the same time, and to a greater degree than government officials or the architects appreciated, the only way to produce a new city was through political mobilization and struggle. The architects' desire to insulate design from politics was understandable but misguided. To succeed, they instead had to make their plans a political cause, aligning their vision for a new San Juan with larger popular visions of a New Argentina.

PROTEST AND THE PROFESSIONS IN 1945

In January 1945, one year after the disaster, a striking publication appeared in Argentina: a short book titled *The Other Earthquake*. Printed abroad to avoid censorship, the book argued that the military had not redeemed San Juan but destroyed it, falling upon the city like a second temblor. Drawing on detailed accounts from local property owners, the seventy-page book portrayed the relief effort as a gigantic fraud, with victims abandoned to their fate while the military pocketed contributions and plundered valuables from the wreckage. If the donations for San Juan were a "measure of our national solidarity," their misappropriation was a measure of military malevolence. The regime had torn apart a basically functional society, the book claimed, trampling on the rights of all—and especially of the propertied.[1]

The book was notable for its direct attack on the military and forceful defense of the fuerzas vivas. In this account, the current state of the city was entirely due to the military government. Nothing about San Juan needed to be rethought: once the "Nazi-fascist" Perón was thrown out, rebuilding would be simple and swift. Instead of seeing the ruins as the starting point for a broader transformation, the book used them to justify a return to the status quo ante.

Remarkably enough, this fierce defense of the mistreated bodegueros of San Juan was written by the leaders of the Argentine Communist Party. This was the party's first publication in 1945, as well as the first attempt on the national stage to use San Juan against Perón. Drawing on the liberal tradition, it portrayed the military as a barbarous horde, throwbacks to Rosas, and local elites as the proper heirs of Sarmiento.[2] In aligning Communists with the liberal tradition, it also aligned them with the fuerzas vivas, in order to roll back social reforms and drive the military out. The left's decision to defend the powerful and oppose social transformation would ultimately prove devastating and open up important space for Perón. But it was not so surprising, given the wartime strategy of broad alliances against fascism and the widespread conviction that this was a "Nazi-fascist" regime. *The Other Earthquake* set out the rhetorical and political strategies that most of the opposition to Perón would adopt over the year.

Frustration over rebuilding was central to the emergence of a political opposition in San Juan in 1945, led by engineers and leftists. The local opposition built its critique of military rule around a defense of propertied interests and a rejection of planning, an argument with visceral appeal but striking ideological narrowness. San Juan resonated deeply at a national level, and was crucial to driving engineers and architects into the opposition, although their shared frustration with military rule led to opposite conclusions about the course rebuilding should take.

In broad terms, local politics followed the pattern familiar from national studies: the emergence of an opposition invoking liberal heroes and based in the middle and upper classes, the faltering response of the military government, the apparent triumph of the opposition—followed, as the next chapter shows, by the countermobilization of labor and nationalist groups that led to Perón's victory in open elections and created an enduring political divide.

But San Juan is not simply another local example of an already understood national phenomenon. It was a testing ground for the New Argentina. It was where the ambitions of modernist architects to build the New Argentina were first tried and rejected by a local opposition led by their professional rivals in engineering. This devastated province was a decisive site for defining how the military, on the one hand, and the opposition, on the other, proposed to transform the nation. Since the issue in San Juan was precisely how the province would relate to the nation, whether local changes could model national changes, it was a particularly important theater for these struggles over the future of the nation.

An Insurgency of Engineers

By June 1945, after a year under the Reconstruction Council, locals had lost patience with its mysterious plans and slow progress. The papers were openly mocking Reconstruction, wondering what its two hundred employees could possibly be doing, and even—remarkably—longing for the return of the MOP, which at least got things done.[3] A commemoration of the hundredth anniversary of Sarmiento's *Facundo* sparked a series of barely veiled attacks on military rule. "When we contemplate these beloved ruins of San Juan," one left-leaning teacher declared, "suddenly Sarmiento appears before us," dressed for work and holding a mason's trowel, "a guerrilla warrior for civilization" and a "tireless builder" calling others to tear down tyranny and raise up houses.[4] As national business and civic groups turned against the government, with the "Manifesto of the Fuerzas Vivas" decrying labor reforms and the national engineering association (the CAI) calling for a freeze on public works, the local engineers decided to make the confrontation explicit.

On 1 July, the San Juan Center of Engineers issued a sharp statement that forged diffuse complaints into a coherent protest movement. Within a month, the national leaders of the CAI would go even further, making San Juan their central exhibit against military rule. But the San Juan engineers started more modestly. "No technical reason" could justify the delay in rebuilding, the engineers claimed. It could only be explained by "inadequate leadership and ineffective planning." Hennekens had failed across the board. By banning property sales, he had violated "constitutional guarantees" and kept the province in limbo. By dissolving the Council, he had "disconnected" his agency from the community it served. By being dishonest with locals, he had squandered their trust. And by firing two teams of architects, then hiring a third on an impossible timetable, he had guaranteed failure. After this performance, the engineers argued, it was time for a new approach and a new leader—who should be a civilian, and an engineer.[5]

The statement was written by Remberto Baca and Alberto Costantini, the president and secretary of the local engineering association. Baca was a patrician Socialist with several works to his credit, most notably the completion of the state rail line to Jáchal. A critic of planning, he had personally scrapped the Guido-Carrasco plan when he served as provincial minister of public works, during the short-lived liberal intervention after the 1943 coup. Costantini was an ambitious young outsider. He came to San Juan with the national road department in 1940, a new graduate of the University of La Plata, and then rose swiftly, winning appointments as a university professor, director of the provincial road department, and then dean of the engineering faculty, while becoming a faithful Graffigna ally.[6]

The engineers simply invoked their prestige and dismissed Hennekens as incompetent. They did not enter into specifics about rebuilding. They were not interested in comparing particular schemes but in judging them all to be extravagant failures. Their aim was to gain control of rebuilding and lift all constraints on property—while ensuring generous national funding. The local associations of lawyers, auctioneers, and notaries immediately echoed their call to remove property restrictions.[7] This was only just, the Graffigna paper argued, for though property owners had been the "most harmed by the cataclysm," they "had not received even a little aid"—even as many others "benefited without having lost anything."[8] As this assertion highlighted, the opposition resented not only government inaction on rebuilding but also government action on social policy. The campaign was launched, and the newspapers soon filled with declarations of support from the usual suspects— as well as a few new allies, like the Communist-led construction workers union.[9]

Hennekens reacted as clumsily as ever. First, he challenged Baca to a duel. The timely intervention of others prevented any bloodshed, but the challenge made Baca the moral leader of the opposition.[10] Second, Hennekens declared that the debate was over, as the national authorities had already approved the Mendióroz plan and would begin work immediately. But when Hennekens actually presented the major ideas in the plan, he met stiff resistance. This was due partly to the rushed, secretive, and distant origins of the plan. But it was also a response to its specifics. The plan's ruling that four neighborhoods were "not rebuildable" prompted anger and also puzzlement from the communities slated for abandonment. After all, if Reconstruction officials believed that geology did not justify moving the city as a whole, why would it justify moving these neighborhoods?[11]

Baca quickly built the engineers' revolt into a broader movement, conven- ing a meeting of forty-two groups on 15 July. "Until now, we have left the full solution of our problem to officials who do not know our world," he began. Although "we are still smothered by the dust of our homes and saddened by the persistence of rubble," he argued, "we are a sovereign people" and must reassert "our natural dominion." Instead of being "humiliated by the cluster of ranchos that grows denser and more uncivilized every day," he argued, san- juaninos should take charge and rebuild a city that would again "radiate civilization."[12]

While Baca aimed to keep the focus on rebuilding, debate quickly spiraled outward from the stalled effort to those the crowd held responsible, the makers of false promises, Farrell and Perón. Soon, the group passed motions in favor of the locals who had resigned from the Reconstruction Council, students recently arrested for pamphleteering, and—remarkably—even the architects fired six months earlier. They formed a Popular Assembly for Re- construction to organize a large public demonstration. This Popular Assem- bly then voted to elect Baca as their leader, to exclude anyone who had "collaborated" with the government, and to demand an immediate start to rebuilding—and an immediate return to constitutional rule.[13]

In leadership and tactics, the Popular Assembly marked a shift from the Del Bono Commission of the year before. While the Del Bono Commission cloaked itself in tradition, aligned with the Church, and chose its members among Conservative bodegueros, the Popular Assembly invoked the liberal Sarmiento, kept its distance from religion, and elected its leaders from Socialist engineers and doctors. There were important continuities, as the new group also took a narrow view of rebuilding and included a few figures from the old, notably the engineer and Graffigna ally Francisco Bustelo. But the new group took a more confrontational stance—organizing a mass demonstration, not private lobbying—and cultivated ties with the national opposition.

It also posed a potential threat to established political powers. After decades on the margins of local politics, Socialists and Radicals saw the chance to lead a popular cause and perhaps overcome the dominance of Conservatives and Cantonistas. The bodegueros thus viewed the Popular Assembly with sympathy, but also some alarm. The Maurín Conservatives, already distanced from the military, praised the movement. Even the Graffigna Conservatives, still entrenched in the provincial administration, began to distance themselves from military leaders. Clearly, the shared contempt for Reconstruction could overcome most rivalries, at least temporarily.[14] But not all rivalries: the Popular Assembly made no overtures to the Cantonistas, and for now, neither did the military.

Labor on the Defensive

Of course, the military regime itself, and especially its labor supporters, were threatened the most by the Popular Assembly. However hard Tejada had pushed for rebuilding, he was so closely tied to Hennekens, and to Perón, that the opposition could easily tar him as another meddling fool who deserved to be sacked, if not imprisoned. It was also clear that the opposition was coming after the labor reforms. The local Socialists had denounced the STP as unconstitutional, and its reforms as unnecessary.[15] Shortly after the engineers issued their statement, the Socialist Party expelled Tejada and his allies.[16] The night Baca formed the Popular Assembly, Tejada's labor confederation held an emergency meeting and voted to demand rebuilding, with priority for workers' housing. The labor confederation then flooded the city with pamphlets denouncing the Popular Assembly as a plot of "displaced politicians and ambitious capitalists."[17]

But Tejada knew that a stronger response was required, and a week later he took a labor delegation to Buenos Aires. Joined by the two top officials of the CGT, the national trade union confederation, they met for two days with President Farrell, Vice President Perón, Interior Minister Teisaire, Reconstruction President Hennekens, and Interventor Berreta. For all that the delegation praised the "wise and just social policies initiated by the STP," their report to the authorities painted a "somber" picture, with "most if not all workers" living in misery, often lacking shelter and work. Labor claimed that, so far, most aid had gone to merchants, bodegueros, and the well-connected. From this point forward, workers should receive more aid and have a greater say in the agencies distributing it. "Those barrios built out of the solidarity of the people of the Republic," the labor delegation lamented, "have not managed to rebuild the lives undone by the earthquake" or "produce the healthy recovery of morale" they initially promised. With planning complete, it was time to "free San Juan from its anguish" and begin rebuilding, in order to "provide a home to each family" and employment for all.[18]

This time, government response was swift. President Farrell released five million pesos for immediate rebuilding, and directed that the remaining thirty million pesos of the collection be spent on grants and scholarships for victims and two thousand more emergency homes.[19] He dismissed Hennekens within a week, and Beretta soon afterward. Perón, who met with the delegation first, was obviously the decision maker here, and he had finally decided to go on the offensive, with the consequences we will see in the next chapter. This was part of a broad shift, as the military government lifted the state of siege, legalized the Communist Party, promised elections, and handed two crucial ministries, interior and foreign relations, over to civilian politicians.

The labor delegation's trip to Buenos Aires made several things clear. First, labor was now the backbone of Perón's support and had assumed a far larger role in local politics than before. Fifteen months earlier, it was bodegueros who spoke for the province; now it was railroad workers and barrel-makers. Government action showed labor's power: the delegation was welcomed home by a boisterous crowd, and the CGT leadership trumpeted their own role in advancing rebuilding.

But labor was also in a treacherous position, as the overall tone and specifics of their report to the authorities showed. They could not deny that the city was still in ruins, the aid collection largely unspent, and emergency barrios a decidedly mixed blessing. The promise of a more just and robust new city was undercut by the persistence of the rubble. In short, they were vulnerable to the same attacks as Perón. And indeed, the local opposition immediately objected to the new approach for spending the collection and the deference given to Tejada, "who is very far from representing a significant value in the life in San Juan."[20]

Arriba San Juan

From the beginning, the Popular Assembly had demanded immediate re-building and immediate return to constitutional rule. They had also called for lifting all restrictions on property. In a statement before the August rally, the Popular Assembly insisted again on a minimal plan for rebuilding, extensive consultations of locals, improvements to emergency shelter, and freedom for owners to dispose of their property as they pleased. The aid collection should be spent "as donors intended," not on scholarships or aid for the poor, as the government proposed. Overall, this was the bodeguero program presented as a popular cause.[21]

The Socialists introduced one deviation from orthodoxy: a call for the government to provide a "single family home" for everyone living in San Juan when the earthquake struck, "whether or not they owned property." The opposition was proposing rebuilding for all and, even more remarkably, challenging landlord power—since the goal was a "*single* family home" for everyone. But there was little behind the call to back it up, as the houses were to be financed with mortgages issued according to "possible future earnings," and low earnings were precisely why most sanjuaninos did not own property already. Equity and inclusion remained minor concerns. The protest was about propertied citizens reclaiming their rights and repudiating a dictatorship.

The rally was on 8 August 1945, the first of a flurry of national protests. Carefully planned, the demonstration featured a broad selection of speakers, professionally printed banners, and even its own song, "Arriba San Juan," by the *Tribuna* journalist and poet Luis Bates. Aware of the emerging class divide, the organizers made a special effort to attract workers—and isolate Tejada—as the Chamber of Commerce urged private employers to close down for the day but pay their workers.[22] Over fifteen thousand people filled Plaza Laprida, the largest public assembly in San Juan in a decade, rivaled only by Perón's visit eleven months earlier.[23]

"Whatever credos separate us in the field of national politics, we are united" by our common local problem, Baca said at the outset. The speakers were drawn from a broad array of groups: there were engineers, lawyers, and businessmen, but also representatives from student, worker, and women's groups, from two "non-rebuildable" areas, and even from the Communist Party. The only ones missing from the podium were bodegueros, discreetly present in the crowd, and Cantonistas.²⁴ It did seem like a unifying moment, and several speakers remarked on this "strange and wondrous coincidence of all."²⁵

The Popular Assembly's demands were clear enough, and while a few speakers insisted only on the need for "immediate rebuilding," many more moved quickly from denouncing the ruins to denouncing the government, with loud support from the crowd.²⁶ The official banners featured anodyne demands, such as "San Juan Deserves Immediate Reconstruction," but the crowd shouted more forceful ones: "Reconstruction not promises!" and "Houses not tents!" There were also a few hand-printed banners, ranging from an ironic quote of Perón—"Deeds not words; achievements not promises"—to a direct repudiation of the military: "Workers from the 4 June Barrio: We want a change of name and a change of life."²⁷

Speakers attacked every aspect of the government. "This is a technical problem, yes, but above all it is a social and institutional problem," argued Benito Marianetti, the Mendoza Communist leader, and "the reconstruction of San Juan is not independent of the institutional reconstruction of the country." The growing popular movement against those who "suppressed liberties . . . annulled the constitution . . . misappropriated the collection . . . and sent our fellow citizens to prison" would soon bring the republic back under law and "plant a poster on the ruins of the dictatorship with the words: non-rebuildable zone."²⁸

Criticism of the government focused especially on labor, Reconstruction, and housing. The head of the Chamber of Commerce, for example, declared that Perón's social reform "cannot be implemented, is not just, and means enormous economic upheavals for the province," while the speaker representing "authentic" workers, the Communist organizer Miguel Barzola, drew particular applause when he mocked the "confused anticapitalism of the little traitor Tejada."²⁹ In short, these measures deceived workers and subverted proper order.

The brief against Reconstruction was familiar: the plans were unnecessary, unwanted, and unaffordable. The government should put an end to experiments, scrap the plans, and let property owners rebuild as they wished. There was little attention to the specifics of any plan, just a blanket dismissal of them all. "We cannot accept unachievable fantasies," one speaker declared, citing fiscal limitations. Before the quake, the total provincial debt had been ten million pesos, so Hennekens's talk of investing four hundred million pesos caused some unease, especially when he suggested the government might eventually recover three-quarters of it. The local press had concluded that this would require plundering "the patrimony of the province of San Juan, buying its lands at 10 pesos to resell them at 1,000."[30]

"We don't ask for gigantic or marvelous works of modern architecture," declared Juana Rodríguez de Marchessi, speaking on behalf of local women, "we want our modest provincial city, simple, decent, and clean." She rejected the rule of outsiders and insisted on the importance of local efforts under local leadership. "We want to raise up again the fortresses that were our homes and work there, in the disciplines of order, cleanliness, and economy," she declared, to lay the "moral foundations" of the city to come, with "hygiene and decency."[31]

Rodríguez de Marchessi also suggested why housing was such a visceral matter: most sanjuaninos still felt uprooted, having lost their loved ones, their physical home, and perhaps their sense of moral grounding. Restoring this order was clearly crucial. And the greatest daily affronts to it were the "denigrating spread" of improvised shacks and the "moral decline" of emergency barrios.

There was the "cluster of ranchos that grows denser and more uncivilized every day," as Baca had put it, a stark indication of the limits of government action. Indeed, the Conservative papers had picked up on this before the protest, printing pictures of the "lovely emergency mansion" of a Reconstruction employee alongside images of popular "ranchos and tents" in "the worst hygienic conditions." The contrast was clear—luxury for Reconstruction, nothing for the people—and did much to undermine the government.[32]

But the true lightning rod for criticism was the large emergency barrios. The opposition did not criticize, or even mention, the other two kinds of emergency shelter: the wooden structures given to individual property owners and the "workers' housing" projects taken over by the elite. Instead, they concentrated on the large barrios assigned mostly—but not at all exclusively—to those of "modest means." The barrios were appalling to elites, as seen in the last chapter, because they were forced to confront how the poor majority lived, and because that majority indeed lived poorly, but also because that majority was, in limited but important ways, beginning to organize and mobilize in those barrios in ways the elite found threatening.

Everyone from Socialist doctors to Catholic Action leaders responded to the three dimensions of the challenge with dark talk of "moral decline" in the barrios.[33] They recommended not only better housing but also forceful instruction, to "strengthen the natural moral knowledge of sociability and mutual respect" that the poor supposedly lacked.[34]

After the disaster, the Socialist doctor Adán Marún claimed, "The government competed with the earthquake . . . to see which could destroy the most." He asked his audience to take an imaginative flight alongside the spirit of Guillermo Rawson, the nineteenth-century sanjuanino doctor who founded public health and campaigned for better housing, into the depths of the emergency barrios. What they would find there was an affront to human dignity, "fetid pigsties where the germs of the most terrible diseases are cultivated and thrive." Marún, head of obstetrics at the provincial hospital, claimed infant mortality had nearly doubled since the quake—and it had been very high before. He argued that the military wanted to reduce the province to submission. The issue at stake was simple: the right of sanjuaninos to determine their own future. The authorities must know, he declared, that "we are not tenants on our own land!"[35]

What did the protestors want for San Juan? Above all, they wanted an end to experiments: the government should shelve its plan and allow property owners to rebuild immediately. Rooted in the perspective of the powerful, this rhetoric of simplicity ignored the challenges of rebuilding and obscured the persistent structures of domination that had made the quake so deadly in the first place.

In many ways, Adán Marún's eloquent harangue was emblematic of the establishment view. The delays and failures he outlined were all too real. Yet the responsibility for them extended far beyond the present military regime. Marún spoke as an outraged property owner; that was what gave his declaration that "we are not tenants on our own land" its force. But this could hardly have the same power for most locals, who had never been anything but tenants.

The imaginative flight Marún had proposed was revealing: to understand the province, citizens had to assume the viewpoint of a liberal statesman and observe the city and the barrios from above. While there undoubtedly were residents of the large barrios at the protest, as the banners prove, photographs and newspaper accounts also suggest that most were from the upper and middle classes and viewed emergency housing largely from the outside.

For all its failings, emergency housing did not charge rent, a vast improvement for most locals. The problems with emergency housing were the product of not only government errors but also the continuing effects of the earthquake and, most importantly, the larger structures of power in the province. Even as Marún denounced health conditions after the quake, he admitted in passing how terrible they were before. Indeed, official statistics placed infant mortality at 162 per 1,000, the second-highest in the nation.[36] Yet Marún spoke as if this long-standing disaster had little to do with him, head of obstetrics at the main hospital, or his Socialist peers in the leadership of the Medical Association, who for two decades had been fierce opponents of Cantoni and willing junior partners to every Conservative government.[37]

The Conservative press mocked the "mansions" for Reconstruction employees, comparing them to the "ranchos and tents" of the poor. But they never drew the more obvious contrast, between those "ranchos and tents" and the "workers' housing" seized by the wealthy. Here was another example of how attacks on Reconstruction, however justified, served to obscure the workings of privilege.

The Refusal of Vision

The protest closed with words from Baca and a procession to the foot of the province's most important statue, where thousands shouted "Sarmiento Yes! Rosas No!" One remarkable feature of the political mobilization of 1945 was that the key leaders on both sides—Baca and Tejada—were Socialists. Both were opposed to Cantoni and suspicious of Conservatives. But particularly for Baca, the attempt to chart a new path for the future led inexorably to embracing much of the past.

At the very moment when the European parties they admired were demanding planning and reform, the local Socialists made an absolute virtue of property rights. Four days after the August demonstration, sixty opposition leaders gathered to celebrate the victory of the Labor Party in Great Britain. They were unconcerned that the state planning they so forcefully rejected in San Juan was the basis of the Labor triumph in Europe they praised.[38] By this point, there were no substantive differences between a Socialist or a Conservative vision for the future. All the Socialists were fighting for was the chance to lead the restoration of the province they had known. But that chance would prove fleeting.

After the August protest, the Conservatives once more became the dominant voices on how to rebuild. One measure of their sincerity had come shortly before the protest, when Reconstruction finally issued a building code. Since the quake, Conservatives had been insisting that a move was unnecessary and soil conditions were irrelevant, because all that rebuilding required was an effective building code and concrete construction. When the code was issued, the Graffigna Conservatives praised it not only for requiring concrete but also for recognizing "the fundamental importance of the subsoil" to stable buildings—the very thing they had strenuously denied for a year.[39] The Maurín Conservatives had also advocated concrete as the alternative to the move—

but now that the move was dead, they rejected both concrete and a building code as excessive.[40]

The Graffigna Conservatives defended the idea of planning but opposed every plan proposed since the quake. There were a few elements of the Mendióroz plan they found worthy of praise—not surprisingly, those derived from the old Guido-Carrasco plan. The fact that even now they judged proposals on how closely they matched a vision produced before the earthquake shows how narrow their thinking remained. And indeed, their endless mockery of "dreams" left quite clear how little change they were willing to contemplate.

The Maurín Conservatives were more straightforward: they rejected all planning and insisted the government need only "set the line."[41] Just before the rally, they published their vision for the future city: a spare map of downtown showing the three existing plazas, five proposed new ones, and nothing else. Around the edge of the map, the editors provided an exhaustive registry of the varying widths recommended for each street: expand General Acha along one side only, leave Salta alone, expand all of Tucumán to the width of the block between Mitre and Santa Fé, and so on. As for the plazas, the paper claimed, in tortured prose, to follow "other modern cities . . . where scholars, after detailed scientific studies, have reached conclusions that produced the result of making evident the need to create small parks and plazas in the very heart of cities." The five new plazas were sited according to symmetry: since there was an existing plaza three blocks west and two blocks north of the center, there should be a new plaza three blocks west but two blocks south. There was no justification for the symmetry or why property owners on those particular blocks—otherwise so strenuously defended by the press—should lose their homes.[42] And the drawing ended at the four avenues; nothing outside them was of concern.

Yet even if the demands of the urban periphery were largely ignored by the bodegueros, they too were important in the August protest. Each of the areas ruled "not rebuildable"—the neighborhoods of Santa Lucía and Concepción in the capital and Villa Independencia and Villa Colón in Caucete—insisted that their soil was stable and proper construction techniques would ensure safe rebuilding. They pointed out contradictions in the Mendióroz plan: if Santa Lucía was so dangerous, community leaders asked, why was workers' housing adjacent to the "not rebuildable" area? Residents of Concepción, for their part, opposed the planned concentration of government buildings downtown, arguing that many could be built cheaply in their neighborhood, on property donated by community members.[43] Perhaps their communities were poorly laid out and built, Caucete leaders recognized, but this was because public authorities had failed to drain the waterlogged land. Indeed, they had failed to deliver on the projects promised after a smaller earthquake in 1941, which were all the more urgent now. Caucete's problems were not due to geology, leaders insisted, but to politics—and the solution was public works.[44]

Since the entire future of their communities was at stake, these protests drew broad support—one gathered the signatures of more than half of local residents. But while they astutely critiqued the proposal for their community, they failed to tie those critiques into an overall vision for the province. As the Caucete leaders suggested, it was precisely their marginality that made them vulnerable in the first place. And this critique of the concentration of power in the province—a demand for planning—was never taken up by the Popular Assembly.

For all the insistence on local knowledge, not one speaker made any specific proposal for how to rebuild the city. In part, this was because it was unnecessary: the entire rally was premised on restoration, and even those who might entertain more radical aims, like the Socialists and Communists, had renounced any particular ideas for the city. Down the line, however, this refusal of vision would haunt the opposition—and to the degree they won the symbolic battle, it would haunt the province as a whole.

"San Juan has chosen a path it will never abandon," the Maurín Conservatives enthused afterward, and the only way forward is to "elaborate new plans, adapted to the economic reality of our province."[45] All the national papers published favorable editorials and letters of support arrived from businessmen across the country: bakery owners in Córdoba, shopkeepers in Santiago del Estero, and chambers of commerce across the province of Buenos Aires.[46]

But there were at least three possible paths after the demonstration: to accept the Mendióroz plan but push harder for immediate rebuilding; to reject the Mendióroz plan and demand swift execution of a radically scaled-back plan; or to defer rebuilding and instead push for restoration of constitutional rule. Given the level of resistance to the Mendióroz plan and the apparent fragility of the national government, many in the Popular Assembly claimed to back the second option but really wagered on the third. As the next chapter will show, the government tried to retake the initiative by starting construction on the Mendióroz plan. But the opposition was not interested.

Instead, the opposition built on this successful protest to launch a political challenge. The August demonstration to demand rebuilding led directly to a September rally to demand constitutional rule. The rally was opened and closed by Popular Assembly leaders, with speakers from every party except the

Bloquistas.[47] The Communist labor leader Barzola denounced emergency housing as "immense concentration camps" and emphasized that "our local problem is part and consequence of the great institutional problem facing the Nation as a whole." Remarkably enough, he even brought up the expulsion of three designers from the province in 1944 to prove the regime's authoritarian intent. Nonetheless, the opposition imagined that all that was necessary was to "set the line"; opposition leaders made the "three engineers" into symbols but ignored their actual proposals—and profession.[48]

Others were even more aggressive. That same week, a Communist-led committee in Trinidad launched a blistering attack on regime leaders: "What should we thank these gentlemen for? The dispersion of families . . . unemployment, miserable shacks, the unhealthy concentration camps of the emergency projects, promiscuity, disease, moral regression . . . We do not thank them, we repudiate them: we repudiate and denounce those who became our enemies and treated us like an occupied people . . . traitorous elements like Tejada and . . . the Colonel who would be President."[49]

The declaration was notable more for its fury than its analysis: for activists on both sides, reconstruction was becoming far more useful as a political symbol in a national struggle than as a site from which to rethink local politics. As the opposition seemed about to drive the military from power, the earthquake as political symbol had almost entirely displaced any consideration of the problems the earthquake had revealed. This was especially evident within San Juan, but it also was becoming clear to the professionals who had staked so much on rebuilding.

Professional Identity and Political Commitment:
Engineers and Architects

The political tumult of late 1945 extended into professional spheres. While the positions engineers and architects took toward the regime were shaped by many factors, debate within both professions returned obsessively to the question of San Juan. The CAI leadership even sent a delegation of prominent engineers to the August protest. This closing section of the chapter will trace the different ways the two professions faced the impasse of reconstruction and the rise of protest.

Architects and engineers had responded differently to the military regime when it was ascendant and took contrasting stances as it fell apart. For engineers, professional opposition to regime plans for rebuilding led directly to political opposition to the regime itself. Starting in July 1945, the notables of the profession became leaders of the opposition, in San Juan and nationally. From their standpoint, defending the profession required opposing the government.[50]

But for architects, political commitments and professional interests were cross-cutting rather than mutually reinforcing. Architects, like engineers, came from a social world that in 1945 turned overwhelmingly against the government. Yet in professional terms, many government actions that seemed threatening to engineers seemed promising to architects. If engineers saw military rule as subverting their authority, architects could point to inspiring, if incomplete, triumphs. The military had strengthened their legal position, named their colleagues to leading posts, and aggressively pursued the policies they advocated, especially in housing and planning. Architects were hardly ready to discard these achievements. San Juan was the clearest example: most architects had supported a bold approach to rebuilding. In 1945, the engineers complained that the military had gone too far. Most architects objected that it had not gone far enough. Thus even when rank-and-file architects did turn against the government, their opposition came later and was more conflicted.

In July 1945, the CAI dedicated the entire issue of its journal to a critique of military rule, with the rebuilding of San Juan the centerpiece.[51] Rejecting the military's "all absorbing statism," the CAI called for "greater freedom" for the private sector and an immediate halt to all public works.[52] They wanted everything back in its proper place: workers disciplined and obedient; military officers removed from positions where they had shown such "contempt for our personal and professional dignity"; and engineers restored to the leadership of universities and government agencies.

San Juan was the main exhibit in this far-ranging critique. For the CAI report authors, the "evident misjudgment," clumsy restrictions, and "incomprehensible slowness" of rebuilding exemplified "the reigning abnormality" of military rule. The crucial error had been the idea of moving the city, "the principal source of the vacillations that caused such pernicious delay." It had been compounded by secrecy: the public had no way to evaluate what had been done, what it had cost, or why it had taken so long.[53]

The engineers called for open debate but did little to promote it. They stressed the arbitrariness of official actions, not the vitality of competing visions for the future of the city. There was no need to rethink the city; only to put proper professionals in charge. The CAI tersely reviewed the architectural teams so far, ignoring their specific proposals but stressing their isolation from the public. As for the Mendióroz plan that had sparked the protest, the engineers noted simply that there had been insufficient time for the "maturing" of such a complex project.[54] By sidestepping the struggles over planning and property, the engineers hoped to relegate architectural concerns to backstage.

The CAI defended the minimal solution: the government should remove all restrictions and get out of the way. Rebuilding should begin with the propertied. There was only one discordant note, when they acknowledged in passing that part of the delay was due to private interests who "fought with partiality and excess" for advantage. This was the sole hint of any possible flaws in a rebuilding strategy based on a defense of the propertied.[55] According to the engineers, the state's proper role was to ensure the availability of labor and materials and "to *rationally* regulate salaries and prices"—by which they meant keeping salaries low and letting prices rise. Private construction mattered most, and official projects could wait. Indeed, the engineers set out their priorities in revealing order: first private housing, then urgent public buildings like hospitals, later government offices, and finally the least important constructions, rental housing and churches.[56] The list reflected their overall vision: it made no mention of productive infrastructure like dams, assigned low priority to government buildings, and, after two years of the noisy imposition of integralist Catholicism, left churches for last.

The engineers saw rebuilding as simply a matter of restoring the rights of homeowners, who would do the rebuilding themselves. Of course, since only a third of the population of San Juan owned their homes, framing the issue this way meant giving priority to a powerful minority. The CAI argued that collection funds should go to the propertied few, who had lost more, rather than to the propertyless majority, who had less to lose.[57] The engineers did implicitly recognize there were other considerations beyond property rights, since they wanted to prioritize "family homes" over rental properties, but they did not discuss what those considerations might be. And even if they placed "family homes" over rentals in order to penalize speculative capital, that stance meant that rentals—the housing the majority most needed—received the lowest priority in their scheme.

In Buenos Aires, the engineers moved firmly into the opposition, with the CAI president playing a leading role in political organizing, and professional publications peppered with calls for engineers to reassert their authority and "take decisive action" in national politics.[58] Professional identity led directly to political commitment.

The institutional leaders of architecture took a different course. In June 1945, when the CAI president asked the SCA board to join a declaration against military rule, the architects insisted on their "invariable position of absolute neutrality with regard to the political panorama."[59] Privately, the leading architects were divided: most were pragmatists with little interest in the military agenda but healthy appreciation of its institutional benefits, but a powerful minority, mostly Catholic and nationalist activists, were enthusiastic supporters. Several of the latter had served in official posts and implemented some of the policies, particularly in the universities, that had sparked protest. Reluctant to turn on the government, the leadership opted instead for the deliberately "apolitical" line and resisted the calls from members, at every meeting from June onward, to support a return to constitutional rule. In an increasingly polarized context, the government read neutrality as tacit support and months later rewarded the SCA with a subsidy for a new headquarters building.

However strong their support for planning, architects could hardly be encouraged by the course it had taken so far in San Juan. Thus, as the political control of the regime began to slip, architects focused their energies on the critique of rebuilding. Whereas engineers tried to shut down debate, dismiss alternative approaches, and pin all blame on the government, architects attempted to open up debate and more fully explain their thinking.

Consider José Pastor, the young editor of the professional journal. Two years earlier, he had penned dozens of editorials advocating rebuilding on a new site. Now he withdrew from the daily controversy to write two books: one on San Juan and the other on planning more generally. "The better we understand the problems San Juan has raised," he maintained, "the better we will be prepared to face our principal objective of planning the country."[60] For Pastor, San Juan had made clear that the country lacked the capability—in terms of expertise, law, or institutions—to plan a properly modern future.

Because he viewed planning as a matter of technical expertise, never a question of politics, Pastor was far more interested in building this technical capability than in supporting or opposing the military regime. He saw the challenge as overcoming "social and economic chaos" and attributed this "chaos" to an absence of foresight rather than the interplay of conflicting interests.[61] Planners would be successful, in his favorite analogy, if they took care of the public good the way enlightened landowners take care of their private land. Pastor viewed planning not as building a collective project out of divergent interests but instead as gathering the information necessary for architects to fashion the collective project themselves. He called the public willingness to accept expert visions "popular consciousness of planning," and he had found it lacking in San Juan—which meant "Argentine public opinion" was as responsible for the current morass as the military regime, property owners, or architects.[62] Pastor thought the path to greater "popular conscious-ness of planning" was not debate or mobilization but simply education by experts.[63] At the moment, the only way to advance such ideas was publicity in the press.

Beginning in June 1945, architects published a flurry of articles in the technical press and a few key pieces in mass-market publications, laying out the virtues and flaws of each plan with polemical zeal. This was the first time the broader public could examine the various plans in detail. Just as the citizens of San Juan were challenging the official project, and citizens nationwide were taking note of their frustration, the leading experts were making their case to the public. This burst of publications was partly due to Pastor, who opened the professional journal to projects, critiques, and exchanges of letters which turned quite bitter. There certainly had been professional controversies before, but never so openly expressed in the professional publication.

The other motor behind this was Fermín Bereterbide, who first convinced his team to publish its project and then launched a crusade against the Men-dióroz plan, advocating a new site and a property swap as the basis of any proper rebuilding. Since being dismissed, Bereterbide had insisted on the need for more "controversies" to counter the "very undemocratic way things are being done" and ensure that the new city was "a popular creation everyone participates in."[64] Privately, he tried to recruit Ferrari Hardoy, Sacriste, and others to the cause, but while they agreed with much of what he said, they declined to join him.[65] The outcome instead was a cross fire between Bereter-bide and Mendióroz, with occasional contributions from Sacriste and even Villalobos, who revived his insistence on the wondrous effects of government ownership of land.[66]

The technical debate intensified as the regime crumbled. In September, architects began circulating a petition supporting a return to constitutional rule. When the public works minister Pistarini learned that four architects working for him had signed, he fired them immediately. The SCA responded timidly, using the fact that Pistarini was an honorary member to treat this as an internal dispute rather than a question of professional dignity. This inter-pretation did not persuade the four Pistarini had fired or the thirty-five still working for him. Since one of those fired, Carlos Muzio, had worked on San Juan, discussion at a boisterous members' meeting soon turned to the gov-ernment's mishandling of rebuilding, and even the dismissal of the Ferrari Hardoy team months before. The board quickly shut this down and requested only that Pistarini reconsider his actions.

By contrast, the CAI had reacted sharply when Pistarini's second-in-command had fired three engineers in July, calling a mass meeting attended by seven hundred members and successfully demanding the immediate reinstatement of those dismissed. While the architects received little support from their own association, the CAI president (and former MOP architecture head) had their statement published in the press.[67]

On 13 September 1945, a week before the opposition March for the Constitution and Liberty, the architects published their petition, signed by nearly four hundred, a sizable majority of Buenos Aires professionals.[68] They signed as private citizens, not members of their professional association, as they underscored in a follow-up statement defending freedom of opinion among civil servants, asserting that "no architect would accept the posts left empty" by the firings and pointedly thanking the CAI—not the SCA—for support.[69]

Shortly afterward, almost three-quarters of the signatories formed the Agrupación de Arquitectos Democráticos (AAD). The group had a different critique of state action than the engineers: they were disturbed not by the fact of state intervention but by the clumsy course it was taking. Unlike the engineers, few architects were given to far-ranging attacks on "all encroaching statism."[70] Instead, the AAD implored colleagues to be more than "a mere 'Architect' and take an active role in shaping the future Argentina" precisely in order to do planning properly. First "the Colonel" must be defeated, "then we can take care of popular housing, urbanism and planning."[71]

Nearly every architect who had worked on San Juan signed the petition for constitutional rule. Many became active in opposition politics, most prominently Bereterbide and Vautier, and as we will see, some would draw on San Juan to produce a powerful AAD statement against Perón on the second anniversary of the earthquake. But while they were disenchanted with the military, they were suspicious of the opposition as well. Jorge Ferrari Hardoy, for example, was conflicted in revealing ways. He signed the petition and likely joined the AAD. He declined to enter the debate on the Mendióroz plan but repeatedly brought up San Juan at SCA meetings, unsuccessfully trying to register a formal complaint about his team's firing.[72]

While Ferrari Hardoy failed with the SCA, he was pleased when the San Juan engineers took up his case in September 1945. Of course, he was well aware that the reconstruction envisioned by the "democratic" architects faced dim prospects in the "democracy" of the San Juan engineers. The week of the engineers' action, his fellow team member Simón Ungar had written a sharp letter to Alberto Graffigna, editor of *Tribuna* and brother of the Conservative chieftain, congratulating him for so successfully "dragging the union of a people after the earthquake and the most generous aspirations of Argentine designers down to the level of petty disputes."[73] Reporting on the letter's impact, Ferrari Hardoy's closest ally in San Juan, the dissident engineer and provincial mining head Juan Victoria, pressed the point further.

The country needed a radical transformation, Victoria argued, not a return to "the supremacy of a discredited and decrepit class." The calls for "democracy" unfortunately seemed to be serving the interests of conservative elites. Looking across the national political scene, Victoria thought only Perón could carry out this "true social and intellectual revolution"—and only he could build a new San Juan. Victoria insisted to Ferrari Hardoy that he should speak with Perón, as dramatic action was in the works and the political situation was so unstable that Ferrari Hardoy might well regain control of reconstruction himself. For Victoria, this was not a matter of following Perón but of recruiting him for their cause: "Make *them* collaborate with *us*, and not us with them."[74]

Ferrari Hardoy was tempted, as his papers reveal: sometime after Hennekens was dismissed, he carefully worked out a full organization chart for the design side of Reconstruction, with positions for all the modernist architects and the local officials they trusted. He first named himself head of design within Reconstruction, then crossed that out, and gave himself the more lucrative role of chief architect, in private practice. But the temptation passed, he ignored Victoria's advice, and by late September he wrote that Perón "only wants to do demagoguery and enlarge his own figure."[75]

Instead Ferrari Hardoy tried to reframe the debate. His team had been turning their own incomplete project into a book, and when Ferrari Hardoy showed it to two visiting North American architects, they praised it as a pioneering exercise in integrated planning.[76] He was eager to win international exposure, to increase the domestic pressure for a proper rebuilding, and to offer a precedent for the coming reconstruction of Europe. What he had in mind was "constructive criticism, without personal attacks, but firmly denouncing the stumbling blocks we came up against (and which they'll come up against even in Europe itself) when a city and a region must be rebuilt, and the general interest placed before personal interests." He hoped San Juan might offer a lesson to the larger world, "given its small size, where general laws can be applied rightly and surely."[77]

Whether or not he could find "general laws" for overcoming resistance to rebuilding, he hoped this would prevent the return of democratic rule from bringing a return to narrow thinking about the province's future. "If we rush," he wrote in late 1945, "we can publish it by the end of the elections . . .

the moment when the problems of San Juan will be decided on for real, and for good."[78]

Ferrari Hardoy's book undoubtedly would have been opportune, offering a fuller sense of what was at stake than the three volumes that did appear in 1946, two by Pastor and one by Reconstruction staff. But with the team dispersed, the book was never completed, and their project was largely forgotten.

The mobilization of the opposition made rebuilding into a national issue and a mark against Perón. From July on, the four months of intense opposition mobilization in Buenos Aires, San Juan, and elsewhere put Perón on the defensive. But the military regime did not prove as easy to topple as opponents had hoped. And in San Juan, the opposition challenge did not open up a broader discussion about power and citizenship but instead served primarily to close down critical thinking about how to transform the province. Instead of promoting a broad debate over how to rebuild, it produced a narrow dispute over who should be in charge.

However small in size, San Juan loomed large as a symbol, and failure there was embarrassing to the military government. The August demonstration against the military—the first of many nationwide—made clear that stopgap measures were no longer enough. Perón launched a counterattack, as he gave local authority to a seasoned politician, named a competent engineer to lead Reconstruction, and finally enlisted Cantoni for his cause. But this was not enough, locally or nationally, and by October, the opposition was on the verge of toppling the military regime. The mass protest in favor of Perón enabled him to regain the initiative, opening the way to contesting the elections of 1946. Still, while he survived this crisis, he was very far from rebuilding San Juan, and the ruins would become a key theme of debate during the national campaign, a powerful reason for professionals to oppose Perón, and a starting point for rethinking politics locally. But even as struggle over who should rebuild became impassioned, as we will see, the debate over how to rebuild grew stale.

The Return of Cantoni

In response to the August protest, Perón raised the political stakes in San Juan, naming as the new interventor Emilio Cipolletti, a seasoned journalist and Radical politician. Now the provincial government was in the hands of a civilian who was adept at handling the press and building political alliances. Cipolletti was prepared to retake the initiative on the slippery terrain of opinion.[1] The new head of the Reconstruction Council, Enrique Zuleta, was a Radical and civil engineer who had directed the Water Department since the earthquake, winning elite support.[2] He took office determined to start re-building but quite willing to negotiate the details.

After months of vacillation, the new authorities took decisive action. They broke with the opposition within, the Conservatives who still dominated the ranks of the provincial administration. When Cipolletti took office, after more than two years of military rule, he found that Conservative appointees still held nearly every post in the provincial administration—from the judges down to the clerks, almost four thousand in all. He turned against Conserva-tive leaders, started naming a few key replacements, and struck a new alliance.[3] Leaving the Conservatives behind, he turned to Cantoni. In this action, he brought back a mode of politics many had thought was buried, and which he himself had hoped to avoid.

The alliance with Cantoni marked the exhaustion of Perón's earlier strategy. From the start, Perón had aimed to build a broader movement, trying to win support across all classes, rather than pursuing the polarizing strategy that had won Cantoni power but also ensured he could not keep it for long. Perón wanted to transcend existing politics in San Juan, not reproduce them. There-fore he had kept Cantoni at a distance, despite the similarities in their social plat-forms and Cantoni's lonely support for moving the city in 1944. Fearful of mobi-lization he could not control, Perón drew recruits from every local group but the Bloquistas and tolerated for a time those who supported him nationally but sub-verted him locally—above all, the Graffigna Conservatives. When labor organiz-ing began in San Juan, it did not draw on Cantonista grassroots groups but instead was based in largely urban unions, like winery and construction workers, and led by long-standing Cantoni opponents like Tejada and Godoy. Inviting Cantoni to join him marked his recognition that this strategy had failed, as well as his embrace of the polarizing and mobilizing approach he had resisted.

This was a reversal for the Cantonis as well: earlier in the year, Federico Cantoni had told a Chilean journalist that with fascism collapsing and democ-racy returning worldwide, Perón had squandered his opportunity and "can't become president."[4] But after sitting out the August protest, Federico Can-toni saw his chance and, over the objections of his brother Aldo, joined Perón. Conservatives responded immediately: after a year of supporting the regime but resisting Reconstruction, the Graffigna Conservatives now openly moved into opposition.

Counteroffensive

Cipolletti's strategy had three components: to secure control of the state, to accelerate rebuilding, and to deepen social reforms by expanding social subsidies and strengthening labor. The hope was that these efforts could unify a heterogeneous alliance of Bloquistas, Radicals, nationalists, and labor activists. A few weeks into his administration, the interventor took Cantoni and Zuleta to meet Perón in Buenos Aires, to plot a new course for the province.

It was at this moment that social action in San Juan began to resemble the style later associated with Peronism. The arrival of Radical, Cantonista, and laborista leaders as heads of many government departments, replacing long-dominant Conservative functionaries, sparked a constant round of disputes, politicking, meetings, and marches. As a newspaperman (and co-director of the one national paper still with Perón), Cipolletti knew the importance of bringing popular voices into public debate, so he injected cash into *La Reforma*, which had been largely dormant since the quake, and helped fund a laborista broadsheet called *Democracia*. While few issues from these days have survived, the impact of these papers can be measured by the alarm they provoked among Conservative journalists, who had monopolized the local printed page since the quake.

Zuleta brought new energy to Reconstruction, as resources once again flowed from Buenos Aires. In contrast to the secretive Hennekens, he met with opponents, opened a press office, and started publishing plans, making use of his political skill and administrative experience. These meetings were not only for show; the plan was open to modification, and because the opposition lacked a clear overall proposal, these modifications might well win over some opponents. A delegation from Concepción demanded that their neighborhood be rebuilt on the same site and with more government buildings than before, while downtown commercial interests objected to the idea of dispersing businesses from the plaza to a half-dozen neighborhood centers. By distributing patronage around the periphery and catering to the powerful in the center, Zuleta hoped to win enough support to move forward.[5] For a time, he even seemed to have persuaded del Bono himself to join the Reconstruction Council, but this idea was opposed by Cipolletti and eventually abandoned.[6] Watching all of this, the engineer Juan Victoria, local ally of the modernist architects, was appalled to see the comprehensive scheme broken apart "according to the whims of bankers, salesmen and shopkeepers," a "scandal" for everyone from the chief designer—"some Mendióroz fellow who designs the city in his spare time"—down to the shortsighted locals.[7]

Zuleta was willing to make concessions inside the city because his priorities were elsewhere. For him, reconstruction was first and foremost about transforming the province as a whole; he wanted to build dams, not argue about shops. When he took over the Reconstruction Council, he remained in charge of the Water Department. He thus controlled the two largest state agencies in the province. His first action was to put a thousand laborers to work on a new canal, originally proposed thirty years earlier, which could double the acreage under irrigation. Predictably, the national press immediately singled out the canal as something that could wait.[8] He also began extensive demolition, clearing, and surveying operations in the city. With work finally underway, the remaining evacuees steadily returned to their home province.

But his larger objective was to organize a consortium of private construction firms to carry out rebuilding. He proposed to hire the consortium without bidding and pay them project cost plus a guaranteed profit. Despite the intransigent opposition of the CAI, with such generous terms Zuleta managed to persuade six leading Buenos Aires engineer-entrepreneurs to join him, as he announced on 6 October.[9]

None of this sat well with local engineers: the emphasis on infrastructure over housing, the recruiting of outsiders, or the possibilities for malfeasance. After being blocked from rebuilding for over a year, they might now be excluded permanently. Unable to perform themselves the work Zuleta proposed, and fearful of this new consortium, they attacked the timing, scope, and nature of the project.[10] Once more, they were leaders of a mobilized opposition.

17 October 1945, and After

As Zuleta continued working into October, painting mysterious crosses on street corners for an aerial photography survey, the military regime was breaking apart and the opposition seemed about to triumph. Two events shook the local world on October 9: first, a new declaration by the local engineers kicked off another cycle of protest, with students seizing the university and Baca, Constantini, and other engineers briefly jailed as "agitators," and second, in Buenos Aires, Perón was forced to resign from the government. With the engineers apparently vindicated, Conservative newspapers celebrated Perón's dismissal and issued stern warnings to "collaborators."[11]

The course of events in Buenos Aires over the following week is well known. Perón seemed defeated, but on the day he left office, a delegation of four labor leaders, including San Juan union boss Tejada, persuaded him to give a farewell speech, which planted the seeds for a dramatic reversal. By 16 October, CGT leaders were debating whether to mount a general strike on his behalf, and Tejada offered one of the most eloquent arguments for the strike. "We have to live the reality of the movement we belong to," he asserted, and the reality was that Perón's actions had produced "this great mass movement we now have, and not that other ailing movement, where a handful of us activists used to vegetate."[12] Particularly in the interior, Tejada insisted, recent success would have been impossible without Perón. The CGT voted for a general strike on 18 October, and guaranteed of this action, mobilized workers took to the streets on 17 October.[13]

In Buenos Aires, hundreds of thousands of workers from the industrial outskirts made their way to the central plaza in an unexpected demonstration of strength that forced Perón's release and turned back the opposition. That evening, General Humberto Sosa Molina, the former San Juan interventor, was named minister of war and immediately began purging the officers who had turned on Perón. His ally Juan Pistarini, the minister of public works, temporarily assumed the vice presidency. Released from custody and returned to the center of national politics, Perón launched his campaign for the presidency.

The protest on 17 October is often portrayed as a radical reversal of assumptions, an overturning of order. The periphery invaded the center, and the working class seized the city. While there was physical violence, even a few deaths, the most striking violence was symbolic. Leaving factories and government offices alone, workers went after the cultural institutions most clearly opposed to Perón, the press and universities, in a series of highly ritualistic attacks aimed at "negating their authority and symbolic power."[14] These protests revealed and reinforced a sharp class divide, as workers became a powerful force in national politics, no longer identified with the left but with Perón.

In San Juan, as in other provincial cities, the demonstrations came on 18 October, not to demand Perón's release but to celebrate it afterward. Fireworks went off in the morning, and workers spread out across the city chanting slogans, recruiting others, and forcing shops to close. Gathering at the plaza, they met beneath the statue of Sarmiento, sang the national anthem, and then set off with police behind them. Whistling and shouting insults as they passed the engineering faculty and the owner of a Conservative paper, the crowd reached the government offices, where Cipolletti welcomed them and called the day a triumph for workers.[15]

Despite the local tradition of violent protest, this one was peaceful, accompanied by police—greeted by workers with a cheer and the national anthem— and guided by government officials. Protesters controlled the streets, but there was little of the brick-throwing that occurred in other cities. If protesters did not devote as much effort to humbling the powerful, this was partly because the earthquake had already done so. There were few institutions left to humiliate, and little point to shattering windows when the city was in ruins. Even so, the targets of ridicule were clear: the officers of Conservative newspapers, the homes of opposition politicians, and the university. The procession began at the center of public life and ended at the seat of government. Indeed, the October demonstration for Perón began where the August protest for rebuilding and the September rally for constitutional rule had ended: beneath the statue of Sarmiento.

This underscores the centrality of culture and power to the protests. In Buenos Aires, the opposition student chant of "Books Yes, Boots No" inspired workers on 17 October to shout "Alpargatas Yes, Books No." Alpargatas were espadrilles, the cheap shoes worn by the poor—and the chant was both a response to students and an echo of old Cantonista slogans. The opposition took this exaltation of shoes over learning as confirmation of the backwardness of the popular classes. Yet the chant was directed less at books than at the cultural authority they represented; as another cry put it, "Less culture, more work!" The chants were assertions, as Daniel James argues, that "working class experience had its own value and cultural worth."[16] In San Juan, protesters went even further: with the anthem and the invocation of Sarmiento, they were arguing that theirs was *the* legitimate culture, pointing up the falsity of a cultural order that had mouthed liberal pieties while ruling by exclusion and fraud. Insisting on the value of their own ideas, they were also rejecting the opposition claim to speak for the city.

Across the country, the opposition and the press portrayed the pro-government protestors as marginal, illegitimate, and out-of-place. In Buenos Aires, Socialists and Communists asserted that the protestors were not true workers, because they failed to observe proper decorum and discipline and above all because they backed a "Nazi-fascist."[17] It was not just their cause that was offensive; Buenos Aires papers portrayed their mere presence as an offense to the city.[18]

"That is not the people," San Juan Conservatives had already declared of pro-government rallies.[19] After 17 October, every party but the Bloquistas issued a joint communiqué denouncing the "monstrously counter-sensical" protest in which "workers, who in all places and times have occupied the vanguard of the struggle for liberty and democracy, appear as defenders and sustainers of the dictatorship."[20] For the press, the demonstrators sowed chaos and made "the shape of the city" change, while the true "people" merely observed their actions from a distance and, providing "a high example of culture," did not respond to insults.[21]

In the San Juan press, the dominant note was not novelty but familiarity. When Perón was arrested, the local press had denounced the "insolent, aggressive and corrupting" provincial administration, filled with "regressive figures" who returned to "repeat the same gestures . . . from those dark times when the honor, life, and property of people were in their hands." For the national press, the slogan "Alpargatas Yes, Books No" seemed to encapsulate the ignorance and foolishness of popular protests. When the local press took up the theme, they attacked the demonstrators, blamed Cantonistas, and invoked Sarmiento in editorials with titles like "Let's Talk a Little about Civilization and Barbarism." Yet they were fighting a losing battle, because Cantonismo had already shown how to champion the alpargata as a political symbol while also claiming the mantle of Sarmiento.[22] As the political moment slipped out of their hands, the opposition press watched the movement they thought they had banished returned to center stage.

Cantoni had assumed a larger role than many of Perón's supporters in San Juan would have liked, but his rivals still had important roles to play. After 17 October, Ramón Tejada retained his local influence and helped found a national Labor Party to support the election of Perón. The party called itself "a new consciousness on the march," and Tejada and his allies hoped it would enable them to seize the leadership of the popular movement from Cantoni, once and for all. Unions would indeed play an important role in Peronist San Juan, though Cantonistas did not exit the provincial stage.

San Juan in the 1946 Campaign

San Juan was a cause célèbre during the 1946 presidential campaign, an embarrassment for the government and a rallying cry for the opposition. With the second anniversary of the earthquake falling five weeks before the election, few critics could resist the opportunity to measure the conditions in 1946 against the promises of 1944. Rather than demonstrating government commitment to social justice, San Juan had become opposition shorthand for official incompetence.

Two forceful critiques of Perón's actions in San Juan appeared in newspapers on the second anniversary of the earthquake: a simple advertisement by the opposition alliance, the Unión Democrática, and a detailed reckoning from the dissident architects of the AAD. For the architects, San Juan was a powerful indictment of military rule: "a polished mirror in which the country can contemplate the great fraud of this government and those who would continue it." According to the architects, reconstruction had been frustrated by the bombastic ambitions and shortsighted calculations of military leaders. Turning the regime's rhetoric against it, the architects insisted that "instead of speaking and decreeing," leaders should be "organizing and acting." Instead of holding designers back, political leaders should give them the reins, and "entrust the problem of general well-being to the capability of technical experts, rather than using projects left undone as propaganda banners."[23]

But for all the architects' efforts to pin the blame on a brutish national state, they could hardly ignore the other obstacles they faced. The foremost obstacle was the propertied interests of San Juan "who, under the guise of defending the province, dedicated themselves to defaming the experts . . . in a libelous campaign against anyone who believed in a comprehensive solution." The wealthy had used their newspapers to turn the population against "graduates of Argentine universities who they even now refer to as 'outside experts.'" According to the architects, the government had only worsened matters by blocking "technical experts from any connection with the people, any surveys, or any exchange of ideas." The fruit of this division was the "suicidal and rushed" Mendióroz proposal, which capitulated to local elites and resurrected the old street plan. To the "democratic architects," this surrender to the propertied few proved that military leaders "who call themselves pro-worker and anti-capitalist, who speak of morality and social justice, are really just at the service of the speculators of the hour." Even now, the architects declared, "the government has not made or even planned a single tile, door, or brick."[24]

The venom of the manifesto was noted by the government, which took the architects to court, and the local press, which denounced "the bellicose association of architects."[25] But in a deeper sense, the manifesto failed to fully make its case. The large number of architects who had worked on San Juan undermined the claim of official indifference, although it heightened the sense of official "incoherence." The architects denounced the state as authoritarian, but their real frustration was that it was not authoritarian enough and had failed to impose the correct project. The architects who now declared themselves "democratic" had been eager to work for the dictatorship. And even now, those they accused of blocking reconstruction were the backbone of the "democratic" opposition in San Juan.

The architects' manifesto tried to make a complex point. By contrast, the advertisement taken out by the opposition parties was simplicity itself: a full-page image of the devastated city below the words "San Juan is Still Waiting. Unión Democrática." This was a difficult argument to refute: if Perón had not delivered for San Juan, how would he deliver for the country? The press, by now overwhelmingly opposed to Perón, echoed the charge. At best, this was a case of "revolutionary ineptitude" due to a "lack of solidarity."[26] At worst, this was a deliberate attempt to humble the city into obedience: emergency barrios were "concentration camps" and the failure to rebuild proof of "how Nazi Perón is."[27]

The opposition invoked the ruins to undermine the military, but never to offer a different vision. All the blame was assigned to the military regime: its authoritarian bent, utopian delusions, and disrespect for property and culture. There was no recognition of local responsibility, and no sense that justice demanded anything but restoration of the previous city. The parties of the Unión Democrática promised immediate reconstruction, full stop. But they did not worry about how to rebuild. Putting the right people back in charge would be enough.

Instead of debating how to rebuild, the opposition focused on how aid had been mismanaged. Attacking the collection became the most effective way to discredit Perón and any plan for the future. Of course, it was the collection that had first won Perón prominence and popular support, opening the way to a broader reform project and paying for the first stage of relief: twelve million pesos had been spent in 1944 on everything from emergency shelter to the salaries for provincial workers. But after April 1944, when the Interior Ministry wrested control of the collection away from the STP, disbursements stopped and uncertainty grew about how to use the remaining thirty million pesos. Despite two proposals for how to spend the money, nothing was done until July 1945, when the discovery of some skimming from the original collection and, as seen in the last chapter, the emergence of an opposition asking aggressive questions finally prompted government action.[28]

When the opposition took to the streets after August 1945, all that mattered was the obvious. Everyone knew that forty-two million pesos had been collected, some knew that twelve million had been spent, but no one knew what had happened to the rest. "Where's it gone, where's it gone, the money for San Juan" became a favorite chant at opposition rallies nationwide.[29] After the 17 October demonstration launched Perón on the path to the presidency, some opponents claimed he had used the collection to hire workers for the demonstration or was using it to fund his campaign.[30] On the surface, these claims were absurd, as Perón's powers over the state were too extensive to require the use of such a comparatively paltry fund. As the campaign heated up, the government clarified repeatedly that the supposedly missing thirty million pesos were actually sitting in official accounts, earning interest. The one newspaper supporting Perón claimed the "eloquence of these figures" would "silence the voices of calumny."[31]

But the criticism was never strictly about the numbers. The opposition focused on the collection for its symbolic power, not its exact amount: this money, entrusted to Perón for the good of the victims, had been of much use to his career but little to their welfare. While the government could reasonably argue that it had spent a great deal in San Juan, this hardly settled the matter. Indeed, the reality that the collection was unspent was even more puzzling than the possibility that it had been misdirected. The fight over reconstruction had obviously held up the distribution of aid. But the delay only strengthened opposition claims that the government hardly knew how to rebuild the province, much less the nation.

These claims were also reinforced by the nasty response of the government and its few press allies. Surprisingly, those defending the government made little use of the vast body of assembled technical evidence to explain the collapse and argue in favor of rebuilding. They rarely even presented drawings of the future city.[32] Instead, they sputtered that the province "had received all the aid any government could give," that "no one lacked a roof in San Juan," and that the opposition was "speculating with pain" by talking about the earthquake."[33] One article even offered comparative excuses: San Francisco had taken five years to rebuild, and the Chilean city of Chillán had not rebuilt after seven, so Argentines could hardly expect completion after only two years had passed.[34] But as the defensive tone of this article suggested, the best way for Perón to address San Juan was just to change the subject.

The Debate within San Juan

Virtually every established party in San Juan joined the opposition coalition, the Unión Democrática. But they had little in common other than opposition to Perón and his schemes for rebuilding. Thus, in a familiar sequence, the unity of the August 1945 protest quickly fragmented into separate candidate lists for the Graffigna Conservatives, Maurín Conservatives, Socialists, Communists, and several Radical factions. Rather than consolidating a new unity led by Socialists, the mobilization of the opposition revived an older dispersion dominated, as ever, by Conservatives.

The Graffigna Conservatives claimed they were the only ones capable of rebuilding and renamed themselves the "Party of Reconstruction." Their program was a distillation of the August protest: houses yes, plans no. The Maurín Conservatives made the same claim, with the same narrowness of vision and a certain provincial pride. The Maurín paper took note of the dissident architects' manifesto on the anniversary. "The tragedy of San Juan has always been wanting to fix our problems from the Federal Capital," the Conservatives responded, and the architects who knew the city from books and came "to indulge their fantasies" were just the latest in a long series. "The small town press, as the bellicose association of architects dubbed us," had simply represented public opinion in its campaign against the move, the designers, and any planning: "Never was there such a close identification between a people and their press."[35]

Perón's supporters had little difficulty refuting Conservative claims of competence, either by pointing to the rubble of the Conservative-built City Hall or by evoking still-fresh memories of stolen ballots, beatings, and assassinations.[36] In sharp and clear language, the Cantonista paper attacked Conservative greed, defended government expertise, and dismissed the idea that bodegueros spoke for the province as a whole. "The work has not begun because the Conservative interests who own two-thirds of the city center opposed it," the Cantonistas stated flatly. "They achieved their objective. The city stayed where it was. But it stayed like it is."[37] When a visiting leader of the national opposition claimed that the city had been "utterly abandoned," the Cantonistas stressed that much of local "pain and misery" was due to the rapacity of local elites, the "very individuals who now served as guides" for the visitor, who "took everything intended for earthquake victims," including workers' housing, "whole neighborhoods seized by aristocrats."[38] But while Cantonistas could highlight the depredations of elites and the class bias in their complaints of "moral suffering," neither argument cast official relief in a particularly positive light. Arguing that the revolution had not reached San Juan certainly explained the power of local elites and the challenge for the future. But it hardly accounted for San Juan's prominent place at the origins of the revolution.

The day of the anniversary, a visiting labor leader wrote back to Buenos Aires of a province "where the houses are on the ground but the people are on their feet," yet even here, he emphasized not the challenge of rebuilding but rather the irrelevance of the past and even the fallen buildings. Local energy was "unified in a single goal: political and labor unity to defeat the eternal enemy of the People, the Oligarchy."[39]

Like the opposition, regime supporters used reconstruction mostly as a generic symbol. They easily undercut opposition rhetoric but shied away from the challenge of offering a specific program of their own. They certainly did not trumpet the actions of the Reconstruction Council. This was not so troubling for many supporters, who were understandably suspicious of opposition talk of property, rights, and efficiency. Shifting debate to whether those who had built the collapsed city should be the ones to build its replacement was an effective tactic. But the reluctance of Perón's supporters to advance a compelling vision of their own for the future city would soon prove politically crippling.

Perón's backers were an unruly lot: laboristas, Cantonistas, and dissident

Radicals, with a leavening of nationalists, newcomers, and opportunists. Each group had some organizational core to provide funding and structure: Cantonistas had a revived party structure, laboristas had unions, and dissident Radicals had Interventor Cipolletti and his administration. But no group was institutionally strong, and they were held together by little beyond their adherence to Perón. Each claimed to be Perón's only true followers: Cantonistas because of their long-standing support among the poor, the laboristas because of their advocacy for workers, and the others because they had no cause besides Perón.

For his part, Perón tried to play these groups against each other, building on each without giving any supremacy. His control was limited, as the movement was dynamic but not especially orderly. But his authority was the ultimate trump card in the war for electoral position between competing groups. Nationally, Perón was growing wary of the power of the independent-minded laboristas, and in San Juan he remained unwilling to simply delegate authority to Cantoni.

The conflict came to a head when Perón came to San Juan, two years and twelve days after the disaster. Thirty thousand supporters filled the stadium, a crowd perhaps twice the size of the August protest. Not surprisingly, the Cantonistas were the largest contingent. But the rally would produce unexpected results.

"The fierce struggle of Perón . . . is our struggle in San Juan taken to a larger stage," Federico Cantoni told the crowd: first this city, then the entire nation needed rebuilding. But even as he endorsed Perón, Cantoni reasserted his own originality, claiming to be the source of Perón's key ideas.[40] This was not all that made Perón uncomfortable. When each local leader rose to speak, rivals shouted him down: the Radical leader could hardly be heard, the laborista Tejada was partly drowned out, and even Cantoni had a few hecklers. When Perón came to the podium, the noise died down. But his promise of immediate rebuilding brought another chorus of boos and whistles, from dissident Bloquistas led by Aldo Cantoni. Only the forceful intervention of Federico Cantoni made it possible for Perón to finish his speech. He left early and headed straight out of town. A few days later, Cantoni's party endorsed Perón, while issuing an electoral platform at odds with key pieces of his nationalist program.[41]

Cantonismo had proven insubordinate and even insolent, hardly the local base Perón had in mind. A week later, he ruled out supporting Cantonista and laborista candidates for office, opting instead to back two STP officials: legal advisor Alvarado for governor, and regional delegate Ruperto Godoy for vice-governor.[42] Until a week before the election, Cantonistas continued to back Perón for president while promoting their own candidate for governor—Elio Cantoni, the quiet brother. But when Perón insisted on Alvarado, Federico Cantoni switched sides. Overnight, his paper went from fierce defenses of Perón's democratic credentials to ritual denunciations of the "Nazi-fascist" regime. Significantly, the Cantonistas invoked rebuilding to justify their decision. They claimed to have allied with Perón for two reasons: "the similarities of his social and labor policies" to their own and his "formal promise . . . to immediately begin reconstruction." But Bloquista activists grew disenchanted with the limited progress, expressing "hostility when Perón spoke of reconstruction" on his visit, which wounded his "pride."[43] Local power mattered far more than policy differences. But it was the failure to rebuild that made Cantoni and his supporters waver and then switch. This last-minute decision would cast a long shadow over provincial politics.

Every important actor in local politics, supporters and opponents of Perón alike, focused more on who should rebuild than what the rebuilt city should look like. In other words, they focused more on politics than on envisioning a new city—or province. In so doing, they confirmed the bracing critique of rebuilding penned by Juan Victoria at the end of 1945. Victoria, the engineer who led the Mining Department, had worked closely with modernist architects but enthusiastically supported Perón. While agreeing with many of the frustrations of the "democratic" architects, he found the local sources of delay more important than the national ones and saw Perón as the only leader who could remake San Juan.[44]

For Victoria, "very few people have understood the true meaning, and above all, the scope of this matter." If the early insistence that the government simply "set the line" and get out of the way could be ascribed to the "confusion and impatience of the moment," it also revealed that civic leaders were more interested in pursuing individual advantage than a collective project. Victoria recalled the bodeguero demands for compensation after the earthquake, and how others had followed their lead:

> How to explain the temperament of the people of San Juan, tied to their customs, their little mud houses, their narrow streets and plazas, in contrast to that of other peoples who make such efforts to liberate themselves from the weight of the past and create and build great things? Note the care with which buildings are taken down here, brick by brick and almost with tenderness, while in the United States they blow up skyscrapers with dynamite.[45]

Reconstruction had a "social and economic meaning" far greater than the width of the streets, Victoria argued. The future of the city would be determined by the future of the river valley: "this is the foundation of reconstruction, from which all planning and action must proceed." As San Juan had reached "the limits of agricultural development allowed by [current] river water," reconstruction should mean reshaping the landscape, partly with dams, to control the river, expand irrigation, and provide electricity for industry. This was what the fuerzas vivas had blocked, with their intransigence and disdain for expertise. This is what university leaders had missed, by making "political pronouncements" about democracy instead of seizing "the opportunity . . . to make San Juan a model for the country and . . . a center of urban studies." For Victoria, this demonstrated the "archaic" character of Argentine universities, the isolation of "capable experts," and the cramped vision of local leaders.

"In reality," Victoria concluded, "the reconstruction of San Juan has already failed." A few months later, the editor who had published Victoria's polemic, a distinguished local intellectual, inadvertently offered decisive proof of his point. In a long article, the editor addressed with great care what he saw as the central and perhaps insoluble problem with the new rebuilding plan: too few parking spots in front of city hall.[46]

PART 4

"RUBBLE OR NO RUBBLE, WE WANT PERÓN," 1946–1962

On 4 June 1946, exactly three years after the military coup, Juan Perón took office as the elected president of Argentina. In the thirty months since the earthquake, the once-obscure military officer had become a charismatic and polarizing national figure. With an unlikely and somewhat haphazard coalition of supporters, he had prevailed over the opposition of a surprisingly unified national establishment. While his numerical margin of victory was narrow, only 52 percent to 48 percent, he won all but four provinces, and as his triumph became clear, the opposition quickly fell apart.

When he delivered his inaugural address to the reconvened Congress in Buenos Aires, over a million people filled the plaza outside—in a city of three million. There was a palpable sense of promise and new beginnings. Perón confidently sketched out ambitious reforms to expand rights, increase prosperity, and strengthen industry. In many ways, his vision for the nation in 1946 echoed his earlier visions for San Juan, stressing the importance of robust labor organizing, vastly improved popular housing, and even extensive irrigation projects.[1]

Over the coming months, the administration's policy agenda came together in the First Five-Year Plan, a blueprint for turning Argentina from a colonial "farm" into an industrial "power." As the official slogan put it, Argentina would become a "socially just, economically free and politically sovereign" nation.[2] A reorganization of the banking system soon enabled the government to pay off the foreign debt, nationalize many foreign-owned enterprises—including, by 1948, the entire rail network—and deepen import-substitution industrialization.[3] The overarching framework for these policies was the First Five-Year Plan, which promoted the idea of comprehensive planning that had animated official visions for rebuilding San Juan. This was especially clear in its utopian hopes for a New Argentina, and the sizable role of expanded state authority in achieving them. "Planning is the key to the entire system of work and prosperity," the minister of agriculture later declared, "the benefits . . . will reach the furthest corners and touch the most humble inhabitant of the territory."[4] According to one pro-government newspaper, "The Plan is our very life in these five years: this is the idea that is gathering force among the masses."[5] Whatever the limitations of the Five-Year Plan in terms of economic policy or administrative effectiveness, it clearly was a great success in making planning synonymous with progressive social reforms.

Yet San Juan itself could no longer serve as the model for national planning. Perón's opponents had lost the election, but they had won the rhetorical battle over rebuilding.[6] Even Perón's supporters had grown reluctant to defend his vision for the nation based on his accomplishments in San Juan. Within the devastated province, he enjoyed increasing support, but this support came despite the state of rebuilding, not because of it. As one journalist put it after the overwhelming victory of a government candidate a few years later, sanjuaninos had declared that "Rubble or No Rubble, We Want Perón."[7]

The political opening that followed Perón's victory marked a divergence between the project for San Juan and the project for the nation. That divergence was clear in the contrast between two inaugural addresses: Perón's confident and ambitious speech in June 1946 and the defensive and concessionary one given two weeks earlier by Juan Luis Alvarado, the elected Peronist governor of San Juan.

This final section thus reveals another dimension of the relationship between the project for San Juan and the project for the nation: San Juan represented first a call to build a New Argentina, second a model for the task, and third a cautionary warning against heeding that call. In this fourth section, I show how San Juan was eventually rebuilt, but as a shadow of what it might have been, a ruin of the promise of a New Argentina.

In a sense, the center of gravity of this account now shifts. If the rebuilding of San Juan was a key leading case for national processes up to this point, now that those processes were unfolding, it became far less important as a leading case, or even a point of national reference. While it continued to have signal importance for architects and engineers, they viewed it rather less optimistically. For locals, of course, rebuilding was still a very specific challenge and in many ways the matrix through which they experienced Perón's rule. Or to make the point differently: while national attention shifted away from San Juan, within the province rebuilding finally began, and the struggles over plans gave way to struggles over practice.

Before turning to these final chapters, a brief sketch of Perón's years in elected office is in order, to highlight the dynamics of national political economy that shaped the range of the possible—especially the organization and funding of rebuilding. Overall, Perón's presidency breaks down into three periods: an ascendant period of economic expansion, institutional experimentation, and freewheeling political conflict from 1946 to 1948; a somber period of economic austerity and political consolidation from 1949 to 1952; and a tense period of renewed economic growth but deepening political conflict from 1953 to 1955, culminating in the military coup that removed him from office. After that came a military dictatorship, from 1955 to 1958, which tried but failed to suppress labor and eliminate Peronism altogether while pursuing sharply contractionary economic policies.

When Perón took office in 1946, the government had a massive wartime surplus, which it quickly began spending. The outline for this was the First Five-Year Plan, as orchestrated by the chief economic policymaker, Miguel Miranda, president of the Central Bank. First came the boom: dramatic wage increases and expansionary credit drove powerful growth, with 8 percent annual increases in GDP from 1946 to 1948. Three actors in particular were crucial: workers, who dramatically increased in buying power as wages rose 40 percent in real terms; industry, which received most new credit and flourished with growing consumer markets; and the state, which assumed a greater role in the economy by nationalizing bank deposits, utilities, and railroads and, above all, by becoming the clearing house for all agricultural exports and using this role to control prices and redistribute resources.

Politically, these were the years of building a governing party, with an explosion of popular mobilization prompting intermittently successful attempts by Peronist officials to channel that energy into strengthening their institutional power and isolating their rivals. Unions grew rapidly, tripling in size by the fall of Perón, and proving their power in several strike waves.[8] But they were increasingly incorporated into the party and subordinated to political power. The old-line union leaders who had been crucial in Perón's rise were promoted if they agreed—the Socialist Ángel Borlenghi became interior minister and the Socialist Juan Atilio Bramuglia foreign minister—and forced aside if they did not, opening up space for a younger generation in labor and political posts. Looking to counterbalance the power of labor, the administration welcomed the support of politicians from peripheral provinces, where labor was weak, and began to reach the poor outside of the unions, particularly through Eva Perón and her Foundation. The regime acted to constrain the opposition across the board, gradually shutting down many independent newspapers and indirectly buying up nearly every radio station. This period was capped by a new constitution in 1949, which granted women the vote for the first time nationally and incorporated a wide range of social guarantees, including the rights to housing, work, retirement, and a just wage.

But then came the crisis: inflation shot up, agricultural exports collapsed, and industry, starved of imported capital goods, contracted as well. From 1949 to 1952, the economy stalled and even shrank slightly, and the dramatic increases in wages and popular consumption peaked and began to reverse. This economic contraction was accompanied by a political tightening, as the government consolidated party organization, tightened control over unions, and expanded its influence over the press. The government redrew electoral districts and harassed the opposition, at first sporadically, then more intensely after a failed coup in September 1951. This was the high point for Eva Perón, as her foundation took over many social welfare tasks, and she became the centerpiece of a powerful propaganda apparatus. But while her power was great, it proved fleeting, as her campaign to win the vice-presidency in 1951 was blocked by the military and then the swift onset of cancer took her life, only a few months after Perón was reelected by a commanding margin.

Finally came reorientation and renewed expansion: Perón began his second term with a Second Five-Year Plan, in many ways a reversal of the first. By contracting credit and redirecting resources from industry to agriculture, the administration cut inflation and restarted growth, which rose to over 5 percent annually. But Perón did not profit politically from this adjustment, as his attempts to shoehorn the citizenry into increasingly elaborate corporatist bodies met with little popular enthusiasm and less success. In many ways, Perón lost his judgment and alienated some of his original supporters, turning the military and the Church against him and embarking on a series of increasingly bitter conflicts that polarized the country and paved the way for the coup.

For all the ups and downs, the overall pattern was clear: the redistribution of wealth, the strengthening of the state, the construction of public works, and the promotion of industry (with a later tactical retreat). The share of national income going to the wealthiest one percent of the population dropped from a 1942 high of 29 percent to a 1952 low of 14 percent.[9] Meanwhile, the wage share of national income leapt from 37 percent in 1945 to 50 percent in 1950. Real wages peaked in 1948, but even with dips, remained far above 1945 levels.[10] The increase was greatest in the interior: in San Juan, local wages were 76 percent of the national average in 1945 and 90 percent of a much higher national average in 1955.[11] In strictly economic terms, Perón did indeed deliver for the majority of the country. That fundamental achievement, and the social and political opening for the majority that accompanied it, were essential to his popular appeal.

The three chapters in this final section trace the rebuilding of the city and the remaking of the political order in San Juan after 1946. Chapter 10 focuses on the brief but consequential first elected Peronist administration in San Juan, explaining why Governor Alvarado took office renouncing the rebuilding project Peronism had championed. Chapter 11 turns to a broader examination of the social experience of rebuilding, looking at the political strategy and architectural plans that shaped Peronism and the rebuilt city. The focus here is on the administration of Ruperto Godoy (1947–50), a period of great social and political dynamism which saw the consolidation of the new political order, the final choice of a plan for rebuilding, and the muscular beginnings of physical reconstruction. Finally, chapter 12 discusses the legacy of the disaster and reconstruction for the province after the fall of Perón.

CHAPTER 10 AGAINST THE "SOVEREIGNTY OF EXPERTS"

REBUILDING ON LOCAL TERMS, 1946–1947

On 25 May 1946, Peronist governor-elect Juan Luis Alvarado laid out his political agenda in an inaugural speech to the new legislature. Across the nation, for Perón and his supporters, this was a moment for bold plans. But in San Juan, the moment seemed to demand something else. Instead of proclaiming his dreams for the future, Alvarado wanted to bring the dreaming to an end.

He began by surveying the meager progress of rebuilding, and he did not have to look far: the legislature was meeting under the stands of the stadium. But Alvarado did not blame national authorities. On the contrary, he maintained that they had acted swiftly in 1944 and had "done nothing since but order action, favor action, and push for action." The problem was not with Perón. The problem was with the "outside experts" across the road from the stadium at Reconstruction headquarters.[1]

According to this Catholic Action lawyer, Reconstruction and its technical experts were latter-day "builders of the Tower of Babel" who had succumbed to "the delirium of intellectual pride." Alvarado claimed they had acted behind Perón's back and seized power for themselves. "None of us believes in such sovereignty of experts," Alvarado declared. Sobriety, modesty, and provincial control were now the order of the day. "Rebuilding a city is not like founding a new province in the desert," he stated, but a matter of "raising up the homes and social institutions of people who are already there."

Just as Perón was overturning the established order, this Peronist staked his future on a return to the past. In order to deflect the blame from Perón, Alvarado made scapegoats of the architects—outsiders chosen by Perón, just like he was. Ignoring local resistance, he attributed all the delays and problems to the experts' "delirium of intellectual pride." He completely dismissed their authority, even mocking the idea of earthquake-proof building.[2] Instead, he tried to claim the mantle of the local cause. He argued that rebuilding must begin with respect for property rights and insisted, on the basis of his reading of the constitution, that it was a task for the province, not the nation, to undertake.[3]

His speech made opposition demands into Peronist policy—and was naturally well received among the powerful in San Juan.[4] This speech marked a public split between the project for San Juan and the project for the nation, as he renounced ambitious plans, but underscored how vital rebuilding remained to Peronist success. Alvarado himself would remain in office less than a year, but the course he set and the alliances he forged would prove decisive in the province's future.

On first consideration, Alvarado would not seem a likely recruit for the cause of local Conservatives. A decade earlier, he was a founder of FORJA, a nationalist movement within the Radical Party, and penned withering critiques of the Conservative state, its "anti-national" subservience to foreign interests, and its staff of "experts for rent."[5] Even now, he continued to believe that Argentine universities had been deliberately "trimmed of their fruitful branches" so that the country would reject its own experts but mindlessly "admire any drunk foreigner who landed in the port of Buenos Aires."[6] But in San Juan, he ignored these nationalist convictions. Instead, he adopted the arguments of the "experts for rent"—one of his targets in the 1930s, the engineer Antonio Vaquer, was in 1945 president of the CAI and an outspoken Reconstruction critic—and denounced the leading Argentine architects as incompetent outsiders. This would-be defender of Argentine technical expertise then appointed lawyers with no technical training to head up the province's two technical ministries.[7]

But as we will see, Alvarado took this stance for clear reasons: political calculation, religious conviction, and, above all, his personal history with Cantoni. To understand his actions and their larger consequences, we need first to consider more closely the election results.

Building a Ruling Coalition

While Perón had won a decisive victory across the nation, he had his worst performance in San Juan, where he captured only a third of the vote. But even here, the Peronist ticket won the largest plurality and thus gained the governorship, two of three seats in the national chamber of deputies, and the largest bloc in the provincial legislature. There is a simple explanation for this paradoxical result: Perón lost the majority when Cantoni defected, but he still won more votes than anyone else. Peronists received 33.2 percent, Cantonistas 28.6 percent, Conservatives 21.7 percent, Radicals 14.9 percent, and Socialists 2.5 percent.[8] Voting followed a clear geographical pattern: Conservatives won narrowly inside the four avenues; Peronists triumphed outside them—especially in the so-called "concentration camps" of emergency housing—and across most of the central valley; and Cantonistas prevailed almost everywhere else.[9] The unicameral provincial legislature reflected a divided polity, with twelve Peronists, ten Cantonistas, four Graffigna Conservatives, one Maurín Conservative, and three Radicals.

But this fragmentation should not obscure the fact that voters had completely rejected the old political establishment. The two populist tickets—Perón and Cantoni—together captured almost two-thirds of the vote and a majority in every legislative district. They did especially well in emergency barrios. None of the antipopulist opposition parties won even a quarter of the vote. If Cantoni had not broken with Perón, the opposition would have been shut out of the provincial legislature. But because he did, they had eight seats—and a key mediating role.

Alvarado held the governorship, but to actually govern he needed allies and a legislative majority. Peronism was a future project, not a consolidated party. One option was reconciliation with Cantoni, but that was nearly impossible for him. Alvarado had first entered politics as a protégé of Governor Amable Jones, and when Cantonistas killed his mentor, he left the province for twenty-five years. It was Cantoni who had driven him out, and Cantoni who had complicated his return by refusing to follow Perón's orders, switching sides, and proving once more how untrustworthy, dangerous, and popular he remained. None of this recommended him to Alvarado.[10]

A second option was to call a new election. Women had voted in provincial elections for twenty years, but not in national contests, and in 1946, because national electoral rolls were used, they were excluded. This was ample reason to call another provincial election, as Cantoni had done under similar circumstances fifteen years earlier, and a revote would undoubtedly give Alvarado a stronger mandate.[11]

But with Peronism in the ascendant nationally, Alvarado chose to pursue a third option, that of seducing the opposition. As the magnitude of Perón's national victory sank in, fierce opposition melted away. "Right about now," La Reforma observed two weeks after the election, Peronists "make up something like 99% of the population."[12] Thus Alvarado could ignore Cantoni, as he was eager to do, and brush aside the laboristas, who were proving more demanding than he liked, and try to win over the opposition, dominated by Conservatives. Although Alvarado had worked as a labor lawyer, he ultimately saw workers more as a group to be helped than a force to be led.[13] He thus cast his lot with those he trusted—Catholic activists. As a carrot, he used the province's two national Senate seats, which were chosen by the provincial legislature, not popular vote. On the advice of José Conte-Grand, the young Catholic Conservative who had been Sosa Molina's chief of staff, he offered the seats to two Catholic Action members: the Conservative judge Pablo Ramella and the Radical doctor Oscar Tascheret, who lived in Buenos Aires.[14] In exchange, all but one of the opposition legislators forgot their furious denunciations of the "Nazi-fascist" Colonel and lined up behind Perón.[15]

Across the country, there was a growing rift within Peronism between politicians and labor leaders, between the experienced professionals of party politics who had allied with Perón and the labor activists whose allegiance to Perón had drawn them into party politics for the first time. Laboristas had been Perón's most dynamic supporters, but to rein in their unruly independence, Perón was beginning to favor their opponents, with San Juan an especially stark example.[16] The San Juan laboristas did not give up: they chanted anti-Conservative slogans during victory celebrations, plastered anti-Ramella posters everywhere, and finally called for a general strike to demand the resignation of everyone just elected.[17] Their frustration was understandable: workers had voted down the Conservative order, only to send a leading Conservative intellectual to the Senate. Ramella was certainly an unlikely champion of the disenfranchised; he had recently advocated restricting voting rights, for example, claiming that "what matters is not whether many or few vote, but that those who do, vote consciously."[18] His closest allies had led the opposition, and he himself may have voted against Perón.[19] But the tide was turning against the laboristas, and when public employees refused to join the strike, their hope for "another October 17" gave way to resignation.[20] Labor would certainly have an important place in Peronist politics, but not on the autonomous terms laboristas had demanded.

Thus the stance Alvarado took in his inaugural speech was the product of political compromises and personal conviction. He hoped to govern in a conciliatory spirit, balancing the national initiatives of Perón with the local interests of the powerful. He staffed his administration with well-known figures, including many from the opposition. "Slogans expressed on 8 August 1945 are now hidden away as youthful indiscretions," a business group noted, as ardent opponents were now "honored" to serve Perón.[21] A new Department of Social Justice was established, to expand aid to the poor, but it was led by Catholic activists and staffed by the same society ladies who had done "charity" before 1943.[22]

Quickly forgetting their last-minute opposition to Perón, Cantonistas spent the months after the election making overtures to the laboristas and sniping at Alvarado, while keeping tabs on his backroom maneuvers.[23] There was still enough fluctuation in Peronism that they still hoped to push aside Alvarado and make themselves the backbone of the local party. As the laboristas grew troublesome and Alvarado overly independent, Perón decided it was time to draw the Cantonistas back in. This he did in the simplest way possible: he named Federico Cantoni Argentina's first ambassador to the Soviet Union.[24] At the Bloquista convention, Cantoni in turn obliged his followers to dissolve their party and join Perón's newly formed Unified Revolutionary Party.[25] With the troublesome Cantoni soon off to Moscow, the far more amenable Eloy Camus became not only the point man for the ex-Bloquistas but also the local head of the newly unified party founded by Perón.[26]

"Our political world . . . no longer develops according to the laws of a slow and gradual evolution, but by sudden and extremely violent mutations," the Cantonista paper suggested, as "political parties with apparently deep roots among the citizenry and alleged firmness in their doctrinal positions . . . have simply collapsed after the resonant electoral triumph of Peronism." Peronism was swallowing all the rivalries and contradictions of local politics, to produce "something cast from a new mold" unified so far only by a desire for social reform and an admiration for a single leader.[27]

Having cobbled together a governing coalition, securing at least nominal adherence from virtually every political group in the province, Alvarado now staked his administration on taking over rebuilding. Like Ramella, his status as an outsider made him an especially fervent convert to the cause of provincial autonomy.[28] He established a new provincial Reconstruction Ministry to shadow and eventually replace the Council, naming his close advisor José Conte-Grand to head it.[29]

The Legislature Debates Rebuilding

The setting for Alvarado's campaign was the national Congress. When it reconvened in July 1946, it simply ratified most of the twenty thousand laws and decrees issued under military rule. But the controversy and scope of the reconstruction of San Juan, the largest public works project facing the country, demanded more direct attention. If Alvarado thought he had achieved unity, he was soon disabused of this idea: the five congressmen from San Juan presented four distinct bills, which differed dramatically on the authority, scope, and financing of rebuilding. Their only common commitment was to subsidized mortgages for previous homeowners. Three bills had clear objectives and political backing: Alvarado's bid to gain provincial control of rebuilding, put forward by his two Senate appointees; the Reconstruction Council's attempt to strengthen national control, presented by its former member Tejada; and the economic "wizard" Miranda's quirky scheme to annex rebuilding to the Central Bank, sponsored by the ex-Cantonista Camus. The fourth was a narrow proposal focused entirely on mortgages from the ex-Radical Arévalo Cabezas, who soon dropped it to sign on to the Senate bill. Two months of contentious negotiation, in Congress and back in San Juan, would yield a surprising outcome that recast the local political landscape. In order to appreciate these changes, we must examine each of these bills more closely.[30]

Governor Alvarado advanced a constitutionally solid proposal to grant the province sole authority over rebuilding. The province would take over Reconstruction and the collection, and the federal role would shrink to rebuilding government facilities and providing subsidies and mortgages. Funding would come from four sources: the collection, highly subsidized mortgage loans, sixty million pesos in federal grants, and one hundred million pesos in provincial bonds. The bill enacted the program of the fuerzas vivas: all it specifically required of the new city was wider streets, and in any case rebuilding plans had to be finalized only ninety days after the bill became law.[31]

The Tejada bill came from within Reconstruction itself, as suggested by its extensive documentation of official efforts so far. When the bill was introduced, it was also published as a book, and the Mendióroz plan for the city was placed on display at the state oil company offices a few blocks from the Congress.[32] The bill kept the federal government in charge, reaffirmed the Reconstruction Council, and proposed not only rebuilding the city but also reshaping the ecology (and economy) of the province by building canals and dams. In the central valley, where half the irrigation water was currently lost to evaporation and diversion, Reconstruction proposed sealing and expanding the canal network, doubling the land under irrigation, and building several small hydroelectric dams. After this first stage, financed by four hundred million pesos in national bonds, Reconstruction president Zuleta hoped for a second stage which would expand irrigation in the province's depressed north, his long-standing passion.[33]

The Camus bill was short on detail. For him, the specifics mattered less than integrating the rebuilding of San Juan into the overall rebuilding of the

Argentine economy. As a long-standing defender of provincial autonomy, and the only prominent Cantonista to join the 1945 protests, Camus naturally wished to abolish Reconstruction. But he was also a close ally of Miguel Miranda, the Mendoza industrialist now directing the Central Bank and national economic policy, who wished to bring rebuilding under his own purview.[34] Thus his bill transferred rebuilding to the Central Bank. Removing any mechanism for local representation, the Camus bill reduced rebuilding to widening streets and subsidizing housing and made the province responsible for repaying a three-hundred-million-peso loan. This proposal was adamantly opposed by Reconstruction President Zuleta, who saw it as an attempt to win construction contracts for Miranda and his friends.[35]

None of the proposals envisioned any role for architects or engineers in planning. The political debate over rebuilding took little note of the intense parallel debate among architects. All the attempts to demonstrate authority had failed to win architects a role. Senator Ramella defended the authority of professionals, insisting that rebuilding could not "be done seriously without architects," but he ignored their specific ideas. Tejada stressed irrigation and financing, barely mentioning plans for the city; Camus assigned bankers full responsibility; and Arévalo Cabezas overlooked architects entirely, entrusting all future buildings to "registered engineers or construction companies."[36] In the entire debate, there was only one mention of an individual designer, when Tejada offered passing praise for the "engineer" José Pastor.[37]

Debate centered instead on the financing, scope, and political authority for reconstruction. This started out on a predictable note in Congress, with the opposition blaming Perón for failing to rebuild, and in San Juan, with the Conservative papers lining up behind their ally Alvarado and the Cantonista paper supporting Camus with contorted arguments about how assigning rebuilding to the Central Bank was the best way to secure provincial autonomy.[38]

But then positions began to shift. First Alvarado had abandoned his reformist and nationalist ideals to mount a conservative defense of provincial autonomy, and now Conservatives began to abandon their defense of provincial autonomy to secure a place within the reformist and nationalist project. In July, *Tribuna* reversed its long-standing position and admitted that "the province lacks the personnel and technical and financial elements necessary to carry out a work of this magnitude."[39] By August, one year after the mass protest against Reconstruction, the paper was defending the bill written by Reconstruction officials and sponsored by Tejada.[40] They were skeptical of Alvarado's proposal: the bond issue was too small for the "immense task" ahead, yet so large that repaying it would bankrupt the province. Incurring painful debt for piecemeal reconstruction was dangerous and unsatisfying: "Why not begin on a grand scale?"[41] After years of insisting on austerity and modesty in rebuilding, the paper now argued for a new city that was "solid, healthy, safe, and properly laid-out according to modern standards." Despite Alvarado's efforts to win over Conservatives, they turned against him in almost daily editorials.[42]

This was not a reversal of conviction; the "voice of the wineries" had not suddenly embraced the workers' cause. Conservatives remained faithful to their oldest traditions: it was Alvarado who had misunderstood. The central issue was never provincial autonomy, as the local elite had often asked for national intervention against their rivals, but rather local power and taxation. In its scrupulous defense of provincial autonomy, the Alvarado scheme incurred a heavy financial burden that would eventually fall on the fuerzas vivas. It soon emerged that, sure enough, Alvarado was considering doubling the wine tax. For Conservatives, this "impossible tax" proved that Alvarado was an impractical dreamer who would harm the industry responsible for "more than 95%" of the local economy. Once more, the bodegueros refused to pay taxes for infrastructure, even if that infrastructure was the entire city around them. To save themselves from the burdens of provincial autonomy and avail themselves of a generous national administration, Conservatives were, remarkably enough, making their peace with Reconstruction. After two years as the most committed and recalcitrant opponent of ambitious planning—recall that the architect Simón Ungar had identified the paper as the single most important barrier to rebuilding—the editor of *Tribuna* reversed course and accepted a job with the "useless bureaucracy" he had mocked.[43]

The Congress ultimately approved a modified Tejada bill, keeping the Reconstruction Council in place and increasing national funding. But there was no unity yet: the sanjuanino legislators were so at odds that the final bill was drafted by sympathetic opposition legislators.[44] Alvarado had been defeated, but the direction of local Peronism was not yet clear.

In Search of Support

When Alvarado was elected, he had noticed how consistently and successfully the fuerzas vivas had resisted any attempt at rethinking the city and decided they could be a stable anchor for his administration. If he could keep the support of Perón and the allegiance of workers, while also winning over the fuerzas vivas, he would have the broadest coalition in local political history. Moreover, if he could take over Reconstruction, he would have an extraordinary amount of institutional power over the province. All he had to do was win over the fuerzas vivas. Thus he started out by embracing their cause.

But along the way, he had lost sight of the weakness of his local support, after twenty-five years away from the province, and the dangers of confronting an institution which did after all report to Perón. Above all, he had misunderstood the Conservatives. While many had indeed switched sides after Perón's electoral victory, few were interested in Alvarado's high-minded vision of rebuilding. The Graffigna Conservatives cast their lot with a more generous national state, while others continued to argue for "setting the line," only now as Peronists.

In any case, Alvarado returned from Buenos Aires diminished. He had been proven unwise and weak.[45] Much of local Peronism was moving away from him, and his vice-governor was getting comfortable in the seat of authority.[46]

Alvarado knew he had to win over the press. Newspapers in San Juan had long been ferociously partisan, providing the staff and symbolic weapons for local struggles—and often the literal weapons as well. More recently, they had been the foremost obstacle to government plans for rebuilding, the most resilient space of local opposition. But the comparatively peaceful 1946 election and shifting views on rebuilding seemed to indicate a growing calm. According to the Bloquista paper, this was largely due to a new union, the Journalists Circle, which had "strengthened the consciences of workers of the pen" and turned "the battle fortress" of earlier days into "the club of good understanding."[47] Even though *Tribuna* had switched sides during the legislative debate, Alvarado was the one who had drawn the Graffigna Conservatives into Peronism, and he still needed their support to govern. Alberto Graffigna had directed the paper for years, and his family had provided much of its funding, but legally it belonged to the Conservative Party, which remained opposed to Perón. To strongly support Alvarado, therefore, the Graffigna Conservatives needed to drive out their rivals, which they did, with police assistance, on 9 January 1947.[48]

To win over the "club of good understanding," Alvarado began hiring leading *Tribuna* and *La Acción* journalists to state posts. Conservative journalists switched sides for various reasons: some genuinely converted to the Peronist cause and would remain faithful long after Perón was overthrown. Others came to see Peronism as the best vehicle for fulfilling their Conservative ideals. Still others saw Peronism as the best vehicle for their mercenary ethic and joined simply to draw a salary.

But Alvarado was well aware that he needed to build his own political base, and, as ever on the local scene, the first step was to found a newspaper.

Together with four allies, in late 1946 he founded a paper whose name expressed his hope for rebuilding: *La Nueva Ciudad*.

Despite his legislative defeat and strange alliances, Alvarado sincerely embraced the larger Peronist project and saw himself as its local agent. If others stood in the way, they were not true Peronists. "Our local Quijote," as opponents started to call him, seemed unable to grasp that his version of the populist national project was alienating local popular sectors. Instead, he strenuously defended true Peronism to dwindling crowds of his supporters, drawn largely from the ranks of the Conservatives who had fought Perón a year earlier.[49] For the first anniversary of 17 October, already becoming a crucial date for the movement, he tried to organize an event to honor the workers who had defended Perón, but most unions boycotted his event for a parallel one of their own. Two weeks later, construction workers went out on strike against both private builders and the government and were joined within a week by winery workers. "Soon the majority of the unions in the province will join them," the Bloquistas exulted, as "San Juan returns to what it had always been: fertile ground for social struggles."[50] While Alvarado prevented the strike from expanding and managed to resolve it within two weeks, it still revealed the limits of his appeal to workers—and of his control over the administration, as one of his own ministers subverted his efforts during the strike and had to be dismissed afterward.[51] Then, after Alvarado struggled through the last months of the year, the weakness and contradictions of his position came to a head on the third anniversary of the earthquake.

The Third Anniversary

There were two main events for the anniversary: a series of official ceremonies and a coordinated protest by the propertied. The day before, there was a labor demonstration in support of Perón. On the day itself, there was a mass for the dead; the inauguration of the Sosa Molina Barrio, the first permanent housing project since the earthquake; and the installation of a newly expanded Reconstruction Council. In the afternoon, there was a groundbreaking for the votive temple overlooking the valley, as a memorial of the dead and a marker of rededication to the faith. The main event, the reconvening of the Reconstruction Council, took place in the central plaza of the largest emergency barrio, Captain Lazo, with the presence of the governor, the interior minister, and many officials, and was broadcast live on national radio. To underscore this sense of purpose, the next day Senator Ramella introduced a bill to establish an architecture school in San Juan, so the province could take a more active role in its rebuilding. The government was honoring the dead, beginning the first memorial, recognizing the importance of labor, inaugurating the first permanent piece of the new city—and announcing the future leadership of the rebuilding project, from the spot where it had began.[52]

For Reconstruction, this was a moment of triumph. Enrique Zuleta had taken over Reconstruction at its nadir, when it was the subject of derision, and he had navigated through the tumult, survived several direct political attacks, achieved legislative victory, and now left the agency at the height of its powers, to direct the National Water Authority. During his tenure, the agency had produced a master plan, a rigorous building code, the first cadastral map of the city, detailed studies of water and soil resources, and extensive projects for dams and canals. It had set up a factory to produce ceramics, another to produce concrete blocks, and a school to train masons and craftsmen. It had expanded from three hundred employees at the end of 1945 to nearly three thousand employees a year later, carrying out studies, clearing rubble, and digging canals. It had just completed the first permanent housing project built after the earthquake: the Barrio Sosa Molina, a carbon copy of the pre-quake workers' housing project.[53] The Mendióroz team had finalized their master plan, and their first housing project had gone out to bid. Zuleta had not only allowed anti-seismic construction in the four areas initially labeled "non-rebuildable"; he also decided that the first major housing project, with four hundred units, should go precisely in one of those areas, Concepción.

But there were obvious limits to what Reconstruction had achieved. Zuleta had spent a year tweaking city plans to elite taste in order to win support for his dams. The result was a shelf full of studies, but only a few buildings underway. Many expropriation cases were ending up in court—a sign that property owners regarded Reconstruction as weak and the Conservative-dominated judiciary as supportive.[54] Back in 1944, an outside lawyer had predicted that the fraudulent property registry would make expropriations difficult. Accurately determining the market value of properties, he had argued then, required a large number of sales records—precisely the information lacking here.[55] Now, after three years of frustration, Reconstruction's offers were not overly generous, and property owners were likely to view any offer as too low—and denounce assessors for their "war without mercy against anyone who owns anything."[56] Even so, Reconstruction had survived and was now embarking on a new phase, broadcast to the nation.

It was undoubtedly difficult for Alvarado to smile and speak encouraging words at this ceremony honoring an institution he had pledged to destroy. But it was equally complicated to see those he had tried to recruit, the fuerzas vivas, use the occasion to attack him. According to the Chamber of Commerce, rebuilding was stalled and the future was dark. "We are already up to our necks in plans," they complained, and rebuilding was likely to further slip in importance before "the vastness of the Five Year Plan."[57] A few months earlier, the Chamber had claimed that government actions had only harmed property owners:

> Who have been the victims of the catastrophe of 1944? The working class? No: the workers of San Juan lost nothing... beyond some family suffering, they "benefited" from housing never known before, work to a degree never seen, and... aid that was as effective as it was pernicious... Workers lost nothing, absolutely nothing in the face of the massive losses of commerce and industry, the activities that have something to lose.[58]

This was a stark distillation of the resentment of the powerful: thousands of deaths were written off as "some family suffering," and all loss was measured in capital. These successors to the Del Bono Commission marked the anniversary with a lockout and protest convoy through the city.[59] So far, they claimed, rebuilding had violated local autonomy and property rights: a continually changing city plan, no progress on public structures, little finance for private efforts, arbitrary expropriations, growing "collective anxiety," and "the barriers of a complicated, onerous, and demanding building code."[60] They blamed everything on the government. Their complaint about the building code revealed the narrowness of their vision: any code would be "onerous" in a province that had never had one. Clearly, their earlier advocacy of anti-seismic housing had been an instrumental stance, easily abandoned once radical schemes for rebuilding were defeated.

As the protest was being organized, Alvarado's paper had pointed out that its leaders "were candidates for the Unión Democrática, declared that 'San Juan is Still Waiting,' asked 'where is the money for San Juan' and led the August demonstration." In short, he tried to discredit them by recalling their previous opposition to Perón.[61] But if they were so untrustworthy, why had Alvarado written an inaugural address for their ears and so assiduously pursued their support? The protest simply revealed the failure of Alvarado's strategy: the fuerzas vivas he had tried to win over rejected him for failing to give them complete control of rebuilding and trying to burden them with taxes to pay for it.

The sharpest take on the protest came from a laborista paper in Mendoza. The powerful had little reason to complain, the paper observed, "especially those renting out their own houses while living in homes the state built for workers." Having received ample assistance after the disaster, "the rich seem...

to have enriched themselves even more with Reconstruction." They might praise "private initiative," but they kept their money in the banks. There were few houses under construction, but many lawsuits against expropriation underway. The only locals showing a "spirit of rebuilding," the paper argued, were "patient and long-suffering workers," holding back their justified complaints because "they have faith in Perón, and Alvarado."[62]

This account was certainly correct about popular support for Perón, but it provided little sense of where that support came from. The depiction of the elite rapaciousness was accurate, but there was not much suggestion of what Peronism was offering instead. There was no unifying vision for the future city that might convince workers and overcome the resistance of the propertied. At a time when popular insurgency was transforming politics across the nation, all the newspaper could praise sanjuanino workers for was their resignation.

When Alvarado lost the fuerzas vivas, he lost his post. First, he wagered everything on taking over rebuilding, but failed. Then, he turned on his rivals, and finally on his allies, denouncing virtually every other local Peronist for conspiring against him in a bout of self-fulfilling paranoia. With unrest rising and his control slipping, the provincial legislature voted to impeach him on trumped-up charges. On 12 February 1947, Godoy, Camus, and an envoy from Perón returned from a trip to Buenos Aires. Met at the station by an enthusiastic crowd of Reconstruction workers, they had come to remove Alvarado, and he quickly resigned. Less than a year after proclaiming a new era for San Juan, Alvarado returned to Buenos Aires, repudiated and alone.[63]

PERONISM IN ONE PROVINCE, 1947–1955

Each of the rival groups who had pushed Alvarado out—laboristas, Cantonistas, and Conservative turncoats—thought it could remake local Peronism in its own image. None gave much thought to the man they made governor, Ruperto Godoy. But they underestimated the man and misjudged the movement. Within months, he had outmaneuvered his rivals, appropriated their ideas, and isolated or captured their followers. Like Peronist leaders across the country, Godoy brought insurgent labor under control with an adept combination of incorporation and repression. With national support and a popular touch, he forged a political machine from second-tier journalists, ward-heelers, and enforcers—what rivals described as "the leftovers of every political party that ever existed in the province."[1] When he died of a heart attack in May 1950, four days after beginning his second term, there was a massive public funeral and genuine popular sorrow at the loss of "the first Peronist governor of San Juan."[2]

In his three years in power, Godoy set the pattern for the political and material rebuilding of the province. Those who came to power with Godoy remained until Peronism was overthrown in 1955. These years were when Reconstruction marshaled its institutional power, plans were finally set, and the foundations were poured. The changes in terms of political culture and social rights were clearly evident in popular responses to Peronism, especially around the reelection of Godoy as governor in 1950 and the reelection of Perón as president in 1951. But only a few months later, in 1952, a second earthquake would offer a telling measure of the limits and achievements of Peronism.

Consolidating Power

Unlike the stiff and reserved Alvarado, Godoy was all backslapping and bonhomie, a skillful operator and cafe gadfly who knew how to work a crowd and a deal. Jovial and rotund, with a slight limp from childhood polio, Godoy was a man of humble bearing but distinguished lineage: he bore the same name as his grandfather and his father, who were both statesmen and governors.[3] But Godoy was an only son and inherited little beyond his name: when his father died, his mother remarried and then shipped him off to boarding school. After a few years as a labor official with the provincial government of Santa Fe, he returned to San Juan to earn a modest living as an auctioneer, marry the daughter of a Conservative power broker, and lead the local branch of the Santa Fe–based Progressive Democrat Party.[4] His earlier experience and political connections won him the post of provincial labor secretary during the short-lived liberal intervention after the 1943 coup, and he held on after the STP annexed all provincial labor agencies, becoming first Perón's local point man, later a dependable choice for vice-governor, and finally a safe replacement for the prideful Alvarado.[5]

It was with Godoy that rebuilding finally began. Provincial life regained the sense of possibility last seen in the boom years of the second Cantoni administration two decades earlier. This dynamism was largely due to national policies, particularly funding for Reconstruction, subsidies for the province, and expanded credit. But it was lived with particular intensity, as the shattering of the disaster and the squabbling afterward gave way to a clear political direction, a frenzy of construction, and a sense of new beginnings. The last of the evacuees returned to the city, and even new migrants were drawn by building work.[6]

Because he seemed agreeable and innocuous, Godoy proved successful at "the pacification of spirits," defusing the factionalism of local political life by spreading resources around. He was effective because he was weak: the fact that he was not a polarizing leader in the mold of Cantoni or Graffigna made him trustworthy. Many allied with him thinking they were getting the better of the deal, and some undoubtedly were. But Godoy proved effective in Perón's shadow, as the accommodating local delegate of the compelling and polarizing national leader.

From early on, Godoy had a popular touch: his years as labor delegate had taught him how to work with unions and employers and had given him a sense of the vibrancy of popular culture at this insurgent moment. When Alvarado was governor, he proposed a week of ceremonies honoring Sar-

35 Governor Ruperto
Godoy, 1946. CREDIT
AGN.

miento, centered on public readings of the master's texts, but while Alvarado
was away, Godoy refashioned the events into a popular festival with gauchos
and folkloric music. However untrue to the spirit of Sarmiento, this adjustment showed a keen appreciation of the political uses of popular culture and
of the direction Peronism was taking.[7]

When he became governor in February 1947, Godoy immediately began
consolidating power. He had several points in his favor. For one, he had
personal ties to Conservatives, through his wife's family and his stepbrother,
Eusebio Baltazar Zapata, a former enforcer for Maurín Conservatives who
was now the Peronist speaker of the provincial legislature. Building on these
connections and Alvarado's earlier efforts, Godoy soon reached a stable arrangement with the fuerzas vivas. This alliance began when Conservatives
defected to Peronism, deepened when they supported the Tejada bill on Reconstruction, and solidified when they accepted the overthrow of Alvarado.

Godoy turned Alvarado's informal seduction of the press into an estab-

36 Governor Ruperto Godoy at school event, ca. 1947. From left: Deputy Eloy Camus, Vice-Governor Elias Amado, Governor Ruperto Godoy. Archbishop Rodríguez y Olmos is behind the woman speaker. CREDIT JOSÉ MAZUELOS FRÍAS, COURTESY LEOPOLDO MAZUELOS.

lished system. In September 1947, *La Nueva Ciudad*, the paper Alvarado had founded, was reborn as *Diario de Cuyo*, under the ownership of Godoy and other government officials.[8] This was part of a broader national pattern, as the government employed its control of various tools—congressional investigations, imports of newsprint, bank loans, and official advertising—to favor allies and marginalize critics. "Not a single independent newspaper is left," an opposition legislator declared in July 1948; he claimed that they were "stuffed full of Peronist gold."[9] But this should not be understood solely in terms of coercion and bribery. In San Juan and likely elsewhere, newspapermen aligned with the Peronist cause out of enthusiasm rather than resignation. Conservative newspapermen were prominent in Godoy's inner circle, and they came to wield greater influence with him than under their former Conservative bosses. Indeed, for Godoy's critics, the Journalists Circle was "the central barracks of the antipatriotic conspiracy."[10]

In locating the problem specifically in a union, critics highlighted a central

37 Governor Ruperto Godoy, Deputy Eloy Camus, and Secretary Juan Victoria, ca. 1947.
COURTESY FUNDACIÓN BATALLER.

aspect of Godoy's power. Laboristas had played an essential role in building local Peronism, as we have seen. But by 1946, labor leaders like Tejada were so focused on high politics that they drew challenges from the rank and file, and so passionate about labor autonomy that they drew opposition from Peronist loyalists. This was a common dynamic nationwide, and it played out quite clearly in San Juan, where Tejada quickly lost his few allies among the local political class. After his time as STP delegate, Godoy knew how to win over many workers and activists. Thus by late 1946 Tejada was caught in a pincer movement between grassroots mobilization and high-level maneuvering: his rivals formed a parallel labor central, aligned themselves with Godoy, and then began to deliver results for workers. When Godoy elbowed aside the laboristas in March 1947, shortly after becoming governor, Tejada called for the intervention of the province. This led the pro-Godoy labor federation to denounce Tejada as a traitor to Peronism. The rhetorical struggle and physical confrontations continued for a year, but by early 1948 Tejada and his allies had been pushed aside and the labor movement unified in the new federation led by Godoy's allies—with its press releases written by his staff.

Even so, workers were a minor presence among local Peronist leadership, unlike other provinces. One former bus driver did eventually replace Ramella as senator, and a handful of labor leaders entered the provincial legislature, but officials came more from the second tier of older parties than from unions. Godoy had learned well, during his time at the STP, how to control, accommodate, and defuse popular mobilization.

Godoy's only real rivals were the Cantonistas. The laboristas were easily outmaneuvered; the Catholic activists had limited popular support; the Conservatives were resigned to backroom influence—and each group's foot soldiers steadily defected to Godoy. But the Cantonistas retained significant autonomy. For their help in overthrowing Alvarado, Cantonistas won three key posts in February 1947: public works minister, reconstruction minister, and mayor of San Juan. From these positions, as we will see, they successfully managed to take over the Reconstruction Council and pass a new provincial rebuilding law. But by that November, Godoy had outwitted them, firing the mayor and one minister and winning the other one to his cause. After that, Cantonistas would remain within the Peronist fold but split into two groups: an orthodox group that answered to Camus and a dissident group that tried and failed to radicalize local Peronism. In 1949, when the dissidents tried to block Godoy's reelection, he had them expelled from the Peronist Party and then rewrote the electoral law to prevent them from running for office on either a Peronist or Bloquista ticket. Federico Cantoni himself had resigned his ambassadorship and returned from Moscow by that point, but after being welcomed by adoring crowds, he retreated to his estate in the provincial north and remained uncharacteristically silent throughout Perón's rule.[11]

"The revolution has not reached San Juan," the dissident Cantonistas repeated once they were turned out of power, reflecting the disenchantment of a broad range of activists.[12] Cantonistas denounced the ex-Conservatives in Godoy's inner circle; Catholics denounced the ex-Cantonistas; others denounced the ex-laboristas. One Catholic activist claimed that Godoy "enthrones the scum of all the old parties, people who by their nature disdain and mistreat those who have always been the underdogs, the *descamisados*." For this activist, the provincial government was "a true system of anti-Peronism" erected precisely in the name of Perón.[13]

Continually surprised by the support Godoy received from above, these accounts treated his government as an anomaly. What they failed to grasp was that this was the form Peronism took on the periphery. While the challenge to previously existing authority was central to Peronism's appeal, the people leading the challenge were mostly lesser functionaries of that previous authority. In part this was because the kind of political awakening Peronism represented nationally could only come once, and had already come to San Juan with Cantonismo two decades before. These fissures were impossible to overcome, and they ultimately resulted in an internally divided movement that was unable to build the future it promised but remained unassailably superior to the past it renounced.

To be sure, Godoy and his successors took major steps toward social justice on a local level. Provincial government spending doubled in real terms after the quake and, except for a dip in 1953–54, continued at that level through 1955 (see appendix). The national government dedicated considerable resources to San Juan, primarily through the Reconstruction Council. This national spending oscillated, first rising dramatically then dropping precipitously, due to struggles within Reconstruction and shifts in national economic policy. But at the peak in 1948, the Reconstruction budget equaled the provincial budget. Overall, then, government spending had roughly quadrupled. Yet local taxes hardly rose, which helped secure the grudging support of local elites. Instead, most of the increase was funded by federal transfer payments and bond issues.[14]

The Godoy administration was marked by an expansive spirit, due to rising wages, increased government spending, flourishing wineries, and the construction boom. These were the most prosperous years the local poor had known, and even if many continued to live in emergency housing, they had far greater access to all kinds of public services—schools, medical care, and social aid. The construction boom was primarily due to the energy of the Reconstruction Council and its encouragement of private building. But it was also connected to other public works, especially canals, as we will see. The construction sector expanded dramatically, from a dozen firms in 1944 to over two hundred by 1949, as everyone from the president of the legislature to the chief justice of the Supreme Court started their own.

Water and Wine

Before taking over Reconstruction, Enrique Zuleta had directed the Water Department, and he retained that earlier focus even after assuming the larger mission. While he had folded irrigation projects into the national rebuilding law passed in October 1946, he also appreciated that his successors at Reconstruction might not see them as equally essential. Therefore, he took the dam projects with him when he took over the national water authority in January 1947. From there, he built the province's first hydroelectric dam, increasing locally generated power thirty-fold, and began planning for others (although they would not be completed for decades).[15] As one provincial legislator put it, these dams were the triumph of "civilization over barbarism" and fulfillment of Perón's promises of transformation. "Our poverty is solely due to a lack of leadership over fifty years of misgovernment and abandon," he said,

38 North Canal (Canal Perón), 1950. CREDIT AGN.

but now Perón had recognized the province's potential and provided "the instrument that will make us . . . dignified heirs of patriotic glory: dams."[16]

Zuleta left behind two crucial irrigation projects funded by one hundred million pesos in bonds: the completion of the northern canal (which was inevitably named the Perón Canal) and the sealing of the entire network. These projects were shepherded to completion by Godoy's technical advisor Juan Victoria, the ally of the modernist architects who was committed on expanding irrigation, and by two disciples of Zuleta who became ministers for Godoy, Juan Melis and Rinaldo Viviani. The irrigation projects provided steady employment for thousands, opened ample opportunities for contractors, and expanded the irrigated area by at least a third. The government created a new registry of property ownership and irrigation rights. Since the right to irrigation water was associated with particular plots, and this registry had not been updated since 1894, this was a crucial step in democratizing access to fertile land.[17]

Public investments in irrigation certainly allowed for greater social mobility, and viñateros increased in number and prosperity, even managing in 1948 to finally establish a union to represent their interests.[18] Viñateros revived the proposals for cooperative wineries, so important to the most ambitious early visions for rebuilding, but by now the government showed little interest. Talk of reversing monoculture remained just that: the hectares under vine increased by a third, and production increased even more, as attempts to develop alternative crops fizzled, limited to a few thousand olive trees. The lonely insistence of a Communist militant in 1947 that building a just San Juan required a redistribution of property and a diversification of the economy went unheeded. Instead, the most comprehensive reshaping of land, water, and property in fifty years expanded access to land but deepened the commitment to grape monoculture.[19]

Similarly, Peronist reforms greatly strengthened unions and viñateros, but many bodegueros still came to terms with Godoy. Social and labor reforms were not open to negotiation, which greatly reduced their profits and power, but subsidies, regulations, and economic policy certainly were open to consultation. Like most industries, wineries prospered, especially until 1949. Rising wages nationwide meant expanding consumer markets and significant winery profits. Bodegueros never did receive the compensation they had been demanding since 1944. But instead, they were granted generous loans, including a special industrial credit—with long terms and negative real interest rates—which enabled them to modernize the wineries and strengthen their position.[20] Slow to rebuild their own homes, bodegueros were fast to expand industrial capacity.[21] When the early bonanza came to an end, and price controls on wine began to cut into winery profits, the government allowed bodegueros to water down their wine, passing the costs on to growers.

In short, bodeguero power was confined, but not overturned. There were some who resisted, and a few leading Graffigna Conservatives kept their distance from the government, losing access to official credit and influence over policy. But Graffigna himself won a place at the table, took over the Chamber of Commerce, and led it into Perón's corporatist business organization, the Confederación General Económica. The Graffignas remained dominant in local media: despite scarcities of imported newsprint, their newspaper *Tribuna* received all it needed, and when two government-influenced networks bought up all the radio stations, they left the Graffigna station as the last independent broadcaster in the country. In turn, the large wineries would become a leading source of funding for the Peronist party itself.[22]

Yet however effective Godoy proved at mediating between interest groups and improving the lives of everyday citizens, the true test of his success remained rebuilding the city—and here the central actor was the Reconstruction Council, which Godoy could influence but did not control.

Bringing Reconstruction to Heel: Lines of Authority

When Zuleta departed in January 1947, Reconstruction seemed to have consolidated its power: Alvarado's takeover attempt had failed, the Mendióroz plan had become law, the province had its first construction code, and work had begun. But behind the scenes, Reconstruction staff were eroding that achievement, and a second takeover attempt was on its way.

"There is nothing more dangerous than an architect from Buenos Aires with an HB pencil and a roll of trace paper": that was the watchword of Manuel Aramburo, the local road builder who had become technical chief at Reconstruction. His words showed that he was familiar with the tools of design—and held them in contempt.[23] He was hardly afflicted by the "delirium of intellectual pride" Alvarado had diagnosed among Reconstruction officials; indeed, he fancied himself a practical man standing up against the dreamers. He had been Zuleta's emissary in the successful attempt to win establishment support for Reconstruction by making concessions, and he had taken that spirit to heart. In late 1946, Aramburo led the agency to temporize on a number of key issues. In the city center, heavily damaged commercial buildings were allowed to make repairs, even when their location conflicted with the future street line, if owners promised to bring the building into compliance within ten years.[24] Similarly, every plan since the earthquake had included a minimum lot width. This was crucial to ensuring light, air, and anti-seismic safety for future homes. But the very thing that made the requirement urgent, the narrow dimensions of existing lots, made it politically unpopular. So Reconstruction abandoned the effort, granting waivers to owners of narrow lots if they promised to purchase the neighboring parcel when available for sale.[25] Thus core elements of the Mendióroz plan were already weakened before Zuleta left.

Then the second takeover attempt began, led by Central Bank President Miguel Miranda, who had lost the round in the Congress but had not given up. He could still count on his friend Eloy Camus, the ex-Cantonista who was influential both in the national and provincial legislatures, and now aligned himself with Aramburo inside Reconstruction. Miranda also had direct influence over the Reconstruction Council, since most of its members were now bank representatives whom he had named. The interior minister appointed the president of Reconstruction, but Miranda was soon running the show. Thus as soon as the Council convened, a bank representative proposed a "readjustment" of the just-completed Mendióroz plan, and the new president agreed.

Entrusted with the task, technical chief Aramburo radically scaled back rebuilding. He kept the buildings architects had proposed but abandoned larger efforts at planning, giving up on reordering streets or increasing public space. Claiming that difficulties with the first housing project in Concepción were "eloquent" proof of the futility of expropriations, he argued for abandoning the effort and redrawing streets along their previous lines.[26] Inside the four avenues, he slashed expropriations to a tenth of the Mendióroz plan, and outside the four avenues, he dropped them almost entirely.[27] Since the earthquake, the one thing everyone had agreed the city needed was more public parks. But to save on maintenance, Aramburo slashed them "to the smallest possible area," a quarter of the Mendióroz plan, leaving nothing of the "garden city" architects and opponents alike had promised since 1944.[28] The plan was only marginally competent: Aramburo's team designed a new train station but forgot to provide for the tracks. This was urban design as a bureaucrat's amusement: all the attacks on "useless experts" had left no one at Reconstruction with useful expertise. Rather than a "cornerstone of national planning," the new city would be a dusty replica of its former self.

Having quietly guided the "readjustment" from afar, Miranda raised the stakes in April 1947: he went to San Juan, declared that Reconstruction had "done nothing," and cut off funding.[29] The "readjustment" was approved, but Zuleta's replacement then prudently resigned, after only six months in office.[30]

The first step of the takeover was the installation of a new Reconstruction President: Gerónimo Zapata Ramírez, the longtime San Juan branch manager for the National Bank.[31] Loyal to Miranda and close to the Cantonistas, Zapata Ramírez was the first local to head Reconstruction. At this moment, Camus and the former Cantonistas had full control of two provincial ministries and the federal agency as well. Zapata Ramírez made a dramatic debut: his first step was to fire everyone who worked for the agency (although Aramburo naturally remained).[32] On hearing the news, La Acción set off its roof siren in triumph. An opposition paper acidly observed that "this was all that was missing to make the reconstruction of San Juan a complete disgrace."[33]

Since 1945, Reconstruction had hired over two thousand workers, making it the province's largest employer and the home of its most powerful union. The union had been winning significant battles over wages, schedules, and work rules.[34] It was an important stronghold for laboristas—and also for Communists, who opposed Perón but now supported many Peronist initiatives—and thus a threat to both Cantonistas and Godoy.[35] The firing thus aimed at crippling a potentially troublesome union. Labor leaders mounted demonstrations, sent a delegation to Buenos Aires, and even convinced a few Cantonistas to try to dismiss administrative staff instead of workers, but they had no success, and the firing stood.[36]

Zapata Ramírez's second step was to offer a ten-thousand-peso subsidy to any property owner who started building immediately.[37] By breaking the union, Zapata Ramírez effectively cut wages and made workers available for private construction—or private companies contracting with the state. This was not a matter of suppressing labor as a whole—labor activism continued to rise, and the workers soon found less lucrative employment with private contractors—but of subordinating it to political power.[38]

The third step of the takeover was perhaps the most surprising: Camus and the former Cantonistas became the provincial champions of a narrowed vision of rebuilding, in alliance with Miranda and Zapata Ramírez. For over twenty years, Cantoni's party had been the foremost local advocates of housing for all, defending both social reform and provincial control. Now they renounced the reform in favor of the control. After consistently blaming Conservatives for the failure to rebuild, Cantonistas shifted the blame and even adopted Conservative rhetoric and explanations. No longer was the root of the problem the obstinancy of the fuerzas vivas. Now Cantonistas located the "primary cause" of the failure in the "outside experts," who had made ridiculous plans and "betrayed the disinterested and patriotic hopes of the President of the Republic."[39] The Cantonistas attacked the "legion of outsiders" and the "luxuriant and sterile bureaucracy" at Reconstruction.[40] They backed up this attack with revealing examples, denouncing "experts" for designing workers' homes that cost thirty thousand pesos and believing that "people could have a luxurious house without the resources needed to maintain it."[41] The party that had once demanded housing for all now mocked thirty-thousand-peso houses as too expensive for workers, even as they insisted that no "decent" home for the all-important middle class could possibly be built for less than fifty thousand.[42]

Centering the attack on "outside experts" served to obscure what Cantonistas had always seen as central: the exercise of power within the province itself. By this point, such attacks were entirely about discrediting radical visions, not about undermining the actual "experts" at Reconstruction: after all, the most passionate critic of "outside experts" and "architects from Buenos Aires" was Aramburo, who was now the chief "expert" at Reconstruction. By associating "outside experts" with radicalism, and discrediting both, the Cantonistas completed the task their Conservative opponents had begun, emptying rebuilding of its potential for transformation. Rebuilding should not create a new order, only perfect the old one.

"San Juan cannot be the testing ground for urban . . . fantasies," the Cantonistas argued.[43] They took Aramburo's "readjustment," added a central avenue running west from the main plaza, and presented it as a bill to the provincial legislature. In an enthusiastic midnight vote six weeks after the mass firing, the legislature passed the "readjusted" plan. Two years and a day after the 1945 protest, the government had finally "set the line"—and this Conservative goal had been achieved by Cantonistas.[44]

The one new feature introduced by legislators—the central avenue—was presented as a familiar, local, and simple idea. It was indeed familiar, as some version of it had appeared in the Guido-Carrasco and even Mendióroz plans.[45] But it was hardly local: the model was the sixty-year-old Avenida de Mayo in Buenos Aires, the very definition of nineteenth-century urbanism.[46] And far from being a simple task, it required significant expropriations and the demolition of perhaps half the major historic buildings to survive the earthquake. The designs of the elite might be less ambitious, but they were just as disruptive of property and dependent on Buenos Aires models as any design by an "outside expert."

At Reconstruction, Zapata Ramírez opened the floodgates. He increased subsidies, expanded low-interest loans, and granted nearly two thousand building permits on the "readjusted" layout. But problems soon emerged. The dream of Cantonista dominance proved fleeting. By the end of 1947, Godoy maneuvered them out of his cabinet, and Zapata Ramírez naturally fell into line with the governor. The dream of quick rebuilding along "readjusted" lines did not last long either: the incompetence of Aramburo's team soon became evident, and even the Chamber of Commerce, stalwart advocates of minimal solutions, admitted that Aramburo's work "contained errors of such magnitude that before long it will be modified again."[47] Zapata Ramírez recognized that he needed designers to provide what he called "an urbanistic direction."[48]

By chance, he stumbled upon the one architect still committed to rebuilding but not yet burned by official vacillations. José Pastor, who had tirelessly advocated moving the city in professional journals—and two books—was also a staff architect of the National Bank, in charge of designing the new branch office. Zapata Ramírez met him in September 1947, looked over his writings, and then called him with an offer in late December. Within a month, Pastor traveled to San Juan, suggested a plan of attack, and was appointed chief "urbanistic advisor."[49] Four years after the disaster, the decisive moment for planning had finally arrived.

Bringing Reconstruction to Heel: The Pastor Plan

In 1944, with the country apparently united behind Perón, Pastor had called San Juan "a large-scale 'test' of what will have to be done later in every city in the country."[50] By late 1945, with ambitious early plans discarded and the country divided by Perón, he had watched with frustration "as the door slowly closes on an opportunity for progress that goes far beyond a mere plan for San Juan." Yet even with this defeat, he had also held out hope that planning might still advance, however slowly.[51]

While "the greatest urban opportunity of the era," the reconstruction of San Juan, was taking a dispiriting course, Pastor had reasons for guarded optimism, as expanding state authority brought architects many new opportunities. By remaining politically neutral in 1945, the professional association of architects had kept itself in Perón's good graces and now reaped the benefits—unlike the engineering association, which was intervened in by the government.[52] Designs for a few key government buildings were chosen through SCA-run competitions, fulfilling an old professional dream. Julio Otaola, from the Mendióroz team, was named rector of the University of Buenos Aires and finally established an independent faculty of architecture. Even many of the architects who had worked on San Juan and then joined the opposition in 1945 had returned to prominent government posts. Ernesto Vautier continued to work for the MOP and became the first chair of urbanism in the new faculty. Eduardo Sacriste, Hilario Zalba, and Jorge Vivanco turned the new architecture school in Tucumán into a center of modernist experimentation, even starting work on a massive new university campus. Finally, and most ambitiously, Jorge Ferrari Hardoy and Juan Kurchan replaced the Mendióroz team as planners for the city of Buenos Aires and began to put 2into action the radical plan for remaking the city they had hatched with Le pCorbusier a decade earlier.[53]

But there remained San Juan itself. After visiting late in 1946, as the finishing touches were being put on the Mendióroz plan, the modernist Sacriste judged rebuilding a failure. The opportunity for a "laboratory" of architecture and urbanism had been lost. Instead the locals had gotten the streets they wanted, and "what is built on those new streets expresses vanity, emptiness and falsehood, it is inadequate, it is not architecture."[54] Mendióroz immediately and bitterly complained in the professional journal, leading Sacriste, who counted him as a friend, to tone down his critique. Mendióroz's defensive response underscored how embarrassed the profession's leaders were at the course rebuilding had taken, and how determined they were to avoid debate about it.[55]

This reluctance to debate took a chilling direction following an incident in 1947 involving Fermín Bereterbide, the effective leader of the first San Juan team after the earthquake. Bereterbide played an active role in the opposition, then returned to state employment while continuing to lobby against the

Mendióroz plan. During the congressional debate on the rebuilding law, for example, he and Vautier unsuccessfully asked the SCA to advocate a more far-reaching approach.[56] In May 1947, Bereterbide was a winner in a design competition for the new Air Force headquarters and used the prize ceremony to register his protest: he went on stage but refused to shake Perón's hand, causing a scene and prompting the other nineteen contestants to file a complaint with the SCA. For the president of the association, Federico de Achával, architects had a duty to remain "apolitical": "The SCA is not interested in analyzing or discussing power as a fact nor authority as a right, nor the matter of the origins of power or the particular form social authority takes. It can only occupy itself 'in helping to govern.' "[57] Annoyed at Bereterbide's insult to authority and insistence on airing the messy San Juan business, the SCA president charged him with violating professional ethics, and a general assembly voted to expel him.[58] The defense of an "apolitical" mission thus led to the first political expulsions.[59] Although Bereterbide continued to practice architecture and even won local government contracts, the drive to shut down debate was clear. It was obviously inspired by the leadership's ideas about authority in general, but there were also more instrumentalist reasons for silencing Bereterbide, because in the time between the incident and the expulsion vote, the SCA had gained control of the nation's largest building project, the reconstruction of San Juan.

Pastor joined Reconstruction fully aware that radical transformation was now off the table. Although he considered "readjustment . . . a true embarrassment for Argentine urbanism," he agreed to work within it.[60] In many ways, this proved a political blessing. With the overall shape of the city set, Pastor could resolve the remaining issues—especially roads and railroads—and start designing housing immediately. He could also greatly strengthen the institutional power of architecture and, from his position as the editor of the professional journal, establish himself as a leading voice in planning.

Overall, Pastor was trying to accomplish four things: first, to plan a city and its buildings comprehensively according to broadly modernist principles; second, to establish a national and even international precedent for such planning and its specific technical forms (the master plan, zoning code, and so forth); third, to provide colleagues and allies with the opportunity to build an extraordinary range of buildings within that plan; and fourth, to establish a national precedent for architects to design public buildings through competition. While the conditions under which he accepted set severe limits on the planning itself, they actually made it easier to pass and publicize plans—even if they were less ambitious than he would have liked, for the first time they

Pastor plan, 1948

1 Cathedral / Civic Center
2 Railroad Station
— Proposed Streets
— Historic Streets

0   1   2 km

would have legal force. This also allowed him to move quickly to assigning work to teams of professionals, through competitions, and thus inaugurate a new method for running large complex projects. Pastor began work in January, submitted his plan in April, and saw it enacted as law in June. The building design competitions began soon afterward. This was the first successful implementation in Argentina of a land use zoning code, a building code, and a regional master plan.[61]

"Without being extraordinary or utopian, as others were, the new plan is viable and correct," the Mendoza newspaper concluded.[62] Like every architect since the quake, Pastor envisioned the new city as a collection of neighborhoods, each organized around a school, church, plaza, and cluster of stores. This was part of a broader decentralizing of urban functions. But the details were well thought out, even if more shaped by powerful constraints than driven by the pathbreaking innovation Pastor evoked. Each of these neighborhoods had a new housing project, seven in all, for a total of seven hundred units along with the four hundred already underway in Concepción. Pastor and his allies also designed new schools and clinics in this renewed effort. The plan called for parks, building setbacks, and a ring highway. It also greatly broadened the streets, which was crucial to ensuring that buildings would not collapse onto each other or the public in earthquakes. Pastor made every street twice as wide, which ended the danger of collapse and opened up space for the trees and canals reformers had long advocated. Within the city, adobe was banned and all future construction had to meet the anti-seismic code; outside the city, new construction in adobe was permitted, as long as it was light and structurally stable.[63] Pastor recruited a team of Italian engineers to develop an irrigation system, working steadily to find a practical means to produce a city of shaded streets, a goal every architect had proclaimed but no one had done much to advance.

Pastor persuaded Reconstruction to choose the designers of major public buildings through professional competitions run by the SCA. If the city did not exemplify large-scale modernist urbanism, it would at least be composed of modernist structures—and offer architects a new mechanism of institutional power. Pastor thus spent months developing a legal framework for the relationship between private architects and the state. Clearly, this project was a spearhead: not only would these hundreds of buildings guarantee many professionals work for years to come but guaranteeing private architects a role in future state projects promised even more down the line.

If not a "laboratory" for urbanism, San Juan would at least be a laboratory for the professional authority of architects. While the overall scope of the project was already set, and not as Pastor would have preferred, the architects were still able to systematically and collaboratively design every building in a new city center. Of course, architects were mostly acting in their traditional role of designing urban symbols of power. But the scale of the task— some seventy firms ultimately won contracts—meant this could significantly strengthen the position and broaden the scope of architecture as a liberal profession doing government work. By February 1949, there were winning designs for all major public buildings, including the Cathedral, banks, city hall, civic center, legislature, courthouse, and prison. Pastor, meanwhile, filled the pages of the professional journal with a profusion of documentation of the project and all its pieces.[64]

Bringing Reconstruction to Heel: Reversal

Zapata Ramírez supported Pastor enthusiastically, and funds were flowing freely. But when signs of economic trouble appeared in January 1949, Perón removed Miranda as chief economic policymaker, and Zapata Ramírez lost his patron. Within days, economists who wanted to reverse Miranda's expansive policies sent investigators to look at spending on Reconstruction. They had key inside allies, most importantly the technical chief Manuel Aramburo, who was still angry that his "readjustment" of the plan had been discarded.[65]

Aramburo embarked on a year-long bureaucratic war against the architects. Invoking a law that barred state officials from serving as independent contractors to the state, he set out to shred Pastor's carefully constructed design competition. Many competition winners had part-time state jobs, like Pastor's National Bank post, and Aramburo argued this meant Reconstruction could not pay them.[66] He also had the Reconstruction Council slash Pastor's proposed architectural fee scale. Aramburo was trying to separate design from construction, in order to pay architects as little as possible and redirect the projects to his local engineer allies.[67] While Pastor insisted that professional compensation should be set just like workers' wages, "according to the cost of living proportional to the social class each belongs to," the Council ignored him.[68] Under the final agreement, an Aramburo ally on the Council boasted that they had obtained "the lowest rate of payment in any category for any state body," while leaving the question of whether architects could direct projects at all to be resolved in the future by the provincial reconstruction minister, an engineer.[69] Aramburo was exultant to his staff about his sabotage of the architects. The fees and project control mattered a great deal to architects yet constituted a trivial part of the costs of rebuilding—but Aramburo's campaign held up work for a year.[70]

In the meantime, Zapata Ramírez, after losing his patron Miranda, tried to make himself indispensable to the interior minister by embarking on a publicity campaign. After all the press attacks on Reconstruction, he had hit upon a counterstrategy, as he told Senator Ramella in a letter: he bought favorable coverage from all the major dailies, in San Juan and elsewhere.[71]

This campaign began in earnest just as the investigator finished his report.[72] Thus readers of Buenos Aires newspapers were told how, after only five years, the "gigantic task of Reconstruction" was virtually complete. Instead of a "San Juan problem," there was a "fruitful harvest of realities." The city was well on its way to becoming "the most modern and rational of our cities." The "Peronist Revolution has shown the social measure of its doctrines," claimed one report, in this "masterwork of the Interior Ministry" that firmly established the "willpower of the New Argentina." Indeed, one provincial legislator argued that the rebuilt city was a rebuke to the "bad Argentines" who had tried to use the ruins against Perón, while he "at every moment stretches out his generous hand to make San Juan the city Sarmiento dreamt of: great, strong and beautiful."[73]

These claims were exaggerated but not fictional. Reconstruction was indeed completing hundreds of houses and schools, but this talk of "unceasing work" that enabled San Juan "to know itself more deeply" offered the most optimistic take possible.[74] And for all that the triumphal tone concealed conflicts, some notes of controversy filtered through. When an account declared that "the little model houses from the [1946] exposition are now beginning to become real houses of normal dimensions," a careful reader might note that after three years they were only *beginning* to do so. The insistence that "the apparent slowness" of reconstruction only "conceals a profusion of technical preparation work" was accurate but fit poorly with the overall image of a future already achieved.[75] A half-million-ton cement purchase from Chile confirmed the progress of rebuilding but cast doubt on the claims of readily available raw materials and a supposedly functioning cement plant in San Juan.[76]

The frenzy of positive coverage could not last. In January 1950, Zapata Ramírez was dismissed, Pastor was fired, the irrigation system was scrapped, the architects of individual buildings were removed, and everything was put on hold for a new round of austerity cuts. The Pastor plan would remain as the guide, but rebuilding would proceed slowly, held back by fluctuations in funding, changes in Reconstruction leadership, and above all the influence of the technical chief. For the final winner of these struggles was Aramburo, who directed contracting work to his allies and deferred projects as he tinkered with them to protect the interests of the fuerzas vivas. He would leave evidence of his handiwork all over the rebuilt city, in the strange turns and mysterious narrowing of streets he had modified to favor one well-connected bodeguero or another.[77]

Reelection

In 1948, after the official candidate won a massive victory in a special legislative election, one newspaper drew the clear conclusion: "Rubble or no rubble, we want Perón."[78] Indeed, whatever the vagaries of rebuilding, Perón's popularity remained great and his project largely unquestioned. In April 1949, he finally returned to the province to inaugurate the new northern canal and to visit the dozens of projects underway. Fifty thousand sanjuaninos came out to see him, many bearing banners with the names of their emergency barrios, as the governor thanked him once more for the aid collection and rebuilding and called upon the citizenry to "produce works worthy of Perón." For his part, the president was gracious and vague, glad to join in the work of raising up the province again.[79]

When Godoy ran for reelection a year later, his campaign centered on housing and public works. On the sixth anniversary of the earthquake, a week before the election, Godoy inaugurated the María Eva Duarte de Perón barrio. This was the project of 420 homes in Concepción begun two years before.

The ceremony was carefully staged: the homes were built by the Reconstruction Council on behalf of the province, which turned the keys over to the Eva Perón Foundation, which distributed them to representatives of forty-two unions, which then handed them to individual members. The intricate choreography of Peronist institutions was characteristic of this moment of social change by bombastic means, with the repeated gesture of the gift, the by-now constant echoes of Evita's name, and the presence of so many officials—the governor, both senators, a national deputy, and a Reconstruction Council member.

Godoy drew attention to the new houses and the broader benefits provided by the government, explicitly pointing back to the disaster and its role in Perón's rise. "The collection and reconstruction" might have provided "the opposition . . . their preferred weapons for combating . . . General Perón," Godoy admitted. He argued that those attacks were wrong, as "the collection" had been employed "with scrupulous and irreproachable honesty and immense collective benefits" to compensate merchants, aid the poor, and provide emergency housing for thousands.[80]

Opponents mocked Godoy's administration as "a government of peons," and he naturally turned this disdain into a badge of honor. Indeed, he claimed, "they could not have offered greater praise to my work," as "my government is a government of peons" in both senses: it ensures peons, like all workers, have a voice, and it puts them to work for the general benefit. Indeed, Godoy claimed his administration had accomplished more "than all the others from the last half century combined."[81]

Raised salaries and increased consumption meant these were the most prosperous years most locals had known. But this buoyancy was barely reflected in the physical city. On the key question of housing, the balance of Godoy's government was ambiguous. While workers are "living in housing savages would have disdained," dissident Cantonistas complained, "the oligarchs are living for free in the true workers housing located in the Sosa Molina, Rawson and Rivadavia barrios."[82] Those were the highest-quality houses available, planned as "workers' housing" but largely assigned to local elites. Despite some changes, and repeated criticism, over the years, this

39 President Juan Perón and Deputy Eloy Camus (to his left) in Mendoza, 1948. CREDIT AGN.

40 Evita Perón, Governor Ruperto Godoy, and President Juan Perón, San Juan, 1949. COURTESY FUNDACIÓN BATALLER.

41 María Eva Duarte de Perón barrio, Concepción, San Juan, 1950. CREDIT AGN.

pattern of occupation held, as an official census of seven small projects confirmed. At a time when two hundred pesos was a high monthly wage for a worker, very few project residents reported earnings under four hundred pesos, most were between four and eight hundred pesos, and a handful over two thousand. These reports are likely low: the minister who ordered the census appeared on it himself with no reported income.[83] Even in official circles, this state of affairs caused nervousness, and after Godoy was reelected, his paper went after the "oligarchs" who refused to give up their state-built homes.[84]

In terms of permanent structures, the barrio in Concepción was complete and seven further barrios designed by Pastor were under construction. Perhaps a thousand private homes had been built with official subsidies. The government had also distributed several thousand wooden structures since 1946 and added more units on the edge of emergency housing barrios. These emergency structures generally violated the new building code—although some were built with *simulated* reinforcing columns—but they were, as an embarrassed deputy admitted in the one debate on San Juan in the national Congress, "a solution for the poor" because they charged no rent.[85] Beyond that, however, there had been only minor improvements to the largest barrios,

42 Housing built by Reconstruction Council, 1950. CREDIT AGN.

such as 4 June and Captain Lazo. Godoy's signal initiative was to sell emergency housing to its occupants for a nominal sum. Condemned by his local critics, this measure accomplished a central national objective of Peronism—housing for workers—by rhetorical sleight of hand.

Absurd as this initiative was, it did capture a shift taking place in the emergency barrios: residents' growing sense of ownership of the community. The incipient forms of social organization evident since late 1944, such as Catholic organizations and local clubs, now reached full flower. The emergency barrios were the centers for the most lively base organizations for the Peronist party and the homes of folklore peñas (musical gatherings) as well as the often-criticized open-air dance halls. Most notably, the barrios began forming football clubs and established a provincewide tournament. Here was a striking metaphor of the new San Juan: while the established football teams were generally associated with bodegas, like Del Bono and Graffigna, the new teams were associated with barrios. This emerging barrio identity was naturally tied to popular and Peronist identities. And even if the regime was going relatively slow in providing a decent home for barrio residents, it certainly did open up a range of new institutions to them, from better-paying work in construction and light industry to schools with greatly expanded enrollments.[86]

Insisting on building a "home for every family," Godoy won reelection easily, proud that so much had changed over four years: the canals, the con-

43 Plaza 25 de Mayo, west side, 1950. Compare with figure 7. Note the missing Cathedral, just before the Del Bono building, and the Zunino hardware store sign, in the foreground. CREDIT AGN.

struction boom, the emergency houses, and hundreds of permanent homes as well.[87] He didn't mention the recovery of the city center, but that was also a point in his favor. Except for the Cathedral, every building on the western side of Plaza 25 de Mayo was still standing, a surviving remnant. There were many ramshackle buildings along the streets and gaps in the skyline, but socially and commercially, the downtown was remarkably lively.

These themes were prominently featured in Perón's reelection campaign in 1951. A local pamphlet trumpeted "one hundred years of progress" in only "five years of Peronist administration." It invoked achievements familiar from the national campaign: twice as many hospital beds, twice as many kilometers of road, expanded canals, the first hydroelectric dam, and more diversified and industrialized production. It also highlighted policies specific to this devastated province, such as the eight million pesos from the collection distributed as maternity grants, scholarships, and building subsidies. Most strikingly, the pamphlet described "a rebuilding experience unique in the world" that had produced eight thousand homes, all of them "anti-seismic." This had taken place in a climate of "social justice, tranquility of spirits, administrative morality, and social and political peace."[88]

The count of homes was decidedly optimistic, including everything from private homes that had received small subsidies to planned public projects that were theoretically "under construction." Outside San Juan, such claims were credible because of the extraordinary number of public works Peronism actually was completing. Inside San Juan, they were more suspect, but with the recent boom and the clear sense of direction, they seemed attainable in the near future.

One further point stood out from the pamphlet: Godoy's successors valued "tranquility of spirits" so much that they laid claim to it twice. Indeed, for all the tensions within Peronism itself, these were remarkably calm years in local political history, the first time in thirty years one elected administration succeeded another. Thanks to the success of the government and the weakness of the opposition Radical party, Perón won the November 1951 elections easily, gaining 78 percent of the vote in San Juan, one of his best results nationwide.[89]

The Earthquake of 1952

On 10 June 1952, six days after Perón began his second term, with Evita dying and political polarization sharpening, another earthquake struck. Once more it came in the early evening, driving terrified crowds outside, this time into the winter cold. The temblor was stronger than in 1944 but did far less damage, leaving only five dead—one from falling rubble, four from exposure.[90]

The earthquake was less destructive partly because it was strongest in the rural areas, where there was less to destroy, and partly because many of the most vulnerable structures in the city had been destroyed eight years earlier. Still, damage was heavy in the countryside, particularly near Pocito to the southwest, where architects had wanted to raise the new city in 1944. Though thousands of quincha shacks collapsed, no one was hurt, highlighting both the material's structural flaws and its social virtues.

This time, local response was swift and effective, with the quick arrival of the governor, provision of aid, and inspection and repair of buildings. In the countryside, two just-completed residential schools, originally inspired by the need to care for the orphans of the first quake, opened their doors to those who had lost homes in the second quake. The Eva Perón Foundation provided one hundred families from emergency barrios with just-completed permanent homes and moved victims of the second quake into the places this opened up.[91] Beyond this, however, the government was not eager to repeat the barrio experiment. New emergency structures were erected, following 1944 precedents with three important changes: the materials were simple, labor was local, and the structures went up wherever they were needed, but not in barrios. A thousand were built in a month.[92]

In the city, damage was less extensive but more embarrassing: many buildings repaired after 1944 proved unsound, starting with Reconstruction headquarters itself, a converted school which had to be demolished.[93] A few new structures also failed. For one engineer, this suggested that some were still doing shoddy work and the lessons of 1944 had not sunk in fully.[94]

The Reconstruction building code was the main reason the city weathered the earthquake so well. One newspaper tallied eight thousand anti-seismic structures, all undamaged, "categorical" proof of the code's virtues. This "brilliant triumph" showed the code must remain and every building in the province "from the most modest to the most luxurious should have a supremely solid frame of iron and cement, no matter how expensive."[95]

This was an enormous challenge, as the paper recognized, for "in truth, reconstruction was just getting underway" when the second quake struck. The 1949 Constitution guaranteed every Argentine the right to dignified housing, and in San Juan only anti-seismic housing fit the bill. Yet most of the province was in adobe homes that provided only the illusion of safety, or tattered emergency shelters that offered few illusions at all. When the national press began to describe San Juan "returning to normal," *Tribuna* protested that everything had been "abnormal" for eight years and still was: less than a quarter of the population lived in safe buildings. The earthquake was a reminder that recovery had been limited. The only way out was "building more, much more."[96] Indeed, considering the urgent need, the paper suggested exploring "proven systems" beyond reinforced concrete, "whether light and elastic or heavy and rigid."[97]

"Speeding up the construction of public buildings is fundamental," one local engineer noted, because they become the center of "professional, commercial, and industrial activities." While "satellite neighborhoods" like those underway might be a "modern" idea, so far they only represented "great costs" in infrastructure, lovely fragments around an empty core.[98] Thus Reconstruction renewed its efforts, during Perón's second term, to finish the complex of monumental buildings on the central avenue: the sleek new post office, the headquarters of official banks, the new courts and other administrative offices. And these building efforts were accompanied by a new effort to train professionals, as the architecture faculty established on the initiative of Senator Ramella finally opened for instruction.

The government also redoubled efforts to build homes and establish novel institutional mechanisms for doing so. Governor Viviani was an engineer who had just taken office himself, and he quickly established a Provincial Housing Institute to ensure "as General Perón said, a house for every family"—

especially those of workers. San Juan was following Perón's Second Five-Year Plan, which shifted focus away from direct state construction of houses toward subsidized mortgages and standardized plans that allowed homeowners to build on their own. The new Housing Institute would build projects using a permanent fund, financed by a new tax on empty lots, a wage tax, sliding-scale rent for residents of permanent barrios, and monthly payments from new homeowners. New homes would be assigned according to need, with lenient loan terms. Crucially, workers would be paying for new homes as a sign of their earning power, not receiving them as gifts, and this arrangement would enable building to continue over time.[99] All these new initiatives set the standard for later policy, even if they did not bear immediate fruit in the intense atmosphere of political conflicts after 1952. In short, the second earthquake reaffirmed the effectiveness and the limitations of rebuilding so far.

During his government, Perón visited San Juan only a few times, doubtless fearful that warm memories of the collection might be overshadowed by darker feelings about Reconstruction. Yet the limited attention he paid to the province after 1946 did not affect his popularity there. From 1946 until 1955, despite the efforts of economic elites and opposition politicians, all fights over the future of the province took place within Peronism. This did not mean they were narrow in scope but that local Peronism stretched to incorporate virtually the entire political spectrum. The frustrations and missteps of rebuilding only deepened this dynamic.

While Perón lost San Juan in 1946, he won in 1951 by one of the widest margins nationwide. This was not because locals had tangible proof that "Perón delivers," in the form of a rebuilt city. On the contrary, the province remained in ruins. But two factors were at work. First, any *local* denials of social justice increased support for a *national* government that was committed to social justice. Second, national Peronism was strengthened, in San Juan and elsewhere, by local divisions, which national Peronism could then step in to resolve. Local conflicts requiring mediation were as important as Perón's authoritarian leanings to the emergence of a top-down party structure. It was precisely because supporting Perón was all that contending groups could agree on that Perón gained such support.[100]

The Peronist unity of San Juan became a unity of impasse. A decade on, there was little sense of conquest in popular ownership of emergency housing. And Conservative elites found small consolation in preserving their relative power, as they too were living in emergency housing. But this impasse also represented a rare moment of cordiality in the fractious history of the province. Thus the intense partisan conflict of Perón's second term was partly muted in San Juan by the newfound placidity of local politics. When the national showdown came between Perón and the Catholic Church, his supporters in San Juan had no churches to burn, because none had been rebuilt. Local Catholic activists did spend nights praying outside the emergency Cathedral, and the government did knock the structure down a short time later, in a convenient implementation of long-delayed plans.

But real as the conflict was, it had a distinctive character in San Juan. At the height of the polarization, just before the government was overthrown, Governor Viviani urged a massive crowd to "give their life for Perón," with the virulent and partisan language common nationwide. But when Viviani went on to identify the essential local achievement of Peronism, he did not emphasize social justice, or even rebuilding, but simply peace. "We should remember our past, the persecution, the permanent discrimination, the electoral frauds and misery" and compare it to the calm of the present, which was due largely to the late Governor Godoy, "who took great pride in being called 'the peacemaker of San Juan.' "[101] While this assertion might seem strange, it is worth noting that, for all the rivalries and oppositions within local Peronism, it had indeed accomplished something remarkable. The nine years Godoy and his circle held power, from 1947 to 1955, were the longest period of political stability in the province since independence. Peronism may not have completed rebuilding, but in many ways it had laid the essential groundwork.

The earthquake and reconstruction were intimately connected to Perón's rise, yet he never made the rebuilding project fully his own. It was key to launching his larger project and served as an important testing ground, before frustrations in San Juan and successes elsewhere led rebuilding to fall behind the larger project for the nation. Perón did devote an enormous amount of time and energy to rebuilding, particularly during the first four years. Yet once it ceased to promise symbolic returns, or to serve as a laboratory for new policy, attention and resources shifted elsewhere.

Rebuilding went forward but lost priority within the regime. The clearest indication of this is the institutional responsibility for the task. All of the other major public works initiatives of Peronism had a powerful champion at the highest ranks of the state: the Ezeiza airport complex promoted by the public works minister Pistarini, the new hospitals advocated by the health minister Ramón Castillo, and the array of social welfare buildings pushed by the Eva Perón Foundation. No similarly powerful administrator controlled rebuilding for very long: Pistarini was in charge for five months, Zuleta for eighteen, and Zapata Ramírez for nearly thirty, each ultimately vanquished by elite resistance. The sequence is also illuminating: rebuilding was the responsibility first of a major minister (Pistarini), then of an important technical figure (Zuleta), but later of a politically connected bank manager (Zapata Ramírez). After Pistarini lost control, everyone else answered to the Interior Ministry, which never gave rebuilding the political priority or technical supervision it required. The Reconstruction Council was an ad hoc creation coordinating a complex policy across various realms, but after some dynamism under Zuleta, it devolved into a highly localized and isolated institution, a mechanism for ruling the province rather than transforming it.

So while rebuilding remained an enormous public works endeavor, the second largest project of a government known for public works, and a matter of great consequence to architects, engineers, and locals, it lost its central claim on the Peronist imagination. Across many domains, the Peronist state governed in a similar way. After beginning with multiple, aggressive, and often contradictory policy initiatives, a kind of reconnaissance in force for reform, Peronist officials then chose the initiative which seemed to work best, throwing everything behind it and leaving the others to wither away or be incorporated into the winning approach. This kind of scattershot advance on policy can be seen in areas ranging from housing and healthcare to rural land reform. In housing, the government moved from expanding the mortgage market to direct construction of housing projects, only to grow frustrated with limited results and shift back to broad funding of standardized construction, primarily of individual homes. Designing and building new housing proved slower and more difficult than the government had envisioned: even the signal initiatives, the barrios that became symbols of Peronist social policy, were produced later and in far smaller numbers than initially planned. For example, a model Buenos Aires housing project that the architect Mendióroz, leader of one key team for San Juan, designed in 1944 did not open until 1949. In this sense, then, delayed rebuilding in San Juan was less an outlier than an exemplification of a broader phenomenon. But in the city of ruins, delay had an existential cost. For all the stability and progress Perón had brought the province, for all the canals and the numerous buildings that had been built, this remained a landscape as haunted by promises as filled with achievements.

CHAPTER 12 THE "BULLDOZER KID" AND THE REBUILT CITY, 1955–1962

When Perón fell, the rebuilding of San Juan was still far from complete. Indeed, those who overthrew him in September 1955 claimed it had hardly begun. Once again, there was talk of an entire nation in ruins, needing reconstruction, with San Juan presented as an exemplary case. Soon enough, the new authorities tried to turn San Juan to their own ends. The debate began as soon as Perón fell but only moved to the center of political discussion with the January 1956 visit by the new president, General Pedro Aramburu.[1]

"Twelve years ago, San Juan lived through a great tragedy" and the nation responded, Aramburu recalled. But Perón had squandered that response and compounded the tragedy, "defrauding not only the people of San Juan but the nation as a whole." Now, Aramburu, a military dictator who claimed to be restoring democracy, insisted he would raise up the fallen province, "not only to meet the obligations of our common humanity, but also to banish a national shame, which offends and humiliates us." He vowed to deliver results, instead of "making everyone see houses where there are only empty lots." Locals had heard such promises before but allowed themselves to hope again, as they had little choice, and Aramburu was quite specific about what needed to be done.[2]

Rebuilding would take an ironic course in these seven years, as first a military then a civilian government led by Perón's opponents tried to prove they had overcome Peronism by finishing the project Perón's government had planned but left incomplete. But to understand the actions and legacies of these anti-Peronist governments, and to gain proper perspective on the rebuilt and consolidated city that celebrated its four hundredth anniversary in 1962, the first step is to explore how the military came to remove Perón and seize power.

"The Liberating Revolution"

The coup that overthrew Perón in September 1955 had been long in the making: after three failed attempts, this one succeeded because the opposition had grown broader, bolder, and more intransigent. Since 1945, opposition to Perón had been socially homogeneous but politically diverse, based in the upper and middle classes, expressed through the Conservative, Socialist, and (increasingly) Radical parties, and supported by some military officers, especially from the Navy. But after 1952, as politics became more polarized, the government began to lose its earlier supporters, particularly Catholics, nationalists, and Army officers. By 1953, the Catholic Church came into conflict with the government, becoming the backbone of the opposition and the target of popular Peronist ire.

Escalating confrontation led to definitive rupture in June 1955, when the traditional Corpus Christi march in Buenos Aires became a massive opposition protest. Perón organized a counterdemonstration and the Navy tried to launch a coup by bombing the crowds. They killed 355 civilians, failed to win Army support, and sparked Peronists to attack churches and set fire to the Cathedral.[3] Despite attempts to defuse the situation, a deep split had opened up. Three months later, Navy and Army units rose again, with "Christ is Victorious" as their countersign. While most of the military remained loyal, Perón held them back, declined to mobilize civilian supporters, and, after a few days of fighting, resigned and went into exile. The political machine that had dominated the country for a decade simply collapsed.

The new military regime proclaimed itself a "Liberating Revolution," adopting the slogan of the liberal overthrow of the dictator Rosas a century before.[4] Military leaders spoke of returning the country to a democratic path. The first military president, General Eduardo Lonardi, tried to strike a conciliatory line, declaring there would be "Neither Victors nor Vanquished"— another slogan from those who overthrew Rosas. Lonardi and his Catholic and nationalist allies wanted to preserve Peronist social reforms while purging the party and banishing its leaders. They launched an Investigative Commission to document and punish high-level corruption. If Peronism could be cleaned up and could learn to respect institutional limits, perhaps Lonardi might contemplate its participation in free elections.

But the hatreds brewed over more than a decade could not be wished away. Lonardi faced great pressure from hard-line anti-Peronist soldiers and civilians, a sizable minority, who did not want to purify Peronism but to wholly destroy it. Within two months, Lonardi was deposed by Aramburu, who set a far harsher course.[5]

While loudly proclaiming liberal democratic ideals, Aramburu launched a vengeful attack on Peronism, outlawing what had been the majority party and jailing its officials for treason.[6] Aramburu crushed a general strike, intervened every union, and banned anyone who had occupied any government or union post between 1949 and 1955 from ever holding public office again. He expanded the purview of the Investigating Commission from top leaders to anyone associated with the government. In March 1956, he went even further, decreeing illegal all symbols, images, songs, or phrases associated with Perón. Simply saying the name of the former president (or his wife) was now a criminal offense.[7]

According to the military, Peronism was the local equivalent of fascism and thus had to be uprooted by force. The military drew on a long tradition within Argentine liberalism that stressed the need to defend culture against barbarism with violence. No wonder Sarmiento was a favorite. The drive to symbolically annihilate Perón was clear. The military and their civilian supporters gleefully set bonfires of Peronist writings and memorabilia in the street. The regime razed the palace where Evita had lived as first lady and then kidnapped and hid her embalmed body.[8]

San Juan experienced these same rituals of denunciation: smashed statues, burned publications, and generalized vandalism. Recent converts to the opposition were often the most avid destroyers.[9] As elsewhere, this vindictiveness was driven as much by the enthusiasms of anti-Peronist civilians as by the orders of military officials. Every canal, dam, hospital, school, and barrio was stripped of its Peronist name and rededicated to the heroes and holidays of the patrician republic. The seven different housing projects named for Evita, for example, were renamed for the city's founder, the heroines of independence, and various nineteenth-century liberals.[10] The mausoleum of Ruperto Godoy was turned into a "Provincial Pantheon" for illustrious liberals—and Godoy's body was spirited away. Plaques honoring Perón and Godoy were melted down and recast as busts of Sarmiento.[11]

In the schools, anti-Peronist students mounted lively and usually successful protests to demand the resignation of teachers, directors, and authorities. In these paradoxical mobilizations, students shouted insults and seized buildings to protest "the absolute lack of any discipline" during "the tyranny" and demand the reestablishment of proper authority.[12] Generic calls to restore quality quickly hardened into specific demands to expel the poor. One protest leader flatly declared that the teachers' school had declined because it had "filled up with girls from 4 June and Captain Lazo."[13] Framing the conflict in terms of civilization against barbarism, as anti-Peronists often did, allowed them to tie Peronism's socially transgressive aspects to its more obviously authoritarian features and repudiate both at once.

The widely documented brutality of the Liberating Revolution was evident in San Juan as well. Government officials insisted this was not a "revolution for the bosses," but the rollback in the workplace was swift, palpable, and surprisingly indiscriminate.[14] Military interventors in the unions started firing activists immediately; employers slashed wages and ignored union complaints. Grape growers asked the government to break up the viticultural workers union, which under Perón had expanded from representing solely permanent winery staff to include the much larger group of seasonal grape pickers.[15] Public agencies revived the Conservative practice of paying workers in scrip rather than cash, dismissing anyone who objected.[16] This continued for months, until the interventor himself discovered (or admitted) the practice and condemned it as an "act of sabotage against the Liberating Revolution." The fact that his own administration was doing this and, for months, he was unaware or unworried underscores the extent of social revanchism and the limited ability of the interventor to resist it. A residential school for girls built by the Eva Perón Foundation was handed over to an upper-class doctor, who hired out many students as domestic servants, appropriating their wages for herself, forced the others to stage elaborate banquets for her family and friends, and so abused her power that her subordinates reported to authorities that all the children were openly and "lamentably" wishing "if only Perón would return."[17] The colonel who was named mayor of San Juan was so eager to impose his will that a minor objection from the leader of the municipal workers prompted him to physically attack the worker, smashing his face and kicking him with his boots. This brutality was especially notable because the union leader was actually a Socialist and an enthusiastic supporter of military rule.[18]

On first glance, then, the repression in San Juan looked much like the rest of the country—indeed, by early 1956, San Juan too began to experience the fleeting protests, everyday sabotage, and occasional pipe bombs of the incipient "Peronist resistance."[19] But the repression of Peronism, while real, was on balance less intense in San Juan than elsewhere. It was certainly far less intense than the bombings, beatings, and assassinations that had followed each overthrow of the Cantonis—or, for that matter, that had punctuated factional struggles among Radicals, Cantonistas, or Conservatives. Paradoxically, this relative calm was also a legacy of Peronism.

In part due to the repression of workers and supporters of "the tyrant," this was a hopeful moment for the "democratic citizenry" aligned with the military.[20] From the beginning, military leaders were committed to a rapid return to civilian rule. Nationwide, they allied with the most resolutely anti-Peronist parties: Radicals, Socialists, and Conservatives. In San Juan, where Radicals and Socialists were weak and most Conservatives had become Peronists, these parties were even less representative than elsewhere, but the military still turned to them.[21] This provided anti-Peronist parties with influence and funds—but not popular backing.

Perón's former supporters were in disarray, fragmenting into a dozen factions and semi-legal parties.[22] The main local papers, which had both been resolutely Peronist, changed their ownership and allegiance. *Diario de Cuyo* offered a qualified defense of Perón until Aramburu took office, then was sold to new owners, who lined up behind the military.[23] *Tribuna* returned to the Catholic and nationalist themes of the past, hoping to capitalize on the lively rallies celebrating patron saints that had punctuated local Catholic mobilization against Perón.[24] But on the same day the major national dailies taken over by Perón were returned to their owners, a judge seized *Tribuna* from the Graffignas and returned control to the rump Conservative party.[25] In addition to losing the paper, the Graffignas also lost the opportunity to lead a Catholic party, as unity proved fleeting and activists scattered across a range of local parties.

Surprisingly, the only galvanizing local figure was Federico Cantoni, who emerged from political retirement after the coup. The military and other parties ignored him, but the massive crowds who turned up to see him showed that Bloquismo had outlasted Perón's government and might yet inherit his supporters.[26] To avoid this, the Liberating Revolution needed to establish credibility on the central issue of the day: rebuilding.

The Legitimacy of the Bulldozer

When Perón fell, San Juan was a hollow city: there were new neighborhoods around its edges and a handful of impressive monumental buildings at its core, but little in between except rubble and false starts. The nearly nine thousand new anti-seismic homes—a fifth built by the government and the rest by private builders, often with subsidies—were dispersed in barrios on the outskirts.

Praiseworthy as it was, the building effort had managed to replace barely half the homes lost in 1944. Because the population had grown, this meant that new construction housed only a third of city residents. There were nearly that many in emergency barrios. "There are ten year olds who know nothing but life in these camps," a National Housing Commission delegation observed, "with shared bathrooms that don't work and the perennial spectacle of family intimacy made into a public matter."[27]

Within the four avenues, there was a new central boulevard, extending four blocks east of the main plaza, flanked by a half-dozen landmark government buildings. This was one of few completed major projects: the provincial administration was in temporary quarters, the legislature under the stadium, and many other buildings simply blueprints. Even the other half of the central boulevard, west of the main plaza, was only partly cleared and ended in the still-closed train station, not the projected civic center. In the center, there were several blocks of active businesses and a smattering of new houses, but little else. A frenzy of land speculation, with a quarter of the province's properties changing hands annually, had left little besides profits for the fortunate.[28]

Most importantly, Reconstruction had not "set the line." Propertied interests had colonized Reconstruction, producing endless revisions to the street layout. Nearly every street had been widened on paper, but few of those changes were evident on the pavement. Neither were the changes evident in buildings, as Reconstruction had granted many older structures temporary repair waivers. Lacking any certainty that streets would indeed be widened, many property owners delayed building. When they did build, their outposts of progress were so deep inside the block that they were invisible from the street.

In short, the achievements of the past decade were isolated complexes, and the broken city was the material expression of a divided and distrustful polity. "A new city rises, without reflecting a new spirit," the housing delegation observed, "the same streets, haphazard constructions, a total absence of trees, [and] despair among the inhabitants."[29]

Rebuilding had proven far more costly and less straightforward than either architects or the establishment had imagined. Peronism had met its funding commitments, at least in nominal terms. Reconstruction had spent the entire collection and nearly all of the four hundred million pesos authorized in 1946. But this was less impressive after taking inflation into account: with the peso worth a sixth as much in 1955 as in 1946, the government had spent considerably less than planned in real terms. And completing the task would obviously require more.

Whatever its failings, however, locals now thought the Reconstruction

44 City center, 1956. CREDIT AGN.

Council should remain in charge. "Only the very short-sighted" would do away with it, *Tribuna* argued, since discarding its expertise would cause further delays and possibly undermine "the building code and strict controls" vindicated by the 1952 earthquake.[30] All the Council needed to do was repent of its sins, "wash itself in the waters of the Jordan," and finish the task.[31]

This was what President Aramburu found in January 1956. He decided to make San Juan a symbol of national resolve once more—this time, the resolve to overcome Peronism. After consulting with experts who had surveyed conditions, he issued a detailed decree in February specifying funding, projects, and a timetable for rebuilding. He ignored the demands of local elites, who were clamoring for such things as subsidized car loans, and instead presented a plan for action that was generously funded and took note of past operational failings. While slashing government spending overall, Aramburu decided to splurge on this one landmark project.

He entrusted the task to retired general Mariano Bartolomé Carreras and solved the perennial jurisdiction conflict by naming him both interventor of the province and president of the Reconstruction Council. Carreras found allies already in place. Across the nation, Aramburu rewarded leading engineers for opposing Perón: after spending the past decade in private practice, anti-Peronist engineers now assumed nearly every technical post in government, from state railroads to the MOP itself.[32] Consistent with this, Aramburu had already appointed Remberto Baca and Alberto Costantini, the two engineers who had led the 1945 protest against Perón, to the Reconstruction Council.[33]

Carreras brought the two local engineers onto his team: he named the Conservative Costantini provincial minister of public works and second-in-command at Reconstruction, and the Socialist Baca mayor of the city. When Baca took office, Carreras praised him as a latter-day Sarmiento who had battled "tyranny" to show that "ideas cannot be killed," while Baca's predecessor, the colonel who assaulted workers, lamented his failure to "suppress . . . the Peronist elements" among public employees and hoped Baca would do better, as "a democratic citizen without any stain of Peronism." Baca declared his own intention to "heal the wounds produced by the earthquake of 1944 that the malice and disorder of the dictatorship [of Perón] could not and would not alleviate."[34]

After twelve years, the fuerzas vivas had finally taken full control of rebuilding. Costantini, who was forty years old, assumed operational command and showed such zeal in moving forward, at long last, that locals dubbed him the "Bulldozer Kid." His basic approach was simple. Only forceful public action could "constitute the city." Only the larger collective framework of streets and walls would enable individual projects for homes. Thus the Pastor plan should be implemented without further debate. Costantini did not follow the Pastor plan because he agreed with it but because it was settled. First Reconstruction would "set the line," carrying out the expropriations, demolitions, and paving necessary to bring every street to its proper width. Then private construction would return to the center, overcoming the "depressing effect" of ruins and jump-starting a rebuilding process which otherwise "might take fifty years."[35]

His focus was on encouraging private building in the city center. To free up materials and funding, he slashed public housing construction, finishing three projects underway but going no further. To speed progress, Reconstruction issued two thousand long-pending building subsidies. The city government raised taxes on vacant lots and lifted them on new construction. Most importantly, the National Mortgage Bank agreed to fully finance all new construction, including rentals and commercial buildings, at low interest for up to fifty years.[36]

Having spent the past decade as a private contractor building roads and houses with government subsidies, Costantini naturally felt this was the model to follow. He thus detailed as much work as possible to other agencies or private contractors. Instead of building a permanent staff, he drafted temporary help from the provincial ministries. Remarkably enough, he even assigned all design work to the MOP. This was a measure of the bankruptcy of establishment ideas. Even with complete control, the fuerzas vivas still could not finish the job without "outside experts"—and they turned to the MOP, their original enemies, the very body the Reconstruction Council had replaced back in 1944.[37]

Costantini staged demolitions with a theatrical flair. Reconstruction first walled off empty lots, then "set the line." This meant destroying homes. Old streets were 6 meters wide, with buildings flush to the narrow sidewalk, but new streets were at least 18 meters wide, with a 9 meter roadway and 4.5 meters on each side for sidewalks, trees, and an irrigation canal. Costantini and Carreras were wary of protest, so they established owners' groups on each block to settle conflicts. But they were also ruthless, and when the deadline passed, they sent the bulldozers. To open up the western half of the central avenue, Reconstruction leveled prominent landmarks, starting with the Cervantes Cinema and the Archbishop's Palace on the west side of the plaza. In total, they demolished 765 buildings.[38]

There were confrontations, most memorably in March 1957, at the Zunino hardware store on the central plaza. Since 1944, Zunino's newspaper, *La Acción*, had been the most strident defender of the idea that all rebuilding required was to set the line. Yet Zunino refused to bring his own store into compliance and threatened to shoot anyone who dared approach with a bulldozer. In this, he was emblematic of the many in the local elite who had advocated a minimalist approach and then used connections to escape even minimal strictures. Carreras himself drove the bulldozer; Zunino stayed inside but held his fire; the façade was ripped down.[39]

Reconstruction also erected many buildings. In eighteen months, Reconstruction (and other agencies) built twenty-six schools, fourteen town halls, the city market, the prison, the insane asylum, the police headquarters, and four police stations. It opened two new plazas downtown and finished one hundred homes. It put the final touches on major buildings nearly completed under Perón and then claimed credit for them.[40] Overall, the Liberating Revolution was spending as much on rebuilding as Peronism at its high point in 1948 (see appendix).[41]

Under Costantini, Reconstruction focused its efforts inside the four avenues and did little work outside them.[42] This effort was largely successful on its own terms: Costantini set the material and institutional framework for a

45 Reconstruction
Council headquarters,
1956. CREDIT AGN.

later building boom. There were already a thousand new homes underway in
1957, the most since the quake.[43] That year, San Juan had the highest per
capita cement consumption in the country, 40 percent above the national
average.[44] But since there was still no cement factory, this required importing
one hundred thousand bags every month.[45]

The achievements of Carreras and Costantini cannot be isolated from
their larger political context: they were able to act swiftly because they were
the armed representatives of a military dictatorship during a state of siege.
They began knocking down buildings in June 1956, just as the regime crushed
a Peronist uprising in Buenos Aires by summarily executing twenty-seven
"rebels"—including, it later emerged, at least twelve innocent workers grabbed
off the street.[46] Nothing like that happened in San Juan, though the violence
elsewhere certainly colored how the administration was viewed locally.

Overall, the initial anti-Peronist fury faded quickly in San Juan, as local
parties realized it could not produce future stability. Within a year of Perón's

overthrow, the local political world began to accept the resilience of the changes he had brought. This was not because they remained firmly Peronist; most had been allies of convenience and broke away as soon as possible. The interventor before Carreras had noted how prominent journalists had been in local Peronism and how easily they cast off those connections—an observation so astute that the journalists, who could hardly deny it, instead tried to portray it as a harsh attack on freedom of the press.[47] But by incorporating nearly every local group, including both opponents and supporters of Cantoni, Peronism had indeed created the conditions for the "pacification of spirits" Godoy so often proclaimed. In a province with a history of persistent division, this remained an appealing idea. So many had allied with Peronism at some point and had come to appreciate tranquility that the anti-Peronist cause lost steam as it became clear it could not produce a new unity.

Elsewhere in Argentina, the Investigating Commission was a primary vehicle for vengeance. But in San Juan, the local commission mostly revealed the waning of the drive for revenge. Its first president lasted only a day, the second a month, the third two months, and while the fourth stayed on to the end, his reports to national authorities traced a steady decline in enthusiasm and support for the work. After five months, the commission brought seventy-three cases to trial, mostly accusing former government officials of illicit enrichment. The major case involved the diversion of thirty million pesos from a crop insurance fund into the province's operating budget. Even if some funds had ended up in officials' pockets, this was more artful accounting than outright fraud. The commission did conduct a few suggestive audits, such as one engineer's close look at a provincial housing project, which documented a rich array of procedural irregularities, overcharging, and kickbacks, estimating that fraud accounted for as much as 40 percent of the project's one-million-peso cost.[48]

Yet there was no serious investigation of the places where large-scale fraud might be found, such as loans from official banks or the many public works projects, from canals to Reconstruction buildings. Private contractors who worked for the state were left alone. The subcommission on the canals barely met, and it did not dig very deep, as one of its two members was Eduardo Grano Cortinez, a nationalist who had been in and out of Peronist administrations and now was directing the tax authority and leading the elite Social Club.[49] The Reconstruction Council itself was untouched, because it fell under the jurisdiction of the federal commission on the Interior Ministry, which proved more interested in police repression than the misdeeds of bureaucrats in the provinces. Costantini, who for a decade had made his living as a contractor with the state, declined to push further. In the end, the investigations singled out low-level functionaries and politicians, leaving the largest beneficiaries untouched and aligned with the military government.[50]

For different reasons, Carreras himself charted a less confrontational course. While loyal to the national authorities, he was less of an anti-Peronist ideologue than his superiors (or many of his peers elsewhere). He did support some of the more extravagant local attacks on Peronism, such as the removal and (brief) disappearance of the body of Ruperto Godoy, but he focused more on the common task of rebuilding than the divisive project of rolling back social reforms. He resisted raising Reconstruction wages but defended unions. He forced a wage increase for grape pickers during the bounty harvest of 1957 and fought back various elite campaigns to tailor government actions to their particular interests. In short, he proved far more independent than provincial elites wished. But while he lost their support, he also taught them several crucial lessons.

The most important lesson was this: if even a faithful delegate of this aggressively antiworker government could not destroy unions, gut social reforms, and redirect state largesse to elites, then the basic changes Peronism had brought were here to stay. The familiar local pattern of seizing the state and securing patronage had been broken. And the program first set forth by Cantoni in 1919, the reforms that elites had fought against for two generations, was now the law of the land.

This was driven home by the way Carreras left office. As the Liberating Revolution foundered, local politicians broke with Carreras, some because he was too anti-Peronist, others because he was not anti-Peronist enough, and all because he was so little inclined to indulge their demands. Carreras had proven himself in pragmatic terms, by advancing rebuilding, which had created jobs and revived the boom feeling of a decade before. Acutely conscious of his distance from the establishment and his prestige with the public, Carreras resigned in a very familiar way.

One night in May 1957, Carreras took to the radio, the medium so deeply associated with Perón, to contrast how "the people" supported him with how "the pseudo-politicians" plotted against him. His opponents "perhaps believed this government, indirectly controlled by them, should be the guarantor . . . of their schemes" and, when he refused to go along, they filled with "resentment . . . and blindly refused to accept . . . that injustice is not eternal . . . and that liberty is not the ally of speculators." Thus he was resigning to open the way for democratic elections, confident that locals were "sick of the lies of bad politicians, the shocking prevalence of the privileged and the untouchables, the false promises of saviors and protectors, and the avarice of the insensitive, the indifferent, and the insatiable."[51]

This was surprising rhetoric for a military leader. Like Cantoni or Perón, he pitted the virtue of the people and the diligence of the government against the greed, opportunism, and "dark interests" of the fuerzas vivas. The next morning, the press reported, "columns of workers, on foot, on bicycles, and in trucks, filed through the streets" to protest his resignation.[52] The description echoed accounts of hundreds of Peronist mobilizations, and especially the paradigmatic one: 17 October 1945. While Carreras could not be convinced to stay, the way he left made an impression. This was the first time anyone could recall public sorrow, much less protest, at the departure of an interventor. This was certainly the only moment, nationwide, when any sizable group of workers expressed support for the Liberating Revolution.[53]

What workers were praising, of course, was Carreras's inability to live up to the Liberating Revolution. Having failed to eliminate Peronism, he ended up reproducing its symbolic framework and defending its key values. He had redrawn the streets, but not the polity.[54]

Even so, as the Liberating Revolution fell apart, military leaders desperately tried to capitalize on the rebuilt San Juan, one of their few achievements. One month before voters were to elect delegates to a new constitutional convention, President Aramburu returned with Carreras for the anniversary of the city's founding. One month before voters were to elect a new president and legislature, Vice President Isaac Rojas returned with Costantini for the earthquake anniversary. But while Carreras and Costantini were certainly popular, they delivered few votes for the regime or its favored candidates. And the apparent local success of rebuilding was quickly swallowed by the larger failures of the regime. In 1956, Aramburu had proclaimed rebuilding the starting point of a new Argentine democracy, but eighteen months later he was unable to summon anything but boilerplate about San Juan, dwelling instead on the crises of his collapsing government.[55] Rojas found it easy to denounce "two successive disasters . . . the earthquake itself . . . and the political earthquake of the totalitarian dictatorship" and to mock Perón's supporters as "masses who are as helpless intellectually as they are socially," but he proved far more interested in invoking Sarmiento to explain why most of the country was unworthy of the vote than in drawing any positive lessons from rebuilding.[56]

The favored candidates of the Liberating Revolution, the promilitary faction of the Radical Party, did poorly in both elections. In the July 1957 contest to choose delegates to write a new constitution, the exiled Perón told his supporters to submit blank ballots, and across the country blanks were the largest plurality. The only exception was San Juan, where the revived Blo-quista Party won.[57] The Constitutional Convention was a fiasco, quickly losing its quorum as parties withdrew, underscoring the weakness of the military regime. In the February 1958 presidential elections, Perón threw his support to the antimilitary Radical faction, which tripled its share of votes, easily winning the presidency and, thanks to a split among Bloquistas, even the governorship of San Juan.

While Carreras returned to retirement and political obscurity, the young Costantini, who was originally from Buenos Aires, became a hero to the engineering profession. The day they both resigned, Costantini was named director of the Sanitary Works Authority and professor at the University of Buenos Aires. He became dean of engineering within a year, then national minister of public works, and finally president of the CAI, the professional association of engineers, from 1967 until his death in 1992. Like other leading engineers, he strongly defended "democratic" values while supporting in-creasingly brutal military regimes, and even served briefly as rector of the University of Buenos Aires after the 1976 coup. The one constant would be his opposition to Peronism.[58] The "Bulldozer Kid" did make one attempt to return to San Juan, running for governor as a Conservative in a decisive election in 1962. It is to that year, the four hundredth anniversary of the foundation of the city, that the closing section of this chapter now turns.

Reconstruction Fulfilled—and Denied

At first glance, the Liberating Revolution fulfilled the long-standing dream of the fuerzas vivas: it "set the line," funded private rebuilding downtown, and ignored the rest of the province. This could be taken as final proof that the architects had been wrong all along. But the rhetoric of the fuerzas vivas was never fully honest. After his newspaper had stridently advocated setting the line for a decade, Zunino, the anti-Peronist businessman, pulled a gun on workers when they tried to set the line on his property. After the fuerzas vivas had endlessly insisted that local expertise was good enough, Costantini had to call in architects from the MOP, the hated "outside experts," to finish the work. And even as Costantini apparently brought the establishment program to completion, nearly everyone else in local debates was belatedly embracing modernism.

When surveying the provincial scene, even *Tribuna* now echoed the argu-ment modernist architects had been making since 1944: rebuilding should begin with the economic transformation of the province, and the design of the city and its homes would follow. After years of opposing any comprehensive plan, the paper now ruefully noted that if such a plan had been enacted, "we would already be well on our way to material rebuilding . . . and finishing off the housing problem." While the paper naturally did not dwell on its own central role in frustrating any such plan, this was a noteworthy shift in perspective, and by the time the Liberating Revolution left office, it was evident across the political spectrum.[59]

Perhaps the clearest sign of a change in attitudes was the campaign to save the School of Architecture. Back in 1947, Senator Ramella, the one establishment figure who defended technical expertise, had sponsored the creation of an architecture faculty in San Juan, part of the multicampus University of Cuyo. The new school came together slowly, and like the engineering and enology faculties also located in San Juan, was still meeting in emergency sheds in 1955. Sensing an opportunity, the government of Mendoza lobbied to have it transferred there, since the neighboring province was already home to eleven of its twenty-seven professors, a (supposedly impressive) four-hundred-volume library, and other faculties of the university. The arguments for the move were weak, and the symbolism of removing the school just as rebuilding was finally getting underway was terrible. Local architecture students launched a campaign to keep the school in San Juan, which became a great provincial cause, winning the enthusiastic support of civic groups, labor unions, business associations, and every political party in the province. This was a distant and ironic echo of 1944: once the fuerzas vivas had lined up against architects as useless "outside experts," but now they defended architects as essential to the provincial future.[60]

The students used the campaign as a platform to address larger issues, organizing a week-long conference for architecture students nationwide and then issuing a combative statement about the future of the profession and the province.[61] The architecture school must remain, they insisted, but the Reconstruction Council must change. According to the students, the Council had lost "popular trust" and would not regain it without admitting its errors and naming those responsible. The students had very specific errors in mind, from the inexplicable changes in street layout to the abandonment of the irrigation system for trees, but they also wanted to remind the public that these particular missteps were the result of the rejection of comprehensive solutions.[62] Back in 1944, they recalled, the local establishment had rejected the bold solutions proposed by a series of leading architects, figures like Ernesto Vautier, Eduardo Sacriste, and Jorge Ferrari Hardoy, who had gone on to international acclaim. If the mediocre had failed at Reconstruction, the students suggested, perhaps it was time to think boldly again.[63]

The successful campaign to keep the architecture school prompted reconsideration of how rebuilding should proceed. A key background player was the architect and professor Carmen Renard, who had worked for Bereterbide and Vautier in 1944, authored an impassioned argument for rebuilding on a different site, and later returned to the province after winning the competition to design a large public school. The daughter of an admiral, an unmarried female professional with a sports car and projects across the province, Renard cut a glamorous and charismatic figure. After advising the students in their campaign, she formed a study group of architects, engineers, and builders to shape a future strategy for reconstruction. Her group drew together everyone from Enévaro Rossi, the dean of local architecture, to the young modernist Alberto Pineda, the head of the housing authority. Despite his work for many figures in the elite, Rossi had favored the move in 1944, and when colleagues later began to rebuild on the same site, he went to the United States for a year to learn proper anti-seismic construction techniques.

Over the following years, Renard and her allies and students took the lead in designing and building the future city: this cadre of architects occupied most important technical posts in San Juan and designed thousands of units of government-sponsored housing. Equally importantly, in private practice they designed the homes of the wealthy, which set the standards for emulation by others. After years of mocking modernist designs and "utopian schemes," the establishment now embraced them for their own houses. Once denounced as hopelessly opposed to provincial life, these designs were now valued as the proper expression of provincial modernity.

While the Liberating Revolution was in power, this new generation of local architects built a few notable projects, including a striking modernist office for the new provincial tourism authority, next to Sarmiento's childhood home. But they began to build more extensively and to shape discussion more directly after Costantini departed and the elected Radical government took office in 1958. Taking a page from the military playbook, the elected government named an engineer president of Reconstruction, and later provincial minister of public works. The new leader was Juan Victoria, the longtime modernist ally who had corresponded assiduously with Ferrari Hardoy and darkly foreseen the failure of ambitious reconstruction in 1945. He would continue in the post for four years, a record at this unstable bureaucracy. In that time he would further expand irrigation, begin rural electrification, advance planning for dams, expand the state winery, and entice a private company to finally build the long-promised cement factory. But most importantly, he would preside over a private building boom and a flurry of public construction of schools, buildings, and especially housing.

While Perón was in power, most residential construction had taken place outside the four avenues, initially in emergency barrios, and later in permanent barrios, some built by the government, others by subsidized private developers. In Costantini's bid to "constitute the city," he focused his efforts within the four avenues and limited his work outside to town halls and a handful of projects already underway. When Victoria took over, he allowed private construction to flourish within the clear boundaries Costantini had set and refocused his attention on the periphery where most of the city now lived—and the valley beyond. During his four years at the helm, Reconstruction finally turned the emergency barrios of 4 June and Captain Lazo into permanent settlements. In a complex choreography, the Council moved some residents out to new barrios, then razed the emergency structures and built a far less dense barrio of concrete homes for those who remained. Beyond the conversion of emergency housing, Victoria also promoted a range of other barrios, built by the government or private developers.

In short, Victoria brought the city into its lasting form: individual homes on the central grid and a dense patchwork of barrios outside. This was a matter of not only the material layout of the streets but also the social organization (and political culture) of communities, modeled on the "neighborhood units" advocated by architects and planners. Before 1944, many certainly thought of their nearby surroundings as a neighborhood, but this had no legal or political status and relatively weak social roots. After 1944, and particularly after 1956, these barrios came to provide a new basis of social organization and solidarity across the city. These arrangements would deepen and endure. Anyone looking at a map of the city after 1960 would have to take note of the hundreds of officially acknowledged barrios outside the four avenues. Six decades after the quake, San Juan still has one of the highest percentages of government-built housing in the country, nearly all in barrios.

Under Victoria, the Council also addressed the most remarkable deficit in rebuilding so far: churches. It was only in 1958 that the Desamparados Chapel was completed, the first of the many destroyed churches to be raised again. The foot-dragging of the fuerzas vivas, bureaucratic inertia of Reconstruction, and intense Church-state conflicts after 1953 had all contributed to making the buildings many valued the most the last ones to be restored. These projects were naturally powerful symbols, perhaps even more than the complex of government buildings along the central avenue or the new hotels on the main

46 City center, looking east, 1962. Note Cathedral campanile in the lower center; entirely new west side of Plaza 25 de Mayo (compare with figure 43); new buildings lining the central avenue; commercial blocks above the plaza rebuilt at the same density. COURTESY FUNDACIÓN BATALLER.

plaza. The Cathedral proper was a modernist design by the Mendoza architect Daniel Ramos Correa, and Reconstruction drove hard to complete two components by 1962: the crypt and the campanile. Now there was no longer a void at the center of the rebuilt city but the spare lines of the bell tower rising above the Plaza 25 de Mayo, an evocative distillation of the city's attenuated modernity.

Housing had been radically transformed, turned inside out, with the blank walls and inward-looking patios of the past replaced by front gardens and outward-facing buildings. The dun-colored city of adobe was replaced by a white city of concrete. Ramshackle constructions gave way to rows of variations on a few themes, spread out in many neighborhoods under stretches of trees. Soon most of the population were homeowners. Observers noted that anti-seismic construction had become "the only acceptable kind of housing" for locals. Almost 49 percent of the capital's housing stock was anti-seismic, by far the highest percentage along the entire Andes, an extraordinary technical achievement.[64]

Every city destroyed by an earthquake vows to rebuild in a way that will endure, but hardly any actually do. For all of Reconstruction's failings, this was a singular achievement. Part of Victoria's task during his time at the helm was to find a way to put this expertise to broader use. Under pressure to declare rebuilding complete, he expanded the agency's mandate to include responsibility for seismology and anti-seismic building standards for the entire nation—a decade later, the agency declared its original task fulfilled and dedicated itself entirely to those new tasks.[65] Over the years, Reconstruction was the training ground for a generation of architects, engineers, geologists, and seismologists, who became the core of several university departments, the leadership of the local construction industry, and a central component of the much-expanded provincial middle class. For years, construction generated the jobs demanded by population growth, not only for workers but also for liberal professionals.

Out in the countryside, the vines still reigned supreme, although the power of the large bodegueros had been checked. There were thirty thousand hectares under vine in 1943, forty thousand when Perón was overthrown in 1955, and fifty-two thousand by 1966. Thus in the two decades after the earthquake, vineyards expanded 70 percent.[66] Wine production nearly tripled: annual output averaged 1.6 million hectoliters in the three years before the quake (1941–43), 3 million in the last three years under Perón (1953–55), and 4.4 million in the three years after the Liberating Revolution (1959–61).[67] But instead of challenging grape monoculture, reconstruction had come to complement it.[68]

The pattern was set by 1962, when Victoria left office. By that time, looking up at the Cathedral tower and around at the scores of massive concrete buildings downtown, many declared the city rebuilt and put the earthquake definitively behind them. That was an election year and the four hundredth anniversary of the city, a fitting moment to turn the page. We will look in a moment at the ultimate outcomes of rebuilding, in politics and in memory. But first, we should take note of some of its more evident limits.

Back in 1944, and for years afterward, rebuilding had meant rethinking the social and spatial structure of the province, to diversify production, decentralize population, and integrate all of the territory on a new basis. But over the years, possibilities had narrowed. Peronism built canals, expanded irrigation, and broadened access to land. But its policies only deepened the hold of grape monoculture and reinforced the geographic concentration of power within the province.

Instead of making the rest of the province more prosperous, resilient, and interconnected, rebuilding deepened its impoverishment, fragility, and isolation. By the 1960 census, every department in the province was shrinking, except for the capital and its suburbs. This trend was evident in Caucete, the second city of the province, as early as 1956. While Caucete had the province's most productive vineyards, there was a stark "contrast between its agricultural wealth and urban poverty." The city had little urban life, as "landowners, industrialists and even professionals preferred to live" in the capital, a process only "accentuated" by the completion of a paved road. Thus after 1944 there was no "significant renewal," as "houses were rebuilt with their previous structure and the same materials, fundamentally adobe." This was a "typical case" of the decline in local life across the province.[69]

Indeed, the prevalence of anti-seismic construction diminished with distance from the capital: 22 percent of houses in the suburbs, 11 percent in Caucete, across the central valley, and less than 5 percent in Jáchal, outside the central valley.[70] Similarly, it was only in the capital that most houses had strong roofs and finished floors (concrete or wood): everywhere else, most houses had quincha roofs and earthen floors.[71]

This imbalance between the capital and the rest of the province was the most extreme in the country. By 1969, the capital accounted for 62 percent of the province's population—and 86 percent of its business activity.[72] A geographer assessing the comparative possibilities for more balanced development in San Juan and Mendoza reached a stark conclusion. The provinces were quite similar in terms of geography, ecology, and of course agro-industry, and both were dominated by a single capital city. But while a thriving network of towns had developed in Mendoza, creating a more prosperous and less centralized economic geography, in San Juan the geographer ruefully concluded that concentration had become irreversible.[73]

When an even more powerful earthquake came in 1977, it left the capital intact and cost sixty lives, instead of ten thousand. But it devastated Caucete and the poorer areas of the countryside, all places neglected in rebuilding after 1944. Such were the benefits and limits of rebuilding.

The New Establishment

When Federico Cantoni died in July 1956, one of those expressing his condolences in the newspaper was a young nephew with a striking name: Aldo Graffigna Cantoni.[74] Here was an early sign of the new establishment emerging after Perón: the two clans whose rivalry had so shaped the province had entered into tentative alliance. The scourges of the fuerzas vivas were becoming their allies.

This process came to fruition in 1962 under Leopoldo Bravo. Widely understood to be the illegitimate son of Federico Cantoni, Bravo was a savvy lawyer who had followed his father to the Soviet Union then stayed behind, eventually becoming ambassador himself. On returning to San Juan, Bravo found that the political experience and the social process of the years of rebuilding had made this divided, unequal, and tempestuous province far more moderate, egalitarian, and even-tempered. Above all, during Peronism the local elite had found a way to work together, resisting past impulses to settle internal disputes by subverting institutions and invoking outside authority. The social reforms Cantoni had advanced and the fuerzas vivas had opposed were now an unassailable political fact: the problem for elites was no longer how to block reforms but how to live with them. Peronism had offered one path, which was largely closed after it was overthrown and banned. Instead, Bravo offered a revived Bloquista Party.

Out of the remnants of the Peronist project, Bravo fashioned for the first time a stable provincial order. He first won the governorship in 1962, crushing a field of rivals that included the Conservative "Bulldozer Kid"—and though that election was annulled by a national coup, Bravo won again the following year. His governorship was brief, until another military coup in 1966, but Bravo became the central player in local politics for three decades, the fixer and operator, creating a bastion of relative peace using the skills he had learned from his father, his father's opponents, and ten years of diplomatic duty in Eastern Europe. During years of intense instability and weak political parties on a national level, Bravo built surprising stability and a strong provincial party on the local level, with a base among the winemaker elite, state functionaries, the urban middle class of viñateros and professionals, and the rural poor. Over time, after the electoral ban on Peronism was lifted in 1973, the province settled into two-party rivalry, with Cantoni's former bodyguard Camus the leader of the Peronists and Perón's former ambassador Bravo the leader of the Bloquistas. Since 1962, a Peronist or Bloquista has been on the winning ticket for every gubernatorial election save one. Even when the military were in charge, they tended to name Bloquistas or Peronists as their local delegates—including Bravo and the son of Godoy—in a tacit recognition of their power.

Peronism had provided the blueprint for the province, from streets to buildings to institutions. Or perhaps a better metaphor, considering the centrality of concrete, is that Peronism built the formwork for the future province, the sometimes haphazard-looking wooden frame that determined the shape within which (and against which) the concrete city would set. These origins had to be obscured, as the "ultramodern" city was presented as a product of local (and now Bloquista) wisdom, and the surprising stability of the local political world after 1955 was portrayed as timeless and natural. The connection between Peronism as a national movement and the local tragedy faded away, even for local Peronists themselves. While national funds continued to flow in for rebuilding and education, local politics narrowed its horizons to the strenuous defense of provincial autonomy. The once-insurgent Bloquista Party, champion of the rights of workers and the vote for women, became the very definition of a conservative provincial establishment.[75] Horacio Videla, one-time Conservative vice-governor and secretary of the Del Bono Commission, became the leading historian of the province, retelling a story of provincial virtue and distinctiveness that silenced radical ideas and dismissed as "impossible imaginings" the plans that had made rebuilding possible.[76]

Perhaps the most striking aspect of the rebuilt city was its forgetfulness. There was a flourishing of local literature after 1944, first in a book of eyewitness accounts and then in a series of chapbooks of melancholy poetry which interspersed laments for the lost city with evocations of the glorious landscape.[77] But at that point the innovation ceased, and as a local critic later noted, "What could have been the eruption of new currents, emerging and enabled by the horrid drama of that geological collapse, was trapped in the voice of poets as the pain and weeping for the lost city." Even the laments soon faded away. "Instead of forging our present, and trying to interpret it, actively participating in it," the critic noted, regional literature came to dwell obsessively on two themes: the liberal heroes of the nineteenth century and the evocative force of the provincial countryside.[78] This trend was already evident in the massive volume published for the four hundredth anniversary, which dispatched the new city with pious assertions of its "ultramodern" character and curious claims that rebuilding had begun immediately after the earthquake and then devoted the rest of its many chapters to the legends, myths, and heroes of the distant past.[79] In a sense, San Juan became an "ultramodern" city by silencing its recent history.

Despite all that had been wagered on rebuilding in the same spot, despite the thousands of direct connections with the past, there was a rupture. Photographs were put away, stories went untold, and locals discovered they could "bury their pain in concrete."[80] Every public building had a plaque recognizing the government role in building or repairing it. No public or private buildings had a plaque remembering what had stood there before. The only memorial was the forlorn votive temple dedicated in 1947, on a hilltop forty kilometers out of town. The entire city was rebuilt, without a single marker of the worst disaster in national history. The party that had once championed a local revolution, and the party that had once made reshaping the province the starting point for reshaping the nation, both buried those hopeful pasts as well, obscuring not only the violence of politics but also its promise of a better world.

FINAL RECKONINGS

"Full-blown Peronism made it as far as Córdoba, no further," observed a character in Bernardo Verbitsky's novel about workers in a Buenos Aires shantytown, *Villa miseria también es América* (1957). Inland from there, the character continued, "it stumbled along a little more, but arrived tired, worn out."[1] This pithy observation summarizes the scholarly consensus since: Peronism is a movement that began at the center, Buenos Aires, and only much later reached the distant corners of the republic. Moreover, "full-blown" Peronism is to be found at the core and should be studied there, where the state was most powerful, unions most mobilized, and plebeian demands most effective. In fact, this scholarly approach extends beyond the study of Peronism to the study of twentieth-century Argentina in general; in this scholarship, local politics either do not matter at all or matter in radically particularistic ways. Major processes of social and political change are best studied from the center. This was where institutional power was located, and where it faced its strongest challenges.

Certainly there is a measure of truth in this, particularly in the greater dynamism and combativeness of Peronism in the industrial core. But it is evidently not the whole picture, especially when one considers that from 1948 on, Peronism won its largest electoral majorities in the interior.[2] More to the point, this book has shown how the scholarly consensus emphasizing the center is wrong in several ways.

First, the case of San Juan underscores the degree to which Peronism was born in the interior. To be sure, the aid campaign after the earthquake was powerful precisely because it was national and run from the center. But it was San Juan that provided the spark to act and the political challenge to confront.

This challenge was foundational to Peronism, which began with an attempt to transform the periphery—and to turn its vision for San Juan into a vision for the nation. It was not a late arrival on the periphery; it started out at the periphery.

Second, if Peronism did not fully deliver on its promise to transform the periphery, that was because it was defeated, not because it "arrived tired." If the leadership of the military regime had aimed solely to win over local elites, they would have granted those elites control of rebuilding at the outset. Instead, the military regime mounted a fundamental challenge to their power and authority. That response to the disaster may well have been foolish, and ultimately it failed to mobilize the necessary local support, but it was hardly weak. If anything, radical rebuilding failed because it came too early, not too late. As we have seen, by the time Perón had vanquished his rivals within the regime, in July 1944, the locals had already battled the first plan for rebuilding to a draw. In the following year, labor organizing took off nationwide, in incremental efforts that finally achieved a powerful cumulative effect, while rebuilding stalled in San Juan, precisely because of the massive scale of the initial push required. By the time Perón and his allies recognized that rebuilding demanded an aggressive mobilizing political strategy within San Juan, in August 1945, official plans for rebuilding were already drained of much of their ambition—and their credibility. The great insurgent energy of the first years after Perón's election, the moment when Peronism truly came together as a movement, came too late for ambitious plans in San Juan.

Third, then, the point could be reversed: it was not that Peronism was "worn out" when it reached San Juan but that the province had "worn out" much of the promise of Peronism early on. It was in San Juan that the utopian early goals of forging a New Argentina by moving a city and remaking an entire region were first pursued—and defeated. The fact that labor-based politics at the core (especially in greater Buenos Aires) came to be a defining feature of Peronism is, I suggest, closely related to the abandonment of the more comprehensive and ambitious goals on the periphery. Put another way, the less aggressive course that Peronism ultimately took on the periphery, and the fact that its most powerful challenge to the status quo ultimately came near the capital, should not be taken as a given but rather as the result of a defeat in one place, a relative victory in another, and an accommodation to the resulting balance of forces.

At the same time, as the last chapters have shown, Peronism did have a pervasive impact on the physical landscape and political culture of San Juan. While the transformation fell well short of early hopes, it was a transformation nonetheless. I have argued that the course it took, moreover, was powerfully shaped by actors whom previous scholarship had largely ignored, from provincial elites to architects and engineers. I have highlighted the creative role these groups played in shaping Peronism—and national history more generally. However intransigent the fuerzas vivas were in their larger strategy of preserving power, they proved quite adaptive in their tactics. Their concerns may have been parochial, but their strategies were national, as their successful cultivation of engineers shows. The scholarly consensus that writes off local politics as particular, petty, and distant from the life of the nation bears a strong resemblance to the early strategy of various key actors—military officials, architects, and to a degree Perón himself—who failed to seriously engage local politics at the outset and thereby doomed the more ambitious plans for rebuilding. On the other hand, of course, Peronism later demonstrated a protean ability to adapt to circumstances: Godoy may well have sacrificed a broader challenge to the local order, but he created a far more stable and egalitarian province, no small achievement, especially given the prior history.

Finally, if Peronism reshaped the landscape and political culture of San Juan, San Juan also continued to shape Peronism. Consider the setting of the novel from which the opening comment was drawn: a Buenos Aires shantytown. These were a new phenomenon in 1957, and largely an unintended consequence of two major Peronist successes: the industrial expansion that drew hundreds of thousands of provincial migrants to the capital, and the combination of a rent freeze and easy credit that drove landlords to sell existing rental properties to tenants but deterred them from building any new rentals to meet demand. The novelist Verbitsky thus chose these new shantytowns, which held less than half of one percent of the population of the city of Buenos Aires, as a revealing vantage point on the limits of Peronism. The Liberating Revolution selected these shantytowns, which it termed "villas de emergencia," as one of the two sites to focus development of its own housing policy. The other site was, not surprisingly, San Juan—and the policy was produced by a commission filled with the architects and engineers who have populated this book, most notably José Pastor.

It was because Perón had made the provision of decent housing for all a foundational political goal—enshrined as a right in the constitution—that Verbitsky's novel packed its punch. San Juan was where the drive to provide housing for all had begun, as I have argued, but in 1957 San Juan, like the shantytowns, offered a stark measure of how distant that goal still remained. Verbitsky's choice of setting, and the Liberating Revolution's choice of focus, underscore how central the goal of decent housing had become to political legitimacy. Both the Communist novelist Verbitsky and the repressive military leadership thought they could undermine the legitimacy of Peronism by showing how it had failed to live up to its promises. But in so doing, they made those promises all the more important. And they highlighted how central housing, planning, and architecture had become to national political debate, as a result of Perón, and ultimately of the San Juan earthquake.

Professional Trajectories

What was the legacy of San Juan for architecture? First consider the idea of rebuilding as a "laboratory for urbanism," a signal opportunity not only to erect modernist buildings but also to carry out modernist planning, to create novel communities in a rebalanced landscape. For all the enthusiasm the idea generated in 1944 and held, despite mounting frustrations, over the following years, the balance two decades later was hardly positive. Here the stops and starts, hirings and firings, had left many architects discouraged at apparently weak professional authority, intense propertied opposition, and vacillating state support. The attempt to reshape the province and the nation had come up short, and a few intriguing buildings and a handful of commissions for leading professionals could not overcome the pervasive sense of squandered opportunity. As Eduardo Sacriste put it in a magisterial overview of Argentine architecture in the twentieth century, San Juan was the greatest test "of our creative and organizational capacity," a test he believed the country had failed.[3]

The experience led at least one architect to rethink his approach to design. After teaching urbanism for several years in Buenos Aires, Ernesto Vautier, the leader of the first San Juan team, took a position in Colombia with the Inter-American Center for Housing and Planning (CINVA). Turning away from a top-down approach to development, he went to work on rural housing and community organizing. Rather than imposing new models from outside, the idea was to build capacities from within—and CINVA's most notable achievement was a simple device for ramming earth, to create more durable earthen structures, and find an inexpensive method for anti-seismic housing.[4] This was precisely the sort of approach that had been missing in San Juan, where the demonization of adobe led to an embrace of concrete that effectively deterred any efforts to build more resiliently in adobe but never managed to provide enough concrete homes for the whole province.[5]

Unlike Vautier, most architects emerged from the experience of San Juan with a deepened commitment to state-led modernization and a sharpened sense of political maneuvering—often accompanied by a wariness of Peronism. In short, they blamed the failures on Perón, not themselves, and embraced a narrowed but still muscular vision for state-led development. Perhaps the results had been disappointing: certainly the José Pastor of 1944 would not have been fully satisfied with the plan drafted by the José Pastor of 1948, much less its implementation by Costantini in 1956. But even if the results did not live up to architects' ambitions, they still could reinforce claims to authority. The rebuilding of San Juan was the moment when planning discourse gained state approval. Perón's Second Five-Year Plan had required master plans of every city; only a few followed through, but a lasting precedent was set. Pastor might have failed to fully persuade the Peronist state of his particular vision, but he had made his larger project indispensable to future state actors. He went on to serve as advisor to many housing and planning agencies during the Liberating Revolution and after, becoming a central figure in the profession and developing master plans for locations from the industrial suburbs of Buenos Aires to the furthest corner of Patagonia.[6] The vocabulary and approach he developed in San Juan would become standard planning practice nationwide.

In 1944, very few buildings in San Juan or in other interior cities were designed by architects. Under Perón, the government built thousands of buildings and hundreds of housing projects across the nation, opening up important spaces for architects. After Perón was overthrown, this trend intensified. The 1960s and 1970s were decades of experimentation in Argentine architecture, as most government buildings and many housing projects were designed through architectural competitions. This gave the profession direct institutional control over building, and it also cleared the way for the emergence of aggressive and radical young designers, who won in competitions important commissions they would never have obtained through older hierarchical relations of patronage. Both the government buildings and the housing projects were particularly concentrated in the interior. At the same time, perhaps the most powerful and creative strand within Argentine modernism, *casablanquismo*, took particular inspiration from the "casas blancas," the whitewashed adobe homes, of the provinces.[7] In this sense, San Juan was an opening act in a longer drama.[8]

Within San Juan itself, as I argued in the last chapter, architects became for the first time a part of the local establishment, as attenuated modernism became the preferred language of local construction, and barrios designed according to neighborhood unit principles became the major vehicle of urban growth. But if the architects rejected in 1944 became heroes to a new generation of professionals, the uncomfortable questions they had raised about the geographic balance and social development of the province were largely swept aside. Instead of challenging the centralization of power within the province, rebuilding ultimately strengthened it. Even as grape monoculture expanded and new wineries were built, the countryside lost its population and fell behind the cities. Thus the very successes of the local architects were also a measure of their limitations. In the final analysis, however, the richest terrain for surveying the impact of Peronism, modernism, and rebuilding is the landscape of the city itself, to which we now turn.

A Final Ruin

Just as this book opened with a view of the landscape, the "grapes everywhere" and "everything built of adobe" one observer recorded in 1942, so it seems appropriate to close with a return to the landscape, to examine the traces of the transformations it has registered. The most obvious starting point is the countryside, where vines covered even more terrain than before. Grape monoculture was democratized, to some extent, as the number of producers increased and the power of the great wineries decreased, but the industry retained its central role in local politics and economics.[9]

In the city, the haphazard grimy world of adobe gave way to a structured white order of concrete. The inward-looking courtyard houses were replaced by free-standing concrete boxes, the narrow streets by broad avenues. Instead of ledges too narrow for people to pass each other, the streets were now lined with sidewalks wide enough to allow canals and trees beside them. Within the four avenues, at least, those sidewalks had such appeal that locals became famous for washing and even waxing them obsessively.

The center of the local world remained the Plaza 25 de Mayo, surrounded by cafes, clubs, and the Cathedral. To the west and the east, the central avenue stretched out for blocks lined by monumental buildings. Beyond that, the grid inside the four avenues remains the terrain of discrete homes and professional offices. Of course, this structured order was shot through with gaps and exceptions, lonely adobe brick buildings that had survived the disaster and precarious shacks thrown up in the interstices between planned developments, like the shantytown standing three blocks from the Institute for Seismic Prevention, successor to the Reconstruction Council. Still, the city proper may be one of the most successful examples in the world of anti-seismic rebuilding, and it certainly is the most secure city along the highly active length of the Andes.

While the government buildings in the city center and housing projects around the periphery were largely completed by 1962, certain symbolically key projects would remain unfinished for decades to come. The Cathedral tower was completed in 1962, for example, but the building itself did not open until 1979. Three particular projects were icons of rebuilding: the dam, the highway, and the Civic Center. All three were important as symbols, as infrastructure, and as vehicles for federal funds. Every comprehensive plan for rebuilding had stressed the importance of dams to produce power, attract industry, expand irrigation, and increase agricultural production. After Perón's fall, even the fuerzas vivas embraced the idea, and Victoria tirelessly advocated it when he ran Reconstruction. Still, the major dam was not finished until the 1970s—and others proposed by Zuleta were only nearing completion in the first years of the next century. Similarly, every plan since Guido and Carrasco had called for moving the train stations and lifting most of the rail lines, and many plans (although not the more radical Bereterbide or Ferrari Hardoy proposals) had envisioned building a belt highway around the city. But the tracks were only lifted in the late 1960s, and the highway finally completed in the 1990s.

On the west edge of downtown, every plan had envisioned a landmark to replace the train stations, from Guido's and Carrasco's reflecting pool to Pastor's new cathedral. By the late 1960s, a site was chosen for the new Civic Center, a single building to concentrate all the state agencies scattered across the city since the quake. A national competition was held, judged by the SCA, and a team of young modernists from Buenos Aires won. They designed a concrete structure three blocks long and six double-height stories high, by far the largest edifice in the province, an imposing presence on the skyline with spectacular views of the valley and mountains from its roof. The aggressive design was in keeping with the ambitions of state-led development of the era. With its overpowering size, sleek glass skin, and pivotal location at the end of the new central avenue, it was also a fitting capstone to state-led rebuilding. Indeed, serious work on the project began just as Perón triumphantly came back from exile in 1973 to be elected president for the third time. In San Juan, Peronism returned to power, with the two leading figures in the administration—Governor Eloy Camus and Government Minister Pablo Ramella— major actors from the struggles of thirty years before.

The contracts were signed, the foundations poured, the concrete frame went up—and there it stood. For three decades the empty shell towered over the city. During the long downward spiral of the Argentine state after the Peronist administration was overthrown by a savage coup in 1976, the shell remained untouched. Too expensive to complete, too massive to demolish, the Civic Center loomed over the city as an uneasy reminder of both the extent and the limits of state power, what local wags called "a monument to cement." It was a literal ruin of the New Argentina. Promising to remake the city on its own designs but unable or unwilling to carry through, the state had left a void at city center.

But in the surprising recovery of Argentina in recent years, after the default in 2001, a different future opened up for this ruin. As the dire economic crisis receded and prosperity returned, the Peronist governor declared this boom to be the "second reconstruction" of the province, with new housing, another dam, and a new wing for the Rawson Hospital. For some, this phrase evoked the days of Godoy, and for others, those of Carreras, but in either case, it brought a memory of a sense of common purpose. In 2007, two days after the sixty-fourth anniversary of the coup that began Perón's political career, the governor of the province and the president of the nation, a Peronist from the tiny province of Santa Cruz, stood before a crowd to inaugurate the finally complete Civic Center. Resonant as the sense of closure was, the governor decided that his office would not join the provincial agencies moving into the structure. Instead, he would continue to govern from the same place as always, the complex from which the province had been governed for so long: the provisional quarters thrown up in a few weeks in the desperate fall of 1944.[10]

APPENDIX

GOVERNMENT SPENDING IN SAN JUAN (IN MILLIONS OF 1944 PESOS)

Year	Province	Reconstruction Council
1920	2.5	
1925	8.8	
1928	13.4	
1931	10.7	
1935	13.9	
1939	13.9	
1943	12.4	
1944	24.1	22.4**
1945	16.0*	1.5*
1946	16.9*	8.1
1947	22.4	17.2
1948	25.0	21.8
1949	20.9	20.7
1950	22.4	11.6
1951	29.1	17.4
1952	20.1	11.1
1953	14.9	4.4
1954	16.4	4.9
1955	19.1	3.4
1956	20.3	21
1957	20.8	18

*estimated
**includes MOP spending

NOTES AND SOURCES: All amounts in constant 1944 pesos; converted according to government deflator in della Paolera and Taylor, eds., *A New Economic History of Argentina.* No consistent statistics on the size of the provincial economy are available.

Early years included for comparison purposes: fiscally typical Radical administration in 1920; Cantoni administrations in 1925, 1928, and 1931; Conservative administrations in 1935, 1939, and 1943.

Sources for provincial budgets: *Anuario geográfico argentino 1941*; Banco de San Juan, *Serie estadística de San Juan* 1954, 1958, 1962; República Argentina, *Mensaje del excelentísimo señor presidente de la Nación General Edelmiro Farrell y memoria del segundo año de labor*; "Presupuesto general de la provincia," AHASJ, Leyes; *La Reforma.*

Sources for Reconstruction Council budgets: *Memoria del Ministerio de Obras Públicas año 1945*; *Informe y Cuenta de Inversión del Ministerio de Hacienda* [1947–56]; *Boletín del Consejo de Reconstrucción 1948;* Costantini, "Política relativa a la reconstrucción." These figures are approximate, as official data are not complete, transparent, or consistent.

NOTES

Introduction

1. Taylor, *Rural Life in Argentina*, 38.
2. Wine and distilled liquor were important products during the colonial period but declined with the crisis of independence, giving way to livestock trade across the Andes. The late-nineteenth-century boom was a return to this precedent on a far larger scale. On earlier wineries, see Lacoste, "The Rise and Secularization of Viticulture in Mendoza."
3. Sarmiento, *Facundo*. Sarmiento's book was formally about the provincial strongman Facundo Quiroga, but everyone understood it to be aimed at Rosas. Three starting points in the vast literature on Sarmiento are Halperín Donghi, ed., *Sarmiento*; Goodrich, *Facundo and the Construction of Argentine Culture*; and Svampa, *El dilema argentino*. The best overview of the liberal project remains Halperín Donghi, *Una nación para el desierto argentino*.
4. This process has been studied closely in Mendoza, and more summarily in San Juan. For Mendoza, see the excellent Richard Jorba, *Poder, economia y espacio en Mendoza*; Lacoste, *El vino del inmigrante*; Supplee, "Provincial Elites and the Economic Transformation of Mendoza, Argentina, 1880–1914"; Fleming, *Region vs. Nation*. For San Juan, see Avila and Gago, *Proceso y mecanismo de formación de las clases sociales y modos de producción*, and the comparative essays in Richard Jorba, ed., *La región vitivinícola argentina*.
5. Quoted in Arias and Peñaloza de Varese, *Historia de San Juan*, 389.
6. Marianetti, *El racimo y su aventura*.
7. Page, *Perón*, 3–6.
8. Perón quoted in Civita, ed., *Perón, el hombre del destino*, 1: 247.
9. Scalabrini Ortiz, *Los ferrocarriles deben ser del pueblo argentino*, 1; see also Luna, *El 45*, 396; Arturo Jauretche, quoted in Galasso, *Jauretche y su época*, 615.
10. One recent history used a photograph of Perón with victims as an emblematic

image of Peronism, without mentioning the disaster itself: Luna, *Breve historia de los argentinos*.

11. On the economic imbalances, see Rocchi, *Chimneys in the Desert*.

12. Balán, *La cuestión regional en la Argentina*. On federalist structures, see Gibson, ed., *Federalism and Democracy in Latin America*, especially the essay by Gibson and Tulia Falletti.

13. Brennan and Pianetto, "Introduction," vii. One exception is Sawers, *The Other Argentina*, but his approach consists more of demonizing the interior than examining its social or political history.

14. A recent bibliography of Peronism included 3,400 items, but fewer than 20 studies of the interior: Horvath, *A Half Century of Peronism*. But see Rafart and Masés, *El peronismo desde los territorios a la nación*; Macor and Tcach, eds., *La invención del peronismo en el interior del país*; Macor and Iglesias, *El peronismo antes del peronismo*.

15. Segura, "Prólogo" in Jorba, ed., *Cuarto Centenario de San Juan*, 21.

16. Two Peronist administrations served a full term, but in both cases the elected governor was replaced by his vice governor.

17. There are several political histories of cantonismo, largely focused on the years before 1934: Smith, "Radicalism in the Province of San Juan"; Rodriguez, *Lencinas y Cantoni*; Ramella de Jefferies, *El radicalismo bloquista en San Juan (1916–1934)*. Two works have examined Cantoni as a power broker after his overthrow: Hattingh, "Cuyo and Goliath," and Diego Pereyra and Sol Vasini, "El Bloquismo sanjuanino (1930–1941)," in Lacoste, ed., *Populismo en San Juan y Mendoza*. The cultural world of cantonismo has remained largely unexplored, except for suggestive chapters in Westrate, "The Populist Prism and the End of an Era," and Garcés, *La escuela cantonista*. The only work on bloquismo after 1944 is a journalist's fawning biography of Leopoldo Bravo, who is widely reputed to be Cantoni's illegitimate son: Barbosa, *El federalismo bloquista*.

18. Rodríguez, "Cantonismo." Similar parallels are drawn in Mansilla, *Los partidos provinciales*, 11, and Barbosa, *El federalismo bloquista*, 106.

19. Lomnitz, *Fundamentals of Earthquake Prediction*, ix.

20. See Horne, *Small Earthquake in Chile*.

21. Dickie, "The Smell of Disaster," 237.

22. See, for example, García Acosta, ed., *Historia y desastres en América Latina*, or Walker, *Shaky Colonialism*.

23. Rofman, "Teoría y práctica de la planificación regional en América Latina," 353–56. Two major examples are SUDENE in Brazil, a drought-relief program which became a model regional-development initiative, and CORFO in Chile, one part of the rebuilding initiative after the 1939 Chillán earthquake which became the key state industrial development agency.

24. See especially Videla, *Historia de San Juan*.

25. For example, Barton, *Communities in Disaster*. One skillful work in this vein is Oliver-Smith, *The Martyred City*.

26. Scott, *Seeing Like a State*.

27. This book thus represents an in-depth exploration of the processes briefly sketched in the mini–case studies of two post-9/11 books on rebuilding, Vale and Campanella, eds., *The Resilient City*, and Ockman, ed., *Out of Ground Zero*.

28. Liernur, *La arquitectura en la Argentina del siglo XX*; Gorelik, *La grilla y el parque*; Ballent, *Las huellas de la política*.

29. For useful overviews of the historiography on Peronism, see Plotkin, "The Changing Perceptions of Peronism"; and Buchrucker, "Interpretations of Peronism"; and the introduction to Chamosa and Karush, eds., *A New Cultural History of Peronism*.

30. See above all Germani, *Política y sociedad en una época de transición*, and Germani, Ianni, and Di Tella, *Populismo y contradicciones de clase en latinoamérica*.

31. Plotkin, "Changing Perceptions," 43.

32. Ibid., 39.

33. See particularly Murmis and Portantiero, *Estudios sobre los orígenes del peronismo*, and Horowitz, *Argentine Unions, the State, and the Rise of Perón*.

34. James, *Resistance and Integration*, and "October 17th and 18th, 1945."

35. Zanatta, *Del estado liberal a la nación católica*, and *Peron y el mito de la nación católica*; Caimari, *Perón y la Iglesia católica*; Bianchi, *Catolicismo y peronismo*.

36. Plotkin, *Mañana es San Perón*; Gené, *Un mundo feliz*; Puiggrós and Bernetti, *Peronismo*.

37. Cane, *The Fourth Enemy*, Chamosa, *The Argentine Folklore Movement*, and the essays in Chamosa and Karush, eds., *A New Cultural History of Peronism*.

38. Mackinnon, *Los años formativos del Partido Peronista*; García Sebastiani, *Los antiperonistas en la Argentina peronista*; Rein, *In the Shadow of Perón*; Rein and Sitman, eds., *El primer peronismo*; Spinelli, *Los vencedores vencidos*; and the chapter on anti-Peronism by Natalia Milanesio in Chamosa and Karush, eds., *A New Cultural History of Peronism*.

39. Berrotarán, Jáuregui, and Rougier, eds., *Sueños de bienestar en la Nueva Argentina*; Elena, *Consuming Dignity*; Ramacciotti, Valobra, and Acha, eds., *Generando el peronismo*; Cosse, *Estigmas de nacimiento*; Caimari, *Apenas un delincuente*.

40. This is the incident described at the end of chapter 2, mentioned in Zanatta, *Perón y el mito de la nación católica*, 133–35.

Part 1: Revelations among the Ruins, Early 1944

1. The GOU was initially formed by colonels and lieutenant colonels active in nationalist and Catholic integralist circles; after the coup, lodge cofounder Perón expanded the GOU to include virtually the entire junior officer corps. See Potash, *The Army and Politics in Argentina*, 1: 182–282, and Potash, ed., *Perón y el GOU*.

2. "'No traemos anhelos pequeños ni afanes descoloridos,' dijo el Interventor Dr David Uriburu," *Tribuna*, 11 January 1944.

Chapter 1: "Rooted Vines and Uprooted Men"

1. De Fina, Giannetto, and Sabella, *Difusión geográfica de cultivos índices en la provincia de San Juan y sus causas*, 21.

2. The 1943 guidebook optimistically counted 259 "existing" mines, but according to the economic census only a few dozen were actually operating. *Anuario general de San Juan DUA*, 23.

3. By contrast, across the Andes, mines had become the core of the Chilean economy. Mining has remained a centerpiece of utopian projects for the province since Sarmiento.

4. Fourteen of the twenty largest bodegas were located in the capital. The remaining six were elsewhere in the central valley, and three of them were subsidiaries of firms in the capital. "Informe sobre bodegas," March 1944, Archivo Histórico y Administrativo de San Juan (hereafter: AHASJ), Misc., c. 44, d. 8.

5. The 1943 guide listed 318 wineries. The twenty largest were concentrated in the capital, but the rest were more dispersed: 44 percent in the capital, 52 percent elsewhere in the central valley, and 3 percent outside the central valley. *Anuario general DUA*, 398–400.

6. Small is defined as under five hectares; medium five to twenty-five hectares, large over twenty-five hectares.

7. "Cuadro No. 6: Número de Viñedos y superficie por escala de extensión (1938)," Jorge Ferrari Hardoy Papers, Francis Loeb Library, Graduate School of Design, Harvard University (hereafter: Ferrari Hardoy Papers), D-85j2. These statistics are by the size of individual holdings. They do not account for ownership of multiple vineyards, which was common, and do not distinguish between independent vineyards and those run by wineries.

8. Boleda, *La estructura productiva*, 45.

9. Wine was the most common use for grapes: the 1943 harvest was 82 percent wine, 15 percent table, 3 percent other uses. Boleda, *La estructura productiva*, 38. Power dynamics within the industry are astutely described by Mó, *Vitivinicultura*, 161–74. There are no studies of sharecroppers ("contratistas") for San Juan, but one suggestive article for Mendoza: Salvatore, "Labor Control and Discrimination."

10. Raul Bahia, "La industria de conservación de frutas en la provincia," *Boletín Agrícola-Industrial de la Provincia de San Juan* 1, no. 1 (Jan 1935): 31. For a comprehensive overview of a decade of production across all sectors, see *Anuario estadístico de la República Argentina 1948*, vol. 1.

11. Calculated from 1895 and 1947 census figures: Maurín Navarro, *Contribución al estudio de la historia vitivinícultura argentina*, 194. These are statistics for individuals; the decline in household ownership would likely be more dramatic, on the order of 70 percent to 25 percent. While locals were losing land, immigrants were gaining it: immigrants were a negligible percentage of landowners with water rights in the early nineteenth century, but 21 percent by 1870 and 39 percent by 1911. Avila and Gago, *Proceso y mecanismo de formación de las clases sociales*, 23.

12. There was no national census between 1914 and 1947, the latter survey was obviously affected by the disaster itself, and the census categories are problematic in various ways. But the 1947 census provides the best available overview of the social structure. It divided the economically active population into 17 percent owners and

managers, 5 percent self-employed, 3 percent family-employed, 15 percent (white-collar) empleados, and 60 percent (blue-collar) obreros. Nearly half of obreros were unskilled agricultural workers, who thus composed a quarter of the economically active population. República Argentina, Instituto Nacional de Estadística y Censos, *IV Censo General de la Nación año 1947, Cuadros inéditos*, 227.

13. In 1940, San Juan had 162 deaths per 1,000 live births. Marcelo Cañellas, "El Terremoto de San Juan: Problemas de orden económico y su solución," *Revista de Ciencias Económicas* no. 276 (July 1944): 612.

14. "Informe del Departamento Provincial del Trabajo de San Juan," 1938, cited in Westrate, "The Populist Prism," 327. The national rejection rate in 1937 was 28 percent, *Anuario geográfico argentino 1941*, 321.

15. Maurín Navarro, *Introducción a la hygiene social de Cuyo*, 21–23. Even the booster-sponsored city guide in 1943 listed average life span as thirty-eight in the capital and twenty-eight provincewide. *Anuario general DUA*, 576. While the low numbers were primarily due to high infant mortality, striking differences persisted even among those who survived to age five.

16. Guido and Carrasco, *Plan regulador de San Juan*, 7, 14. Abenhamar Rodrigo, "Las dos ciudades," in Bataller, ed., *Y aquí nos quedamos*, 68.

17. "San Juan de Cuyo: La Ciudad de las Estatuas," in Gómez Lucero, ed., *San Juan*, 169, 171. San Juan was first described as "the city of statues" in 1911, less than a decade after most of the statues went up. Capdevila, *Tierra mia*.

18. Gómez de Terán, *Conferencia sobre el terremoto del 27 de octubre de 1894*, 17–18. He noted that mortality rates were higher in San Juan than in Rio de Janeiro, then one of the deadliest cities in the world. Hauthal Commission report quoted in "Nuevo Director General de Arquitectura," *Revista de Arquitectura* 29, no. 278 (February 1944): 85.

19. Bodenbender, "El terremoto argentino del 27 de octubre de 1894," 327–28.

20. When he was governor shortly after the Mendoza earthquake, Sarmiento passed a law to widen the streets, but this was ultimately only applied to the "four avenues." Augusto Landa, "Sarmiento y el ensanche de las calles de la ciudad de San Juan," *La Acción*, 21 March 1944.

21. Juan Siri, "El terremoto de 1894," *La Acción*, 18 January 1945.

22. The post-earthquake census counted 35 percent of households as homeowners. There are no definitive pre-earthquake figures, but newspapers claimed two-thirds of the city were renters, consistent with census data for the broadly similar city of Mendoza. Coghlan, *La condición de la vivienda en la Argentina a través del censo de 1947*, 187, 200.

23. Both Jáchal in the north and Caucete in the southeast had around four thousand urban residents. Obras Sanitarias de la Nación, which ran the water service and thus had the best population information, estimated the 1943 population at 107,000. República Argentina, Obras Sanitarias de la Nación, *Memoria del año 1943*, 131.

24. *Anuario general DUA*, 576.

25. Antonio L. de Tomaso to Interventor Evaristo Pérez Virasoro, San Juan, 28 October 1939, AHASJ, Misc., c. 51, d. 5.
26. Juan Moreira was a bandit celebrated in popular literature, here used to refer to the supposedly barbarous past. Federico de Achával, "Los 2000 estilos porteños," *Revista de Arquitectura* 29, no. 288 (December 1944): 538.
27. One did live east of the plaza—but only one block east.
28. The professions broke down as follows: legal, 76 lawyers and 50 notaries; medical, 111 doctors and 51 dentists; agro-industrial, 26 agronomists, 110 enologists, and 67 chemical or mining engineers; construction, 12 architects and 40 civil or architectural engineers. Calculated from *Anuario general DUA*.
29. República Argentina, Comisión Nacional del Censo, *Tercer Censo Nacional, levantado el 1 de junio de 1914*.
30. Calculated from "Informe sobre bodegas," March 1944, AHASJ, Misc, c. 44, d. 8.
31. Conte-Grand, *La ciudad en ruinas*, 59.
32. "San Juan de Cuyo," 171.
33. Estimated annual newspaper circulation was 268 per capita in Buenos Aires, 38 in Mendoza, and 8 in San Juan. The local figures are undoubtedly too low, but the stark contrast is telling. Taylor, *Rural Life*, 266.
34. Sedán, *La Reforma*, 17–18.
35. On the Cantonis' political trajectory, see especially Smith, "Radicalism in the Province of San Juan," and Ramella de Jefferies, *El radicalismo bloquista en San Juan*.
36. One such tale in Juan Carlos Bataller, "El lado humano del poder: Anecdotas de la politica sanjuanina I," *El Nuevo Diario*, 12 May 2001, 3. On photos of Cantoni, see Mansilla, *Los partidos provinciales*, 16. On the political style of Cantoni, and the prevalence of this kind of story, see Garcés, *La escuela cantonista*.
37. *El Porvenir*, 20 August 1919, quoted by Garcés, *La escuela cantonista*, 166. Cantonista crowds in 1919 called for "Fewer parasites, more alpargatas!" Westrate, "The Populist Prism," 151.
38. Fernando Darousa, "Cantoni, lider del Bloquismo, afirma: Perón no será presidente," *Ercilla*, 13 February 1945.
39. For a comparative analysis of taxation in Mendoza and San Juan, see Westrate, "The Populist Prism."
40. On Cantonismo as the moment when state authority reached the periphery, see Escolar, *Los dones étnicos de la nación*, 157–83, and the fictionalized memoir by Mugnos de Escudero, *La maestrita de los yarcos*.
41. Carlos Ciro Gutierrez, quoted in Persello, *El Partido Radical*, 49. A montonera was a gaucho band, like those Sarmiento had deplored.
42. Importantly, Cantoni's most important national allies were the Conservatives and right-wing Radicals who opposed the dominant Yrigoyen wing of the Radical Party.
43. On three separate occasions, assassins killed the man next to Aldo or Federico but missed their target.

44. The Conservatives provided the slogan, and the rest of the elite followed out of common loathing for Cantoni.

45. Smith, "Radicalism in the Province of San Juan," 273–74.

46. Ramella, *Anteproyecto de código impositivo para la provincia de San Juan*, 8. The two previous interventions against Cantoni had also slashed provincial tax collections: during the first, from 1925 to 1926, they dropped to 60 percent of their previous level; during the second, from 1928 to 1931, they fell to 23 percent. República Argentina, Ministro de Hacienda, *Primera Conferencia de Ministros de Hacienda*, 106.

47. "La Acción Católica representará el dia 25 de diciembre el Belén Dramatizado en el Estornell," *Democracia (San Juan)*, 22 December 1945.

48. On Catholic activism in the 1930s, see Caimari, *Perón y la Iglesia católica*.

49. Quoted in Westrate, "The Populist Prism," 334–35.

50. Ramella, *Reformas a la constitución de San Juan*, 18, 48.

51. Ramella, *La prepotencia y otros temas*, 80.

52. *Memoria de Obras Sanitarias de la Nación 1944*, 183.

53. On widespread irregularities in the election, see Hattingh, "Cuyo and Goliath," 201–22.

54. The three largest beneficiaries were the leading Conservative bodegueros Santiago Graffigna, Francisco Bustelo, and Bartolomé del Bono. See Hattingh, "Cuyo and Goliath," 142.

55. Guido and Carrasco, *Plan regulador*, 7, 8, 65, 70, 10.

Chapter 2: In a Broken Place

1. Rúben Juncos, "El terremoto de San Juan del día 15 de Enero de 1944: Importancia de la construcción antisísmica," in de Lorenzi, ed., *Contribución a los estudios sísmicos en la República Argentina*, 57–58. On the earthquake itself, see Castano, *La verdadera dimensión del problema sísmico en la provincia de San Juan*, 21; Laura Patricia Perucca and Juan de Dios Paredes, "Fallamiento cuaternario en la zona de La Laja y su relación con el terremoto de 1944, departamento Albardón, San Juan, Argentina," *Revista Mexicana de Ciencias Geológicas* 20, no. 1 (2003): 20–26.

2. "Escenas impresionantes relata una persona migrada de San Juan," *Los Andes*, 16 January 1944.

3. Luis Romero, "Horas de terror y de ruina," *Revista CACYA*, February 1944, 193–94.

4. "No ha quedado en San Juan casa alguna que pueda ser habitada," *La Voz del Interior*, 21 January 1944; Manuel Gilberto Varas, "Enfoques de la tragedia," *Tribuna*, 18 April 1944.

5. Romero, "Horas de terror," 198.

6. Interview of Juana Antonia Lima de Orozco, San Juan, 1997, quoted in Ferrá de Bartol, dir., *Historia contemporánea*, 1, 46–48.

7. Harrington, *Volcanes y terremotos*, 224; Josephs, *Argentine Diary*, 334.

8. Di Leo, *Acá cerca*, 72–73.

9. Arnaldo Ulises Varas, "Todo dependía de un solo hilo," *El Viñatero*, 16–23 November 1991.

10. Francisco Compañy, "El problema religioso en la ciudad destruida," *Boletín Oficial de la Arquidiócesis de San Juan de Cuyo* 28, no. 2–3 (February–March 1944): 63.

11. "Benito Elizondo, El Salvavidas," *Diario de Cuyo*, 15 February 2004.

12. Interview of Margarita Usin de Molina, San Juan, 1997, quoted in Ferrá de Bartol, dir., *Historia contemporánea*, 2, 35.

13. Romero, "Horas de terror," 195–96.

14. Ibid., 196.

15. Varas, "Todo dependía de un solo hilo."

16. Cantoni's presence was noted in the late edition of *Los Andes* on 16 January 1944; Edgardo Mendoza, "El personal de la salud," *Diario de Cuyo*, 11 January 2004. His brothers Aldo, who had been in Calingasta, and Elio joined him in relief work in the following two days. Interview of Aldo Hermes Cantoni by Aldo Gaete, San Juan, 1 August 2002.

17. "A tres décadas largas del terremoto que destruyó a la ciudad de San Juan," *La Nación*, 24 November 1977.

18. Bogni, *Terremoto del 44*, 19.

19. Odin Gómez Lucero, "La vida en una cárcel argentina," *Tribuna*, 1 June 1944, and "Visitaron la cárcel de Marquesado varios magistrados," *Los Andes*, 8 February 1944. Earlier reports incorrectly spoke of mass flight—"Pidióse la salida de los que pueden hacerlo," *La Voz del Interior*, 18 January 1944—or claimed the release was a matter of simple compassion—"Bajo palabra de regreso, el director de la cárcel de Marquesado puso en libertad a los presos," *El Pueblo*, 21 January 1944.

20. Interview of Cruz Lidia Lazzo by author, San Juan, 11 July 2001.

21. Romero recalled aftershocks at 11:15 p.m., 1:28 a.m., and 4:10 a.m. Romero, "Horas de terror," 196.

22. Interview of Tulio del Bono (padre) by Aldo Gaete, San Juan, 14 July 2002.

23. Compañy, "El problema religioso," 64–65.

24. Varas, *Crónica de mi San Juan*, 129.

25. Compañy, "El problema religioso," 64.

26. Interview of Manuel Leiva, San Juan, 1997, quoted in Ferrá de Bartol, dir., *Historia contemporánea*, 1, 83.

27. Romero, "Horas de terror," 198.

28. "De San Juan llegaron anoche a esta capital muchos viajeros," *La Prensa*, 18 January 1944.

29. Pablo Ramella, "Reflexiones acerca de la tragedia de San Juan," *El Pueblo*, 23 January 1944; Fr. Bernardo Arias, "A un mes de la catastrofe de San Juan," *El Pueblo*, 17 February 1944.

30. "Desolación y estupor muestra la gente que ambula por San Juan," *La Prensa*, 17 January 1944.

31. Erikson, *Everything in Its Path*, 198.

32. "Declaraciones del Secretario Provincial de Obras Públicas," *La Voz del Interior*,

17 January 1944; Varas, *Terremoto en San Juan*, 63, 67–68. Many doors also carried survivor's notices: "Telegrama original," *Ercilla*, 26 January 1944; Patricia Pelaytay and Susana Tello, "Aquellos días interminables" in Bataller, *Y aquí nos quedamos*, 16.

33. Erikson, *Everything in Its Path*, 177, 186.

34. Although several churches were partly standing, including the Cathedral, the authorities ruled all of them unsound, except for the reinforced concrete chapel at Don Bosco School.

35. See the drawing reproduced in Carlos Mendióroz, "El planeamiento en la reconstrucción de San Juan," *Revista de Arquitectura* 31, no. 310 (October 1946): 422.

36. "Es imponente la ayuda de todo el país a la desesperada población de San Juan," *Los Andes*, 17 January 1944; "Designaronse las comisiones para la reconstrucción de San Juan," *La Prensa*, 2 February 1944; Angel Martin to Luis Maria de Pablo Pardo, Ministro de Gobierno e Instruccion Publica, 18 January 1944, AHASJ, Gobierno 2, c. 9bis, d. 24.

37. Cañellas, "El terremoto de San Juan," 613.

38. "Todo para la reconstrucción," *Tribuna*, 27 March 1944.

39. Castellanos, *Anotaciones preliminares con motivo de una visita a la ciudad de San Juan*, 27.

40. Pablo Ramella, "Legislación de la propiedad en zonas expuestas a movimientos sísmicos," *El Pueblo*, 4 February 1944. Catholic Action leader Ramella had been appointed judge by the Conservative administration in 1942.

41. "Meditando," *El Censor*, 25 January 1945. The building's architect was Eduardo Carrizo Vita, former secretary of public works and Guido's and Carrasco's main source in preparing their plan.

42. "Cerca de 100 médicos locales actuaron en San Juan el 15 de enero," *Los Andes*, 25 January 1944; Fr. Bernardo Arias, "A un mes de la catastrofe de San Juan," *El Pueblo*, 16 February 1944 and 17 February 1944.

43. "Dió la nómina de los ofrecimientos de la Salud Pública," *Los Andes*, 22 January 1944.

44. "Fue extraordinario el servicio que los médicos prestaron en San Juan," *La Prensa*, 31 January 1944; "Se precipitó un avión que partió de Mendoza para San Juan: Once muertos," *Los Andes*, 21 January 1944.

45. "Solo 50 casas quedaron en pie en San Juan," *Ercilla*, 26 January 1944. While emergency cremation was common in large disasters, it had not been employed before in Argentina. There certainly was typhus: survivors report deaths among rescue volunteers—Varas, *Terremoto en San Juan*, 77—and unofficial figures suggest that mortality rates from the disease quadrupled—República Argentina, Obras Sanitarias de la Nación, *Memoria del año 1944*, xlii. But the greatest danger, contamination of the water supply, was ruled out within two days. Enrique Real, "Obras Sanitarias de la Nación en la catástrofe de San Juan," *Boletín de Obras Sanitarias de la Nación* 7, no. 89 (November 1944): 349.

46. Interview of Adalcina Ramona Pereyre de Garate, San Juan, 1997, quoted in Ferrá de Bartol, dir., *Historia contemporánea*, 2, 61. Such incidents were reported in the

press in Chile, but not Argentina. "Solo 50 casas quedaron en pie en San Juan," *Ercilla*, 26 January 1944. Interview of Mercedes Alonso, San Juan, 1997, quoted in Ferrá de Bartol, dir., *Historia contemporánea*, 2, 61.

47. Josephs, *Argentine Diary*, 333; Emiliano Lee, "Tren de evacuados," *Tribuna*, 28 August 1944; "Telegrama original," *Ercilla*, 26 January 1944.

48. Interview of Jorge Rosendo Domínguez, San Juan, 1997, quoted in Ferrá de Bartol, dir., *Historia contemporánea*, 2, 61.

49. Interview of Isabel Guerrero de Carchano, San Juan, 1998, quoted in Ferrá de Bartol, dir., *Historia contemporánea*, 2, 66.

50. Interview of Jorge Abelin, San Juan, 1997, in Ferrá de Bartol, *Historia contemporánea*, 1, anexo documental; interview of Domingo Eloy Garay, San Juan, 1997, in Basualdo Miranda et al., *El testimonio oral*, 150.

51. Interview of Magdalena Arancibia by author, San Juan, 15 July 2001; interview of Tulio del Bono by Aldo Gaete, San Juan, 14 July 2002. A Mendoza anthropologist heard reports of such movements the day the burning started: Carlos Rusconi, "Recuerdos del Terremoto de San Juan, 1944," *Revista del Museo de Historia Natural de Mendoza* 16, no. 1 (1964): 74.

52. Federico Prolongo to Ministro de Gobierno, 11 February 1944, AHASJ, Misc., c. 69, d. 8.

53. Juan Valenzuela to Ministro de Gobierno, 22 April 1944, AHASJ, Misc., c. 69, d. 8. Ten months after the Conservative governor Valenzuela was deposed, his brother still directed the Civil Registry, the key post for electoral fraud.

54. On 26 January, the provincial government estimated that 2,500 bodies had been cremated, but only 436 had been identified: "En torno a la falta de identificación de las víctimas de San Juan," *La Nación*, 4 February 1944. A rough count by the head of police was never completed, a local suggestion that neighborhood committees draw up lists of victims was brushed aside, and an emergency request to change the procedures for registering a death was apparently ignored—for the suggestions, see Guillermo Petra Sierralta, "Los problemas de San Juan," *Los Andes*, 25 January 1944. In the absence of official information, the press developed its own estimates. Drawing on the limited government reports, information from relatives, and local reporting, in late January the Mendoza paper estimated the death toll at 5,000.

55. "Urgentes problemas," *Los Andes*, 25 January 1944. The newspaper later conducted a survey that concluded there was one death for every tenth family in San Juan, 1,500 in all. But this number was far below even the early estimates for cremations. "Después de veinte años de su destrucción San Juan brilla por un milagro de la voluntad de sus habitantes," *Los Andes*, 15 January 1964. The first published account to settle on 10,000 seems to be Chilean: "Diez mil muertos causó la noche triste de San Juan," *Ercilla*, 19 January 1944.

56. República Argentina, Dirección Nacional de Estadística y Censos, *Informe demográfico de la República Argentina, 1944–1954*, 185, 264. Unofficial aggregate statistics from the OSN indicate that mortality in San Juan doubled from 1943 to 1944. It is unclear whether these numbers include quake victims, but if they do, that would

indicate a death toll of roughly 3,000. República Argentina, *Memoria de Obras Sanitarias de la Nación 1944*, xlii.

57. During Holy Week 1944, the ashes were taken to the Dominican emergency chapel. According to the prior, the urn contained the remains of perhaps a thousand dead. Varas, *Terremoto en San Juan*, 81.

58. Josephs, *Argentine Diary*, 333.

59. "La evacuación de la ciudad será el exodo forzoso de 50.000 almas," *La Prensa*, 18 January 1944. At a moment when the press was under new government scrutiny, there was considerable self-censorship. There was external censorship as well: an article critical of Army relief actions earned the Communist activist Angel Bustelo a year in prison. Bustelo, *Vida de un combatiente de izquierda*, 1: 20.

60. "La catástrofe excede a cuánto puede concebir la imaginación," *La Prensa*, 19 January 1944. The rumors might have some basis: the archbishop himself claimed the bombing was set for January 22, then cancelled. "El Arzobispo de Cuyo nos habla de su viaje a San Juan después del terremoto," *Tribuna*, 9 April 1944.

61. "La catástrofe de San Juan vista por un funcionario de la Compañía," *Redes Argentinas* 13, no. 8 (February 1944): 6–7.

62. "El Arzobispo de Cuyo nos habla de su viaje a San Juan después del terremoto," *Tribuna*, 9 April 1944.

63. "El dolor de San Juan reflejado en sus miras," *Los Andes*, 19 January 1944.

64. The provincial government reported "approximately" 21,572 evacuated. Intervención Federal en San Juan, *Informe elevado al Ministerio del Interior por el Interventor Interino, corresponde al Gobierno del Interventor Federal, General de Brigada Don Humberto Sosa Molina*, 81.

65. "El problema de la vivienda," *Los Andes*, 14 March 1944.

66. "Telegrama original," *Ercilla*, 26 January 1944.

67. "Benito Elizondo, el salvavidas," *Diario de Cuyo*, 15 February 2004.

68. "A United Press e suas informacoes sobre a catastrofe," *Correio de Manhã* (Rio de Janeiro), 19 January 1944.

69. Varas, *Terremoto en San Juan*, 48.

70. "Telegrama original," *Ercilla*, 26 January 1944.

71. Interview of Tulio del Bono (padre) by Aldo Gaete, San Juan, 14 July 2002.

72. Interview of Segundo Vilas by author, San Juan, 17 July 2001.

73. Félix Ríos quoted in Jorge Rodríguez, "Memorias del horror" in Bataller, ed. *Y aquí nos quedamos*, 14–15.

74. Rodríguez, "Memorias," 14.

75. His son was seriously wounded, but there were closer hospitals, such as Mendoza. Both his departure and the failure of others to take charge underscored the weakness of the local state. See "Un alto funcionario sanjuanino que huyó abandonando su puesto, ha sido exonerado," *La Voz del Interior*, 22 January 1944, and "Hizo una aclaración el ex director general de hidráulica de San Juan," *Los Andes*, 27 January 1944.

76. "El Arzobispo de Cuyo nos habla de su viaje a San Juan después del terremoto," *Tribuna*, 9 April 1944.

77. Interview of Father Pedro Roger Quiroga Marinero by author, San Juan, 9 July 2002. Rodríguez y Olmos had been archbishop since 1940. On this incident, see Zanatta, *Perón y el mito de la nación católica*, 133–35. Criticism of the archbishop was so strong that the prominent politician and Catholic activist Horacio Videla had to personally accompany him on visits to ruined sites, to vouch for him to locals. *Al Dr. Horacio G. Videla*, 47.

78. "La palabra irradiada y la palabra escrita: Ejemplo típico la tragedia de San Juan," *El Pueblo*, 10 March 1944; see also "El Arzobispo de Cuyo nos habla de su viaje a San Juan después del terremoto," *Tribuna*, 9 April 1944, and Francisco Compañy, "El problema religioso en la ciudad destruida," *Boletín Oficial de la Arquidiócesis de San Juan de Cuyo* 28, no. 2–3 (February–March 1944).

Chapter 3: "The Measure of our National Solidarity"

1. Vice-Consul La Plata to Foreign Office, "Report on Public Opinion in January," 31 January 1944, Public Record Office, Foreign Office (hereafter PRO, FO), file 118, folder 726, document 24.

2. Eduardo Sacriste, "Arquitectura popular de San Juan," *Revista de Arquitectura* 29, no. 281 (May 1944): 216.

3. This strand of criticism was evident in the works of Raúl Scalabrini Ortiz, Eduardo Mallea, and Ezequiel Martínez Estrada.

4. Perón had taken over the backwater Department of Labor on 27 October, expanding its responsibilities, annexing other agencies, and elevating it to Secretariat level. He gave the first speech on 2 December, when he officially became secretary of labor. For the speeches, see Perón, *El pueblo quiere saber de qué se trata*, 31, 34–35.

5. In addition to being secretary of labor, Perón was second in command to Farrell at the War Ministry. While initiatives usually came from Perón, he worked hard "to preserve the fiction" that they came from Farrell. Potash, *The Army and Politics in Argentina*, 1: 210.

6. "Se suspendieron los espectáculos," *La Voz del Interior*, 17 January 1944, and "El decreto sobre el duelo," *La Voz del Interior*, 18 January 1944.

7. Norman Armour to Sec'y of State, 18 January 1944, United States National Archives, Record Group 59, (hereafter: USNA, RG 59), 835.48/17.

8. These struggles were between two factions within the GOU, the secret military lodge—by this point, the liberal, pro-Allied Army generals had been almost entirely pushed aside.

9. "El espíritu argentino, dijo el presidente anoche, es capaz de sobreponerse a cualquier cataclismo," *El Pueblo*, 23 January 1944.

10. Ramírez himself was a pedestrian thinker, more an opportunist than a committed nationalist ideologue—before the coup, when he was war minister, there had been serious talk of making him presidential candidate of a Radical Party–led alliance. But after the coup, he aligned with hard-line nationalists like Lugones and Perón's rivals within the GOU, and they exerted decisive influence over his agenda from October 1943 on. Potash, *The Army and Politics*, 217–18, 225–27.

11. Lugones's plans for authoritarian modernization included nationalizing energy production and protecting domestic industry. See Lugones, *La grande Argentina*. Likely out of despair at his political failure, Lugones killed himself in 1938.

12. During his tenure, between 1930 and 1934, the police arrested roughly ten thousand political prisoners and tortured four hundred using techniques Lugones invented (but apparently did not personally implement), including the first use of the electrical cattle prod. Rodríguez Molas, *Historia de la tortura y el orden represivo en la Argentina*, 95–97.

13. Perón blocked the secret police proposal and allegedly beat up Lugones when he tried to have him tailed. Goñi, *Perón y los alemanes*, 179–80. On Lugones's ambitions, see also Luna, *El 45*, 62; Josephs, *Argentine Diary*, 178, 237.

14. Uriburu, unlike Lugones, apparently was directly involved in torture sessions. Rodríguez Molas, *Historia de la tortura*, 96–97.

15. Lugones (h), *El presidente en San Juan*, 1, 4.

16. Ibid., 2, 6.

17. Ibid., 4.

18. "Discurso del presidente," *La Voz del Interior*, 19 January 1944.

19. "El Interventor Federal en San Juan dirigió ayer un manifiesto al pueblo," *La Voz del Interior*, 21 January 1944. At a farewell banquet when Uriburu left San Juan a week later, he offered a toast to "Germany, which for the good of humanity is winning this war." Interview of Hilario Zalba and Eduardo Sacriste by Alfredo Rezzoagli, Buenos Aires, 1985. Copy in author's possession.

20. "There have been expiatory victims," the archbishop wrote, but most survived. "Pastoral del Arzobispo de Cuyo," *La Nación*, 10 February 1944. Six years later, he would ask "were we, perchance, the victims of propitiation through which God spared our remaining brethren sheltered under our flag of blue?" Rodríguez y Olmos, *Pastoral Letter on the Reconstruction of Our Churches*, 1.

21. Roberto Barberis, "Victima expiatoria, pero conmutada," *El Pueblo*, 27 January 1944.

22. A parallel mass took place in Mendoza, also officiated by a military priest. "Gran solidaridad adquirió el funeral de ayer," *Los Andes*, 26 January 1944.

23. "La Plaza del Congreso convertida en Basílica Mayor de la Patria" and "Ayer en la Plaza del Congreso," *El Pueblo*, 26 January 1944.

24. Andrés Calcagno, "Discurso del Vicario General de Ejército" *Boletín Oficial de la Arquidiócesis de San Juan de Cuyo* 28, no. 2–3 (March 1944): 79.

25. Ibid., 80.

26. Lugones, *El presidente*, 5.

27. Ibid.

28. "En pocas horas háse recaudado para los damnificados por el terremoto alrededor de medio millón de pesos," *La Voz del Interior*, 17 January 1944.

29. "Historia del peronismo," *Primera Plana*, 14 January 1969.

30. "En una reunión quedó constituida la Comisión Nacional de la Colecta," *La Prensa*, 18 January 1944. Military leaders had coordinated ad hoc relief in previous tragedies,

but this time the effort and military involvement were far greater. On the GOU, see Potash, *The Army and Politics*, 1: 182–282, and Potash, ed., *Perón y el GOU*.

31. J. H. Hadow, "Argentine Government," 18 January 1944, PRO, FO 118/726/14a.

32. Perón took over the Department of Labor on 27 October 1943; it was expanded and renamed the Secretariat of Labor and Social Welfare one month later. On transformations in the state, see Campione, *Orígenes estatales del peronismo*. On the transformation of the STP, see especially Torre, *La vieja guardia sindical*, and Horowitz, *Argentine Unions, the State, and the Rise of Perón*.

33. Numerous photographs in the national archives show boxcars plastered with posters for the STP.

34. "Sobre la ayuda a las víctimas habló el Coronel Perón," *La Nación*, 16 February 1944.

35. See Perón, *El pueblo quiere saber de qué se trata*, and Perón, *Obras completas*, vol. 6.

36. In response to complaints, Perón explained himself to a joint meeting of officers and enlisted men. At least one officer, Pedro Aramburu, found this "undignified and demeaning," as an officer need never justify himself to subordinates. Opposed to Perón from this point, Aramburu was key in his overthrow eleven years later and led the repressive dictatorship that followed. Interview quoted in Alexander, *The ABC Presidents*, 14.

37. "La reconstrucción de San Juan," *Boletín de Obras Públicas de la República Argentina* 87 (February 1944), 75.

38. See, for example, "Ya suma veinticinco millones de pesos la contribución popular," *El Pueblo*, 20 January 1944; "Los cinematografos de todo el pais donaran sus ingresos de hoy," *La Prensa*, 16 February 1944; "Estampillas con sobrecargo de beneficiencia pro victimas de San Juan," *La Nación*, 17 February 1944; "Fue inaugurado una muestra pictorica en beneficio de San Juan," *El Pueblo*, 11 April 1944.

39. "La magnitud de la colaboración del pueblo está plenamente a la vista," *El Pueblo*, 22 January 1944.

40. "Por radiotelefonía se propaló un discurso del Coronel Juan D. Perón," *La Prensa*, 20 January 1944. The radical change in thinking about labor and social justice was still to come: No one yet questioned why this man was still working for subsistence wages at age 73 and the very entrance to national government.

41. For the beer workers, for example, see "El aporte de la Federación de Obreros Cerveceros y Afines para ayudar a San Juan," *C.G.T.*, 1 July 1944.

42. "El noble gesto de un viejo barrio porteño," *El Pueblo*, 4 February 1944.

43. "33 milliones de pesos, solamente," *C.G.T.*, 16 April 1944.

44. "La evacuación de la ciudad será el exodo forzoso de 50.000 almas," *La Prensa*, 18 January 1944.

45. "A una nota emotiva dió lugar el arribo del primer tren transportando evacuados," *La Voz del Interior*, 21 January 1944.

46. Emiliano Lee, "Tren de evacuados," *Tribuna*, 28 August 1944.

47. Perón quoted in Civita, ed., *Perón, el hombre del destino*, 1: 247.

48. Notably, the two main sites for receiving refugees were the hotel for European immigrants and the main army barracks.

49. "Ya han sido depositados en el Banco de la Nación cerca de ocho millones de pesos para los damnificados de S. Juan," *El Pueblo*, 23 January 1944. All monetary amounts will be given in Argentine pesos. While exchange rates become more complicated after the onset of inflation in the 1940s, the rough exchange between 1944 pesos and 2009 dollars is 1:2.25. 28 million pesos, therefore, is approximately 63 million dollars.

50. "Recibió el presidente el producto de la colecta pro damnificados de San Juan," *Tribuna*, 5 April 1944.

51. Chancery to Foreign Office, 10 April 1944, PRO, FO 118/728/177.

52. Pablo Ramella, "Reflexiones acerca de la tragedia de San Juan," *El Pueblo*, 23 January 1944.

53. "San Juan," *Los Andes*, 15 January 1946.

54. The deputy was Arturo Illia, a Radical leader from Córdoba who would later become president. *Diario de sesiones de Cámara de Diputados de 1949*, 3: 2042.

55. Two architects working for the provincial government noted that "everybody found it really strange" that he "never showed up." Interview of Hilario Zalba and Eduardo Sacriste by Alfredo Rezzoagli, Buenos Aires, 1985.

56. English support for Argentine neutrality undercut the arguments of both the United States—because Argentina might best contribute to the Allied war effort as a neutral—and nacionalistas—because it was precisely in maintaining neutrality that Argentina served the imperial interests of Great Britain.

57. Robert Potash has convincingly shown that the uprising could not have succeeded without these so-called liberal generals, but this small group was quickly rendered irrelevant by Perón. Potash, *The Army and Politics*, 1: 201–2.

58. On the arms deal gone wrong, see Goñi, *The Real Odessa*, and Newton, *The "Nazi Menace."*

59. For more thorough treatment of this three-way power struggle between England, Germany, and the United States, see Newton, *The "Nazi Menace"* and Rapaport, *Gran Bretaña, Estados Unidos y las clases dirigentes argentinas, 1940–1945*.

60. It also momentarily weakened the diplomatic isolation of Argentina. The United States contributed only X-ray film, but other nations contributed more, and the United States attempt to isolate Argentina failed; when a U.S. diplomat in Peru reluctantly showed up at a mass for earthquake victims, he ran into a host of fellow Allied diplomats who had claimed they would not attend. Jefferson Patterson, U.S. Embassy Lima, to Sec. of State, 26 January 1944, USNA, RG 59, 835/48.

61. Only three weeks before the earthquake, Perón personally wrote Conservative leaders in Mendoza to ask them to support a new interventor. Mansilla, *Los partidos provinciales*, 156.

62. At the time, Pistarini was the head of the arms purchasing mission, Sosa Molina was serving under him, and Campero was the military attaché in Berlin. Perón,

Pistarini, and Sosa Molina had taken part in the 1930 coup. González Crespo, *El Coronel*, 187, 196–97.

63. Only the most aggressive publications were closed, leaving untouched other media subsidized by the German Embassy, including the Catholic paper *El Pueblo*.

64. Since each GOU member had sworn loyalty to Ramírez, the lodge was dissolved on Perón's initiative to make way for removing Ramírez from power.

65. The first letter of resignation Ramírez signed mentioned that he was being forced out of power; when the coup plotters realized that this would jeopardize diplomatic relations, they went back and compelled Ramírez to sign another letter in which he merely delegated authority to Farrell, claiming illness.

66. See Potash, ed., *Perón y el GOU*, 400–454. Perón's delegate did travel to neighboring Mendoza and San Luis. A week later, when sixteen brigadier generals demanded a return to constitutional rule, the garrison commanders stayed loyal to Farrell, the demand was ignored, and the generals cashiered.

Part 2: The Cornerstone of the New Argentina, Early 1944

1. "No se reparará en gastos para la reconstrucción de San Juan," *La Voz del Interior*, 21 January 1944.

2. "A breve plazo se iniciará la reconstrucción: Ignórase aun si la ciudad se levantará en el mismo lugar," *La Voz del Interior*, 20 January 1944.

3. Fermín Bereterbide and Carlos Muzio, "Contribución al estudio de la reconstrucción de la ciudad de San Juan y poblaciones vecinas," January 1944, 2, 5, 8. Report included as appendix 1 in *Memoria de la Comisión de Urbanismo de la Dirección Técnica de Reconstrucción de San Juan*, June 1944. Fermín Bereterbide Papers. Partly reprinted in Fermín Bereterbide, "La Reconstrucción de San Juan" *Revista de Arquitectura* 30, no. 293 (June 1945): 184–96.

4. Ibid., 8.

5. José M. F. Pastor, "San Juan," *Revista de Arquitectura* 29, no. 277 (January 1944): 4.

6. José M. F. Pastor, "La futura San Juan," *Revista de Arquitectura* 29, no. 278 (February 1944): 75.

7. See "Para la reconstrucción de la ciudad se pide la conscripción de 50.000 obreros," *La Voz del Interior*, 17 January 1944; "Se pide la emisión de un empéstito patriótico de 150.000.000," *El Pueblo*, 18 January 1944; construction worker total from Cámara Argentina de la Construcción, *Las actividades de la Cámara Argentina de la Construcción en favor de la Industria de la Construcción en la República Argentina 1936–1947*, 105. Many sensed that conscription was going to be expanded: the British ambassador predicted a call-up of one hundred thousand for 1944, and the military drafted fifty thousand. Kelly to Eden, 24 December 1943, PRO, FO 461/3/47.

8. "Residentes sanjuaninos en esta capital ofrecen su amplia colaboracion," *La Prensa*, 17 January 1944.

9. "La reconstrucción se hará con los recursos normales," *Los Andes*, 30 January 1944.

10. For early opposition, see quotes from "wealthy industrialist and investor Saúl Aubone" in "Varios vecinos opinan que la ciudad no debe cambiar de ubicación," *La*

Prensa, 24 January 1944, or a federal judge in "La ciudad no debe ser reconstruida fuera del ejido en que se halla," *La Prensa*, 28 January 1944.

11. Agricultural statistics from "Las perspectivas agrícolas y la acción de la Dirección De Industrias, Fomento Agrícola y Estadísticas," *Revista Sarmiento* (December 1945): 25. Wage figures from "Hizo una gestión el gobierno en pro de la industria del vino," *Triuna*, 22 July 1944. See also Marcelo Cañellas, "El terremoto de San Juan," 618.

Chapter 4: Utopias in the Dust

1. See Gorelik, *La grilla y el parque*. See also Ballent and Gorelik, "¿País urbano o país rural?,"

2. The University of Tucumán was founded by the province in 1914, nationalized in 1922, and expanded in the thirties with a new architecture school and other faculties. The University of Cuyo was founded by the nation in 1939, incorporating the existing mining and enology schools in San Juan and other facilities in Mendoza and San Luis.

3. See Ballent and Gorelik, "¿País urbano o país rural?"

4. On architecture as a profession, see Cirvini, *Nosotros los arquitectos*.

5. Butty, *La ingenería*, 4.

6. These provinces were Santa Fe, Córdoba, and now Tucumán.

7. Eduardo Sacriste, "Flor de mirar: Casa criolla en San Antonio de Areco," *Estilo* 1 (1943): 44.

8. The fundamental text on this moment in Argentine architecture is Liernur, *Arquitectura en la Argentina del siglo XX*, esp. chaps. 2 and 3.

9. Alejandro Christophersen, "Rumbos nuevos," *Revista de Arquitectura*, 1, no. 1 (July 1915).

10. Liernur, *Arquitectura en la Argentina*. See also Roberto Lint Sagarena, "Building California's Past: Mission Revival Architecture and Regional Identity," *Journal of Urban History*, 28, no. 4 (2002): 429–44.

11. Alberto Prebisch, quoted in Jorge Francisco Liernur, "El discreto encanto de nuestra arquitectura 1930/1960," *summa* 223 (March 1986): 78. Both Prebisch and Vautier expressed similar ideas in later articles.

12. Alberto Prebisch, "Sugestiones de una visita al Salón de acuarelistas, pastelistas y aguafortistas," *Martín Fierro* 4 (15 May 1924): 35. Another article opened with side-by-side photographs of reinforced concrete grain silos and a Greek temple, then contrasted these two positive examples of integrated design with a well-known Beaux Arts building in Buenos Aires. Ernesto Vautier and Alberto Prebisch, "Hacia un nuevo estilo," *Martín Fierro* 21 (28 August 1925): 151.

13. This argument is made convincingly in Liernur, "El discreto encanto," and in Gorelik, "La arquitectura de YPF."

14. CIAM, the International Congress of Modern Architecture, was an international association of modernists.

15. Eduardo Sacriste, "La enseñanza de la Arquitectura," *Revista de Arquitectura* 30, no. 294 (July 1945): x.

16. Jorge Francisco Liernur, "Arquitectura moderna: El Grupo Austral, Argentina, 1938–1942," *Materiales*, no. 4 (1989): 28.

17. Eduardo Catalano, Carlos Coire, and Horacio Caminos, "Planteamiento de un problema urbanístico (un ingenio de azúcar en Tucumán)." *Tecné* 2 (1939): 4.

18. Horacio Caminos, "El problema de la vivienda obrera en Tucumán," *Nuestra Arquitectura*, 13, no. 12 (December 1943): 522.

19. Horacio Caminos, "El pensamiento del siglo XX en arquitectura y urbanismo," *Nuestra Arquitectura* 16, no. 12 (December 1946): 435. In this article, Caminos was repeating the position he and allies took in 1943.

20. Guido and Carrasco, *Plan regulador*, 7, 8, 65, 70, 10.

21. Ibid., 36.

22. Ibid., 39.

23. Ibid., 25, 26, 27, 42.

24. Ibid., 78, 10, 13.

25. This was Guido's remark in presenting another plan in March 1944. "Inauguróse la exposición de maquetas del plan regulador de la Ciudad de Mar del Plata," *La Prensa*, 7 March 1944.

26. Guido and Carrasco, *Plan regulador*, 42.

27. Ley 816, 916, 919, *Boletín General de la Provincia de San Juan*, t. 23, f. 98, 553, 558–568.

28. Guido and Carrasco, *Plan regulador*, 43.

29. Benito Carrasco, "Plan regulador para la ciudad de San Juan," *La Prensa*, 18 January 1944, and "Plan regulador para San Juan," *La Prensa*, 22 January 1944.

30. Bereterbide and Vautier, *¿Qué es el urbanismo?*

31. This is what was being done in the rebuilding efforts in bombed European cities, for example in Rotterdam, where the work was just getting underway in 1944. Han Meyer, "Rotterdam: The Promise of a New, Modern Society in a New, Modern City" in Ockman, ed., *Out of Ground Zero*, 91.

32. Gorelik, *La grilla y el parque*, 119. Argentina had not followed the U.S. precedents in the 1930s that greatly expanded understandings of "eminent domain" and enabled large-scale urban planning. For the United States, see Boyer, *Dreaming the Rational City*.

33. Formally, the report was coauthored by Fermín Bereterbide and Carlos Muzio. While Bereterbide's private papers do not contain drafts of the report, they do contain drafts of nearly everything later published on the project, suggesting that Bereterbide was the primary author.

34. Fermín Bereterbide and Carlos Muzio, "Contribución al estudio de la reconstrucción de la ciudad de San Juan y poblaciones vecinas," January 1944: 6.

35. Ibid., 10. There was a clear precedent for a large park, with perhaps a few major buildings, on the edge of the city: the turn-of-the-century park in Mendoza. See Ponte, *La fragilidad de la memoria*.

36. In his enthusiasm for the virtues of the new site, Bereterbide seemed to forget the tenacity of the resistance that had made it necessary in the first place. See, for

example, Fermín Bereterbide to Horacio Videla, Buenos Aires, 18 June 1944, Bereterbide Papers.

37. "San Juan y su reconstrucción," 12 April 1944, 1, Bereterbide Papers.

38. See, for example, his 1943 housing proposal of modernist towers. Molina y Vedia and Schere, *Fermín Bereterbide*, 162.

39. Thus the colleague who accused them of prioritizing aesthetic considerations completely misread their strategy. Julio Villalobos, "La reconstrucción de San Juan considerada como una nueva planificación económico-social," *Finanzas*, June 1944, 8. On the other hand, their approach was entirely consistent with the 1943 plan to rebuild London, which also cloaked ambitious reforms in a familiar architectural vocabulary (in this case, neoclassicism).

40. "San Juan y su reconstrucción," 12 April 1944, 2–3, Bereterbide Papers.

41. Ibid., 2.

42. The neighborhood unit concept, developed by Clarence Perry in the 1920s, became normative in U.S. planning practice during the 1930s, a building block of redevelopment schemes, new suburban development, and New Towns alike. Perry, *The Neighborhood Unit*. Designers aimed to produce the "sense of a community" by formal means, hoping that "physical design" might "reinstill in the individual the sense of dignity, freedom, and identity that were being threatened by the massive urban agglomerations." Banerjee and Baer, *Beyond the Neighborhood Unit*, 23. This amounted to "Gemeinshaft Ends and Gesellschaft Means," as one scholar notes, "to recreate a face-to-face organic community through the efforts of impersonal bureaucratic agencies": John Fairfield, "Alienation of Social Control: The Chicago Sociologists and the Origins of Urban Planning," *Planning Perspectives* 7, no. 3 (October 1992): 429, 431. This approach was later broadly adopted by Peronism, as a kind of "spatial correlate of a social program." Ballent, *Las huellas*, 148.

43. It was to be twice as spacious—30 versus 16 square meters per person—and also higher quality—180 versus 120 pesos per square meter. Comisión de Urbanismo, *Informe U-4/44*, 3 April 1944, 4, Bereterbide Papers.

44. Bereterbide and Muzio, "Consideraciones," 5.

45. Comisión de Urbanismo, *Informe U-4/44*, 2.

Chapter 5: The Superstition of Adobe and the Certainty of Concrete

1. Salvador Doncel, "La colaboración del pueblo para la reconstrucción de San Juan," *La Acción*, 16 May 1944.

2. Pro-German nationalists dominated military engineering during the thirties: Pistarini's predecessor, the ultranationalist Juan Bautista Molina, was the instigator of many coup plots. White, *German Influence in the Argentine Army, 1900 to 1945*, 103. Pistarini maintained extensive contacts with Axis diplomats through the construction magnate Ludwig Freude and initially gave one of Freude's firms an emergency housing contract, although it was then rescinded. Newton, "*Nazi Menace*," 303–4.

3. Zanatta, *Del estado liberal a la nación católica*, 364. Pistarini's lead advisor was

J. Roberto Bonamino, who edited the Catholic paper *El Pueblo* and held one of the highest posts in the lay organization Catholic Action.

4. Emilio Llorens, "Renta Nacional," *Anales de la Comisión de Estudios y Conferencias de la Corporación de Ingenieros Católicos* no. 1 (1944): 11, 19, 23. The publications of Catholic Action and its affiliates were subsidized by leading industrial firms, including the Graffigna winery, and the guiding figure of the Catholic engineers, the recently deceased Alejandro Bunge, came from a major industrialist family. The "Bunge Group" would formulate much of Peronist economic and social policy, particularly early on. See Claudio Belini, "El Grupo Bunge y la política económica del primer peronismo, 1943–1952," *Latin American Research Review* 41, no. 1 (February 2006): 27–50.

5. "Un pequeño drama aleccionador," *El Pueblo*, 11 January 1944.

6. Rodolfo Vázquez, "El veraneo: Necesidad social," *Boletín del MOP* no. 86 (January 1944): 67; Osvaldo Carlos Fornari, "Barrio San Isidro," *Boletin de la Administración Nacional del Agua* (May 1945): 348; "Mejora económica y social de los trabajadores," *Boletín de OSN* 8, no. 85 (July 1944): 1. To appreciate this "correct path of morality" consider the new regulations for work camps from June 1944. Scandalized by what they found on a tour, MOP officials carefully specified every aspect of the functioning of future camps; they made houses larger and more carefully spaced, prohibiting drinking, card games, or unmarried women; and mandated chapel and lectures on "the fatherland and its growth." "Reglamentando la construcción y organización de las viviendas en campamentos de las obras que ejecute el Ministerio," *Boletín del MOP* 1, no. 2 (3 July 1944): 11–15.

7. "Nuevo Director General de Arquitectura" *Revista de Arquitectura* 29, no. 278 (February 1944): 85; "Discurso del Ministro de Obras Públicas," *La Prensa*, 5 July 1944; "Fijando en el Ministerio, salario mínimo por zonas económicas," *Boletín del MOP* 1, no. 1 (1 July 1944): 2 The new minimum wage of $4.80 was more than the MOP had been paying workers in San Juan. "Se fijará el jornal mínimo para obreros de obras públicas," *La Prensa*, 24 June 1944.

8. Enévaro Rossi, San Juan, to Emil Lorch, Ann Arbor, 1 February 1944, USNA, RG 59, 835.48/36.

9. Miguel Piccone, "Entraña una gran responsabilidad decidir el emplazamiento de la futura San Juan," *Crítica*, 26 February 1944; Miguel Piccone, "No convencen las razones aducidas para reconstruir San Juan en el mismo sitio," *Crítica*, 27 February 1944.

10. Rubén Sarmiento, "¿Reconstruir o fundar una nueva ciudad de San Juan?" *Los Andes*, 17 March 1944.

11. Odin Gomez Lucero, "El saldo de la tragedia: Contemplado con criterio de nuestro suelo argentino," *Tribuna*, 29 March 1944.

12. Juan Rómulo Fernández, "San Juan en el pasado y en el porvenir," *La Prensa*, 5 March 1944.

13. Gil, *Tradiciones sanjuaninas*, 238, 12, 220. Unlike other patricians, Gil saw the 1934

provincial coup against Cantoni as "subversion" rather than the triumph of proper order.

14. See del Carril Quiroga, "*Amigos Sanjuaninos*," 11–37, on the organization, and 81–93, for the petition. See also "Pedido de la Asociación Amigos de San Juan," *La Prensa*, 19 February 1944.

15. Ibid., 91–93.

16. See reference by their critics in "Como se pide," *Tribuna*, 14 April 1944.

17. Ramella outlined his initial proposal in three articles: "Reflexiones acerca de la tragedia de San Juan," *El Pueblo*, 23 January 1944; "Problemas jurídicos que suscita la reconstrucción de San Juan," *El Pueblo*, 29 January 1944; and "Legislación de la propiedad en zonas expuestas a movimientos sísmicos," *El Pueblo*, 4 February 1944.

18. "La reconstrucción se hará con los recursos normales," *Los Andes*, 30 January 1944; "Ofrecen su colaboración entidades de profesionales," *La Prensa*, 9 February 1944.

19. Pablo Ramella, "Idealistas y realistas en la reconstrucción de San Juan," *El Pueblo*, 15 February 1944.

20. Pablo Ramella, "Nuevos problemas jurídicos acerca de la reconstrucción de San Juan," *El Pueblo*, 14 April 1944.

21. "Por la actual ubicación de la ciudad abógase," *Los Andes*, 8 February 1944.

22. Graffigna's allies on the commission included, among others, his brother, his brother-in-law, the archbishop, Videla, and Del Bono. Graffigna kept a low profile locally but accompanied commission leaders to lobby in Buenos Aires. "Una delegación entrevistará al primer mandatario," *Los Andes*, 4 March 1944.

23. "Se creará una comisión que tratará diversos problemas de San Juan," *Los Andes*, 13 February 1944.

24. "Una comisión solicita que no sea cambiada la ubicación de San Juan," *La Prensa*, 7 March 1944; Oliver-Smith, "Anthropological Research on Hazards and Disasters," 309; Kates, "Major Insights," 277. Kates maintained that "there is an ordered sequence of return" during reconstruction "that mirrors the hierarchy of function, person and power in the city," an explanation that takes such power for granted.

25. "Una comisión solicita que no sea cambiada la ubicación de San Juan," *La Prensa*, 7 March 1944.

26. Horacio Videla to Fermín Bereterbide, San Juan, 19 May 1944, Bereterbide Papers.

27. Jorge Vivanco to Amancio Williams, Tucumán, 9 June 1947, Ferrari Hardoy Papers, D-85n2.

28. "Una comisión solicita que no sea cambiada la ubicación de San Juan," *La Prensa*, 7 March 1944.

29. "Se formulan observaciones al decreto de creación del Consejo de Reconstrucción de San Juan," *La Acción*, 8 August 1944. While Videla remained secretary of the Club Social in 1944, the president was Octavio Gil, who, intimately aware of this past, led the pro-move group.

30. President Farrell complained about the locals demanding reconstruction but obsessed with "being repaid for lost cans of sardines." "Los eternos disconformes," *La Reforma*, 7 June 1946.

31. "Ha sido ampliada la moratoria en la provincia de San Juan," *La Prensa*, 16 February 1944.

32. "Como los ricos propietarios dificultan la reconstrucción," *La Reforma*, 8 January 1946.

33. Quoted in Doncel, "La colaboración del pueblo."

34. "El Ministro de Obras Públicas regresó de San Juan anoche," *La Nación*, 18 February 1944.

35. Castellanos, *Anotaciones*, 12, 24.

36. "La ciudad de San Juan," *La Prensa*, 16 January 1944.

37. Pablo Ramella, "Reflexiones acerca de la tragedia de San Juan," *El Pueblo*, 23 January 1944.

38. "La ubicación de la ciudad de San Juan no debe modificarse," *La Prensa*, 30 Apr 1944. Also "Una comisión de técnicos dió a conocer sus conclusiones relacionadas con el sismo," *La Prensa*, 4 May 1944.

39. "Se disertó ayer sobre Urbanismo y Defensa Antiaérea," *Los Andes*, 26 February 1944. Protection from aerial bombardment was the "strategic necessity" the officer had in mind.

40. Harrington, *El sismo*, 22–23; Castellanos, *Anotaciones*, 23–27; Rodolfo Martin, "Nociones de ingenería antisísmica," *Boletín de YPF*, July 1944, 47–71.

41. Harrington, *El sismo*, 20–21.

42. The uses of quincha for anti-seismic construction were only systematically explored starting in the 1960s. For a recent overview, see Fabio Carbajal, Gaby Ruiz, and Cliff Schnexnayder, "Quincha Construction in Peru," *Practice Periodical on Structural Design and Construction* 10, no. 1 (February 2005): 56–62.

43. For example, "El espejismo del adobe: La edificación de Cuyo," *La Accion*, 2 June 1944.

44. *Los Andes* put blackboards at food distribution points; these were the main information source for most sanjuaninos until the local papers reappeared in March.

45. "Propúsese un plan para dar seguridad a las viviendas," *Los Andes*, 26 January 1944.

46. "El estado debe ser el primero en ofrecer el ejemplo en la edificación antisísmica," *Los Andes*, 14 February 1944.

47. "La casa de adobe es una amenaza para la seguridad pública en la zona sísmica," *Los Andes*, 11 February 1944.

48. "Es necesario que el hogar mendocino tenga casa digna y sobretodo, seguro," *Los Andes*, 12 February 1944.

49. "Se prohibió la edificación con adobe en Mendoza," *Los Andes*, 17 February 1944.

50. Founded in 1941 as part of a Conservative plan to diversify Argentine exports, the Consejo para la Promoción del Intercambio turned during the war toward studies of industrial development potential. See, for example, Hopkins, *La estructura económica y el desarollo industrial de la Argentina*.

51. "Posibilidades de la producción de cemento," *La Prensa*, 9 February 1944.

52. "Una comisión de técnicos dió a conocer sus conclusiones relacionadas con el sismo," *La Prensa*, 4 May 1944. Also the report itself: Harrington, *El sismo*, 28–29.

53. Harrington contrasted the endurance of quincha houses on bedrock close to the epicenter with the collapse of identical houses on alluvial soil much further out: *El sismo*, 20.

54. See Harrington, Castellanos, and Erwin Kittl, "Sobre la estabilidad del terreno de la ciudad de San Juan y sus alrededores," *Revista Minera, Geología y Mineralogía* 15, no. 4 (1944): 90–96.

55. Castellanos, *Anotaciones*, 28.

56. Pablo Ramella, "Reflexiones acerca de la tragedia de San Juan," *El Pueblo*, 23 January 1944.

57. Martín Cappelletti, quoted in Juan Kulik, "Fundaciones de los edificios asísmicos," *La Ingenería* 855 (January 1946), 29.

58. "Un estudio geológico del subsuelo requerirá la ciudad a construirse," *La Prensa*, 25 January 1944.

59. Argentina held this position from 1938 until the early 1950s. See Graciela Silvestri, "Cemento," in Liernur and Aliata, eds., *Diccionario histórico de arquitectura, habitat y urbanismo en la Argentina*, 76–78.

60. Freeman, *Earthquake Damage and Earthquake Insurance*, 799.

61. For a discussion of Japanese precedents, see Rodolfo Martin, "Nociones de ingenería antisísmica," *Boletín de YPF*, July 1944, 47–71. The newspapers picked up on this later: "Deben ser transformadas las viviendas de emergencia empleadas actualmente en San Juan," *Los Andes*, 14 December 1944.

62. "La ubicación de la ciudad de San Juan no debe modificarse," *La Prensa*, 30 April 1944.

63. Maisonnave, "Previsiones," 96–97.

64. Castellanos, *Anotaciones*, 27.

65. Maisonnave, "Previsiones," 96.

Chapter 6: Looking for Order among the Ruins

1. "Partió ayer para la ciudad de San Juan el Ministro de Obras Publicas," *La Prensa*, 14 February 1944.

2. Harrington, *Volcanes y terremotos*, 225. Normally the city had fifteen days of rain annually, eight of them in January and February. See "Obervaciones metereologicas de la Estación Experimental de Alto de Sierra," *Boletín Agrícola-Industrial de la Provincia de San Juan* 4 (1938): 7; "La lluvia y el granizo causaron grandes daños a las cosechas en San Juan," *La Prensa*, 4 February 1944.

3. Francisco Compañy, "El problema religioso en la ciudad destruida," *Boletín Oficial de la Arquidiócesis de San Juan de Cuyo* 28, no. 2–3 (February–March 1944): 62.

4. Interview of Father Pedro Roger Quiroga Marinero by author, San Juan, 9 July 2002. Photographs of bodies with ripped pockets suggest looting began early: see Bataller, ed., *Y aquí nos quedamos*, 38.

5. "I know who did the vanishing, but I can't say," he reported six decades later. Interview of Tulio del Bono by Aldo Gaete, San Juan, 14 July 2002.

6. See the well-documented local elite complaints in *El otro terremoto*.

7. "Debe darse rápido albergue a la población de San Juan," *La Prensa*, 24 February 1944.

8. Juncos, "El terremoto de San Juan," 65.

9. Official communiqués discouraged anyone from returning, warning that they faced "the inclemencies of winter and the dangers of promiscuity" and would receive a tent, at best. "El sismo de San Juan y la acción oficial," *La Prensa*, 28 March 1944.

10. See "Concurso de anteproyectos para viviendas rurales del Banco de la Nación Argentina," *Nuestra Arquitectura* 10, no. 1 (January 1940): 440–49.

11. Five years earlier, the modernist architects in the Austral group had proposed mass production of fibercement homes as a solution for rural housing. Austral, "Urbanismo rural, plan regional y vivienda," *Nuestra Arquitectura* 9, no. 9 (September 1939): 1–16, esp. 6.

12. Nine of the twelve relief workers killed in the plane crash had barrios named after them. "Nombres de los barrios de emergencia rememorarán a miembros del gobierno," *La Prensa*, 25 March 1944.

13. "Constrúyense 12 nuevos barrios de casas de emergencia," *Los Andes*, 3 March 1944.

14. In all, there were fourteen public projects in fibercement and two in wood, twenty-three state worker projects in various materials, and two pre-earthquake projects in masonry. See Enrique Real, "Obras Sanitarias de la Nación en la catástrofe de San Juan," *Boletín de Obras Sanitarias de la Nación* 89 (November 1944): 356.

15. "Un barrio de modestas viviendas ha quedado inaugurado en la ciudad devastada," *La Voz del Interior*, 25 January 1944.

16. Intervención Federal de San Juan, *Informe elevado al Ministerio del Interior*, 70.

17. "El adobe en San Juan," *Tribuna*, 17 December 1944.

18. Francisco Domingo Riveros, Comisionado Municipal de Chimbas, to Dr. Roberto Videla Zapata, Ministro de Govierno, 15 July 1944, AHASJ, Misc., c. 63, d. 4.

19. "San Juan después del terremoto: La reivindicación del rancho," *Tribuna*, 27 March 1944.

20. "Elogio de la quincha," *Tribuna*, 14 April 1944; "El adobe en San Juan," *Tribuna*, 17 December 1944. Two geologists suggested adobe construction should be improved, not abandoned, and one architect offered a modernist defense of the material: see Harrington, *El sismo*; Rodolfo Martin, "Nociones de ingenería antisísmica," *Boletín de YPF*, July 1944, 47–71; and Eduardo Sacriste, "Arquitectura popular de San Juan," *Revista de Arquitectura* 29, no. 281 (May 1944): 216–25.

21. The official report claimed 7,794, but the interventor reported 8,500.

22. Emergency facilities were built for fifty-two of the sixty provincial schools but only ten of the thirty-eight national schools. This was apparently due to bureaucratic delay by the National Council of Education. Intervención Federal de San Juan, MOP, *Obra*, 80.

23. *Informe elevado al Ministerio del Interior*, 56, 58–60.

24. *Memoria del Ministerio de Obras Públicas 1944*, x. This was 7.7 percent of the MOP annual budget.

25. República Argentina, MOP, *Obra*, 35, 45, 47.

26. "Dos mil millones de pesos se emplearán para lucha contra el conventillo," *El Pueblo*, 18 March 1944.

27. "Fue clausurada la exposición de la vivienda popular," *El Pueblo*, 20 April 1944.
28. "En el Municipio de San Martín se colocó la piedra fundamental del Barrio Obrero Villa Concepción," *La Prensa*, 9 June 1944. As the words of the director, Pedro Tilli, suggest, this discourse drew powerfully on earlier social Catholic thinking.
29. Perón, "En la concentración de obreros realizada en San Nicolás," *Obras completas*, 6: 314; more complete quote in "Fué afrontado eficazmente en San Juan por el estado el problema de la escasez de viviendas," *El Líder*, 27 August 1949. On the transformation of housing from a need into a right, and from an individual effort into a collective responsibility, see Ballent, *Las huellas de la política*.
30. "Asumió sus funciones el nuevo Interventor Federal de San Juan," *La Prensa*, 1 February 1944.
31. Only when the governor refused to recognize the military government did Sosa Molina remove him from office. Mansilla, *Los partidos provinciales*, 149–50. He was garrison commander from 1940 to 1943. He also employed his military command to pursue infrastructure projects, for instance having soldiers build a new road to Chile in 1943 under guise of a military "exercise." See Pablo Lacoste, "El paso de la cordillera de los Andes por El Portillo argentino: Aportes para el estudio de la integración entre Argentina y Chile," *Revista Universum* 11 (1996): 107–8.
32. He had some ties from his time as regional military commander, for instance, having attended the Conservatives' reopening of the provincial bank in 1943. Videla, *El Banco de San Juan en sus veinticinco años de vida*, 77.
33. Ramella, *La estructura del estado*, 183.
34. "El capitalismo y la reconstrucción," *Tribuna*, 18 April 1944.
35. "Los intereses legítimos," *Tribuna*, 20 November 1944.
36. "El deber de decir la verdad al pueblo," *Tribuna*, 2 April 1944.
37. Intervención Federal de San Juan, *Informe elevado al Ministerio del Interior*, 95.
38. "La Arquidiocesis de San Juan va a ser consagrada al Inmaculado Corazón de María el 25 de Mayo," *El Pueblo*, 9 April 1944; "Consagración de San Juan al Corazón de María," *Boletín Oficial de la Arquidiócesis de San Juan de Cuyo* 28, no. 6 (June 1944): 202–27; and Rodríguez y Olmos, *Pastoral Letter on the Reconstruction of Our Churches*.
39. While the prior size of the provincial health service is unclear, Sosa Molina added 65 doctors and dentists to the payroll. Intervención Federal de San Juan, *Informe elevado al Ministerio del Interior*, 16. The province had 185 doctors and dentists, with 162 located in the capital. *Anuario DUA*, 425, 457–58.
40. The strongest advocate of many of these reforms—in medicine, social work, residential schools, and a master file of social data—was Roberto Bárriga, founder with Octavio Gil of the Amigos Sanjuaninos reform club. See del Carril Quiroga, "*Amigos Sanjuaninos*," 81–93.
41. "Los bodegueros se han reunido en asamblea," *La Razón*, 21 January 1944; "El problema vitivinícola de San Juan," *Los Andes*, 8 February 1944.
42. "Reparan rápidamente la Bodega del Estado," *El Pueblo*, 23 January 1944; "En el Rotary Club se trató un aspecto de la catástrofe de San Juan," *La Prensa*, 10 February 1944.

43. "Se ha dado comienzo a la labor que tiende a reconstruir las bodegas," *La Prensa*, 22 January 1944.

44. "Dispúsose la evacuación de toda la uva de vinificar de San Juan y la desocupación de las vasijas," *El Pueblo,* 22 January 1944. When the growers asked permission to sell to Mendoza, it was denied. "Los viñateros proponen medidas para asegurar el buen exito de la vendimia," *La Prensa*, 1 February 1944.

45. "Juntos, bodegueros y viñateros deben tratar el problema," *Los Andes*, 24 January 1944. The main leader of the viñateros despaired of any unified action at the time. Fermín Bereterbide, "Entrevista con Basañez Zavalla," March 1944, Bereterbide Papers. See also "¿Qué esperan los viñateros?," *El Censor*, 12 January 1945.

46. "Like every year, the official balance is broken again. It would seem like the work of the devil, or of certain bodegueros," an observer noted twelve months later. "La Báscula Oficial como siempre descompuesta," *El Censor*, 26 January 1945.

47. "Fijación oficial del precio de la uva," *La Prensa*, 4 March 1944.

48. "Obreros inscriptos," *La Prensa*, 18 April 1944.

49. "Faltan brazos en San Juan para las labores del agro," *La Nación*, 9 February 1944. Another observer later claimed that ending food distribution resolved the labor shortage: "Soluciones y soluciones," *La Reforma*, 5 May 1948.

50. Later reports indicated most harvest workers made two pesos a day. "Debe evitarse que el invierno de a San Juan nuevas penurias," *Los Andes*, 15 March 1944.

51. "Los evacuados sanjuaninos podrán regresar a su provincia," *Tribuna*, 13 April 1944.

52. The housing for employees of national agencies was distributed by the agencies themselves.

53. "Se exhorta a las personas pudientes a construir su vivienda propia," *La Acción*, 18 March 1944.

54. "Problema de la vivienda de emergencia," *Tribuna*, 30 March 1944. The Maurín Conservatives grudgingly accepted the construction of emergency barrios but argued that they should be exclusively for the poor. "La riqueza de San Juan está en pie," *La Acción*, 16 March 1944.

55. Emiliano Lee, "La casa vacía," *Tribuna*, 21 August 1944; also "Buenos dias," *Tribuna*, 27 March 1944.

56. "Se hicieron mas adjudicaciones en barrios," *Tribuna*, 19 April 1944; also "La adjudicación de vivienda en barrios," *Tribuna*, 12 April 1944.

57. "Adjudicóse mas viviendas," *Tribuna*, 14 April 1944.

58. On 30 March 1944, for example, a *Tribuna* editorial insisting that emergency housing should go only to the poor was followed by a poem by columnist Luis Bates celebrating his new Road Department hut.

59. "Serias irregularidades fueron comprobadas en la distribución de viveres," *La Prensa*, 21 April 1944.

60. "Una resolución moralizadora," *Tribuna*, 23 April 1944; "Colaboración y obstruccionismo," *Tribuna*, 18 May 1944.

61. Varas, *Terremoto de San Juan*, 74.

62. General José Humberto Sosa Molina, Interventor Nacional, al Contraalmirante Alberto Teisaire, Ministro del Interior, San Juan, 12 July 1944, AHASJ, Gobierno, d-34, c-1.

63. Before taking office in San Juan, Romeo Gaddi was minister of public works in Buenos Aires, with Hilario Zalba his head of projects. A fourth architect, the Catalan exile Antonio Bonet, was appointed but left after a week over political disagreements with nationalist officials.

64. Their report was reprinted in "Interesantes apreciaciones sobre la situación de San Juan a sesenta días del terremoto," *La Acción*, 19 March 1944. See also Eduardo Sacriste, "Arquitectura popular de San Juan."

65. "Interesantes apreciaciones sobre la situación de San Juan a sesenta días del terremoto," *La Acción*, 19 March 1944.

66. "Comunicado de la Intervención Federal," *La Acción*, 21 March 1944. See "Declaraciones Tomadas a Zunino, Caminos, Sacriste, Assaf," 19 March 1944, AHASJ, Gobierno, c. 10bis, d. 4.

67. Professional associations of engineers, lawyers, agronomists, accountants, notaries, merchants, and winery owners supported the Del Bono Commission. Political parties were still banned. "Comisión Sanjuanina de Restauración," *La Prensa*, 20 April 1944; "Numerosas son las adhesiones para la reconstrucción de San Juan en su mismo sitio," *La Acción*, 7 May 1944.

68. His successor would be less tolerant, closing newspapers on occasion: "Dispusóse la clausura por 3 dias del diario *La Acción*," *Tribuna*, 23 October 1944.

69. Horacio Videla, "La reconstrucción de San Juan," *Tribuna*, 23 April 1944.

70. "Geología, sismología, astrología," *Tribuna*, 15 April 1944; "¿Dónde debe reconstruirse la ciudad?" *Tribuna*, 29 March 1944; "La reconstrucción de la ciudad, problema fundamental," *La Acción*, 8 October 1944.

71. "El gobernante y el arquitecto," *Tribuna*, 9 April 1944.

72. "El quid de la cuestión," *Tribuna*, 11 April 1944.

73. "Sobre la reconstrucción de la nueva capital sanjuanina," *La Acción*, 28 March 1944.

74. Horacio Videla, "La reconstrucción de San Juan," *Tribuna*, 23 April 1944.

75. Interview of Hilario Zalba and Eduardo Sacriste by Alfredo Rezzoagli, Buenos Aires, 1985.

76. "Hablóse en un acto sobre necesidades urgentes de S Juan," *Los Andes*, 20 March 1944.

77. Centro Argentino de Ingenieros, "Memorial presentado al Ministro de Obras Públicas de la Nación," reprinted in *Nuestra Arquitectura*, 14, no. 5 (May 1944): 165–66.

78. Centro Argentino de Ingenieros, *Hacia el planeamiento integral de la industria de la construcción*, 23, 121, 122.

79. The engineers also were suspicious of the military's ties with their rivals, such as the German construction magnate Ludwig Freude, widely (and correctly) seen as a Nazi spy. On Freude, see Goñi, *Perón y los Alemanes*, 147–50, 182, 206.

80. CAI, "Memorial," 165. Pistarini received the report on 30 March. "Se propuso para San Juan un plan de reconstrucción," *Los Andes*, 31 March 1944.

81. CAI, "Memorial," 165. The two most important experimental institutions were the Portland Cement Institute and the Institute for Material Research.

82. Later in the report, the engineers placed traditional materials first and wood second, recognizing it would be supplementary at best. CAI, "Memorial," 166. Wood had to be imported from Brazil, which proved difficult and led to protracted disputes. See documents in AHASJ, Obras Públicas, c. 3, d.1.

83. See Raul Martínez Vivot, "El problema de la vivienda económica," *La Ingenería* 837 (July 1944): 464.

84. CAI, "Memorial," 166.

85. "Dio su opinión sobre la reconstrucción de San Juan una entidad," *La Nación*, 8 April 1944. Sociedad Central de Arquitectos, "Nota presentada por la Sociedad Central de Arquitectos al Ministro de Obras Públicas de la Nación," reprinted in *Nuestra Arquitectura* 14, no. 5 (May 1944): 162.

86. In January 1944, the MOP ruled that the word "engineer" in the 1876 public works law should be interpreted to include architects, allowing them to hold technical posts for the first time. "De mayo a mayo," *Anuario Sociedad Central de Arquitectos* 4 (1944): 3.

87. After coining the phrase in an unsigned editorial, José Pastor later made it the title of his book.

88. Sociedad Central de Arquitectos, "Nota presentada por la Sociedad Central de Arquitectors al Ministro de Obras Públicas de la Nación," reprinted in *Nuestra Arquitectura* 13, no. 5 (May 1944): 163, 164.

89. While professional leaders like Federico de Achával genuinely agreed with the regime's ideological positions, the ambitious figures who actually ran the journal, like José Pastor, were more interested in drawing parallels between modernist planning and Catholic nationalism, for example in a long piece by Pastor in 1944 on the planning vision of the Jesuit missions.

90. SCA, "Nota," 165. In a gesture to the regime, the architects also stressed the importance of providing a place "dedicated to the worship of their God, their Fatherland, and their home."

91. SCA, "Nota," 164, 163.

92. "La reconstrucción de San Juan," *La Nación*, 6 May 1944; also "La reconstrucción de San Juan," *La Nación*, 22 January 1944. For the Catholic paper, see Pedro Badanelli, "El problema estético de la nueva ciudad de San Juan," *El Pueblo*, 20 February 1944, or numerous articles by Ramella.

93. "Un estudio y una politica tecnologica de la estructura economica argentina," *La Prensa*, 25 June 1944.

94. "Ubicación de San Juan," *La Prensa*, 27 March 1944.

95. "Lo más importante en la ubicación de San Juan," *La Prensa*, 30 March 1944; "Reconstrucción de San Juan," *La Prensa*, 15 May 1944.

96. "La Nueva Ciudad no puede ser igual a la destruida, dice el arquitecto José Pastor,"

Crítica, 3 May 1944. Also "Fuera del lugar de las ruinas debe ser levantada la ciudad, dice Raúl Lissarrague," *Crítica*, 5 May 1944.

97. "En la Nueva San Juan estarán reflejadas todas las aspiraciones de la República," *Crítica*, 15 May 1944.

98. Del Carril Quiroga, *"Amigos Sanjuaninos,"* 34–35.

99. "El General Farrell formuló un llamado a todo el país para que acuda en ayuda a las poblaciones del norte," *La Acción*, 16 May 1944.

100. "Numerosas son las adhesiones para la reconstrucción de San Juan en su mismo sitio," *La Acción*, 7 May 1944. Two second-rank Cantonistas joined, Eloy Camus and Napoleón Battezati, but no party leaders.

101. "Elementos de juicio definitivos sobre la ubicación de la nueva capital sanjuanina," *La Acción*, 6 May 1944; "El traslado de la ciudad no sería cosa alegre y fácil," *La Acción*, 9 May 1944.

102. Salvador Doncel, "La colaboración del pueblo para la reconstrucción de San Juan," *La Acción*, 16 May 1944.

103. Edward Reed to Secretary of State, Report 14521 San Juan Relief Fund, 15 April 1944, USNA, 59: 835.48/38.

104. "Obsequia golosinas a los niños," *La Acción*, 9 May 1944.

105. "Hablará mañana el presidente sobre las provincias del norte," *La Prensa*, 14 May 1944. Note that "an Argentine" remains, implicitly, a resident of Buenos Aires.

106. República Argentina, *Diario de Sesiones de Cámara de Senadores 1946*, 1: 644.

107. "Formuló declaraciones sobre la Reconstrucción de San Juan el Interventor," *La Prensa*, 17 May 1944. When he fired the Sacriste team a month earlier, his justification was the (false) accusation that they had advocated the move. "Como se pide," *Tribuna*, 14 April 1944.

108. "Una cordial despedida se le tributó ayer al Gral. Humberto Sosa Molina," *Tribuna*, 22 July 1944.

109. "Regresó ayer de su extenso viaje por el norte del país el Primer Magistrado de la Nación," *La Prensa*, 13 May 1944.

110. "Homenaje a colegas," *Revista de Arquitectura* 29, no. 284 (August 1944): 381. The architects were Estrada, de la Portilla, Cuenca, and Lima.

111. "Exposición 4 de junio," *Boletín del MOP* 1, no. 87 (11 October 1944): 1141.

112. Manuel Gálvez, "La Revolución del 4 de Junio," *El Pueblo*, 4 June 1944.

113. Carmen Renard, "Por qué San Juan no debe ser reconstruída en el mismo sitio," *Memoria de la Comisión de Urbanismo*, appendix 5.

114. Ernesto Vautier, "Una nueva San Juan fuera de su actual emplazamiento," *Memoria de la Comisión de Urbanismo*, appendix 6.

115. Bereterbide returned to private practice; Vautier and Muzio stayed in government service to work on housing.

116. This was a third of the surface area of the adjacent city of Buenos Aires. On "Operation Ezeiza," see Ballent, *Las huellas de la política*, 243–44.

117. Perlinger's chief advisor, the nationalist intellectual Bonifacio del Carril, was descended from sanjuaninos and had just published a polemic titled *Buenos Aires against the Nation*, but he set up the Council without the participation of any locals,

architects, or even military officers. "Prosigue el estudio de la reconstrucción de la ciudad de San Juan," *La Prensa*, 17 June 1944.

118. Robert Potash, *The Army and Politics in Argentina*, 1: 247–48.

Part 3: From Leading Case to Exemplary Failure, Mid-1944 to Mid-1946

1. "La Espada y la Cruz siempre han ido juntos, por eso ha triunfado nuestra patria, dijo el M.R.P. Gonzalo Costa," *Tribuna*, 10 September 1944; "Una calurosa acogida se dispensó ayer al Coronel Juan Domingo Perón," *La Acción*, 10 September 1944.

2. Ramón Tejada, "Introducción," in Juan Perón, *Queremos restaurar en esta tierra, nuestras instituciones básicas*, 12.

3. Perón, *Queremos restaurar*, 12.

4. Quoted in "Fué afrontado eficazmente en San Juan por el estado el problema de la escasez de viviendas," *El Líder*, 27 August 1949. On this transformation of housing from a need into a right, and from an individual effort into a collective responsibility, see Ballent, *Las huellas de la política*.

5. If the pre-quake population of city and suburbs had been 107,000, according to the sewer authority, the population in late 1944 was only 60,000. Obras Sanitarias de la Nación, *Memoria del año 1943*, 317; and *Memoria del año 1944*, xlii.

6. "Una calurosa acogida se dispensó ayer al Coronel Juan Domingo Perón," *La Acción*, 10 September 1944.

7. "Manifiesto del Comercio y de la Industria," *La Prensa*, 16 June 1945.

Chapter 7: Diverging Paths of Reform

1. Ramella, *Autobiografía y selección de escritos jurídicos*, 32, 34. The work was published as Ramella, *La estructura del estado*.

2. "Sobre la reconstrucción de S. Juan habló el presidente del Consejo con un representante obrero," *La Acción*, 20 August 1944.

3. Eight members were named by the province: Alberto Costantini, Francisco Bustelo, Zacarías Yanzi, Emilio Langois, Enrique Uliarte, Indalecio Carmona Ríos, and Enrique de Bonito. All eight supported the Del Bono Commission. The other four members were named by the national government, to represent the War Ministry, the Public Works Ministry, the National Mortgage Bank, and workers.

4. "Son muy restringidas las facultades del Consejo de Reconstrucción de San Juan," *La Acción*, 12 July 1944.

5. This too could be traced back to Sosa Molina, whose minister Marcelo Cañellas set out the mechanism in an article published under his own name: see Cañellas, "El terremoto de San Juan."

6. "Designaron jefe de la oficina de Reconstrucción," *La Prensa*, 18 June 1944.

7. They also wanted more representatives on the Council, but it soon became clear they had a solid majority. "Se formulan observaciones al decreto de creación del Consejo de Reconstrucción de San Juan," *La Acción*, 8 August 1944.

8. "De acuerdo con la reconstrucción, pero no en su planeamiento," *La Acción*, 27 August 1944.

9. Jorge Ferrari Hardoy, "Relato de trabajo en San Juan," 1945, Ferrari Hardoy Papers, D-85n1.

10. Hardoy, "Borrador de comunicado a la población," July 1944, Ferrari Hardoy Papers, D-85k3.

11. Ibid.

12. Ibid.

13. Ibid.

14. Austral, "Urbanismo rural, plan regional y vivienda," *Nuestra Arquitectura* 9, no. 9 (September 1939): 6–7.

15. On the CIAM, the Athens Charter, and debates within modernist urbanism, see Mumford, *The CIAM Discourse on Urbanism*.

16. "Informe al Sr. Pres. del Consejo de Reconstruccion de San Juan, Coronel Julio Hennekens," 3 October 1944, Ferrari Hardoy Papers, D-85k2.

17. See the list of hundreds of drawings and books in "Declaración jurada de arquitectos," 6 December 1944, Ferrari Hardoy Papers, D-85h4.

18. Liernur and Pschepiurca, *La red austral*, 326. Regularizing the river was key: flows averaged 80 cubic meters per second, but varied from as little as 18 to as much as 3,000. Videla, *Retablo sanjuanino*, 122.

19. "Tradición, leyenda y urbanismo," *Tribuna*, 30 November 1944.

20. Videla, *Ocho conferencias y una más en el cuarto centenario de la fundación de San Juan*, 141–42

21. "Eso es todo," *Tribuna*, 24 October 1944. See also "Lo que cuestan los jardines," *Tribuna*, 17 September 1944, and "Nosotros y la reconstrucción," *Tribuna*, 6 October 1944; "Reconstrucción y propietarios," *Tribuna*, 2 November 1944; "Lo académico y lo real," *Tribuna*, 9 November 1944.

22. "Más vale pájaro en mano . . . ," *Tribuna*, 18 December 1944.

23. Torre, *La vieja guardia sindical*, 80, 83.

24. Horowitz, *Argentine Unions,* 184. Before May no contracts were signed in the interior; from May to December there were 279.

25. Quoted in Horowitz, *Argentine Unions*, 195.

26. "Obreros inscriptos," *La Prensa*, 18 April 1944. STP offices in most provinces established hiring pools, but the one in San Juan was by far the largest and most successful. See *Crónica mensual de la Secretaría de Trabajo y Previsión* for 1944.

27. "Pídese que no se aplique el rigorismo de las leyes obreras," *La Prensa*, 17 April 1944.

28. Administración Sanitaria y Asistencia Pública, "Informes de las visitas efectuadas por las visitadoras de Higiene Social," 31 October 1944, AHASJ, Misc., c.63, d.6–8.

29. "Aprobóse el proyecto de salarios para bodegas," *La Acción*, 3 August 1944.

30. Gobierno de San Juan, *Estatuto del Peón*.

31. "Fue en bicicleta a Buenos Aires para saludar al Coronel Perón," *Tribuna*, 24 December 1944.

32. For praise, see "El camino de la justicia social," *Tribuna*, 6 September 1944, and "El primer aniversario de la Secretaría de Trabajo y Previsión Social," *Tribuna*, 27 November 1944; complaints in "Una solicitud improcedente," *Tribuna*, 23 December 1944.

33. "El problema de la vivienda trató el congreso obrero provincial," *La Acción*, 11 June 1945.
34. "Chapas asfalticas ONDALIT," *Los Andes*, 27 March 1944.
35. Calderón de la Piragua, "0 Grado," *Tribuna*, 10 July 1944; Calderón de la Piragua, "Eternos descontentos," *Tribuna*, 27 September 1944.
36. "Se aprobó el concurso de precios para la asilación térmica en los barrios," *Tribuna*, 3 December 1944.
37. "Deben ser transformadas las viviendas de emergencia empleadas actualmente en San Juan," *Los Andes*, 14 December 1944. This article closely followed Eduardo Sacriste's favorable assessment of adobe and may well have been written by Sacriste himself. It also noted how closely local traditions of lightweight adobe construction echoed emergency constructions in Japan after the 1923 earthquake—without mentioning Japan's subsequent embrace of concrete.
38. "Alrededor del problema de la vivienda de emergencia," *La Acción*, 3 April 1945.
39. Carlos Day to Inteventor Interino Tte. Colonel Rodolfo Luque, 29 October 1944, AHASJ, Gob., c-11bis, d-11. An exchange of several increasingly acrimonious letters followed, ending with the official comment that "this note does not follow proper protocol, and therefore will be archived."
40. Cecilio Cerda to Coronel Crencio Palenque, Ministro de Obras Públicas, 25 December 1944, AHASJ, OP, c-1, d-3. The worker lived in Chimbas, wrote on the letterhead of the Chimbas branch, and was requesting housing in Chimbas. But the fact that the organization was based in the largest barrio, across the city from Chimbas, suggests how these neighborhoods were building new forms of social organization.
41. "Constituye un serio problema la falta de viviendas," *Los Andes*, 9 January 1945.
42. "Debe facilitarse la construcción de la vivienda de emergencia popular," *La Acción*, 26 September 1944.
43. "Buenos Dias," *Tribuna*, 20 September 1944.
44. "Los ruidos molestos," *Tribuna*, 9 December 1944.
45. "Los ruidos molestos," *Tribuna*, 16 October 1944; see also Francisco Manfredi, "De nuestra actualidad: Carta al director," *Tribuna*, 20 November 1944; "La moral, la tranquilidad y las pistas de baile," *La Acción*, 29 January 1945.
46. "Las autoridades distribuyeron obsequios a los vecinos de los barrios de emergencia," *Tribuna*, 25 December 1944.
47. "Meditación de nuestra Nochebuena," *Tribuna*, 24 December 1944.
48. Julio Villalobos, "Algo más sobre la reconstrucción de San Juan," *Política*, 12 June 1946; Jorge Ferrari Hardoy, "Análisis del decreto de cesantía," December 1944, Ferrari Hardoy Papers, D-8514.
49. "La reconstrucción de la ciudad, problema fundamental," *La Acción*, 8 October 1944.
50. There was no basis to these accusations, although the nineteen-page transcript of the interrogation over drafting supplies is quite revealing of military attitudes.

DS/92, 2 December 1944, Ferrari Hardoy Papers, D-85i2; "Declaración jurada de arquitectos," 6 December 1944, Ferrari Hardoy Papers, D-85h4.

51. Julio Villalobos, "Algo más sobre la reconstrucción de San Juan," *Política*, 12 June 1946; Jorge Ferrari Hardoy, "Análisis del decreto de cesantía," December 1944, Ferrari Hardoy Papers, D-85i4.

52. It was only weeks later, after a Buenos Aires radio station mentioned the incident, that the local press discussed it. Juan Victoria to Jorge Vivanco, San Juan, 17 December 1944, Ferrari Hardoy Papers, D-85j2. "Qué ocurre en el Consejo de Reconstrucción?" *La Acción*, 18 December 1944.

53. "Grave conflicto se planteó en el Consejo de Reconstrucción," *La Acción*, 21 December 1944.

54. "San Juan será reconstruido a corto plazo, dijo el Interventor Federal," *La Acción*, 14 January 1945.

55. Vitálico Gnecco, "Oíganos Coronel Berretta," *El Censor*, 19 January 1945.

56. "La sobriedad y la prudencia en la Reconstrucción," *La Acción*, 20 January 1945.

57. The four members were architect Villalobos, labor leader Tejada, Water Department head Enrique Zuleta, and provincial attorney general Federico Prolongo. All but Tejada were state officials.

58. Jorge Ferrari Hardoy, "Otras cosas sobre la Reconstrucción de San Juan," late January 1945, Ferrari Hardoy Papers, D-8504.

59. This new capital was to be located in Media Agua, halfway to Mendoza. Julio Villalobos, "Algo más sobre la reconstrucción de San Juan," *Política*, 12 June 1946.

60. See Julio Villalobos, "El gobierno construyendo casas," *Nueva Argentina*, January 1945, 244, first published in *Finanzas* in August 1944. See also Healey, "The Ruins," 375–86.

61. Julio Villalobos, "La Reconstrucción de San Juan considerada como una nueva planificación económico-social," *Finanzas*, August 1944, 7.

62. Julio Villalobos, "Las grandes obras hidráulicas del Tennessee y su importancia social," *La Prensa*, 29 November 1942.

63. Julio Villalobos, "Una planificación efectiva debe lograr la redistribución racional de la población," *Finanzas*, January 1945, 11; Villalobos, "El gobierno," 244.

64. Villalobos, "Una planificación efectiva," 11.

65. Cándido Villalobos Dominguez, "La política de la tierra: Comprar y no confiscar," *Nueva Argentina,* March 1945, 313. See also Cándido Villalobos Dominguez, *Bases y método para la apropriación social de la tierra*. Villalobos Domínguez had translated Henry George's *The Condition of Labor* into Spanish.

66. Villalobos, "Una planificación efectiva," 11. On his own copy, Fermín Bereterbide marked his puzzlement next to this conclusion: "???" Bereterbide Papers.

67. See Julio Villalobos, "Contribuciones al remodelamiento de la ciudad de San Juan," *Revista de Arquitectura* 32, no. 314 (February 1947): 67–71. Also Roitman de Schabelman, *San Juan*, 143–45.

68. "Autonomía y reconstrucción," *Tribuna*, 18 May 1946.

69. See, for example, "Reconstrucción y burocracia," *La Acción*, 21 April 1945.

70. "Una ponencia envió la Fed. O Sanjuanina al Consejo de Reconstrucción," *Tribuna*, 8 October 1944.

71. "La población de los departamentos concurrirá al acto Pro Reconstrucción," *La Acción*, 24 March 1945; "En un mitín solicitóse la pronta reconstrucción de la ciudad capital," *La Prensa*, 2 April 1945.

72. "En un mitín solicitóse la pronta reconstrucción de la ciudad capital," *La Prensa*, 2 April 1945.

73. Villalobos returned to his previous post at the Consejo Agrario Nacional but maintained an interest in San Juan, for example, proposing a 2,000-family colonization project. "Colonizarán en San Juan 10.000 hectáreas fiscales," *Democracia*, 9 January 1946.

74. Carlos Mendióroz, "El planeamiento en la reconstrucción de San Juan," *Revista de Arquitectura* 31, no. 310 (October 1946): 418. Another prominent team member, Julio Otaola, was a Catholic nationalist who had been appointed mayor of Córdoba by the military.

75. Carlos Mendióroz, "Nueva vida universitaria," *Revista de Arquitectura* 29, no. 283 (June 1944): 262–63. The faculty included engineering, architecture, and the exact sciences.

76. For the one-page drawing, see "El plan esquematico de la reconstrucción," *Tribuna*, 2 August 1945, and "La Reconstrucción de San Juan," *La Nación*, 5 August 1945.

77. "La Reconstrucción de San Juan," *La Nación*, 5 August 1945.

78. Carlos Mendióroz, "La Nueva San Juan: Crítica a la crítica del arquitecto Bereterbide," *Revista de Arquitectura* 31, no. 302 (February 1946): 33.

79. "Fue elevado al Ministerio del Interior el proyecto de Reconstrucción de San Juan, *La Acción*, 31 May 1945.

80. República Argentina, *Diario de Sesiones de Cámara de Senadores 1946*, 1: 653–54.

81. For Perón, the idea of a prior strategy served to underscore his foresight and capability as a popular leader; for the opposition, it served to prove that he was a pro-Nazi schemer for power, a born manipulator.

82. After all, the pragmatic and immediate solution would have been to let local elites have their way.

Chapter 8: The Revolt of the Engineers

1. *El otro terremoto de San Juan.*

2. The opening sentence of the book described the military as a "malón" (Indian raiding party) of "new mazorqueros" (members of Rosas's personal militia): a revival of the barbarism liberal Argentina had fought for a century to suppress. *El otro terremoto de San Juan*, 5.

3. "El peso muerto del organismo de Reconstrucción," *La Acción*, 3 June 1945; see also the longing for attention from Pistarini's staff in "San Juan sigue fuera de las rutas oficiales," *La Acción*, 22 June 1945.

4. "Con ferverosa unción reunion recordóse a Sarmiento," *La Acción*, 3 May 1945.

5. "El Centro de Ingenieros de San Juan dió un comunicado sobre la reconstrucción," *Tribuna*, 1 July 1945.

6. Only four years after arriving, Costantini was vice-chair of the organizing committee for the patron saint festival in Desamparados, the neighborhood where many leading Graffignistas lived. The committee was chaired by Alberto Graffigna, and the festival began with a procession from the Del Bono mansion to the emergency chapel. "Reina gran entusiasmo por los festejos patronales de N.S. de los Desamparados," *Tribuna*, 18 November 1944.

7. "Solicitan la derogación de los decretos del Poder Ejecutivo," *La Acción*, 2 July 1945; "Nuevas adhesiones hicieronse a la declaración del Centro de Ingenieros," *La Acción*, 8 July 1945.

8. "Uso y disposición de la propiedad inmueble," *Tribuna*, 4 July 1945.

9. "La posición del Sindicato O. de la Construcción," *La Acción*, 6 July 1945. This stance followed the position taken by the Communist Party and the national union and met with establishment praise. "Obreros que plantean con claridad el problema económico," *La Prensa*, 22 July 1945.

10. "Solución de un incidente," *La Prensa*, 5 July 1945.

11. "El comunicado del Director General de Reconstrucción," *La Acción*, 6 July 1945; "Inquieta en Villa Colón la no reconstrucción de esa región," *La Acción*, 11 July 1945.

12. "Quedó constituida ayer la Comisión Popular Pro Reconstrucción de San Juan," *Tribuna*, 16 July 1945.

13. "San Juan debe ser reconstruido: El Gobierno Nacional tiene la obligación de hacerlo," *La Acción*, 16 July 1945. The group went by several names but for clarity will here be called the Popular Assembly. The president and secretary were Socialists, and the vice president was a left-leaning Radical. The week it was formed, Baca's political patron, the Radical leader Salvador Doncel, was elected rector of the University of Cuyo by the votes of professors and graduates. "Eligióse Rector de la Universidad de Cuyo al Doctor Salvador Doncel," *La Prensa*, 11 July 1945. The universities had been hotbeds of resistance to the military, and within two weeks the rectors of all six national universities would call for constitutional rule.

14. The Graffigna paper joined the cause the day after the Popular Assembly was formed: "Hay que actuar con hechos," *Tribuna*, 16 July 1945.

15. "Sobre la Secretaría de Trabajo y Previsión dio una declaración la Federación Obrera Sanjuanina," *La Acción*, 21 April 1945.

16. "Buenos dias," *Tribuna*, 9 July 1945. Tejada and allies were expelled for "collaborating" with the military; Tejada pointed out that no penalty was imposed on Baca, who had served as minister when the military dissolved his own party.

17. "Reunión extraordinaria de la Federacion Obrera Sanjuanina," *La Nacion*, 15 July 1945.

18. "El más franco éxito coronó las gestiones hechas por la delegación obrera sanjuanina y autoridades de la central obrera," *C.G.T.*, 1 August 1945.

19. "Comunicado de la Intervención Federal Sobre la inversión de fondos de la Colecta

en Favor de San Juan," *La Acción*, 28 July 1945. The communiqué announced the distribution of collection funds: 14.5 million in bonds with the annual interest used for housing loans; 3.5 million for emergency housing; 1.8 million for pensions; 4.2 million for family subsidies for the poor; 1.5 million for maternity subsidies; 0.9 million for scholarships for children of victims; and 0.3 million in compensation for merchants. The communiqué noted that the project had been drawn up by Berretta's staff and sent to the national government in November 1944—a striking eight-month delay.

20. "El Interventor Federal y el mitín del 8 de agosto," *La Acción*, 3 August 1945.

21. For initial demands, see "Las bases de la solución del problema," *La Acción*, 30 July 1945; for final form, see "El Memorial concreta las legítimas aspiraciones de los sanjuaninos," *La Acción*, 9 August 1945.

22. "El mitin de mañana," *Tribuna*, 7 August 1945.

23. Observers claimed fifteen to twenty thousand at the time, and fifteen thousand a year later. "Buenos dias," *Tribuna*, 9 August 1945; "8 de agosto," *Mercurio*, 10 August 1946.

24. Santiago Graffigna, for example, told reporters this "encouraged the idea of collective restoration." "Cuatro opiniones sobre el mitin," *Tribuna*, 8 August 1945.

25. "El problema se complica inutilmente," *La Acción*, 9 August 1945.

26. "Cuatro opiniones sobre el mitin," *Tribuna*, 8 August 1945; "El Ingeniero Baca expuso fundamentos que inspiraron el movimiento," *La Acción*, 9 August 1945; "No solicitamos dádivas ni holganzas, queremos levantar nuestros hogares," *Tribuna*, 10 August 1945; "Comision Popular Pro Reconstruccion de San Juan," *Tribuna*, 12 August 1945.

27. "¡Sarmiento Sí! ¡Rosas No!," *La Acción*, 9 August 1945. See also *La Nación*, 10 August 1945.

28. "Una inolvidable jornada vivió ayer el pueblo de San Juan," *Los Andes*, 9 August 1945.

29. "En nombre de los Obreros de la Construcción," *La Acción*, 9 August 1945.

30. "Hipótesis sobre la recuperación de los 304 millones," *La Acción*, 4 August 1945.

31. "Queremos que el gobierno oiga este llamado," *La Acción*, 9 August 1945.

32. "Lo que se ve en el problema de la Reconstrucción," *La Acción*, 19 July 1945.

33. "El 8 de agosto habrá un mitin para pedir la reconstruccion de San Juan," *Tribuna*, 23 July 1945; "La Acción Católica ha expresado su adhesión," *La Acción*, 2 August 1945.

34. "El cuidado de la niñez en los barrios," *Tribuna*, 26 July 1945.

35. "Fue examinado el problema de S. Juan," *La Acción*, 9 August 1945.

36. Cañellas, "El terremoto de San Juan," 612.

37. Although generally friendly with Conservatives, the Socialists had fallen into disfavor when the Graffigna Conservatives came into office. Marún had been fired for his antifascist politics; one of the first to support him then was Ruperto Godoy, now the local delegate of the STP. Marún was restored to office by the first military interventor after the 1943 coup. "Dos médicos," *Combate*, 18 October 1947.

38. "Un homenaje al pueblo y democracia inglesa se llevará a cabo hoy," *La Acción*, 12 August 1945. Two months later, an Argentine Labor Party would be founded, but in contrast to the wishes of local Socialists, this party supported Perón and counted among its leaders "the little traitor Tejada."

39. "Código de edificación," *Tribuna*, 13 July 1945.

40. "La Reconstrucción debe inspirarse en la lógica y el razonamiento," *La Acción*, 10 July 1945.

41. "Hablando del ensanche de calles," *La Acción*, 14 July 1945; the Mendióroz plan was published as "La Reconstrucción de San Juan," *La Nación*, 5 August 1945.

42. "Elementos de orden técnico y estético que deberían ser tenidos en cuenta al procederse a reconstruir San Juan," *La Acción*, 27 July 1945.

43. "La Comisión Pro-Reconstrucción de Concepción formuló sugestiones," *La Acción*, 6 October 1945. See also "Un memorial al Presidente elevó la C. Pro-Reconstrucción de Concepción," *La Acción*, 18 September 1945.

44. "El vecindario de Caucete refirmó su oposición al decreto declaratorio de zona no reconstruible," *La Acción*, 1 August 1945.

45. "San Juan ha elegido un camino que ya no abandonará," *La Acción*, 10 August 1945.

46. "Numerosas nuevas adhesiones recibe la comisión popular," *La Acción*, 11 August 1945.

47. The meeting was sponsored by Conservatives, Socialists, Communists, and one branch of the Radicals. "Se realizará el mitin de pro de la normalidad," *La Acción*, 2 September 1945.

48. Of course, they were three architects. "Se dió una declaración sobre el problema fundamental de S. Juan," *La Acción*, 3 September 1945.

49. "Quedó constituida la C. Vecinal de Trinidad Pro-Recons. de San Juan," *La Acción*, 27 August 1945. The group was apparently led by Communists; in 1946, this neighborhood would account for 113 of the party's 114 votes provincewide. República Argentina, Ministerio del Interior, *Las fuerzas armadas restituyen . . .*, 2: 528–30.

50. The minority of civil engineers who did support the government, mostly Catholic activists associated with the Bunge group, were largely marginalized from leadership of the profession.

51. "El Centro Argentino de Ingenieros ante problemas de interés general vinculados a la ingenería," *La Ingenería* 849 (July 1945): 435–69. San Juan alone received as much attention as public works in general. The issue was written by a team led by Francisco de la Fuente, a CAI member and president of the builders' association, the CAC.

52. "El Centro Argentino de Ingenieros," 450–52. After eight years of increasing private construction and decreasing public construction, the trend began to reverse in 1944. Yet public works were still a lower percentage of all construction in 1944 than for any year in the previous decade, when the CAI leadership had been in charge. Cámara Argentina de la Construcción, *40° Aniversario*, 55. See also Healey, "The Ruins," 483–86, 727–28.

53. "El Centro Argentino de Ingenieros," 464–66.

54. Ibid., 467. Mendióroz may have merited greater respect because of his prior service with CAI leaders on a Buenos Aires public housing committee.

55. "El Centro Argentino de Ingenieros," 465–66.

56. Ibid., 465, 468. Italics in original.

57. Ibid., 468. The CAI and the Popular Assembly maintained that aid should be given according to property lost, not according to need, as the government proposal based on family income and number of children suggested.

58. Roberto Gorostiaga, quoted in "Homenaje de La Ingenería en 50 aniversario del CAI," *La Ingenería* 851 (September 1945), 606. See also Healey, "The Ruins," 475–78.

59. See 28 June 1945 entry in *Libro de Actas de la Comisión Directiva de la Sociedad Central de Arquitectos, 24 julio 1944-18 noviembre 1946,* vol. 12, 113–14. The *Libro de Actas* is available in the SCA Library.

60. José M. F. Pastor, "El problema de la tierra y el planeamiento," *Revista de Arquitectura* 30, no. 299 (November 1945): 456.

61. Pastor, *San Juan*, 63.

62. Pastor, *Urbanismo con planeamiento*, 162.

63. Pastor, *San Juan*, 171–95. The idea of the enlightened owner as model for public intervention was common in the writings of British planners, and also in Beaux Arts–era Argentine planning. Gorelik, *La grilla y el parque*, 123.

64. Fermín H. Bereterbide to Angel Martín, Buenos Aires, 17 September 1944, Bereterbide Papers.

65. Jorge Ferrari Hardoy to Fermín Bereterbide, Buenos Aires, 4 May 1946, Bereterbide Papers.

66. The main articles are Fermín Bereterbide, "La Reconstrucción de San Juan," *Revista de Arquitectura* 30, no. 293 (June 1945): 184–96; "Reconstrucción de San Juan: Sistema de financiación," *Revista de Arquitectura* 30, no. 295 (August 1945); 210–16; "La Nueva San Juan: Crítica del plan de reconstrucción aprobado," *Nuestra Arquitectura* 15, no. 11 (November 1945): 403–8, 262–66; and "Carta al Sr. Director de la Revista de Arquitectura," *Revista de Arquitectura* 32, no. 302 (March 1946): 120–22. The responses are Julio Villalobos, "Sobre un sistema de financiación para la Reconstrucción de San Juan," *Revista de Arquitectura* 30, no. 297 (October 1945): 358–60; Carlos Mendióroz et al., "La Nueva San Juan: Crítica a la crítica del arquitecto Bereterbide," *Revista de Arquitectura* 32, no. 302 (March 1946): 30–35; and "El planeamiento en la Reconstrucción de San Juan," *Revista de Arquitectura* 31, no. 310 (October 1946): 418–53.

67. See 10 September 1945, *Libro de Actas*, 174–80.

68. "400 arquitectos han pedido la vuelta del país a la normalidad," *La Prensa*, 13 September 1945. Only Eduardo Sacriste, Julio Villalobos, and the Mendióroz team members did not sign.

69. "Una declaración de arquitectos," *La Prensa*, 14 September 1945.

70. One isolated example was Horacio Moyano Navarro, "Arquitectura y estado," *Nuestra Arquitectura* 15, no. 9 (September 1945): 319. This argument was indicative of liberal blindness about the state more than anything else, as the architect who

claimed that "a strong State" was "anti-culture" itself was a public employee who wrote extensively about public architecture and recently had spoken at a U.S. government–funded institute about state-led plans to rebuild Britain. See Healey, "The Ruins," 506–9.

71. "Carta a Colegas de la Agrupación de Arquitectos Democráticos," n/d, Héctor Morixe Papers.

72. Jorge Ferrari Hardoy to Remberto Baca, 13 September 1945, Ferrari Hardoy Papers, D-85k1.

73. Ungar enclosed a pamphlet, *Rebuilding Britain*, as an example of how other countries were facing the challenge, rather than mocking it. The letter appeared in the rival paper. Simón Ungar, "Carta al director del diario *Tribuna*," *La Acción*, 14 September 1945.

74. Juan Victoria to Jorge Ferrari Hardoy, San Juan, 17 September 1945, Ferrari Hardoy Papers, D-85j2.

75. "Organigrama de Reconstrucción," 31 July 1945 (?), Ferrari Hardoy Papers, D-85u3; Jorge Ferrari Hardoy to Juan Victoria, Buenos Aires, 26 October 1945, Ferrari Hardoy Papers, D-85j2.

76. Clothiel Woodard Smith to Jorge Ferrari Hardoy, Montevideo, 18 July 1945, Ferrari Hardoy Papers, F-65.

77. Jorge Ferrari Hardoy to Juan Victoria, Buenos Aires, 26 October 1945, Ferrari Hardoy Papers, D-85j2.

78. Ibid.

Chapter 9: "San Juan Is Still Waiting"

1. A former Radical national committee member and political editor of the newspaper *Crítica*, Cipolletti was also co-owner of *La Época*, the only remaining pro-Perón daily.

2. See, for example, the celebration organized for him by the Conservative chieftain Juan Maurín. "Las fuerzas vivas de Caucete agasajaron al ingeniero Enrique Zuleta," *La Acción*, 28 September 1944.

3. Emilio Cipolletti, Interventor Federal en San Juan, a Coronel Bartolomé Descalzo, Ministro del Interior, San Juan, 1 October 1945, AGN-Intermedio, MI, SCyR, 51/492. Even so, after a month in office, he had made only ninety-six appointments.

4. Fernando Darousa, "Cantoni, líder del Bloquismo, afirma: Perón no será presidente," *Ercilla*, 13 February 1945.

5. After all the months of silence, Zuleta announced new agreements weekly, or even daily. "Ubicación de los edificios bancarios convenida por 'Reconstrucción' y las entidades respectivas," *La Acción*, 9 September 1945.

6. Emilio Cipolletti, Interventor Federal, to Hortensio Quijano, Ministro del Interior, San Juan, 1 September 1945, AGN-Intermedio, MI, SCyR, 37/871.

7. Juan Victoria to Jorge Ferrari Hardoy, 17 September 1945, Ferrari Hardoy Papers, D-85j2.

8. "Obra pública que puede demorarse," *La Prensa*, 19 July 1945. On the canal project, see "Quien se viste con lo ajeno," *Tribuna*, 2 February 1946.

9. "Una delegación de ingenieros llegó ayer a San Juan," *La Acción*, 2 September 1945. A key intermediary here was Romeo Gaddi, minister of public works in San Juan at the time of the quake. Gaddi had first appointed Zuleta. He also previously worked for the Conservative Manuel Fresco when he was governor of Buenos Aires; Fresco and Gaddi were key to setting up the consortium. "Trata la Reconstrucción de San Juan el Congreso de la Construcción," *El Mundo*, 18 January 1946.

10. The 1947 census registered fifty local construction companies, but only eight did roads and bridges, and only one general (large-scale) construction. República Argentina, Dirección Nacional del Servicio Estadístico, *IV Censo General de la Nación*, vol. 3, 352.

11. "El castigo que se buscaron," *La Acción*, 14 October 1945.

12. "Acta de la reunión" in Torre, ed., *La formación*, 189. See also Torre, *La vieja guardia*, 133–34.

13. Despite his eloquent defense of the strike, Tejada followed his union's orders to vote against it. Torre, *La vieja guardia*, 135.

14. James, "October 17ᵗʰ," 453, 450–51, 452.

15. "Se realizó un paro general en nuestra ciudad," *La Acción*, 19 October 1945.

16. James, "October 17ᵗʰ," 454.

17. Ibid., 451.

18. Many papers, especially on the left, used similar language. Quoted in James, "October 17ᵗʰ," 456–57.

19. "Ese no es el pueblo," *Tribuna*, 27 September 1945.

20. "Dieron una declaración los partidos políticos opositores sanjuaninos," *La Acción*, 20 October 1945.

21. "Se realizó un paro general en nuestra ciudad," *La Acción*, 19 October 1945.

22. "Quijano, su política, su renuncia, y San Juan," *La Acción*, 16 October 1945; "El castigo que se buscaron," *La Acción*, 14 October 1945; "Hablemos un poco de Civilización y Barbarie," *La Acción*, 22 October 1945.

23. "Sobre el problema de San Juan dieron una declaración los arquitectos," *El Mundo*, 16 January 1946. While authorship is unknown, the statement's specificity suggests the involvement of one or more of the architects who worked on San Juan, nearly all of whom were members of the AAD.

24. Ibid.

25. The case was dismissed soon afterward. "Desestímanse denuncias por desacato al Poder Ejecutivo," *La Razón*, 7 February 1946.

26. Many newspapers nationwide issued editorials: for example, "La larga espera de San Juan," *El Mundo*, 14 January 1946; "A dos años del terremoto de San Juan: Ineptitud revolucionaria," *El Diario* (Paraná), 15 January 1946.

27. "Esta es la respuesta: Ruinas, hambre y miseria, dicen los sanjuaninos," *Falucho*, 10 January 1946.

28. "Irregularidades en la Colecta Pro-Damnificados de San Juan fueron comprobadas en Tucumán," *La Acción*, 8 March 1945.

29. See, for example, the satirical poems quoted in Marcelo Caruso, "El año que vivimos en peligro," in Puiggrós, ed., *Discursos pedagógicos e imaginario social en el peronismo*, 88.

30. "Un detalle que debe hacerse conocer al país," *El Fiscal*, 8 January 1946. The claim is widespread in opposition memoirs, for example, Damonte Taborda, *Ayer fué San Perón*, 65.

31. "Informóse oficialmente sobre la inversión de fondos hecha en San Juan," *La Prensa*, 16 January 1946; "Aqui está la verdad sobre los dineros de San Juan: Enmudezcan las voces de la calumnia, " *El Laborista*, 26 February 1946.

32. "Se iniciará en breve la reconstrucción de San Juan," *Democracia*, 23 January 1946.

33. "A propósito de la frase 'San Juan Espera Todavía,' " *Democracia*, 15 January 1946; "Nadie carece de techo en San Juan," *El Laborista*, 17 January 1946.

34. "Hay que conocer y difundir la verdad," *La Época*, 7 February 1946.

35. "Un desahogo pequeño relacionado con la reconstrucción," *La Acción*, 20 January 1946.

36. See "Contraste revelador," *La Reforma*, 4 January 1946; "Un episodio del fraude," *La Reforma*, 3 February 1946.

37. "Como los ricos propietarios dificultan la reconstrucción," *La Reforma*, 8 January 1946; "El egoísmo de los potentados retardó la reconstrucción de San Juan," *La Reforma*, 6 January 1946.

38. "Lo que no sabe y le ocultaron al Dr. Calcagno," *La Reforma*, 1 February 1946.

39. Bruno Arpesella, "Lo que vi en San Juan, la provincia de las casas caidas y la población de pie," *C.G.T.*, 16 January 1946.

40. "Discurso del Dr. F. Cantoni," *La Reforma*, 27 January 1946.

41. Interview of Aldo Hermes Cantoni by Aldo Gaete, San Juan, 1 August 2002; "Los sanjuaninos ya han dado respuesta al coronel Nazi sobre los 42 millones," *La Hora*, 1 February 1946; "Respuesta de la convención de la UCRB," *La Prensa*, 17 February 1946. The Bloquista platform called for limiting the power of the national executive, decentralizing education, and defending provincial autonomy. "Plataforma," *La Reforma*, 30 January 1946.

42. "Telegrama de Perón a Alvarado y Godoy," *La Prensa*, 14 February 1946.

43. "Respuesta de la convención de la UCRB," *La Prensa*, 17 February 1946.

44. Juan Victoria, "Acerca de la Reconstrucción de San Juan," *Revista Sarmiento* 5 (December 1945): 18.

45. Victoria, "Acerca de la Reconstrucción."

46. César Guerrero, "Sobre remodelación estructural de la ciudad de San Juan," *Revista Sarmiento* 7 (April 1946): 1.

Part 4: "Rubble or No Rubble, We Want Perón," 1946–1962

1. Perón, *Pensamiento politico del General de Brigada Juan Perón*, 15, 18; for a powerful account of the moment, see Luna, *Perón y su tiempo*, 11–13.

2. While this phrasing is most strongly expressed in República Argentina, *La Nación Argentina: Libre, Justa, Soberana*, it was already present in Perón's inaugural address.

3. Many of the key staff for carrying out these initiatives had worked on San Juan, from those at the top of the administration, like the public works minister Juan Pistarini and the defense minister Humberto Sosa Molina to the Bunge group economics and engineers who had worked with Pistarini and staffed the new branches of the state.

4. "Los fundamentos de la esperanza argentina," *La Reforma*, 31 March 1948.

5. "El plan: Mística de la multitud," *El Líder*, 11 January 1947.

6. Indeed, Radical activists pointed to the ruins of San Juan as a clear "indication of the nature of the Five Year Plan" and its likely result. "Hubo un acto en la Casa Radical," *La Nación*, 16 January 1947.

7. "Para hablar de San Juan, dejar a los sanjuaninos," *Democracia*, 10 June 1948.

8. Doyon, "La formación del sindicalismo peronista," 369.

9. Alvarado, "The Rich," 45.

10. See Gerchunoff and Antúnez, "De la bonanza peronista a la crisis de desarrollo," esp. tables on 198–99.

11. Rofman and Romero, *Sistema socioeconómico y estructura regional*, 199–200, 242.

Chapter 10: Against the "Sovereignty of Experts"

1. "El mensaje del nuevo mandatario," *Tribuna*, 26 May 1946.

2. He pinned the idea of anti-seismic construction as the solution to all ills on Reconstruction, but as we have seen, it was his own Conservative allies who had been the most obsessive and narrow advocates of this approach.

3. He ignored the fact that he did not meet the provincial constitution's one requirement for a governor: residency in the province for five years before the election.

4. "La piedra de toque," *Tribuna*, 27 May 1946. A tone-deaf Reconstruction Council insisted that "provincial interference" be kept to a minimum. "Reconstrucción de San Juan opina que en las obras debe limitarse al máximo la ingerencia provincial," *Comercio e Industria*, 1 June 1946.

5. Galasso, *Vida de Scalabrini Ortiz*, 216–20. See also Scenna, *F.O.R.J.A.*

6. "Fué clausurada la primera etapa del programa de difusión oficial del Plan Quinquenal," *La Reforma*, 6 January 1947; "Difusión oficial del Plan Quinquenal," *La Reforma*, 9 January 1947.

7. The provincial ministries of public works and reconstruction. These appointments were sharply criticized by laboristas, who argued that the posts required technical expertise. "La Reconstrucción de San Juan," *Pregón Radical Laborista*, 26 July 1946.

8. República Argentina, Ministerio del Interior, *Las fuerzas armadas restituyen*, vol. 2, 528–30.

9. Areas outside the central valley—Iglesia, Jáchal, Calingasta, Valle Fértil, and Sarmiento—were little affected by the earthquake and mostly ignored afterward, so the election there turned more on established local rivalries than the national campaign.

Most Bloquistas and all Radicals elected came from these areas. See Healey, "The Ruins," 542–44.

10. Alvarado had been Jones's secretary of finance. Videla, *Historia de San Juan*, 303.

11. "Política politiquería," *La Reforma*, 30 January 1946. At a similar moment in 1931, Cantoni won without women's participation, then called another election including women and won by an even larger margin. This precedent was often mentioned in the press and was undoubtedly on Alvarado's mind.

12. "Balconeando," *La Reforma*, 7 March 1946.

13. As a Catholic activist, Alvarado was hostile to liberal politicians, attacking the secular-minded local lawyer group shortly after taking office.

14. In his autobiography, Ramella claimed to have met Alvarado through Catholic Action and been offered the Senate seat before the election, but he does not mention it in correspondence until afterward. Ramella, *Autobiografía*, 35. Tascheret was descended from a family of San Juan notables, and his brother Juan had just been elected legislator on the Radical slate. When Tascheret was named senator, his brother switched sides and became president of the Bank of San Juan.

15. "Ha sido traicionado el Coronel Perón y estafada la buena fé política del pueblo," *La Reforma*, 2 May 1946.

16. On these disputes, see Torre, *La vieja guardia*, and Mackinnon, *Los años formativos del Partido Peronista*.

17. "Repudio popular a la candidatura del Dr. Ramella," *La Reforma*, 6 April 1946.

18. Ramella, *Reformas a la Constitución de San Juan*, 19. He held that women, illiterates, and the young should not have the vote and in 1946 proposed the "family vote," a Catholic scheme that assigned male heads of household the votes for their entire family, including minors. Women could vote only if unmarried or widowed. Ramella, *La estructura del estado*, 544–47.

19. Just before the election, Ramella wrote a Buenos Aires friend of Catholic reticence toward Perón, and his friend responded that "we all take for granted a crushing defeat for Perón. I am glad that in San Juan there are no Peronists among the Catholics." Ambrosio Romero Carranza to Pablo Ramella, Buenos Aires, 7 February 1946, Ramella Papers. This decade-long friendship ended when Ramella accepted the Senate seat.

20. "La posición de los empleados y obreros de la Municipalidad," *La Nación*, 13 May 1946.

21. "8 de Agosto," *Mercurio*, 10 August 1946. "We are still living like gypsies," the Chamber stated. "And this virile people, this strong people . . . traditionally proud, cantankerous and intolerant, move along, keep their heads down, and hope that someone will remember them."

22. "Será auspiciada por damas de la sociedad la Dirección de Justicia Social de la P de S Juan," *La Calle*, 28 March 1946. Laborista women activists protested at having to beg Conservative women for help. "Protesta justificada," *La Reforma*, 16 April 1946.

23. For example, when Conservative leaders pragmatically offered to join Cantoni in opposition, giving him a legislative majority, the better-informed Cantoni told

them their deputies had already switched sides and was proven right a few weeks later. Interview of Tulio del Bono by Aldo Gaete, San Juan, 14 July 2002.

24. Since he was following in the footsteps of Sarmiento, ambassador to the United States, the party newspaper put four giant photos on the front page: Cantoni, Perón, Sarmiento, and Stalin. "Las relaciones diplomáticas con la Unión Soviética," *La Reforma*, 29 July 1946.

25. "Un acto político trascendental," *La Reforma*, 22 July 1946.

26. "La organización del Partido de la Revolución en San Juan," *La Reforma*, 23 July 1946.

27. "Filosofando," *La Reforma*, 14 September 1946.

28. Ramella first came to San Juan as part of an intervention and remained through several constitutionally irregular regimes, but he became a powerful critic of national interventions and defender of local autonomy. Ramella, *La estructura del estado*, 237–38, 262–65.

29. Conte-Grand, of course, had been chief of staff to Sosa Molina when he set up Reconstruction back in 1944.

30. The four projects can be found in República Argentina, *Diario de Sesiones de la Cámara de Diputados de 1946*, vol. 5, 261–69. For more detail, see Healey, "The Ruins," 552–72.

31. República Argentina, *Diario de Sesiones de la Cámara de Senadores de 1946*, vol. 1, 638–39.

32. Tejada, *La reconstrucción de San Juan*, 6–10. "Nunca se llegó a concebir una ciudad tan perfecta como la Nueva San Juan," *Ahora*, 3 October 1946.

33. Three hundred million would go to Reconstruction, and one hundred million to repair federal facilities in San Juan. Tejada, *La Reconstrucción*, 9. Zuleta, *Resurgimiento económico del Norte y Noroeste de San Juan*. This north of the province was very similar in ecology and economy to neighboring La Rioja, Zuleta's home province.

34. As the finance minister and president of the Central Bank, Miranda directed the nationalization of the banking system, placing loyalists in key posts. The Camus bill specified that the Central Bank would direct rebuilding through the Instituto Argentino de Promoción y Intercambio (IAPI), Miranda's vehicle for centralizing all agricultural exports sales in state hands and channeling the earnings toward industry. The IAPI has long been seen as the single most disastrous piece of Peronist economic policy. See Schvarzer, *La industria que supimos conseguir*, 196–201.

35. República Argentina, *Diario de Sesiones de la Cámara de Diputados de 1946*, vol. 5, 264–65. Zuleta viewed Miranda as his most dangerous opponent. Interview of Enrique Zuleta Alvarez by author, Mendoza, 2 October 1997.

36. República Argentina, *Diario de Sesiones de la Cámara de Senadores de 1946*, vol. 4, 961. Ramella counted "only three" architects in San Juan, among them surely his fellow Catholic Action member Alfredo Quiroga Flores. There are no letters from architects in Ramella's correspondence.

37. República Argentina, *Diario de Sesiones de la Cámara de Diputados de 1946*, vol. 5,

263. Tejada should have known better, having favorably reviewed Pastor's book several months earlier. "Reconstrucción de San Juan: Piedra de toque del escenario nacional," *El Laborista*, 27 March 1946.

38. República Argentina, *Diario de Sesiones de la Cámara de Diputados de 1946*, vol. 1, 728–37. "Autonomía y reconstrucción," *Tribuna*, 18 May 1946; "Los enemigos de la reconstrucción," *La Reforma*, 10 August 1946.

39. "Ley-convenio," *Tribuna*, 2 July 1946.

40. "Dos proyectos en contraste," *Tribuna*, 9 August 1946.

41. "El tercer proyecto," *Tribuna*, 10 August 1946. After it passed the Senate, Arévalo Cabezas dropped his own bill and supported it in the House.

42. "El anhelo sanjuanino," *Tribuna*, 25 August 1946; "El apoyo de la nación," *Tribuna*, 15 August 1946.

43. Quotes from "El diputado Tejada habla de los proyectos sobre la reconstrucción," *Tribuna*, 17 September 1946; "Un sobreimpuesto imposible," *Tribuna*, 18 September 1946. Reconstruction job noted in "De los corrillos," *La Reforma*, 6 September 1946.

44. Indeed, the opposition made a point of supporting the bill on grounds of national unity. República Argentina, *Diario de Sesiones de la Cámara de Diputados de 1946*, vol. 5, 3479. The final law was more generous than any prior bill, because the four hundred million pesos in funds did not require repayment, and individual mortgages were in addition to this amount.

45. His resignation had been rumored for weeks. "Renunciaría el gobernador de San Juan: La Reconstrucción," *La Razón*, 31 August 1946.

46. As early as July, local wags had been speculating about the vice-governor's ambitions. "De los corrillos," *La Reforma*, 11 July 1946.

47. "Con armas limpias," *La Reforma*, 3 February 1946. For an excellent overview of the unionization of journalists and the transformation of the press under Perón, see Cane, *The Fourth Enemy*.

48. The exact sequence of events would be publicized nine years later, when the paper was returned to the conservatives by an equally questionable court ruling. "Aconsejo el fiscal del estado la derogacion de la medida que despojara al Partido Demócrata," *Tribuna*, 4 February 1956.

49. "De los corrillos," *La Reforma*, 29 January 1947.

50. "Del campo proletario," *La Reforma*, 23 November 1946.

51. "La crisis ministerial," *La Reforma*, 29 November 1946; "Se fijaron los salarios para obreros de la construcción," *La Reforma*, 17 December 1946.

52. "El Consejo de la Reconstrucción de San Juan actúa ya," *La Nación*, 16 January 1947. Across the nation, newspapers critical of Perón portrayed the limited progress in San Juan as a dark precedent for the republic: "La reconstrucción de San Juan," *La Capital* (Rosario), 16 January 1947; "A tres años de distancia," *La Voz del Interior*, 15 January 1947.

53. Prior to the earthquake, the province had originally planned to build four two-hundred-unit barrios, but only two were completed. At the end of his term as

interventor, Sosa Molina had begun action on a third, which was now finished and named for him.

54. See, for example, Ramella's discussion of how strongly he defended property rights in his rulings as judge after the earthquake. Ramella, *Autobiografía*, 33.

55. Jorge Loureiro, "La conveniencia de implantar el catastro en la ciudad de San Juan" in de Lorenzi, Ermete, ed. *Contribución a los estudios sísmicos en la República Argentina,* 110–120.

56. "Los tasadores sanjuaninos de Reconstrucción en contra de San Juan," *La Acción*, 26 April 1947. See also "De los corrillos," *La Reforma*, 17 April 1947.

57. "Apresuramiento injustificado," *Mercurio*, 21 December 1946; "Del dicho al hecho," *Mercurio*, 23 November 1946.

58. "El nuevo Consejo de Reconstrucción," *Mercurio*, 5 October 1946.

59. "En una reunión tratáronse problemas relacionados con la reconstrucción de la Capital," *La Prensa*, 18 December 1946. The name this time was the Union of Entities in Favor of Reconstruction.

60. "Sobre el problema sanjuanino se dió una declaración," *La Acción*, 13 January 1947; "A tres años de distancia," *La Voz del Interior*, 15 January 1947.

61. "Interés privado, política y Reconstrucción de San Juan," *La Nueva Ciudad*, 14 December 1946.

62. "San Juan a los tres años del terremoto," *La Palabra*, 18 January 1947.

63. "Con una clamorosa ovación popular fueron recibidos," *La Reforma*, 12 February 1947. While Camus celebrated, the other four legislators introduced a bill to intervene the province, but it was never voted on. República Argentina, *Diario de Sesiones de la Cámara de Diputados de 1946*, vol. 10, 378.

Chapter 11: "The Pacification of Spirits"

1. "Notas y comentarios," *La Reforma*, 10 May 1948.

2. Partido Peronista de San Juan, *Primer congreso de divulgación de las Veinte Verdades del Justicialismo Peronista*, 1. This publication also included a long explanation by Godoy's son, now an elected official, of the "Peronist truth" that all nepotism and "every political gang is anti-popular and therefore anti-Peronist."

3. His grandfather, Ruperto Godoy de la Rosa, was a minister under Sarmiento, a signatory of the 1853 Constitution, and an interim governor. His father, Ruperto Godoy del Carril, was governor. Two other relatives, Enrique Godoy and Manuel Godoy, also served as governors.

4. His wife was from a Conservative clan: her father was Honorio Basualdo and her uncle Oscar Correa Arce was vice-governor under Maurín. The Progressive Democrats held no offices outside of Santa Fe. In the 1931 presidential elections, with the Radical Party banned, the national opposition put up a joint Socialist-Progressive Democrat ticket, which lost badly, and the local opposition ran Godoy for the vice-governorship, with similar results.

5. Juan Carlos Bataller, "Los gobernadores en la intimidad: Anecdotas de la politica sanjuanina," *El Nuevo Diario*, 23 June 2001.

6. Interview of Joaquín and Vicenta Márquez by author, San Juan, 1 July 2001; interview of Fausto Ortiz by author, San Juan, 14 November 1997.

7. "Sábado ingles," *Mercurio*, 14 September 1946.

8. The new owners were Ruperto H. Godoy, Elias Amado, Juan Melis, Rinaldo Viviani, Carlos Guimaraes, Jose Flores, Jose Segaib, Hiracio Stabile, and Ricardo Roberto Fernandez. All held prominent positions: Amado and Viviani would later be governors of San Juan, and Melis of La Rioja.

9. República Argentina, *Diario de Sesiones de la Cámara de Diputados de 1948*, vol. 3, 192. On this process, see Cane, *The Fourth Enemy*.

10. "Dos definiciones concretas," *La Reforma*, 16 June 1948.

11. Moscow did not suit Cantoni, but it was agreeable to Leopoldo Bravo, the man widely reputed to be his illegitimate son, who stayed behind and eventually became Perón's ambassador. "Más de 25.000 voces sanjuaninas aclamaron al Dr. Cantoni," *La Reforma*, 10 March 1948. Aldo Cantoni, who remained opposed to Perón, died in 1948, and Elio died in 1951.

12. "La marcha sobre San Juan," *La Reforma*, 14 January 1948.

13. Cristóbal Carvajal Moreno to Pablo Ramella, San Juan, 22 November 1949, Pablo Ramella Papers.

14. There were three bonds: the national Reconstruction bonds authorized in 1946 and two provincial bond issues discussed below. Both Reconstruction and the province engaged in extensive creative accounting, funding current expenses by raiding pension and insurance trust funds.

15. Victoria, *Un plan de gobierno*, 6.

16. "Sobre el dique de embalse incluido en el Plan Quinquenal habló ayer el diputado Pedroza," *La Acción*, 15 January 1947.

17. Mó, *Cosas de San Juan*, 1: 49. There were two laws: law 1009, passed on 11 October 1946, authorized sealing the canals; law 1071, passed on 27 June 1947, authorized finishing the north canal. Both debt issues were refinanced in 1949.

18. Mó, *Vitivinicultura*, 176.

19. Joaquín Basanta López, "Los comunistas y la reconstrucción de San Juan," *Orientación*, 9 April 1947.

20. For a sense of the loans received and the state of the leading wineries, see Girbal de Blacha, *Mitos, paradojas y realidades en la Argentina peronista (1946–1955)*, 158–59.

21. "Diversas actividades industriales analizo en un discurso el Ing. D. Francisco Bustelo," *Tribuna*, 5 September 1955.

22. For the 1951 reelection of Perón, for example, the party raised nearly half a million pesos from 68 sources, including 20,000 from Santiago Graffigna, 10,000 from Del Bono, and 6,000 from Juan Maurín's wife. Carlos Guimaraes, "Liquidaciones de las comisiones de hacienda del Partido Peronista para sufragar gastos en las elecciones del 11 de noviembre de 1951," AHASJ, Gobierno, c.55, d.4, f.210–1

23. Interview of Hugo Montes Romaní by author, San Juan, 9 July 2001.

24. "Experiencia inútil," *Mercurio*, 17 August 1946; "Desesperanza," *Mercurio*, 7 September 1946.

25. "El Consejo de Reconstrucción dispuso importantes medidas," *La Reforma*, 29 August 1946.
26. "El Poder Ejecutivo remitió a la Cámara la iniciativa del C. de Reconstrucción," *La Acción*, 7 August 1947.
27. Outside the four avenues, the street plan was only suggested, and thus drawn in dotted lines.
28. "El Poder Ejecutivo remitió a la Cámara la iniciativa del C. de Reconstrucción," *La Acción*, 7 August 1947. A late 1947 Reconstruction report argued that parks would have required excessive water and maintenance. "Reconstrucción de San Juan publicó una reseña de su labor," *La Acción*, 19 December 1947.
29. "No se ha hecho nada," *Los Principios* (Córdoba), 5 April 1947.
30. "Renunció el Presidente de Reconstrucción," *La Reforma*, 3 June 1947.
31. "Las actividades comerciales e industriales," *La Prensa*, 27 January 1944.
32. "Darían $10.000 a cada propietario afectado en S. Juan," *Crítica*, 10 June 1947.
33. "De los corrillos," *La Reforma*, 24 June 1947; "El agravio que faltaba," *Tribuna Demócrata*, 16 July 1947.
34. "Sindicato Obrero de Reconstrucción," *La Reforma*, 14 May 1947.
35. The Communists had organized the national unions for construction workers in the 1930s and were very effective local organizers starting in 1945. Breaking the San Juan union was part of the larger effort to undermine the Communist-led national union, which was eventually replaced by the Peronist Unión Obrera de la Construcción. Independent-minded laboristas and Communists in the construction union were the most common topic in the relatively small number of available San Juan reports to the Interior Ministry. See, for example, Gobernador Ruperto Godoy al Ministro del Interior Borlenghi, San Juan, 25 October 1947, AGN-Intermedio, MI, SCyR, 67/1077 or Sección Orden Social y Político de la Policia de San Juan, Memorandum, 6 December 1948, AGN-Intermedio, MI, SCyR, 77/1310. Camus, for his part, "could not stand labor leaders," recalled his grandson (a union organizer).
36. "Del Sindicato O de la Reconstrucción de la Asoc. de O y Emp del Estado," *La Reforma*, 22 June 1947; "La eficiencia del obrero sanjuanino," *La Reforma*, 23 June 1947; "Consejo de Reconstrucción de San Juan: Se decretaron numerosas cesantías," *La Reforma*, 8 July 1947.
37. "Darían $10.000 a cada propietario afectado en S. Juan," *Crítica*, 10 June 1947.
38. Zapata Ramírez later claimed that on taking office, "the most serious among the evils to be suppressed were the political gangs" among workers; "Reconstrucción de San Juan publicó una reseña de su labor," *La Acción*, 19 December 1947. In a report to Perón, he emphasized that Reconstruction "had employed an elevated quantity of workers" in minor tasks, which "denied them to the activities of private initiative and local industry." Gerónimo Adán Zapata Ramírez, Memorandum para su excelencia el Señor Presidente de la Nación Juan Domingo Perón, San Juan, 10 April 1949, AGN-Intermedio, MI, SCyR, 89/70451.
39. "Los técnicos foráneos, principales responsables del fracaso de la reconstrucción," *La Reforma*, 11 August 1947. Even the Conservatives thought this was going too far,

and recognized San Juan did not have enough technical experts. "Una expresión de deseos inopurtuna," *La Acción*, 7 August 1947.

40. "Notas y comentarios," *La Reforma*, 22 July 1947; "Hay que tener fé en el Gral. Perón," *La Reforma*, 19 June 1947. There were daily editorials along these lines.

41. Juan Zavalla, "Se avecina un nuevo aniversario," *La Reforma*, 16 December 1947.

42. "Las necesidades de la clase media," *La Reforma*, 12 July 1947.

43. "El enfoque del nuevo planeamiento," *La Reforma*, 7 August 1947; "La suerte del famoso planeamiento," *La Reforma*, 18 July 1947.

44. "El planeamiento definitivo de la Reconstrucción de San Juan," *La Reforma*, 9 August 1947. Since 1944, Conservatives had insisted that all the government needed to do was to establish street widths and setbacks and then let owners build as they wished.

45. In the Guido and Carrasco plan, the north-south avenues and the monumental axis between Plaza 25 de Mayo and Plaza Aberastain bisected existing blocks. The main monumental axis, however, ran to the *east* of Plaza 25 de Mayo. In the Mendióroz team plan, a new avenue extended the three blocks between the seat of the Executive and the Legislature.

46. Sarmiento had opposed the Avenida de Mayo because it ratified and celebrated the "traditional city." Gorelik, *La grilla y el parque*, 85.

47. "Una institución opina acerca de los problemas de la reconstrucción," *La Nación*, 28 May 1948.

48. "Interesa a todo el país el plan regulador de San Juan," *Los Andes*, 26 June 1949.

49. "1947," San Juan: Leyes y Decretos, Pastor Papers.

50. José M. F. Pastor, "San Juan," *Revista de Arquitectura* 29, no. 277 (January 1944): 4.

51. José M. F. Pastor, "El problema de la tierra y el planeamiento," *Revista de Arquitectura* 30, no. 299 (November 1945): 463.

52. The association was "intervened" in the same sense as a province: with some legal pretext, the government asserted the right to audit the books and appoint new authorities. Both the CAI and the industrialists association (UIA) were intervened.

53. On this project, see Ballent, *Las huellas de la política*, 438–69, 565.

54. Eduardo Sacriste, "Carta al Director General de la Reconstrucción de San Juan, Ingeniero Enrique Zuleta," *Revista de Arquitectura* 32, no. 313 (January 1947): xix.

55. Eduardo Sacriste, "Carta a Federico de Achával," *Revista de Arquitectura* 32, no. 315 (March 1947): 113–14.

56. See entry for 23 September 1946 in *Libro de Actas de la Comisión Directiva de la Sociedad Central de Arquitectos, 24 julio 1944–18 noviembre 1946*, vol. 12, 350.

57. "La Sociedad Central de Arquitectos renovó su Comisión Directiva," *Revista de Arquitectura* 32, no. 319 (July 1947): 275.

58. "Sesión de Comisión Directiva del 13 de octubre," *Revista de Arquitectura* 32, no. 322 (October1947): s/n; "Acta de la Asamblea Extraordinaria General de la SCA del 9 de junio de 1948," *Revista de Arquitectura* 34, no. 339 (March 1949): lxvii, lxix, lxxi.

59. It is worth emphasizing that all evidence indicates the impulse for this action came from within, not from the government.

60. José M. F. Pastor, "El Plan Regulador de San Juan: Legislación en que se apoya," *Revista de Arquitectura* 35, no. 355 (July 1950): 211.

61. See his summary report in José M. F. Pastor, "La Reconstrucción de San Juan," *Revista de Arquitectura*, 34, no. 236 (May 1949): 100–118.

62. "Interesa a todo el país el plan regulador de San Juan," *Los Andes*, 26 June 1949.

63. "El Consejo de Recontrucción adoptó una importante resolución," *La Reforma*, 30 March 1948.

64. From 1948 to 1950, *Revista de Arquitectura* was full of articles and updates. For his strongest statement of San Juan as national landmark, see José M. F. Pastor, "Housing and Town Planning in Argentina," *News Sheet of the International Federation for Housing and Town Planning*, February 1955.

65. Oficina de Control del Estado, "Consejo de Reconstrucción de San Juan: Su funcionamiento y el estado de las obras que tiene a su cargo," March 1949, Pastor Papers.

66. "Edificios públicos de San Juan," *Revista de Arquitectura* 35, no. 354 (June 1950): 159.

67. José M. F. Pastor, "La Reconstrucción de San Juan y los profesionales particulares al servicio del estado," *Revista de Arquitectura* 35, no. 353 (May 1950): 145.

68. Ibid.,152.

69. Quoted in ibid., 146.

70. Interview of Hugo Montes Romaní by author, San Juan, 9 July 2001.

71. Gerónimo Adan Zapata Ramírez to Senator Pablo Ramella, San Juan, 28 October 1949, Ramella Papers. He wrote Ramella asking for help gaining more funds: at the time of the letter, he was paying subsidies to papers in San Juan, Mendoza, Tucumán, and Buenos Aires.

72. The comptroller report came out in March, and the press campaign began immediately: "Solicitóse que sea investigada la actuación del Consejo de Reconstrucción," *La Prensa*, 4 March 1949; "La Reconstrucción de la vida económica y social de San Juan asume, día a día, proporciones de singular importancia," *El Líder*, 8 March 1949.

73. "Es gigantesca la tarea de la reconstrucción," *El Líder*, 12 August 1949; "Ardua ha sido la tarea, pero el 'Problema de San Juan' ha dejado de ser tal, merced a la preocupación oficial," *El Líder*, 16 August 1949; "San Juan será la más moderna y racional de nuestras ciudades," *Clarín*, 30 August 1949; "La Reconstrucción de San Juan, obra maestra del Ministerio del Interior, demuestra la voluntad de la Nueva Argentina," *La Libertad*, 16 April 1949; "Parece que fué ayer . . . pero el tiempo no ha pasado en vano para San Juan, que vive el milagro de su recuperación," *El Líder*, 12 August 1949.

74. "El saldo positivo de una catástrofe," *Crítica*, 26 August 1949; "El potencial hidroeléctrico de San Juan crece," *Clarín*, 27 August 1949.

75. "San Juan será la más moderna y racional de nuestras ciudades," *Clarín*, 30 August 1949.

76. "El Consejo de Reconstrucción adquirió en Chile 500.000 toneladas de cemento portland," *La Prensa*, 27 December 1949.

77. Interview of Hugo Montes Romaní by author, San Juan, 9 July 2001. One of

the most prominent examples is where a major avenue bends to curve around the home of Horacio Videla, the historian and secretary of the Del Bono Commission.

78. "Para hablar de San Juan, dejar a los sanjuaninos," *Democracia*, 10 June 1948. The deputy elected in 1946, Jabel Arévalo Cabeza, had died; he was replaced by José Conte-Grand, former chief of staff to Sosa Molina and close advisor to Alvarado.

79. "Emoción de patria y nacionalidad, vibrando calidamente en el espacio sanjuanino," *Diario de Cuyo*, 11 April 1949; "El discurso del Presidente estimula mas aún la acción del gobierno en la provincia," *Diario de Cuyo*, 11 April 1949.

80. "Entregáronse las casas de la 'Villa María Eva Perón' en una ceremonia ayer," *Los Andes*, 15 January 1950. Perón was a colonel in 1944 but he was promoted to general before reaching the presidency.

81. In local usage, a peon is an unskilled worker, such as those employed in construction, canal work, or viticulture. "Fue proclamada la fórmula del peronismo anteayer en Trinidad," *Tribuna*, 20 January 1950.

82. "No hay peor sordo que el que no quiere oír," *La Reforma*, 23 April 1948.

83. Ministerio de Reconstrucción, Dirección de Viviendas, "Nómina de adjudicatarios de barrios," 1949, AHASJ, Obras Públicas, c. 4, d. 18.

84. "A seis años del terremoto hay todavia oligarcas que se aferran a las viviendas que el estado les proporcionó al principio," *Diario de Cuyo*, 31 March 1950.

85. República Argentina, *Diario de Sesiones de la Cámara de Diputados de 1948*, vol. 3, 2041.

86. For suggestive thoughts on this, see two unpublished papers by Fabiana González: Fabiana González and Rosa del Valle Ferrer, "La identidad barrial: El Barrio Martín Miguel de Guemes" (San Juan, 2003), and Fabiana González and Dora Moreno, "El campeonato de los barrios como una manifestación popular" (San Juan, 2002).

87. "Un hogar para cada familia, aspiracion de Godoy," *Diario de Cuyo*, 24 May 1950; "Todos los que son honestos acudieron a mi llamado, dijo en su elocuente mensaje el Gobernador Godoy," *Diario de Cuyo*, 27 May 1950.

88. Gobierno de San Juan, *Porque el pueblo de San Juan quiere la reelección de Perón*, 1–10, 13.

89. Electoral results from "Últimas cifras de San Juan," *La Nación*, 8 March 1958.

90. "Otro remezón se sintió en San Juan," *La Nación*, 15 June 1952.

91. Ibid.

92. "Adoptáronse diversas medidas en San Juan," *La Nación*, 14 June 1952; "1073 viviendas de emergencia se han provisto a damnificados del sismo," *Tribuna*, 17 July 1952.

93. "San Juan está aún intranquila," *La Nación*, 13 June 1952.

94. Pablo de la Leña, "Terrible Ensenanza," *Tribuna*, 13 June 1952.

95. "Siempre la reconstrucción," *Tribuna*, 12 June 1952.

96. "No volvemos a la normalidad," *Tribuna*, 18 June 1952.

97. "Construir mucho en poco tiempo," *Tribuna*, 18 July 1952.

98. "Conceptos sobre una concepción urbanística moderna en San Juan," *Tribuna*, 30 July 1952.

99. "El Instituto Provincial de la Vivienda crearíase en San Juan," *Tribuna*, 22 June 1952.

100. For an excellent exploration of this dynamic in other provinces, see Mackinnon, *Los años formativos*.

101. "¡Queremos a Perón!," *Diario de Cuyo*, 1 September 1955.

Chapter 12: The "Bulldozer Kid" and the Rebuilt City, 1955–1962

1. "Nueva etapa de la reedificación de San Juan debe comenzar ahora," *Los Andes*, 15 January 1956.

2. "Habló al pueblo de San Juan el General Aramburu," *Los Andes*, 7 January 1956.

3. On the break with the Church, see Caimari, *Perón y la Iglesia católica*, 249–324. On anti-Peronist crowds, especially Catholics, see Robben, *Political Violence and Trauma in Argentina*, 17–27.

4. The term was coined by regime supporters but continued to be used, with deliberate irony, by opponents and later scholars.

5. For an insightful overview of the Liberating Revolution focused on the military alliance with civilian parties, see Spinelli, *Los vencedores vencidos*.

6. "Disolución del Partido Peronista," *Tribuna*, 2 December 1955.

7. Newspapers took to referring to him as, for instance, "the fugitive ex-dictator."

8. On de-Peronization under Aramburu, see Spinelli, *Los vencedores vencidos*, 63–92; James, *Resistance and Integration*, 43–60.

9. This ferocity easily got out of hand. One government functionary was trashing all the official artwork he could find at city hall when another pointed out that the bearded man whose portrait he was about to destroy was in fact his own uncle, the first mayor of the city, who "died long before he could have become a Peronist." "Galeria de libertos," *Diario de Cuyo*, 29 September 1955.

10. "Nueva nomenclatura tienen los barrios y escuelas provinciales," *Diario de Cuyo*, 1 October 1955; "Dióse nuevos nombres a varias obras hidraulicas de San Juan," *Tribuna*, 8 October 1955; "Suprímense denominaciones," *Tribuna*, 1 November 1955. When the government named a *second* barrio after the city's founder, annoyed residents petitioned to be called simply "Villa América." Unión de Vecinos to Interventor Juan Bautista Picca, 22 November 1955, AHASJ, Gobierno, c. 58, d. 19.

11. See the documentation in AHASJ, Gobierno 2, c. 23, d. 9, especially the letter from Florencio Quiroga Marco. The legal justification for ransacking the Godoy mausoleum was that the decree establishing it praised Godoy for following the doctrine of Perón—and since any mention of this doctrine was now illegal, the decree was invalid and the mausoleum illegitimate. Godoy's body was returned to the Provincial Pantheon in 1964, by the Bloquistas.

12. "Entre estudiantes secundarios de San Juan hubo agitación," *Los Andes*, 4 October 1955; "Elevó ayer su renuncia el rector del Colegio Nacional de San Juan," *Tribuna*, 6 October 1955.

13. These were the two largest emergency barrios. The paper noted that the protestor's

family had prospered under Peronist rule and switched sides at the last moment. "Galeria de libertos," *Diario de Cuyo*, 17 October 1955.

14. "La revolución no es para los patrones," *Diario de Cuyo*, 22 September 1955; Jose Nieto Rodriguez, "Los obreros nada deben temer," *Tribuna*, 27 September 1955.

15. "Por la situación de los obreros rurales aboga la Federacion de Vinateros," *Diario de Cuyo*, 25 July 1956.

16. "A procedimientos se refirio el interventor en San Juan," *Los Andes*, 31 July 1956.

17. Hilda Morales Tello et al. a Manuel Hermida, Ministro de Gobierno, San Juan, 7 February 1957, AHASJ, Gobierno 2, c.14bis, d. 19.

18. "Movimiento político: Partido Socialista," *Tribuna*, 30 November 1955.

19. "Un plan terrorista con propositos de sabotaje, desbarató la policia," *Tribuna*, 22 January 1956; "Un hecho insólito," *Tribuna*, 4 February 1956. On the "Peronist resistance," see James, *Resistance and Integration*, 44–100.

20. See, for example, the article on Aramburu's visit to San Juan: "La ciudadania democrática de la provincia se apresta para tributarle cordial bienvenida," *Tribuna*, 6 January 1956.

21. "La Intervencion Federal creo la Junta Consultiva Provincial," *Tribuna*, 23 December 1955.

22. On the various failed attempts to found neo-Peronist parties, see Rein, *In the Shadow of Perón*.

23. For the six weeks before the switch, the paper ran an acerbic daily series on Peronist defectors called "Galeria de libertos." "*Diario de Cuyo* en una nueva etapa periodistica," *Diario de Cuyo*, 30 October 1955.

24. This was a year of intense ritual activity, because patron saint celebrations had taken on a clear political meaning and twelve of the nineteen patron saint days in San Juan fell between October and January. See coverage in *Tribuna* on 17 October, 20 November, 27 November, and 11 December 1955. On celebrations, see Mariela Escobar, "La lectura de las fiestas patronales como práctica social," in Mosert, ed., *Periodismo y sociedad sanjuanina*, 221.

25. "La resolución jurídica que devuelva *Tribuna* a sus legitimos poseedores," *Tribuna*, 4 February 1956. The judge in the case was the brother of the prosecutor, underscoring the clannish spirit of those allied with the military.

26. "Movimiento politico," *Tribuna*, 1 October 1955.

27. CNV, *Plan de emergencia*, 178.

28. No exact sale list is available, but newspaper evidence indicates most were empty lots downtown. See Banco de San Juan, *Series estadísticas de San Juan 1962*, 74.

29. CNV, *Plan de emergencia*, 177.

30. "El Consejo de Reconstrucción," *Tribuna*, 26 November 1955.

31. " . . . en las aguas del Jordan," *Tribuna*, 12 January 1956.

32. The dissident engineers now in charge included former CAI president Luis Migone at the National Housing Commission; former CAI president Vaquer at the Directorate of Nationalized Industries; Dante Ardigó at the nationalized railroads (and

then CAI president); and Pedro Mediondo, a career MOP engineer fired by Pistarini, as interventor of the CAI, dean of engineering at the University of Buenos Aires, and finally minister of public works. Álvaro Alsogaray, a younger but fiercely anti-Peronist engineer, would become minister of the economy. As a later scholar observed, "engineers as a professional group" first gained political "significance" when Perón was overthrown. José Luis de Imaz, *Los que mandan (Those Who Rule)*, 31.

33. "Se intervino al Consejo de Reconstrucción," *Tribuna*, 19 November 1955.

34. "Asumió su cargo ayer el nuevo intendente municipal de la capital, Ing. Remberto Baca," *Tribuna*, 22 February 1956.

35. Costantini, "Política relativa a la reconstrucción," 13 May 1957, AHASJ, Gobierno, c. 58bis, d.1, f. 2.

36. Ibid., f. 10, 12.

37. Ibid., f. 2.

38. Ibid., f. 6.

39. "Importantes edificios en San Juan deben ser puestos en linea," *Los Andes*, 26 January 1957; Juan Carlos Bataller, "El lado humano del poder: Anecdotas de la politica sanjuanina I," *El Nuevo Diario*, 12 May 2001.

40. Costantini, "Política relativa a la reconstrucción," f. 6–10.

41. Aramburu claimed to be spending even more, but official reports do not back him up. "Fue calurosamente recibido en San Juan el jefe de estado," *La Nación*, 14 June 1957.

42. Even the local press urged a broader approach: "Urbanizar tambien más allá de las avenidas," *Tribuna*, 8 June 1957.

43. Banco de San Juan, *Series estadísticas 1958*, 69. On the other hand, fewer buildings were completed in 1957 than in any year since 1946.

44. Vaquer, *Historia de la ingeneria en la Argentina*, 267. Its only rival was Mendoza, a cement producer which also adopted a concrete-only building code in 1944.

45. "Nuevos aspectos, necesidades y esperanzas en la reconstrucción de la ciudad de San Juan," *La Prensa*, 19 February 1956.

46. The definitive account of these killings is Walsh, *Operación masacre*. The summary executions were the moment when some anti-Peronist parties first broke with the regime, as shown in Spinelli, *Los vencedores vencidos*.

47. "Reunión de los periodistas con el interventor," *Tribuna*, 11 December 1955.

48. J. Amaro Silva, Presidente de la Comisión Investigadora, to Interventor Gen. Bartolomé Carreras, San Juan, 2 April 1956, AHASJ, Gobierno, c. 55, d. 4, f. 7–59; Bernardo Seinhart, 28 March 1956, "Observaciones referentes a la construcción y administración de las obras del Barrio Ferroviario ejecutado por el ex-Ministerio de Reconstrucción de San Juan," AHASJ, Gobierno, c. 55, d. 4, f. 197–205.

49. J. Amaro Silva, Presidente de la Comisión Investigadora, to Contraalmirante (ret) Leonardo McLean, Presidente de la Comisión Nacional de Investigaciones, San Juan, 2 January 1956, AHASJ, Gobierno, c. 55, d. 3, f. 14–18. On earlier accusations against Grano Cortinez, see *El otro terremoto*. On his positions, "Visitaron al Gen-

eral Carreras empleados de la D de Rentas," *Tribuna*, 11 May 1957, and "Nuevas autoridades del Club Social de San Juan," *Tribuna*, 4 May 1957.

50. The national summary of investigations mentioned only a few sanjuanino legislators: República Argentina, Comisión Nacional de Investigaciones, *Libro negro de la Segunda Tiranía*.

51. "Renuncio el interventor federal en la provincia, General Marino B. Carreras," *Tribuna*, 7 May 1957.

52. "Buenos dias," *Tribuna*, 8 May 1957.

53. The acerbic Luis Bates, whose fervent anti-Peronism had drained much of the grace from his daily sonnets on politics, managed a wonderful piece on Carreras: "Falta de costumbre," *Tribuna*, 9 May 1957.

54. The press praised Costantini and Carreras extensively: "La intervención Carreras," *Tribuna*, 16 May 1957; "El gobierno del General Carreras superó factores de estancamiento," *Los Andes*, 27 May 1957.

55. "Fue calurosamente recibido en San Juan el jefe de estado," *La Nación*, 14 June 1957.

56. "Visita a San Juan el Contraalmirante Rojas," *La Nación*, 15 January 1958.

57. July 1957 results: 22 percent Bloquistas (UCRB), 20 percent promilitary Radicals (UCRP), 20 percent blank (Peronists), 13 percent antimilitary Radicals (UCRI), 7 percent neo-Peronists (Trabajadores), 6 percent Conservatives, 12 percent other. February 1958 results: 39 percent antimilitary Radicals (UCRI), 24 percent promilitary Radicals (UCRP), 15 percent Bloquistas (UCRB Traditional), 4 percent dissident Bloquistas (UCRB Convention), and 18 percent other. "Últimas cifras de San Juan," *La Nación*, 8 March 1958.

58. See his praise for military guardians of "democracy" at the height of forced disappearances: Costantini, ed. *Evocaciones*, 6.

59. "La economia de San Juan sigue en su larga espera," *Tribuna*, 7 December 1955.

60. "El movimiento de oposición al traslado de la Escuela de Arquitectura tiene mas adhesiones," *Tribuna*, 12 December 1955.

61. "Temas de arquitectura tratan delegaciones reunidas en San Juan," *Los Andes*, 16 February 1956.

62. Indeed, the specific failures they complained about were the work of technical chief Manuel Aramburo and his allies.

63. "Algo con respecto a la reconstrucción de San Juan," *Tribuna*, 16 February 1956.

64. Organización de Estados Americanos, Programa Interamericano, *Planificación simulada del desarrollo social integrado de la provincia de San Juan*, 178.

65. Julio Aguirre Ruiz, "El terremoto de San Juan, República Argentina, del 15 de emero de 1944 y su influencia en la conciencia sísmica nacional," *Revista geofísica* 5, no. 12 (1976): 135–44.

66. Gago and Picón, *La agroindustria vitivinícola*, 55. The number of individual vineyards increased as well, from just over five thousand to nearly ten thousand.

67. Banco de San Juan, *Series estadísticas de la provincia de San Juan 1962*, 22–24, 49.

68. On the larger dynamics of development after 1955, see Brennan, "Prolegomenon to Neoliberalism."

69. "El progreso urbano de Caucete, en San Juan, es muy lento," *Los Andes*, 27 November 1956.

70. Organización de Estados Americanos, *Planificación simulada*, 178.

71. Instituto de Investigación de la Vivienda, *Tipos predominantes de vivienda rural en la República Argentina*, 65–66.

72. Hardoy, *Las ciudades en América Latina*, 232.

73. Ackerman, "A Spatial Strategy of Development for Cuyo, Argentina," 9, 87, 91.

74. "Anoche dejo de existir el Dr. Federico Cantoni," *Diario de Cuyo*, 23 July 1956.

75. On conservative parties in the interior, see Gibson, *Class and Conservative Parties*.

76. Videla, *Historia de San Juan*, 300.

77. See, for example, de la Torre, *San Juan: Voz de la tierra y del hombre*.

78. Barud, *San Juan en su literatura*, 10.

79. Josefa Jorba, "Palabras preliminares," in Jorba, ed., *Cuarto Centenario de San Juan*, 22.

80. Bataller, "La memoria clausurada," in Bataller, ed., *Y aquí nos quedamos*, 5.

Final Reckonings

1. Verbitsky, *Villa Miseria también es América*, 86–87.

2. As we saw in the introduction, the interior has an outsize electoral weight, which was unchanged in the new Peronist constitution of 1949. Indeed, by at long last making several federal territories into autonomous provinces, the Peronist administration further strengthened the electoral power of the least-populated areas of the country.

3. Eduardo Sacriste, "El paisaje, el hombre, y la arquitectura," *Revista de Arquitectura* 44, no. 378 (December 1960):11.

4. CINVA, *Asismicidad en viviendas economicas*.

5. See *Ernesto Vautier: Un arquitecto con compromiso social*, and Vautier and Fals Borda, *La vereda de Chamimbal*.

6. The most successful of Pastor's many plans was probably for a beach municipality along the Atlantic coast, where he proved himself a skillful shaper of landscape and a much more astute cultivator of local alliances than in San Juan. Naturally, he then turned this into an opportunity to publish a how-to book: Pastor and Bonilla, *Desarollo del municipio*. See also Bruno and Mazza, *Construcción de paisajes*.

7. The two leading figures of the movement were Eduardo Ellis and Claudio Caveri, but the later works of Sacriste himself were also important.

8. See especially the chapter "Desarrollo y utopia" in Liernur, *La arquitectura en la Argentina del siglo XX*, 295–358.

9. After 1980, the wine industry began a long and painful shrinking and restructuring, but even this change only underscored how central wine had remained for nearly four decades after the earthquake.

10. "Los que no creían empiezan a creer," *Diario de Cuyo*, 6 June 2007.

BIBLIOGRAPHY

Archives and Collections Consulted

BUENOS AIRES, ARGENTINA

Archivo de la Subsecretaría de Prensa, Presidencia de la Nación
Archivo General de la Nación, Archivo Intermedio
Fermín Bereterbide Papers, privately held
Biblioteca del Centro Argentino de Ingenieros
Biblioteca del Congreso
Biblioteca de la Facultad de Arquitectura, Diseño y Urbanismo,
    Universidad de Buenos Aires
Biblioteca del Instituto Argentino del Cemento Portland
Biblioteca Nacional
Biblioteca de la Sociedad Central de Arquitectos
Biblioteca Técnica de Obras Públicas, Ministerio de Economía
Biblioteca Tornquist, Banco Central de la República Argentina
Héctor Morixe Papers, Instituto de Arte Americano, Facultad de Arquitectura,
    Diseño y Urbanismo,
    Universidad de Buenos Aires
Ernesto Vautier Papers, privately held

MENDOZA, ARGENTINA

Biblioteca San Martín
Pablo Ramella Papers, privately held
Enrique Zuleta Papers, privately held

SAN JUAN, ARGENTINA

Archivo Histórico y Administrativo de San Juan
Archivo de la Legislatura de San Juan

Biblioteca del Arquidiocesis de San Juan
Biblioteca de la Facultad de Arquitectura y Diseño, Universidad Nacional de San Juan
Biblioteca de la Facultad de Humanidades, Universidad Nacional de San Juan
Biblioteca Franklin
Biblioteca del Instituto Nacional de Prevención Sísmica
Biblioteca de la Universidad Católica de Cuyo
Ramón Tejada Papers, privately held

UNITED KINGDOM
Public Record Office

UNITED STATES
Jorge Ferrari Hardoy Papers, Francis Loeb Library, Graduate School of Design, Harvard University
José M. F. Pastor Papers, Berkeley, California, in author's possession
National Archives, Silver Springs, Maryland
Library of Congress, Washington, DC

Interviews

BY AUTHOR
Honoria del Carmen Alé, San Juan, 10 July 2001
Magdalena Arancibia, San Juan, 15 July 2001
Alicia Autard de Serman, San Juan, 13 July 2001
Vitelmo Bertero, Richmond, Calif., 28 June 2004
Eloy Camus (nieto), San Juan, 21 October 1997
Rosa Collado, San Juan, 7 July 2002
Adolfo Dorfman, Durham, N.C., 18 April 2000
Daniel Laciar, San Juan, 14 October 1997
Cruz Lidia Lazzo, San Juan, 11 July 2001
Rafael Díaz López, San Juan, 13 July 2001
Joaquín and Vicenta Márquez, San Juan, 1 July 2001
Leopoldo Mazuelos, San Juan, 14 July 2001
Hugo Montes Romaní, San Juan, 9 July 2001
Fausto Ortiz, San Juan, 14 November 1997 and 14 July 2001
Fernando Pastor, New Haven, Conn., 27 February 1998
Pedro Roger Quiroga Marinero, San Juan, 9 July 2002
Susana Ramella de Jefferies, Mendoza, 1 October 1997
Carmen Renard, Buenos Aires, 20 November 1997
Maria Luisa Soria, San Juan, 16 July 2001
Segundo Vilas, San Juan, 17 July 2001
Enrique Zuleta Alvarez, Mendoza, 2 October 1997

BY OTHERS

Aldo Hermes Cantoni, interviewer Aldo Gaete, San Juan, 1 August 2002
Tulio del Bono (padre), interviewer Aldo Gaete, San Juan, 14 July 2002
Hilario Zalba and Eduardo Sacriste, interviewer Alfredo Rezzoagli, Buenos Aires,
  1985

Serial Publications

NEWSPAPERS

  SAN JUAN: *La Acción, El Censor, Diario de Cuyo, La Reforma, Tribuna, El Zonda*

  BUENOS AIRES: *Crítica, La Hora, La Nación, Noticias Gráficas, La Prensa, El
  Pueblo, La Vanguardia*

  OTHER: *Los Andes (Mendoza), Ercilla (Santiago, Chile), Libertad (Mendoza), La
  Voz del Interior (Córdoba)*

BULLETINS, JOURNALS, AND ANNUAL REPORTS

  GOVERNMENT PUBLICATIONS: *Boletín del Consejo de Reconstrucción, Boletín
  del Ministerio de Obras Públicas, Boletín de Obras Sanitarias de la Nación, Boletín de
  Yacimientos Petrolíferos de la Nación, Crónica Mensual de la Secretaría de Trabajo y
  Previsión, Diario de Sesiones de la Cámara de Senadores de la Nación, Diario de Ses-
  iones de la Cámara de Diputados de la Nación, Informe y Cuenta de Inversión del
  Ministerio de Hacienda, Memoria del Ministerio de Obras Públicas, Memoria de
  Obras Sanitarias de la Nación*

  OTHER: *Boletín Oficial de la Arquidiócesis de San Juan de Cuyo, La Ingenería,
  Martín Fierro, Nuestra Arquitectura, Revista de Arquitectura, Revista CACYA, Revista Cuyo, Revista del Museo de Historia Natural de Mendoza, Revista Sarmiento*

Selected Published Works (Books, Documents, Articles)

Aboy, Rosa. " 'The Right to a Home': Public Housing in Post WWII Buenos Aires."
  Journal of Urban History 33, no. 3 (2007): 493–518.
———. *Viviendas para el pueblo: Espacio urbano y sociabilidad en el barrio Los Perales:
  1946–1955.* Buenos Aires: Fondo de Cultura Económica, 2005.
Ackerman, William. "A Spatial Strategy of Development for Cuyo, Argentina." Ph.D.
  diss., Ohio State University, 1972.
Acuña, Domingo Mauricio. *El terremoto de San Juan en 1944 y sus huérfanos.* Buenos
  Aires: Editorial Dunken, 2004.
Aguirre Ruiz, Julio. "El terremoto de San Juan, República Argentina, del 15 de emero
  de 1944 y su influencia en la conciencia sísmica nacional." *Revista Geofísica* 5,
  no. 12 (1976): 135–44.
Albala-Bertrand, J. M. *Political Economy of Large Natural Disasters, with Special
  Reference to Developing Countries.* Oxford: Clarendon Press, 1993.

Al Doctor Horacio Gerardo Videla: Homenaje de la Universidad Católica de Cuyo. San Juan: Fondo Editorial de la Universidad Católica de Cuyo, 2001.

Alexander, Robert. *The ABC Presidents.* Westport, Conn.: Greenwood, 1992.

Allub, Leopoldo. *Desarollo de ecosistemas áridos.* San Juan: Universidad Nacional de San Juan, 1993.

Alvarado, Facundo. "The Rich in Argentina over the Twentieth Century: From the Conservative Republic to the Peronist Experience and Beyond, 1932–2004." Working Paper N. 2007–02. Paris: Ecole d'Economie de Paris, 2007.

Amaral, Samuel, and Mariano Plotkin, eds. *Perón: Del exilio al poder.* Buenos Aires: Cántaro, 1993.

Anuario general de San Juan DUA. San Juan: DUA, 1943.

Anuario geográfico argentino 1941. Buenos Aires: Comité Nacional de Geografía, 1942.

Arias, Héctor, and Carmen Peñaloza de Varese. *Historia de San Juan.* Mendoza: Spadoni, 1966.

Auyero, Javier. *Poor People's Politics: Peronist Networks and the Legacy of Evita.* Durham, N.C.: Duke University Press, 2000.

Avila, Laura, and Alberto Gago. *Proceso y mecanismo de formación de las clases sociales y modos de producción: La provincia de San Juan a fines del siglo XIX y principios del XX.* Buenos Aires: CICSO, 1993.

Baer, James. "Buenos Aires: Housing Reform and the Decline of the Liberal State in Argentina." *Cities of Hope: People, Protests and Progress in Urbanizing Latin America, 1870–1930,* ed. James Baer and Ronn Pineo, 129–52. Boulder, Colo.: Westview, 1998.

Balán, Jorge. *La cuestión regional en la Argentina: Burguesías del interior y el mercado interno en el desarollo agroexportador.* Buenos Aires: CEDES, 1977.

Ballent, Anahí. *Las huellas de la política: Vivienda, ciudad, peronismo en Buenos Aires, 1943–1955.* Buenos Aires: Universidad Nacional de Quilmes, 2005.

Ballent, Anahí and Adrián Gorelik. "¿País urbano o país rural? La modernización rural y su crisis" in Cattaruzza, ed. *Crisis económica, avance del estado e incertidumbre política,* 143–200.

Banco de San Juan. *Series estadísticas de la provincia de San Juan.* San Juan: Banco de San Juan, 1958.

Banerjee, Tridib, and William Baer. *Beyond the Neighborhood Unit: Residential Environments and Public Policy.* New York: Plenum Press, 1984.

Barbosa, Adalberto Zelmar. *El federalismo bloquista: Bravo, o el pragmatismo político.* Buenos Aires: Sudamericana, 1988.

Barkun, Michael. *Disaster and the Millennium.* New Haven, Conn.: Yale University Press, 1974.

Barton, Allen. *Communities in Disaster.* Garden City, N.Y.: Doubleday, 1970.

Barud, Nemer. *San Juan en su literatura: Periodo 1944–1974.* San Juan: Universidad Nacional de San Juan, 1976.

Basualdo Miranda, Hugo, Rosa del Valle Ferrer, Graciela Yolanda Gómez, and Gladys Rosa Miranda. *El testimonio oral: Teoría y práctica: Hitos y procesos en la historia contemporánea de San Juan, 1944–1977.* San Juan: Universidad Nacional de San Juan, Facultad de Filosofía, Humanidades y Artes, 2000.

Bataller, Juan Carlos. *El día que San Juan desapareció.* San Juan: Editores del Oeste, 1995.

———, ed. *Y aquí nos quedamos.* San Juan: Editores del Oeste, 1993.

Belini, Claudio. "El Grupo Bunge y la política económica del primer peronismo, 1943–1952." *Latin American Research Review* 41, no. 1 (February 2006): 27–50.

Bereterbide, Fermín. "La Reconstrucción de San Juan." *Revista de Arquitectura* 30, no. 293 (June 1945): 184–96.

———. *La vivienda popular.* Buenos Aires: Stilcograf, 1959.

Bereterbide, Fermín, and Ernesto Vautier. *¿Qué es el urbanismo?* Buenos Aires: Honorable Consejo Deliberante, 1933.

Berjman, Sonia, ed. *Benito Javier Carrasco: Sus textos.* Buenos Aires: Facultad de Agronomía, Universidad de Buenos Aires, 1997.

Berrotarán, Patricia M., Aníbal Jáuregui, and Marcelo Rougier, eds. *Sueños de bienestar en la Nueva Argentina: Estado y políticas públicas durante el peronismo, 1946–1955.* Buenos Aires: Imago Mundi, 2004.

Bianchi, Susana. *Catolicismo y peronismo: Religión y política en la Argentina, 1943–1955.* Tandil: Instituto de Estudios Histórico Sociales "Prof. Juan Carlos Grosso," 2001.

Bianchi, Susana, and Norma Sanchis. *El Partido Peronista Feminino.* Buenos Aires: Centro Editor de América Latina, 1988.

Bodenbender, Guillermo. "El terremoto argentino del 27 de octubre de 1894." *Boletín de la Academia Nacional de Ciencias en Córdoba* 14 (1895): 293–331.

Bogni, Carlos Victor. *Terremoto del 44.* San Juan, 1993.

Boleda, Mario. *La estructura productiva sanjuanina y los sectores sociales.* Buenos Aires: CISCO, 1973.

Bowden, Martyn, et al. "Reestablishing Homes and Jobs: Cities." In Haas, Kates, and Bowden, eds., *Reconstruction Following Disaster*, 69–146.

Boyer, M. Christine. *Dreaming the Rational City: The Myth of American City Planning.* Cambridge: MIT Press, 1983.

Brennan, James P. "Industriales y 'Bolicheros': Business and the Peronist Populist Alliance, 1943–1976." In Brennan, ed., *Peronism and Argentina*, 79–124.

———, ed. *Peronism and Argentina.* Wilmington: SR Books, 1998.

———. "Prolegomenon to Neoliberalism: The Political Economy of Populist Argentina, 1943–1976." *Latin American Perspectives* 34, no. 3 (May 2007): 49–66.

Brennan, James P., and Ofelia Pianetto, eds. "Introduction." In Brennan and Pianetto, eds., *Region and Nation*, vii–xvii.

———. *Region and Nation: Politics and Society in Twentieth-Century Argentina.* New York: St. Martin's, 2000.

Bruno, Perla, and Carlos Mazza. *Construcción de paisajes: Transformaciones territoriales y planificación en la región marplatense, 1930–1965.* Mar del Plata: Universidad Nacional de Mar del Plata, 2002.

Buchrucker, Cristián. "Interpretations of Peronism: Old Frameworks and New Perspectives." In Brennan, ed., *Peronism and Argentina*, 3–28.

Bullock, Nicholas. "Ideals, Priorities and Harsh Realities: Reconstruction and the LCC, 1945–1951." *Planning Perspectives* 9, no. 1 (1994): 87–101.

Bustelo, Angel. *Vida de un combatiente de izquierda.* 2 vols. Buenos Aires: CEAL, 1992.

Butty, Enrique. *La ingeniería: enseñanza—profesión—función social.* Buenos Aires: Centro Estudiantes Ingeniería, 1932.

Cabrera de Roda, Susana, María Lliteras de Maratta, and Mirta Elena Caputo de Larrinaga. *San Juan, mío: La furia y la fuerza de esta tierra en recuerdos de vivencias del terremoto de 1944.* San Juan: n/p, 2002.

Caimari, Lila. *Apenas un delincuente: Crimen, castigo y cultura en la Argentina, 1880–1955.* Buenos Aires: Siglo Veintiuno, 2004.

——.*Perón y la Iglesia católica: Religión, estado y sociedad en la Argentina (1943–1955).* Buenos Aires: Ariel, 1995.

Cámara Argentina de la Construcción, *Las actividades de la Cámara Argentina de la Construcción en favor de la Industria de la Construcción en la República Argentina 1936–1947.* Buenos Aires: Cámara Argentina de la Construcción, 1948.

——. *40° Aniversario.* Buenos Aires: CAC, 1976.

Campione, Daniel. *Orígenes estatales del peronismo.* Buenos Aires: Miño y Dávila, 2007.

Cane, James. *The Fourth Enemy: Journalism and Power in the Making of Peronist Argentina.* University Park: Pennsylvania State University Press, forthcoming.

Cañellas, Marcelo. "El terremoto de San Juan: Problemas de orden económico y su solución." *Revista de Ciencias Económicas* 22, 2nd Series, no. 276 (July 1944): 609–31.

Cantoni, Rosalia. *Aldo Cantoni en mi recuerdo.* San Juan: Talleres Salesianos, 1974.

Capdevila, Arturo. *Tierra mia: Buenos Aires y las catorce provincias argentinas.* Buenos Aires: Espasa-Calpe, 1945 [1911].

Caruso, Marcelo. "El año que vivimos en peligro: izquierda, pedagogia y política." In Puiggrós, ed., *Discursos pedagógicos e imaginario social en el peronismo, 1945–1955,* 43–106.

Castano, Juan Carlos. *La verdadera dimensión del problema sísmico en la provincia de San Juan.* San Juan: INPRES, 1993.

Castellanos, Alfredo. *Anotaciones preliminares con motivo de una visita a la ciudad de San Juan a propósito del terremoto del 15 de enero de 1944.* Rosario: Universidad Nacional del Litoral, 1944.

Castellanos, Alfredo, and Pierina Pasotti. *Cuatro lecciones sobre terremotos.* Rosario: Asociación Cultural de Conferencias de Rosario, 1945.

Cattaruzza, Alejandro, ed. *Crisis económica, avance del estado e incertidumbre política: Nueva Historia Argentina,* vol. 7. Buenos Aires: Sudamericana, 2001.

Centro Argentino de Ingenieros, *Hacia el planeamiento integral de la industria de la construcción.* Buenos Aires: Centro Argentino de Ingenieros, 1943.

Centro de Documentación de Arquitectura Latinoamericana. *Alberto Prebisch: Una vanguardia con tradición*. Buenos Aires: Fundación CEDODAL, 1999.

Centro Interamericano de Vivienda y Planeamiento. *Asismicidad en viviendas economicas*. Bogota: Centro Interamericano de Vivienda y Planeamiento, 1959.

Cerisola, María J. Elsa. *La población de San Juan*. Buenos Aires: INDEC, 1977.

Chamosa, Oscar. *The Argentine Folklore Movement: Sugar Elites, Criollo Workers, and the Politics of Cultural Nationalism, 1900-1950*. Tucson: University of Arizona Press, 2010.

Chamosa, Oscar, and Matthew Karush, eds. *A New Cultural History of Peronism*. Durham, N.C.: Duke University Press, 2010.

Cipolletti, Emilio. *Ante los ojos de América*. Buenos Aires: Ediciones Justicia Social, 1947.

Ciria, Alberto. *Política y cultura popular: La Argentina Peronista, 1946–55*. Buenos Aires: Ediciones de la Flor, 1983.

Cirvini, Silvia A. "Arquitecturas de tierra: Prototipos sismoresistentes en la Mendoza posterremoto (1863–1884)." *DANA*, no. 27 (1989): 9–27.

——. *Nosotros los arquitectos: Campo disciplinar y profesión en la Argentina moderna*. Mendoza: Zeta, 2004.

Civita, César, ed. *Perón, el hombre del destino*. Buenos Aires: Abril, 1974.

Clancey, Gregory K. *Earthquake Nation: The Cultural Politics of Japanese Seismicity, 1868–1930*. Berkeley: University of California Press, 2006.

Coghlan, Eduardo A. *La condición de la vivienda en la Argentina a través del censo de 1947*. Buenos Aires: Industrias Gráficas, 1959.

Conte-Grand, Juan. *La ciudad en ruinas*. Mendoza: D'Accurzio, 1950.

Coraggio, José Luis, ed. *La cuestión regional en América Latina*. Quito: Ediciones Equidad, 1989.

Corporación de Arquitectos Católicos. *Un plan de vivienda popular*. Buenos Aires: Corporación de Arquitectos Católicos, 1940.

Cosse, Isabella. *Estigmas de nacimiento: Peronismo y orden familiar, 1946–1955*. Buenos Aires: Fondo de Cultura Económica, 2006.

Costantini, Alberto, ed. *Evocaciones de precursores de la ingenería*. Buenos Aires: CAI, 1980.

Creskoff, Jacob. *Dynamics of Earthquake Resistant Structures*. New York: McGraw-Hill, 1934.

Cuny, Frederick. *Disasters and Development*. New York: Oxford University Press, 1983.

da Cruz, José. *Disaster and Society: The 1985 Mexican Earthquakes*. Lund, Sweden: Lund University Press, 1993.

Damonte Taborda, Raúl. *Ayer fué San Perón: 12 años de humillación argentina*. Buenos Aires: Ediciones Gure, 1955.

Daus, Federico. "Población de los oasis ricos y de los oasis pobres de la región árida Argentina." *Humanidades (UNLP)* 29 (1944): 53–63.

Davis, Ian. *Shelter after Disaster*. Oxford: Oxford Polytechnic, 1978.

De Fina, Armando, Félix Giannetto, and Luis Sabella. *Difusión geográfica de cultivos índices en la provincia de San Juan y sus causas*. Buenos Aires: Instituto Nacional de Tecnología Agropecuaria, 1962.

de la Torre, Antonio. *San Juan: Voz de la tierra y del hombre*. Buenos Aires: Guillermo Kraft, 1952.

del Carril, Bonifacio. *Buenos Aires frente al país*. Buenos Aires: Editorial Huarpes, 1944.

——. *Memorias dispersas: El Coronel Perón*. Buenos Aires: Emecé, 1984.

del Carril Quiroga, Pablo. *Una asociación de bien público: "Amigos Sanjuaninos," su historia y acción 1943–1964*. San Juan: Editorial Sanjuanina, 1966.

Della Paolera, Gerardo, and Alan Taylor, eds. *A New Economic History of Argentina*. New York: Cambridge University Press, 2003.

de Lorenzi, Ermete, ed. *Contribución a los estudios sísmicos en la República Argentina: El caso de San Juan*. Rosario: Universidad Nacional del Litoral, 1944.

Deutsch, Sandra McGee. *Las Derechas: The Extreme Right in Argentina, Brazil, and Chile, 1890–1939*. Stanford, Calif.: Stanford University Press, 1999.

Dickie, John. "The Smell of Disaster: Scenes of Social Collapse in the Aftermath of the Messina-Reggio Calabria Earthquake, 1908." In Dickie, Foot, and Snowden, eds., *Disastro!*, 237–55.

Dickie, John, John Foot, and Frank M. Snowden, eds. *Disastro! Disasters in Italy since 1860: Culture, Politics, Society*. New York: Palgrave, 2002.

Diefendorf, Jeffry. *In the Wake of War: The Reconstruction of German Cities after World War II*. New York: Oxford University Press, 1993.

——, ed. *Rebuilding Europe's Bombed Cities*. New York: St Martin's Press, 1990.

Di Leo, Washington. *Acá cerca y hace tiempo*. San Juan: Editorial Fundación Universidad Nacional de San Juan, 1996.

Dorn, Glenn J. *Peronistas and New Dealers: U.S.-Argentine Rivalry and the Western Hemisphere (1946–1950)*. New Orleans: University Press of the South, 2005.

Doyon, Louise. "La formación del sindicalismo peronista." In Torre, ed., *Los años peronistas*, 357-404.

Drury, A. Cooper, and Richard Stuart Olson. "Disasters and Political Unrest: An Empirical Investigation." *Journal of Contingencies and Crisis Management* 6, no. 3 (1998): 153–61.

Dujovne Ortiz, Alicia. *Eva Perón: A Biography*. Translated by Shawn Fields. New York: St. Martin's Press, 1996.

Echagüe, Juan Pablo. *San Juan: Leyenda - Intimidad - Tragedia*. Buenos Aires: Emecé, 1944.

Elena, Eduardo. *Consuming Dignity: Citizenship and the Marketplace in Peronist Argentina*. Pittsburgh: University of Pittsburgh Press, forthcoming.

El otro terremoto de San Juan. Montevideo: Editorial América, 1944.

Erikson, Kai. *Everything in Its Path: The Destruction of Community in the Buffalo Creek Flood*. New York: Simon and Schuster, 1976.

Ernesto Vautier: Un arquitecto con compromiso social. Buenos Aires: CEDODAL, 2005.

Escolar, Diego. *Los dones étnicos de la nación: Identidades huarpe y modos de producción de soberanía en Argentina*. Buenos Aires: Prometeo, 2007.

Fairfield, John. "Alienation of Social Control: The Chicago Sociologists and the Origins of Urban Planning." *Planning Perspectives* 7, no. 3 (1992): 418–34.

Ferrá de Bartol, Margarita, ed. *Historia contemporánea de San Juan a traves del documento oral 1944–1977. Tomo 1*. San Juan: Universidad Nacional de San Juan, Secretaría de Ciencia y Tecnica, 1998.

——, ed. *Historia contemporánea de San Juan a traves del documento oral 1944–1977. Tomo 2*. San Juan: Universidad Nacional de San Juan, Secretaría de Ciencia y Tecnica, 1999.

Fishman, Robert. *Urban Utopias in the Twentieth Century: Ebenezer Howard, Frank Lloyd Wright, and Le Corbusier*. New York: 1977.

Fleming, William J. *Region vs. Nation: Cuyo in the Crosscurrents of Argentine National Development, 1861–1914*. Tempe: Arizona State University, Center of Latin American Studies, 1986.

Freeman, John R. *Earthquake Damage and Earthquake Insurance*. New York: McGraw-Hill, 1932.

Gaggero, Horacio, and Alicia Garro. *Del trabajo a la casa: La política de vivienda del gobierno peronista, 1946–1955*. Buenos Aires: Editorial Biblos, 1996.

Gago, Alberto, and Mario Picón. *La agroindustria vitivinicola en el area andina argentina*. Córdoba: Universidad de Córdoba, 1998.

Galasso, Norberto. *Jauretche y su época*. Buenos Aires: Peña Lillo, 1985.

——. *Vida de Scalabrini Ortiz*. Buenos Aires: Ediciones del Mar Dulce, 1970.

Garcés, Luis. *La escuela cantonista: Educación, sociedad y estado en el San Juan de los años 20*. San Juan: Editorial Fundación Universidad Nacional de San Juan, 1992.

García, Rodolfo. "Present Situation of Earthquake Engineering in Argentina." *Bulletin of the International Institute of Seismology and Earthquake Engineering* 28 (1994): 13–31.

García Acosta, Virginia, ed. *Historia y desastres en América Latina*. 2 vols. Mexico City: La RED/CIESAS, 1996.

García Sebastiani, Marcela. *Los antiperonistas en la Argentina peronista: Radicales y socialistas en la política argentina entre 1943 y 1951*. Buenos Aires: Prometeo Libros, 2005.

Gené, Marcela. *Un mundo feliz: Imágenes de los trabajadores en el primer peronismo, 1946–1955*. Buenos Aires: Fondo de Cultura Económica, 2005.

Gerchunoff, Pablo, and Damián Antúnez. "De la bonanza peronista a la crisis de desarrollo." In Torre, ed., *Los años peronistas*, 121–206.

Germani, Gino. *Política y sociedad en una época de transición, de la sociedad tradicional a la sociedad de masas*. Buenos Aires: Paidós, 1962.

Germani, Gino, Octávio Ianni, and Torcuato S. Di Tella. *Populismo y contradicciones de clase en latinoamérica*. Mexico City: Era, 1973.

Gibson, Edward. *Class and Conservative Parties: Argentina in Comparative Perspective*. Baltimore: Johns Hopkins University Press, 1996.

——, ed. *Federalism and Democracy in Latin America*. Baltimore: Johns Hopkins University Press, 2004.

Gil, Octavio. *Tradiciones sanjuaninas*. Buenos Aires: Peuser, 1948.

Girbal de Blacha, Noemí. *Mitos, paradojas y realidades en la Argentina peronista (1946–1955): Una interpretación histórica de sus decisiones político-económicas*. Bernal: Universidad Nacional de Quilmes, 2003.

Gironés de Sánchez, Isabel. "La ciudad perdida: Memoria urbana de San Juan pre-terremoto, 1930–44." M.A. thesis, Universidad Nacional de San Juan, 2001.

Giuliani, Francisco. "Presentación del proyecto de normas de estabilidad antisísmica de Mendoza."*Actas de las Primeras Jornadas Argentinas de Ingenieria Antisísmica*, vol. 2, 511–606. Buenos Aires: Coni, 1962.

Gobierno de San Juan. *Estatuto del peón*. San Juan: Gobierno de la Provincia, 1944.

——. *Porque el pueblo de San Juan quiere la reelección de Perón*. San Juan: Gobierno de la Provincia, 1951.

Gold, John. *The Experience of Modernism: Modern Architects and the Future City, 1928–1953*. New York: E. and F. N. Spon, 1997.

Goldar, Ernesto. *El peronismo en la literatura argentina*. Buenos Aires: Freeland, 1971.

Gómez de Terán, Leopoldo. *Conferencia sobre el terremoto del 27 de octubre de 1894*. San Juan: Tipografía y Librería Sarmiento, 1895.

Gómez Lucero, Odin, ed. *San Juan: Libro de lectura*. San Juan: Talleres Gráficos del Estado, 1936.

Goñi, Uki. *Perón y los alemanes: La verdad sobre el espionaje nazi y los fugitivos del Reich*. Buenos Aires: Sudamericana, 1998.

——. *The Real Odessa: How Peron Brought the Nazi War Criminals to Argentina*. London: Granta Books, 2002.

González, Fabiana, and Rosa del Valle Ferrer. "La identidad Barrial : El Barrio Martín Miguel de Guemes." Unpublished conference paper, 2003.

González, Fabiana, Rosa del Valle Ferrer, and Dora Moreno. "El campeonato de los barrios como una manifestación popular." Unpublished conference paper, 2002.

González Crespo, Jorge. *El Coronel*. Buenos Aires: Ayer y Hoy Ediciones, 1998.

Goodrich, Diana Sorensen. *Facundo and the Construction of Argentine Culture*. Austin: University of Texas Press, 1996.

Gorelik, Adrián. "La arquitectura de YPF, 1934–1943: Notas para una interpretación de las relaciones entre estado, modernidad e identidad en la arquitectura argentina de los años 30." *Anales del Instituto de Arte Americano*, no. 27 (1987): 97–105.

——. *La grilla y el parque: Espacio público y cultura urbana en Buenos Aires, 1887–1936*. Bernal: Universidad Nacional de Quilmes, 1998.

Gray de Cerdan, Melly Amalia. "La ciudad de San Juan: Su influencia regional y su proyección en la red de ciudades de Cuyo." *Revista Geográfica (*Mexico*)*, no. 81 (1974): 47–79.

Guido, Angel, and Benito Carrasco. *Plan regulador de San Juan*. San Juan: Gobierno de San Juan, 1942.

Gutiérrez, Ramón, ed. *SCA: 100 años de compromiso con el país.* Buenos Aires: Sociedad Central de Arquitectos, 1990.

Gutiérrez, Ramón, and Fernando Alvarez. "La participación de Austral-Le Corbusier en el concurso de Mendoza." *DANA*, no. 37/38 (1995): 114–18.

Haas, J. Eugene, Robert Kates, and Martyn Bowden, eds. *Reconstruction Following Disaster.* Cambridge, Mass.: MIT Press, 1977.

Halperín Donghi, Tulio. "The Buenos Aires Landed Class and the Shape of Argentine Politics (1820–1930)." In Huber and Safford, eds., *Agrarian Structure and Political Power,* 39-66.

——. *La Argentina y la tormenta del mundo: Ideas e ideologías entre 1930 y 1945.* Buenos Aires: Siglo Veintiuno Argentina, 2003.

——. *Una nación para el desierto argentino.* Buenos Aires: Centro Editor de América Latina, 1982.

——. *La República Imposible.* Buenos Aires: Ariel, 2004.

——, ed. *Sarmiento: Author of a Nation.* Berkeley: University of California Press, 1994.

——. *Vida y muerte de la República Verdadera.* Buenos Aires: Ariel, 1999.

Hardoy, Jorge. *Las ciudades en América Latina: Seis ensayos sobre la urbanización contemporánea.* Buenos Aires: Paidós, 1972.

——."Theory and Practice of Urban Planning in Europe, 1850–1930: Its Transfer to Latin America." In Hardoy and Morse, eds., *Rethinking the Latin American City,* 20–49.

Hardoy, Jorge, and Richard Morse, eds. *Rethinking the Latin American City.* Baltimore: Johns Hopkins University Press, 1992.

Harrington, Horacio. *El sismo de San Juan del 15 de enero de 1944.* Buenos Aires: Corporación para la Promoción del Intercambio, 1944.

——. *Volcanes y terremotos.* Buenos Aires: Editorial Pleamar, 1944.

Hasegawa, Junichi. "Governments, Consultants and Expert Bodies in the Physical Reconstruction of the City of London in the 1940s." *Planning Perspectives* 14, no. 1 (1999): 121–44.

——. *Replanning the Blitzed City Centre: A Comparative Study of Bristol, Coventry and Southampton, 1941–1950.* Buckingham: Open University Press, 1992.

Hattingh, Alistair. "Cuyo and Goliath: The Province of San Juan and the Argentine Federal Government, 1930–1943." Ph.D. diss., University of California, Santa Barbara, 2003.

Healey, Mark Alan. "The Ruins of the New Argentina: Peronism, Architecture, and the Rebuilding of San Juan after the 1944 Earthquake." Ph.D. dissertation, Duke University, 2000.

Hewitt, Kenneth, ed. *Interpretations of Calamity from the Viewpoint of Human Ecology.* Boston: Allen and Unwin, 1983.

Holston, James. *Insurgent Citizenship: Disjunctions of Democracy and Modernity in Brazil.* Princeton, N.J.: Princeton University Press, 2008.

——. *The Modernist City: An Anthropological Critique of Brasilia*. Chicago: University of Chicago Press, 1989.

Hopkins, John. *La estructura económica y el desarollo industrial de la Argentina*. Buenos Aires: Corporación para la Promoción del Intercambio, 1944.

Horne, Alistair. *Small Earthquake in Chile: A Visit to Allende's South America*. London: Macmillan, 1972.

Horowitz, Joel. *Argentine Unions, the State, and the Rise of Perón, 1930–1945*. Berkeley: Institute of International Studies, 1990.

Horvath, Laszlo. *A Half Century of Peronism, 1943–1993: An International Bibliography*. Stanford, Calif.: Hoover Institution, Stanford University, 1993.

Huber, Evelyn, and Frank Safford, eds. *Agrarian Structure and Political Power: Landlord and Peasant in the Making of Latin America*. Pittsburgh: University of Pittsburgh Press, 1996.

Imaz, José Luis de. *Los que mandan (Those Who Rule)*. Translated by Carlos Astiz. Albany: State University of New York Press, 1970.

Instituto de Investigación de la Vivienda. *Tipos predominantes de vivienda rural en la República Argentina: Tipología según materiales de acuerdo al Censo Nacional de Vivienda de 1960*. Buenos Aires: Facultad de Arquitectura y Diseño Urbano, Universidad de Buenos Aires, 1965.

Intervención Federal en San Juan, *Informe elevado al Ministerio del Interior por el Interventor Interino, corresponde al Gobierno del Inteventor Federal, General de Brigada Don Humberto Sosa Molina*, 81.

James, Daniel. *Doña María's Story: Life History, Memory, and Political Identity*. Durham, N.C.: Duke University Press, 2000.

——. "October 17th and 18th, 1945: Mass Protest, Peronism and the Argentine Working Class." *Journal of Social History*, no. 21 (1988): 441–61.

——. *Resistance and Integration: Peronism and the Argentine Working Class, 1955–1976*. New York: Cambridge University Press, 1988.

Jorba, Josefa, ed. *Cuarto Centenario de San Juan*. Buenos Aires: Editorial Cactus, 1962.

Josephs, Ray. *Argentine Diary: The Inside Story of the Coming of Fascism*. New York: Random House, 1944.

Juncos, Ruben. "El terremoto de San Juan del día 15 de enero de 1944: Importancia de la construcción antisísmica." In de Lorenzi, ed., *Contribución a los estudios sísmicos*, 57–81.

Karush, Matthew B. *Workers or Citizens: Democracy and Identity in Rosario, Argentina (1912–1930)*. Albuquerque: University of New Mexico Press, 2002.

Kates, Robert. "Major Insights: A Summary and Recommendations." In Haas, Kates, and Bowden, eds., *Reconstruction Following Disaster*, 261–94.

Katzenstein, Ernesto. "Argentine Architecture of the Thirties." *Journal of the Decorative and Propaganda Arts* 18 (1992): 54–75.

Laclau, Ernesto. *On Populist Reason*. New York: Verso, 2005.

Lacoste, Pablo. *Los "gansos" de Mendoza*. Buenos Aires: Centro Editor de América Latina, 1991.

——. "El paso de la cordillera de los Andes por El Portillo argentino: Aportes para el studio de la integración entre Argentina y Chile." *Revista Universum* 11 (1996): 101–22.

——, ed. *Populismo en San Juan y Mendoza.* Buenos Aires: Centro Editor de América Latina, 1994.

——. "The Rise and Secularization of Viticulture in Mendoza: The Godoy Family Contribution." *The Americas* 63, no. 3 (January 2007): 383–407.

——. *La Unión Cívica Radical en Mendoza y en la Argentina.* Mendoza: Ediciones Culturales de Mendoza, 1994.

——. *El vino del inmigrante.* Mendoza: Universidad del Congreso, 2003.

Lecuona, Diego. *Evolución de los planes de vivienda en la Argentina, 1890–1950.* Buenos Aires: Editorial Dunken, 2002.

Liernur, Jorge Francisco. *La arquitectura en la Argentina del siglo XX: La construcción de la modernidad.* Buenos Aires: Fondo Nacional de las Artes, 2001.

——. "El discreto encanto de nuestra arquitectura 1930/1960." *summa* 223 (March 1986): 60–79.

Liernur, Jorge Francisco, and Fernando Aliata, eds. *Diccionario histórico de arquitectura, habitat y urbanismo en la Argentina.* Buenos Aires: Clarín Arquitectura, 2004.

Liernur, Jorge Francisco, and Pablo Pschepiurca. *La red austral: Obras y proyectos de Le Corbusier y sus discípulos en la Argentina (1924–1965).* Bernal: Universidad Nacional de Quilmes, 2008.

Lint Sagarena, Roberto. "Building California's Past: Mission Revival Architecture and Regional Identity." *Journal of Urban History,* 28, no. 4 (2002): 429–44.

Llach, Juan J. "El Plan Pinedo de 1940, su significado histórico y los orígenes de la economía política del peronismo." *Desarollo Económico* 23, no. 92 (1984): 515–58.

Lomnitz, Cinna. *Fundamentals of Earthquake Prediction.* New York: John Wiley and Sons, 1994.

Loureiro, Jorge. "La conveniencia de implantar el catastro en la ciudad de San Juan" in de Lorenzi, Ermete, ed. *Contribución a los estudios sísmicos en la República Argentina,* 110–20.

Lugones, Leopoldo. *La grande Argentina.* Buenos Aires: Editorial Huemul, 1962 [1930].

Lugones, Leopoldo (hijo). *El presidente en San Juan.* Buenos Aires: Subsecretaría de Informaciones, 1944.

Luna, Felix. *Breve historia de los argentinos.* Buenos Aires: Planeta, 1994.

——. *Buenos Aires y el país.* Buenos Aires: Sudamericana, 1982.

——. *El 45.* Buenos Aires: Sudamericana, 1971.

——. *Perón y su tiempo.* Buenos Aires: Sudamericana, 1992 [1984–86].

Mackinnon, María Moira. *Los años formativos del Partido Peronista (1946–50).* Buenos Aires: Siglo Veintiuno, 2002.

Macor, Darío, and Eduardo Iglesias, eds. *El peronismo antes del peronismo: Memoria e historia en los orígenes del peronismo santafesino.* Santa Fe: Universidad Nacional de Litoral, 1997.

Macor, Darío, and César Tcach, eds. *La invención del peronismo en el interior del país.* Santa Fe: Universidad Nacional del Litoral, 2003.

Maisonnave, Emilio. "Previsiones Antisísmicas." In de Lorenzi, ed., *Contribución a los estudios sísmicos,* 89–98.

Mansilla, César. *Los partidos provinciales.* Buenos Aires: CEAL, 1983.

Maramaras, Emmanuel, and Anthony Sutcliffe. "Planning for Post-War London: The Three Independent Plans, 1942–3." *Planning Perspectives* 9, no. 4 (1994): 431–53.

Marianetti, Benito. *El racimo y su aventura: La cuestión vitivinícola.* Mendoza: Editorial Platina, 1965.

——. *Las luchas sociales en Mendoza.* Mendoza: Ediciones Cuyo, 1970.

——. *Mendoza, la bien plantada: Circunnavegación y reconocimiento de una provincia argentina.* Mendoza: Ediciones Silalba, 1972.

——. *Problemas de Cuyo.* Mendoza: n/p, 1948.

Marzo, Miguel. *La conquista del espacio territorial sanjuanino.* Mendoza: Universidad Nacional de Cuyo, 1968.

Maskrey, Andrew. *El manejo popular de los desastres: Estudios de vulnerabilidad y mitigación.* Lima: ITDG, 1989.

Massolo, María Laura. "Gracias Difunta Correa! Popular Religion in San Juan, Argentina." Ph.D. diss., University of California, Berkeley, 1995.

Maurín Navarro, Emilio. *Contribución al estudio de la historia de la vitivinicultura argentina: Producción, industria y comercio de San Juan, desde su fundación hasta principios del siglo XX.* San Juan: Editorial Sanjuanina, 1967.

Maurín Navarro, Juan. *Introducción a la hygiene social de Cuyo.* Buenos Aires: Comisión Nacional de Cultura, 1945.

McGee Deutsch, Sandra, and Ronald Dolkhart, eds. *The Argentine Right: Its History and Intellectual Origins, 1910 to the Present.* Wilmington: Scholarly Resources, 1993.

Meller, Helen. *Towns, Plans and Society in Modern Britain.* Cambridge: Cambridge University Press, 1997.

Mendióroz, Carlos, et al. "El planeamiento en la Reconstrucción de San Juan." *Revista de Arquitectura* 31, no. 310 (October 1946): 418–53.

Michelini, Pedro. *Anecdotario de Perón.* Buenos Aires: Corregidor, 1995.

Miguens, José, and Frederick Turner, eds. *Perón and the Reshaping of Argentina.* Pittsburgh: University of Pittsburgh Press, 1983.

Mó, Fernando. *Cosas de San Juan: Para descansar e informarse.* 3 vols. San Juan: s/n, 1989–94.

——. *Vitivinicultura. mitología, leyenda, historia: Problemas vitivinícolas argentinos.* Buenos Aires: Depalma, 1979.

Molina y Vedia, Juan, and Rolando Schere. *Fermín Bereterbide: La construcción de lo imposible.* Buenos Aires: Ediciones Colihue, 1997.

Mora y Araujo, Manuel, and Ignacio Llorente, eds. *El voto peronista: Ensayos de sociología electoral argentina.* Buenos Aires: Sudamericana, 1980.

Morey, Francisco. *Los temblores de la tierra: Mendoza sísmica.* Mendoza: D'Accurzio, 1938.

Mosert, Beatriz, ed. *Periodismo y sociedad sanjuanina: El humor en los periódicos sanjuaninos de la década del veinte.* San Juan: Editorial Fundación Universidad Nacional de San Juan, 1997.

——. *Periodismo y sociedad sanjuanina: El imaginario cultural sanjuanino desde el periódico local, 1930–1944.* San Juan: Editorial Fundación Universidad Nacional de San Juan, 2002.

Mugnos de Escudero, Margarita. *La maestrita de los yarcos.* Buenos Aires: s.p., 1957.

Mumford, Eric. *The CIAM Discourse on Urbanism, 1928–1960.* Cambridge: MIT Press, 2000.

Murmis, Miguel, and Juan Carlos Portantiero. *Estudios sobre los orígenes del peronismo.* 2 vols. Buenos Aires: Siglo Veintiuno, 1972.

Muro, Victor Gabriel, ed. *Ciudades provincianas de México: Historia, modernización y cambio cultural.* Zamora, Michoacán: El Colegio de Michoacán, 1993.

Musset, Alain. "Mudarse o desaparecer: Traslado de ciudades hispanoamericanas y desastres (siglos xvi-xviii)." In García Acosta, ed., *Historia y desastres en América Latina,* 41–70.

Newton, Ronald. *The "Nazi Menace" in Argentina, 1931–1947.* Stanford, Calif.: Stanford University Press, 1992.

Novick, Susana. *IAPI: Auge y decadencia.* Buenos Aires: Centro Editor de América Latina, 1986.

Ockman, Joan, ed. *Out of Ground Zero: Case Studies in Urban Reinvention.* New York: Prestel, 2002.

Oliver-Smith, Anthony. "Anthropological Research on Hazards and Disasters." *Annual Review of Anthropology,* no. 26 (1996): 303–28.

——. *The Martyred City: Death and Rebirth in the Andes.* Albuquerque: University of New Mexico Press, 1986.

——. "Post Disaster Housing Reconstruction and Social Inequality: A Challenge to Policy and Practice." *Disasters* 14, no. 1 (1990): 7–19.

Oliver-Smith, Anthony, and Roberta E. Goldman. "Planning Goals and Urban Realities: Post-Disaster Reconstruction in a Third World City." *City and Society* 2, no. 2 (1988): 105–26.

Oliver-Smith, Anthony, and Susanna Hoffman. *The Angry Earth: Disaster in Anthropological Perspective.* New York: Routledge, 1999.

Organización de Estados Americanos, Programa Interamericano. *Planificación simulada del desarrollo social integrado de la provincia de San Juan.* Buenos Aires: Imprenta del Congreso de la Nacion, 1967.

Page, Joseph. *Perón: A Biography.* New York: Norton, 1983.

Palacios, Alfredo. *Pueblos desamparados: Solución de los problemas de noroeste argentino.* Buenos Aires: Guillermo Kraft, 1944.

Panella, Claudio, and Oscar H. Aelo, eds. *El gobierno de Domingo A. Mercante en Buenos Aires, 1946–1952: Un caso de peronismo provincial.* La Plata: Asociación Amigos del Archivo Histórico de la Provincia de Buenos Aires, 2005.

Partido Peronista de San Juan. *Primer congreso de divulgación de las Veinte Verdades del Justicialismo Peronista.* San Juan: Ediciones del Buró de Difusión Partidaria, 1951.

Pastor, José M. F. *San Juan, Piedra de toque del planeamiento nacional.* Buenos Aires: Editorial Arte y Técnica, 1945.

——. *TVA: Planificación del valle del Tennessee.* Buenos Aires: Contempora, 1961.

——. *Urbanismo con planeamiento: Principios de una nueva técnica social.* Buenos Aires: Editorial Arte y Técnica, 1946.

Pastor, José M. F., and José Bonilla. *Desarollo del municipio: Cómo organiza su progreso un vecindario.* Buenos Aires: Instituto de Planeamiento Regional y Urbano, 1961.

Pavón Pereyra, Enrique. *Perón: Preparación de una vida para el mando.* Buenos Aires: Ediciones Espino, 1952.

Peattie, Lisa. *Planning: Rethinking Ciudad Guayana.* Ann Arbor: University of Michigan Press, 1987.

Pereira, Antonio. *Juan Perón: Crónica de cuatro décadas.* Buenos Aires: Corregidor, 1997.

Perón, Juan. *Obras completas.* 28 vols. Buenos Aires: Docencia/ Fundación Universidad a Distancia Hernandarias, 1997.

——. *Pensamiento político del General de Brigada Juan Perón : directivas del presidente de la nación.* Buenos Aires: Subsecretaría de Informaciones, 1946.

——. *El pueblo quiere saber de qué se trata.* Buenos Aires: Freeland, 1973 [1944].

——. *Queremos restaurar en esta tierra, nuestras instituciones básicas.* Buenos Aires: Secretaría de Trabajo y Previsión, 1944.

Perry, Clarence. *The Neighborhood Unit.* New York: Routledge, 1998 [1929].

Persello, Ana Virginia. *El Partido Radical: Gobierno y oposición, 1916–1943.* Buenos Aires: Siglo XXI Argentina, 2004.

Piñeiro, Elena. *La tradición nacionalista ante el peronismo: Itinerario de una esperanza a una desilusión.* Buenos Aires: A-Z Editora, 1997.

Plotkin, Mariano. "The Changing Perceptions of Peronism: A Review Essay." In Brennan, ed., *Peronism and Argentina,* 29-56.

——. *Mañana es San Perón.* Buenos Aires: Ariel, 1994.

Ponte, Jorge Ricardo. *La fragilidad de la memoria: Representaciones, prensa y poder de una ciudad latinoamericana en tiempos del modernismo: Mendoza, 1885–1910.* Mendoza: Ediciones Fundación CRICYT, 1999.

——. *Mendoza, aquella ciudad de barro: Historia de una ciudad andina desde el siglo xvi hasta nuestros días.* Mendoza: Municipalidad de la Ciudad de Mendoza, 1987.

Potash, Robert. *The Army and Politics in Argentina: From Perón to Frondizi, 1945–1962.* Vol. 2. Stanford, Calif.: Stanford University Press, 1980.

——. *The Army and Politics in Argentina: From Yrigoyen to Perón, 1928–1945.* Vol. 1. Stanford, Calif.: Stanford University Press, 1969.

——. *Perón y el GOU: Los documentos de una logia secreta.* Buenos Aires: Sudamericana, 1984.

Puiggrós, Adriana, ed. *Discursos pedagógicos e imaginario social en el peronismo, 1945–1955.* Buenos Aires: Galerna, 1995.

Puiggrós, Adriana, and Jorge Luis Bernetti. *Peronismo: Cultura política y educación.* Buenos Aires: Galerna, 1993.

Quarantelli, E. L. *Sheltering and Housing after Major Community Disasters: Case Studies and General Conclusions.* Newark: University of Delaware Press, 1982.

———, ed. *What Is a Disaster? Perspectives on the Question.* New York: Routledge, 1998.

Quevedo, Hugo Orlando. *El Partido Peronista en La Rioja, 1943–1959.* Córdoba: Lerner, 1991.

Quiroga Salcedo, Cesar Eduardo. *El terremoto de San Juan del 27 de octubre de 1894: Sus efectos en el contexto cultural de la provincia.* San Juan: Universidad Nacional de San Juan, 1987.

Rabinovitz, Bernardo. *Sucedió en la Argentina (1943–1956): Lo que no se dijo.* Buenos Aires: Gure, 1956.

Rafart, Gabriel, and Enrique Masés. *El peronismo desde los territorios a la nación: Su historia en Neuquén y Río Negro (1943–1958).* Neuquén: Editorial de la Universidad Nacional del Comahue, 2003.

Ramacciotti, Karina Inés, Adriana María Valobra, and Omar Acha, eds. *Generando el peronismo: Estudios de cultura, política y género, 1946–1955.* Buenos Aires: Proyecto Editorial, 2003.

Ramella, Pablo. *Anteproyecto de código impositivo para la provincia de San Juan.* San Juan: Uribe Yanzón, 1938.

———. *Autobiografía y selección de escritos jurídicos.* Buenos Aires: Imprenta del Congreso de la Nación, 1994.

———. *La estructura del estado.* Buenos Aires: s/p, 1946.

———. *La prepotencia y otros temas.* Buenos Aires: Editorial Difusión, 1943.

———. *Reformas a la constitución de San Juan.* San Juan: Uribe Yanzón, 1943.

Ramella de Jefferies, Susana T. *El radicalismo bloquista en San Juan (1916–1934).* San Juan: Gobierno de la Provincia, 1986.

Rapaport, Mario. *Gran Bretaña, Estados Unidos y las clases dirigentes argentinas, 1940–1945.* Buenos Aires: Editorial de Belgrano, 1986.

Real, Juan José. *Organizar y educar.* Buenos Aires: Anteo, 1946.

Rein, Mónica Esti. *Politics and Education in Argentina, 1946–1962.* New York: M. E. Sharpe, 1998.

Rein, Raanan. *In the Shadow of Perón: Juan Atilio Bramuglia and the Second Line of Argentina's Populist Movement.* Stanford, Calif.: Stanford University Press, 2007.

———. *Peronismo, populismo y política: Argentina, 1943–1955.* Buenos Aires: Editorial de Belgrano, 1998.

Rein, Raanan, and Rosalie Sitman, eds. *El primer peronismo: De regreso a los comienzos.* Buenos Aires: Lumiere, 2005.

Reini Rutini, Rodolfo. *400 años de vitivinicultura: La lucha de Cuyo contra el desierto y el centralismo.* Buenos Aires: Edición del Instituto de Publicaciones Navales, 1971.

República Argentina. *Mensaje del Excelentísimo Señor Presidente de la Nación General Edelmiro Farrell y memoria del primer año de labor: Primer aniversario del gobierno de la Revolución.* Buenos Aires: Imprenta Lopez, 1944.

———. *Mensaje del Excelentísimo Señor Presidente de la Nación General Edelmiro Farrell y memoria del segundo año de labor: Segundo aniversario del gobierno de la Revolución.* Buenos Aires: Imprenta Lopez, 1945.

———. *La Nación Argentina: Libre, Justa, Soberana.* Buenos Aires: Peuser, 1950.

República Argentina, Comisión Nacional de Investigaciones. *Documentación, autores y cómplices de la irregularidades cometidas durante la Segunta Tiranía.* Buenos Aires: Gobierno de la Nación, 1958.

———. *Libro negro de la Segunda Tiranía.* Buenos Aires: Gobierno de la Nación, 1958.

República Argentina, Comisión Nacional del Censo. *Tercer Censo Nacional, levantado el 1 de junio de 1914.* Buenos Aires: Talleres Gráficos de L. J. Rosso, 1916.

República Argentina, Comisión Nacional de Vivienda, Plan de emergencia: Informe elevado por la Comisión Nacional de Vivienda al Ministerio de Trabajo y Previsión. Buenos Aires: Ministerio de Trabajo y Previsión, 1956.

República Argentina, Dirección Nacional de Estadística y Censos. *Informe demográfico de la República Argentina, 1944–1954.* Buenos Aires: Ministerio de Hacienda, 1956.

República Argentina, Dirección Nacional del Servicio Estadístico. *IV Censo General de la Nación,* vols. 1–3. Buenos Aires: Ministerio de Asuntos Técnicos, 1948.

República Argentina, Instituto Nacional de Estadística y Censos. *IV Censo General De La Nación Año 1947, cuadros inéditos: Características económicas de la población.* Buenos Aires: INDEC, 1979.

República Argentina, Ministerio de Hacienda. *Cuarta Conferencia de Ministros de Hacienda.* Buenos Aires: Subsecretaría de Informaciones, 1950.

———. *Primera Conferencia de Ministros de Hacienda.* Buenos Aires: Subsecretaría de Informaciones, 1946.

———. *Segunda Conferencia de Ministros de Hacienda.* Buenos Aires: Subsecretaría de Informaciones, 1948.

———. *Tercera Conferencia de Ministros de Hacienda.* Buenos Aires: Subsecretaría de Informaciones, 1949.

República Argentina, Ministerio del Interior. *Las fuerzas armadas restituyen el imperio de la soberanía popular.* Buenos Aires: Ministerio del Interior, 1946.

———. *Intervención federal en las provincias.* Buenos Aires: Ministerio del Interior, 1933.

República Argentina, Ministerio de Obras Públicas. *Obra de emergencia en San Juan.* Buenos Aires: MOP, 1944.

República Argentina, Ministerio de Relaciones Exteriores y Culto. *Primer Congreso Argentino de Urbanismo.* Buenos Aires: Gobierno de la Nación, 1938.

———. *Primer Congreso Panamericano de la Vivienda Popular.* Buenos Aires: Gobierno de la Nación, 1940.

Richard Jorba, Rodolfo. *Poder, economia y espacio en Mendoza 1850–1900: Del comercio ganadero a la agroindustria vitivinicola.* Mendoza: Universidad Nacional de Cuyo. Facultad de Filosofia y Letras, 1998.

———, ed. *La región vitivinícola argentina: Tranformaciones del territorio, la economía y la sociedad, 1870–1914.* Bernal: Universidad Nacional de Quilmes, 2006.

Robben, Antonius C. G. M. *Political Violence and Trauma in Argentina: The Ethnography of Political Violence.* Philadelphia: University of Pennsylvania Press, 2005.

Rocchi, Fernando. *Chimneys in the Desert: Industrialization in Argentina during the Export Boom Years, 1870–1930.* Stanford, Calif.: Stanford University Press, 2006.

Rock, David. *Authoritarian Argentina: The Nationalist Movement, Its History and Its Impact.* Berkeley: University of California Press, 1993.

——. *Politics in Argentina, 1890–1930: The Rise and Fall of Radicalism.* Cambridge: Cambridge University Press, 1975.

——. *State Building and Political Movements in Argentina, 1860–1916.* Stanford, Calif.: Stanford University Press, 2002.

Rodriguez, Celso. "Cantonismo: A Regional Harbinger of Peronism in Argentina." *The Americas* 34, no. 2 (1977): 170–201.

——. *Lencinas y Cantoni: Populismo cuyano en tiempos de Yrigoyen.* Buenos Aires: Universidad de Belgrano, 1979.

Rodríguez, Jorge. "Memorias del horror," in Bataller, ed., *Y aquí nos quedamos,* 14–15.

Rodríguez, Nora Inés, ed. *Nueva historia de San Juan.* San Juan: Editorial Fundación Universidad de San Juan, 1997.

Rodriguez Lamas, Daniel. *Rawson / Ramírez / Farrell.* Buenos Aires: Centro Editor de América Latina, 1983.

Rodríguez Molas, Ricardo. *Historia de la tortura y el orden represivo en la Argentina.* Buenos Aires: EUDEBA, 1985.

Rodríguez y Olmos, Audino. *Pastoral Letter on the Reconstruction of Our Churches.* Buenos Aires: Nocena & Raño, 1950.

Rofman, Alejandro. "Teoría y práctica de la planificación regional en América Latina." In Coraggio, ed., *La cuestión regional en América Latina,* 340-380.

Rofman, Alejandro, and Luis Alberto Romero. *Sistema socioeconómico y estructura regional en la Argentina.* 3rd ed. Buenos Aires: Amorrortu, 1998.

Roitman de Schabelman, Dora. *San Juan: La ciudad y el oasis.* San Juan: Editorial Fundación Universidad Nacional de San Juan, 1995.

Ross, Peter. "Justicia social: Una evaluación de los logros del peronismo clásico." *Anuario IEHS* 8 (1993): 105–24.

Rouquié, Alain. *Poder militar y sociedad política en la Argentina.* Vol. 1. Buenos Aires: Emecé, 1981.

Rozario, Kevin. *The Culture of Calamity: Disaster and the Making of Modern America.* Chicago: University of Chicago Press, 2007.

Ruiz Jiménez, Laura. *La Argentina con porvenir: Los debates sobre la democracia y el modelo de desarrollo en los partidos y la prensa, 1926–1946.* Madrid: Biblioteca Nueva / Fundación José Ortega y Gasset, 2006.

Salvatore, Ricardo. "Labor Control and Discrimination: The Contratista System in Mendoza, Argentina, 1880–1920." *Agricultural History* 60, no. 3 (1986): 52–80.

Sarmiento, Domingo Faustino. *Facundo: Civilization and Barbarism.* Translated by Kathleen Ross. Berkeley: University of California Press, 2003.

Sawers, Larry. *The Other Argentina: The Interior and National Development.* Boulder, Colo.: Westview, 1996.

Scalabrini Ortiz, Raúl. *Los ferrocarriles deben ser del pueblo argentino (tierra sin nada, tierra de profetas)*. Buenos Aires: n/p, 1946.

Scenna, Miguel Angel. *F.O.R.J.A.: Una aventura argentina*. Buenos Aires: Editorial de Belgrano, 1983.

Schvarzer, Jorge. *La industria que supimos conseguir: Una historia político-social de la industria argentina*. Buenos Aires: Planeta, 1996.

Scobie, James R. *Secondary Cities of Argentina: The Social History of Corrientes, Salta, and Mendoza, 1850–1910*. Stanford, Calif.: Stanford University Press, 1988.

Scott, James. *Seeing Like a State: How Certain Schemes to Improve the Human Condition Have Failed*. New Haven, Conn.: Yale University Press, 1998.

Sedán, Thuky. *La Reforma: Historia de acontecimientos, hechos sociales, económicos, políticos, cotineidadaes de la vida de la provincia a través de su lectura*. San Juan: n/p, 2004.

Segura, Jorge. "Prólogo." In Jorba, ed., *Cuarto Centenario de San Juan*, 13-22.

Shanken, Andrew. *194X: Architecture, Planning, and Consumer Culture on the American Home Front*. Minneapolis: University of Minnesota Press, 2009.

Smith, Carl. *Urban Disorder and the Shape of Belief: The Great Chicago Fire, the Haymarket Bomb, and the Model Town of Pullman*. Chicago: University of Chicago Press, 1995.

Smith, Robert T. "Radicalism in the Province of San Juan: The Saga of Federico Cantoni." Ph.D. diss., University of California, Los Angeles, 1970.

Spektorowski, Alberto. *The Origins of Argentina's Revolution of the Right*. Notre Dame, Ind.: University of Notre Dame Press, 2003.

Spinelli, María Estela. *Los vencedores vencidos: El antiperonismo y la "Revolución Libertadora."* Buenos Aires: Editorial Biblos, 2005.

Steinberg, Ted. *Acts of God: The Unnatural History of Natural Disaster in America*. New York: Oxford University Press, 2000.

Supplee, Joan Ellen. "Provincial Elites and the Economic Transformation of Mendoza, Argentina, 1880–1914." Ph.D. diss., University of Texas, Austin, 1988.

Svampa, Maristella. *El dilema argentino: Civilización o barbarie: De Sarmiento al revisionismo peronista*. Buenos Aires: El Cielo por Asalto/Imago Mundi, 1994.

Taylor, Carl. *Rural Life in Argentina*. Baton Rouge: Louisiana State University Press, 1948.

Tcach, César. "Neoperonismo y resistencia obrera en la Córdoba libertadora, 1955–1958." *Desarrollo Económico* 35, no. 137 (1995): 63–82.

——. *Sabattinismo y peronismo: Partidos políticos en Córdoba, 1943–1955*. Buenos Aires: Sudamericana, 1991.

Tejada, Ramón. *La reconstrucción de San Juan*. Buenos Aires: Ministerio del Interior, 1946.

Tiratsoo, Nick, ed. *Urban Reconstruction in Britain and Japan, 1945–1955: Dreams, Plans and Realities*. Luton: University of Luton Press, 2002.

Toledo, Nora. *Impacto de las politicas urbanas en San Juan*. San Juan: Cuadernos de Ciencias Sociales, Universidad Nacional de San Juan, 1992.

Torre, Juan Carlos, ed. *Los años peronistas. Nueva Historia Argentina*, vol. 8. Buenos Aires: Sudamericana, 2002.

——, ed. *La formación del sindicalismo peronista*. Buenos Aires: Legasa, 1988.

——, ed. *El 17 de Octubre de 1945*. Buenos Aires: Espasa Calpe, 1995.

Torre, Juan Carlos, and Elisa Pastoriza. "La democratización del bienestar" in Torre, ed. *Los años peronistas*, 257–312.

——. *La vieja guardia sindical y Perón: Sobre los orígenes del peronismo*. Buenos Aires: Sudamericana, 1990.

Vale, Lawrence, and Thomas Campanella, eds. *The Resilient City: How Modern Cities Recover from Disaster*. New York: Oxford University Press, 2005.

Vaquer, Antonio. *Historia de la ingeneria en la Argentina*. Buenos Aires: Eudeba, 1968.

Varas, Arnaldo Ulises. *Crónica de mi San Juan*. San Juan: SADE San Juan, 1984.

Varas, Manuel Gilberto. *Terremoto en San Juan*. Buenos Aires: Luis Lasserre, 1945.

Vautier, Ernesto, and Orlando Fals Borda. *La vereda de Chamimbal: Estudio y acción en vivienda rural*. Bogotá: CINVA, 1958.

Verbitsky, Bernardo. *Villa Miseria también es América*. Buenos Aires: Sudamericana, 2003 [1957].

Victoria, Juan. *Un plan de gobierno para el desarrollo economico y el progreso cultural de San Juan*. San Juan: Unión Cívica Radical Intransigente, 1961.

Videla, Horacio. *El Banco de San Juan en sus veinticinco años de vida*. San Juan: Fondo Cultural del Banco de San Juan, 1968.

——. *Historia de San Juan*. Buenos Aires: Plus Ultra, 1984.

——. *Ocho conferencias y una más en el cuarto centenario de la fundación de San Juan*. San Juan: Fondo Cultural del Banco de San Juan, 1963.

——. *Retablo sanjuanino*. Buenos Aires: Peuser, 1956.

Vilas, Carlos María. *Between Earthquakes and Volcanoes: Markets, State, and Revolution in Central America*. Translated by Ted Kuster. New York: Monthly Review Press, 1995.

Villafane, Elbio. "Realities of Earthquake Engineering in Argentina." *Bulletin of the International Institute of Seismology and Earthquake Engineering* 26 (1992): 17–38.

Villalobos Dominguez, Cándido. *Bases y método para la apropriación social de la tierra*. Buenos Aires: Ruiz Hermanos, 1932.

Violich, Francis. *Cities of Latin America: Housing and Planning to the South*. New York: Reinhold, 1944.

Walker, Charles. *Shaky Colonialism: The 1746 Earthquake-Tsunami in Lima, Peru, and its Long Aftermath*. Durham, N.C.: Duke University Press, 2008.

Wallace, Anthony. *Human Behavior in Extreme Situations*. Washington: National Academy of Sciences, 1956.

Walsh, Rodolfo. *Operación Masacre*. Buenos Aires: Continental Service, 1964.

Walter, Richard. *Politics and Urban Growth in Buenos Aires, 1910–1942*. New York: Cambridge University Press, 1993.

Westrate, Nancy. "The Populist Prism and the End of an Era: Culture, Politics and Economics in San Juan and Mendoza, Argentina, 1890–1930." Ph.D. diss., Duke University, 1993.

White, Elizabeth B. *German Influence in the Argentine Army, 1900 to 1945*. New York: Garland Publishers, 1991.

Willis, Bailey. *La casa segura contra terremotos*. Stanford: Stanford University Press/Carnegie Institution, 1924.

Yujnovsky, Oscar. *Claves políticas del problema habitacional argentino, 1955–1981*. Buenos Aires: Grupo Editor Latinoamericano, 1984.

Zanatta, Loris. *Del estado liberal a la nación católica: Iglesia y ejército en los orígenes del peronismo, 1930–1943*. Buenos Aires: Universidad Nacional de Quilmes, 1996.

———. *Peron y el mito de la nación católica: Iglesia y ejercito en los origenes del peronismo: 1943–1946*. Buenos Aires: Sudamericana, 1999.

Zuleta, Enrique. *Resurgimiento económico del Norte y Noroeste de San Juan y zonas circunvecinas*. San Juan: Reconstrucción de San Juan, 1946.

INDEX

Page numbers for illustrative materials are indicated by the use of italics.

58; firms, 207; traditional Argentine, 120–21

construction materials: concrete, 120–23, 276, 284, 296; fibercement, 130, 163, 169–70; quincha, 34–35, 116–18. *See also* adobe construction

Conte-Grand, José, 135, 228–29

cooperative wineries, *104*, 245–46

Corpus Christi march protest, 268

Correa, Daniel Ramos, 284

Costa, Gonzalo, 55

Costantini, Alberto: achievements of, 274–76; "The Bulldozer Kid," 274–75; as engineer, 280; Investigating Commission and, 277–78; on Reconstruction Council, 274; statement by, against Hennekens, 185

coups: in 1930, 68, 91–92, 107; in 1934, 36, *45*, 46; in 1943, 21, 72, 76, 146; in 1955, 268–71

Crítica (Buenos Aires), 149

dams: hydroelectric, 244, 261; proposals for, 122; slow completion of, 297

Day of National Mourning, 67

defense minister, 342n3

Del Bono, Bartolomé: Del Bono Commission leadership of, 112; family of, *37*; winery of, 27, 39, 167

Del Bono building, 38, *38*, *39*

Del Bono Commission: building code criticized by, 236; experts ignored by, 122; on expropriations, 113–14; on geology, 112–13; as "keepers," 106, 112–13; labor demonstration backed by, 176; leadership of, 112; Reconstruction Council and, 151, 161

Democracia (San Juan), 206

demolition: by "The Bulldozer Kid," 275; materials recovered from, 130–31; repression-assisted, 276

Department of Social Justice, 228–29

Desamparados, 33

Diario de Cuyo (San Juan), 241, 271

Dickie, John, 12

dictatorship (1955–58), 221, 266–71, 275, 279, 293

disasters and rebuilding, 13

doctors in earthquake relief, 54–55, 58–59, 64–65

downtown business district, 37–38

earthquake fatalities, 56, *59*, 59–61, 310n54

earthquake of 1861 (Mendoza), 31–32

earthquake of 1894, 31–32, 97

earthquake of 1944: aftermath of, 56–65, *59*, 124–25, *126*; damage from, *52–53*, 54–57; in national history, 5; nationalist response to, 68–69; official responses to, 67–71; poor of San Juan, effect on, 125–26; as redemption, 69–71; revealing of local divisions by, 6; in the rise of Peronism, 4–5; social damage caused by, 56; survivors' stories from, 51–54, 56, 60, 63–65; third anniversary events after, 234–37

earthquake of 1952, 262–63

earthquake of 1977, 286

earthquake relief, 54–55, 58–61, 64–65. *See also* relief collection

economic crisis (1949–52), 222

economic issues in moving, 105, 113

economic policy in the Five-Year Plan (first), 220

education policy: of Conservatives, 49; 50; religion in public schools and, 137

elections: in 1946, 210–16, 219, 225–27; in 1951, 261–62, 264; in 1957, 279–80; in 1958, 280

elite of San Juan, 36–37; Cantonismo and, 45–46; in earthquake, 64–65; *La Reforma* criticism of, 214; political power of, 9–10; property of, in Mendióroz plan, 179; reaction of, to reform, 7. *See also* fuerzas vivas emergency barrios, 127–28; 4 June barrio, 128, 140, 190, 234, 260, 270, 283; building code violations in, 259–60; Captain Lazo barrio, 128, *142*, 170–71, 234, 260, 270, 283; chapels in, 171–72; communities in, 260; dance halls in, 171; Enfermera Medina barrio, *131*; General Pistarini, 128; heterogeneity in, 170–71; map of, *129*; "moral decline" in, 191; as neighborhoods, 128; photographs of, *128*; problems in, 169–72, 191–92; Rawson and Rivadavia barrio, 128–29, 257, 259; Reconstruction Council and, 162–63; rent proposed for, 141; social hierarchy in, 171; sold to workers, 259–60; Sosa Molina barrio, 235

emergency housing: after 1952 quake, 262; allocation of, 140–42; antiseismic construction in, 130; assembly of, *127*; Barzola on, 196; building code violations in, 259–60; building methods used in, 130–31; criticism of, 143; experimental materials in, 127; Ferrari Hardoy plans for, 162–63; fraud in, 141–42; heterogeneity in, 170–71; living standards affected by, 142; masonry homes as, 128–29, 141; materials from demolition for, 130–31; Molina's implementation of, 134; MOP provided, 126–27, 130–32; propaganda around, 132; provincial management of, 129–30, 141–42, 169–70; rent for, 141, 192–93, 259, 264; shortage of, 170; wooden huts as, 129

emergency response plan, 67

engineers: on concrete, 145; exclusion of, from rebuilding debate, 231; fired by Pistarini, 200–201; insurgency of, 184–87; as "keepers," 145–47; opposing military regime, 196–98; political commitment of, 196–98, 207; priorities of, 198; professionalization of,

89–90; protests by, 207; rewarded for opposing Perón, 273–74; Zuleta and, 207

evacuation, 61–63, *62, 64, 75*

Eva Perón Foundation, 257, 262

exports, 88, 221–22

Facundo (Sarmiento), 1, 184

Farrell, Edelmiro J., 67, 77–78, 150

federalism, 177

Fernández, Juan Rómulo, 109

Ferrari Hardoy, Jorge: AAD membership of, 201; Grupo Austral membership of, 93; planner for Buenos Aires, 251

Ferrari Hardoy team: book by, 202–3; communiqué by, 162–63; emergency housing plans by, 162–63; firing of, 173; letters by, on rebuilding, 174–75; modern urbanism applied by, 163; plans by, 163–67, *166*, 172; priorities of, 162; Reconstruction Council and, 161–62, 172–73; water systems by, 164

fibercement, 130, 163, 169–70

Five-Year Plan (first), 219–21

Five-Year Plan (second), 222, 264, 295

FOS (Federación Obrera Sanjuanina), 168

four avenues: as barriers, 165; barrios outside, 171; as city limits, 40; inside of, 33, 49, *57*, 179, 248, 272, 296; outside of, 33, *58*, 179, 248, 283; residential construction outside, 283; in street grid, 31; Videla on, 145

fuerzas vivas: in Alvarado coalition, 232–33; anti-seismic construction supported by, 120; control by, of rebuilding, 274; demands of, 84–85, 280; Godoy's arrangement with, 240; Hennekens' conflict with, 172–73; manifesto of, 157, 185; modernism supported by, 280–82; opposing move, 99–100, 150; in *The Other Earthquake*, 183–84; on Reconstruction Council,

Prebisch, Alberto, 83, 91–92
Prego, Costantino, 111
La Prensa (Buenos Aires), 149
presidential campaign of 1946, 210–13
press: on anti-government protesters, 209–11; architects' use of, 200–201; censorship of, 21, 222; co-opted by Alvarado, 233–34; on Ferrari-Hardoy plan, 166–67; influence of, 39; opposition of, to move, 144–45, 213–14; ownership of, by officials, 241; Reconstruction Council and, 184; in relief collection, 72, 74. *See also* journalists; newspapers
press releases, 67
priests in earthquake relief, 54–55
priority of rebuilding, 265–66
prisoners in earthquake relief, 55
propertied classes: anniversary protest by, 236–37; against architects, 211; defense of interests of, 198
property expropriation: as argument against moving, 112; in Bereterbide-Vautier plan, 98–100; costs of, 113; issues in rebuilding, 98; market values and, 235; in Mendióroz plan, 180; Ramella's proposal for, 111; tax evasion and, 114
property ownership: Del Bono Commission and, 112–13; engineers on, 185–86; moving San Juan and, 98–100; Villalobos on, 175–76
property registry, 113–14, 235
property rights: Bereterbide on, 97–98; lifting restrictions on, 185–86, 189, 190, 192; Popular Assembly on, 185–86, 189; rural, 29–30; Villalobos's views on, 175–76
property taxes, 114, 274
protests: anniversary, 234, 236–37; anti-Peronist students', 269–70; April 1, 1945, 176–77; Arriba San Juan, 189–93, 194, 203, 213; Corpus Christi, 268;

March for Freedom and the Constitution, 157, 195–96; October 17, 1945, 207–9
provincial archives, 19
provincial demographics, 27
provincial elite. *See* elite of San Juan
Provincial Housing Institute, 263–64
provincial prison, 55
public and civic spaces, 30, 35, 102–3, 179
public buildings: designed through competitions, 252, 254; prioritized, 198, 263
public health, post-quake concerns, 59–60
public works: in Buenos Aires, 88; CAI calls to freeze, 185, 197; by Cantonismo, 43–44; in Caucete, 195; by Conservatives, 49; as cure for poverty, 137; fraud in, 277–78; under Godoy, 244, 257, 262; during "The Infamous Decade," 88–89; local elite resisting, 122–23; in "Manifesto of the fuerzas vivas," 185; rebuilding as, 265–66
public works minister. *See* Pistarini, Juan
public works minister, provincial, 82
El Pueblo (Buenos Aires), 148–49

quincha, 34–35, 116–18, *132*

Radicals: in 1946 election, 227; in 1958 election, 280; as Perón supporters, 214–15
railroads: in Bereterbide-Vautier plan, 102; earthquake damage to, 57; in evacuation, 61–63; in Ferrari-Hardoy plan, 165; Guido-Carrasco plan for, 94; nationalization of, 219; slow completion of, 297; in urban landscape, 33; wine industry and, 25
Ramella, Pablo: concrete advocated by, 120; on construction controls, 57–58; on electoral fraud, 48; as a "keeper,"

110–12; on order, 135; on property lines/swaps, 111–12; Senate appointment of, 228; "The Structure of the State," 159; on "the superstition of adobe," 116–17, 120

Ramírez, Pedro Pablo, 67–69, *70*, 71, 76–79

Ramos Correa, Daniel, 284

ranchos: Baca on, 186, 191; emergency, 127; of poor, 193; of quincha, 34, 116

Rawson barrio, 128–29

Reconstruction Council: achievements and limits of, 235–37, 275–76; architectural competitions held by, 254; bill of on rebuilding, 230; budget of, 244; building code issued by, 193–94; criticism of, 190–91, 235–36, 281; Del Bono Commission and, 151, 161; failure of, in urban reform, 180–81; Ferrari Hardoy team and, 161–62, 172–73; fuerzas vivas on, 161, 172–73; headquarters of, *276*; housing built by, *260*; immediate needs served by, 162–63; membership in, 151–52, 159–60, 174; criticism of plans by, 190–91; publicity campaign for, 255–56; takeover attempt and, 247–50; Tejada on, 169, 174; under Zuleta, 203–7, 235

Reconstruction Ministry (provincial), 229, 243

Reconstruction of San Juan. *See* Reconstruction Council

La Reforma (San Juan): bombings of, 46; Cipolletti funding of, 206; criticism in, of elite, 214; in local politics, 44; against Perón, 216

refugees, 62–63, 74

regional master plan, 253

reinforced concrete buildings, 56

relief collection: GOU and, 78; as official response, 67–68; Perón and, 4, 6, 71–76, 188–89, 212, 256–57; Popular Assembly and, 189; STP in, 72–73, 212–13

relief effort, 58–60, 156

Renard, Carmen, 152, 282

rental housing: in Bereterbide-Vautier Plan, 100; loans to rebuild, 274; priority of, 198–99; selling of, 293

retreta, 38

Rivadavia barrio, 128–29

Rodeo, 25

Rodríguez de Marchessi, Juana, 191

Rodríguez y Olmos, Audino (Archbishop), 65, 69–70, *241*

Rofman, Alejandro, 14

Rojas, Isaac, 279

Rosas, Juan Manuel de, 1

Rossi, Enévaro, 109, 282

Rural Workers Statute, 168

Sacriste, Eduardo: on Argentine architecture, 90, 93; assessment of rebuilding, 200, 251, 294; on Mendióroz plan, 251; report by, 144–45; Tucumán architecture school and, 251; vision by, of San Juan, 143–44

Sacriste team, 142–44

San Juan: 1894 rebuilding, 32–33; in 1955, 271–72; anti-Peronism in, 270–71; in campaign of 1946, 210–13; downtown, *32, 273, 284*; Guido-Carrasco plan for, 94–97; impact of, on Peronism, 293; lasting form of, 283; map of, *31*; in national planning, 147–48; as planning model, 220–21; pre-earthquake grid, 30–31; regional position of, 25–26; Spanish street grid of, 95; symbolism of, 203, 220. *See also* New San Juan

San Juan Center of Engineers, 185–86

San Juan families, 37

San Juan press: Alvarado and, 233–34; on protesters, 209–10

San Juan Province: administration of, 159, 174, 244; in aftermath, 124; anti-seismic construction in, 286; debt of,

Zuleta, Enrique: bill of, on rebuilding, 230; concessions of, 206–7; engineers and, 207; Ferrari Hardoy plan and, 164; provincial focus of, 206–7; on Reconstruction Council, 203–7, 235; style of, 206; Water Department and, 206–7; water projects of, in San Juan, 235, 244–46

Zunino, Antonio, 275

Mark A. Healey is an assistant professor in the Department of
History at the University of California, Berkeley. He translated
*Blood, Ink, and Culture: Miseries and Splendors of the Post-
Mexican Condition* (Duke, 2002) and *Clerical Ideology in a
Revolutionary Age: The Guadalajara Church and the Idea of
the Mexican Nation, 1788–1853* (Calgary, 2002).

Library of Congress Cataloging-in-Publication Data
Healey, Mark Alan, 1968–
The ruins of the new Argentina : Peronism and the remaking
of San Juan after the 1944 earthquake / Mark A. Healey.
p. cm.
Includes bibliographical references and index.
ISBN 978-0-8223-4883-2 (cloth : alk. paper)
ISBN 978-0-8223-4905-1 (pbk. : alk. paper)
1. Peronism. 2. Earthquake relief—Argentina—San Juan
(Province)—History—20th century. I. Title.
F2849.H43 2011
982'.6306—dc22   2010035882